Baroque & Rococo

Architecture & Decoration

Baroque & Rococo
Architecture & Decoration

Anthony Blunt
Alastair Laing
Christopher Tadgell
Kerry Downes

Edited by Anthony Blunt

Photographs by Wim Swaan

ICON EDITIONS
HARPER & ROW, PUBLISHERS, New York
Cambridge, Philadelphia, San Francisco,
London, Mexico City, São Paulo, Sydney

Dedication
To the memory of Rudolf Wittkower

BAROQUE & ROCOCO:
ARCHITECTURE AND DECORATION.
Copyright © 1978 by Paul Elek Ltd.

ISBN 0-06-430115-x

LIBRARY OF CONGRESS CATALOG CARD NUMBER:
78-4446

Designed by Harold Bartram

Half title Cartouche from J. B. Probst's *Schilder oder Cartouches der
neuesten Fason, c.* 1735

Title page Borromini, engraving of a detail of the window from the façade
of the Oratory of S. Filippo Neri, Rome (see plate 45)

Contents

Preface

This book is not intended to be a complete history of the architecture and decoration of the Baroque and the Rococo—such a project would take many volumes of this size; it is rather an attempt to define what can properly be covered by the terms Baroque and Rococo and to bring out the salient features of both styles and the modifications which they underwent in the various countries which adopted them. Emphasis is laid on the great figures of the period, but the vernacular style is also discussed, even in areas which did not produce any great masters.

In a sense I am attempting to work out in greater detail the ideas which I outlined in a lecture given at the British Academy in 1972 with the somewhat cumbersome title: *Some Uses and Misuses of the Terms Baroque and Rococo as applied to Architecture*. In this brief sketch I tried to limit the application of the terms Baroque and Rococo to groups of works which had fundamental qualities in common and to eliminate from their coverage certain types to which the terms have commonly been applied, but which, in my opinion, are essentially different from the true Baroque and Rococo as they appeared initially in Rome and France respectively.

This book is the result of close collaboration between the various contributors. The general scheme and the division into sections were the result of joint planning and there has been a continuous interchange of ideas between the various authors. Naturally our approaches vary, partly because of the particular interests of each individual author and partly because of the problems presented in the different sections. In some cases the historical background needed specially detailed investigation, in others considerations of architectural theory were of predominant importance; in some areas decoration was the most important element to be analysed, in others planning and structure were the features of real originality. We hope, however, that in spite of these variations the different sections of the book share a common basic approach and form a coherent picture of the architecture and decoration of the period.

Our intention was to write for the reader who has an interest in the history of architecture but not necessarily a specialized knowledge of it, and therefore the temptation to take short cuts by using technical terms has been resisted as far as possible. In order not to interrupt the flow of the arguments footnotes have been kept to a minimum. They are mainly designed to give the authorities on which the statements made in the text are based and to guide the reader to books and articles where he can find fuller information on particular subjects that interest him.

The illustrations are based on the photographs taken by Wim Swaan, but these were made before the present team of authors was connected with the project and have been supplemented by others from various sources, including engravings and drawings.

This book is dedicated to the memory of Rudolf Wittkower, to whom I personally owe all the training I ever had in the study of architecture and from whom one of the other contributors, Kerry Downes, also learnt much directly. The two younger contributors did not know him personally but join with us in paying tribute to the founder of the modern approach towards Baroque architecture and sculpture.

Anthony Blunt
London 1978

1 *Ecstasy of St Theresa*, marble group by Bernini, *c.* 1644–47, in the Cornaro Chapel, S. Maria della Vittoria, Rome

Introduction

The word 'Baroque' has been and still is used in many different senses, but in this book it will be taken to mean the style which was created in Rome roughly in the period 1620–70, that is to say in the pontificates of Gregory XV, Urban VIII, Innocent X and Alexander VII. It can reasonably be thus defined in terms of papal history because it expressed the spirit which dominated a particular phase in the development of the Roman Church, represented by the popes just mentioned, and although it spread to other areas and was used for different purposes it always retained the fundamental characteristics developed in Rome.[1]

During the second half of the sixteenth century the Roman Church, the very existence of which had been threatened by the Reformation, went through an austere period of internal reform designed to set its own house in order and to give it sufficient strength to reassert its power. This phase was typified by the activities of the Council of Trent which met from 1545 till 1563. The Council laid down new laws for the internal discipline of the church and re-examined the doctrines which had been challenged by the Protestants. The internal reform was stringent and removed many of the abuses which the Protestants had attacked—by condemning simony (the buying of offices) and pluralism (the holding of many offices), by improving the educational system of the clergy, by reaffirming the observance of monastic rules and the need for bishops to reside in their dioceses, and emphasizing the importance of preaching—but in the matter of doctrine, far from adapting themselves to the demands of the Reformers, the Roman theologians affirmed more vehemently than ever many of the points which their opponents had attacked: the sole right of the Church to interpret the Bible and the equal validity of tradition and the scriptures as sources of religious truth, the validity of all seven Sacraments (of which the Protestants only accepted two, Baptism and the Eucharist), the doctrine of Transsubstantiation (the Real Presence of the body and blood of Christ in the bread and wine of the Mass), the veneration of the Virgin Mary and the saints and the worship of their relics.

This movement of administrative and doctrinal reform was accompanied by a wave of religious enthusiasm. It was the time of the great reformers such as S. Carlo Borromeo, the great fighters against the heretics and the infidel, St Ignatius and St Francis Xavier, and the great mystics, St Theresa of Avila and St John of the Cross. Some of these, like St John of the Cross, expressed themselves in good works and magnificent poetry, but most of them took more practical action by creating new orders, or reforming existing ones. The Jesuits, founded by St Ignatius, the Theatines, by S. Gaetano Thiene, the Oratorians, by St Philip Neri, and the Carmelites reformed by St Theresa became the militants of the new way of life, and the means by which the spirit embodied in the Council of Trent was carried into effect.

The decrees of the Council of Trent were expounded in greater detail by some of the reformers of the period. S. Carlo Borromeo and his nephew Cardinal Federico Borromeo, for instance, laid down rules for the guidance of artists and patrons commissioning churches or works of religious art. Paintings and statues must be designed to convey the truth of Christian doctrine, not to satisfy the senses; they must follow the details of the scriptures or the legends of the saints, and they must observe the laws of decorum as far as the painting of nudes was concerned. Churches must be planned to satisfy the needs of liturgy, not merely to be beautiful in form and ornament. In fact the arts had to be the handmaids of religion, and paintings had to be the Bible of the illiterate, as they had been in the great days of the Church in the Middle Ages.

The effects of this approach to the arts can be seen in the painting and architecture of the later sixteenth century in Italy and elsewhere. The great cycles of frescoes in Roman churches of the time deal with carefully thought-out programmes, expounding the mysteries of the Faith, like those of the Cappella Sistina in S. Maria Maggiore, extolling the virtues of the martyrs, as in the horrific frescoes in S. Stefano Rotondo, and sometimes even celebrating recent victories over the enemy, as in the decorations of the Sala Regia in the Vatican, executed in the 1570s, which include not only the 'Victory over the Turks at Lepanto' in 1571 but the 'Massacre of the Protestants in Paris' on the Feast of St Bartholomew in the following year. In the designing of churches fundamental changes were introduced: the Greek cross and circle, much favoured in the early sixteenth century because of their geometrical perfection which was considered a symbol of the perfection of God, were rejected in favour of the Latin cross which was liturgically more satisfactory in that the clearly defined choir allowed for the separation of the clergy from the laity, a point to which theologians of the Counter-Reformation attached importance as it emphasized the sacred character of the priesthood. The long nave provided a good setting for processions and allowed the construction of chapels for the worship of individual saints. The decoration of

19

2 S. Ivo della Sapienza, Rome, interior (after restoration) by Borromini, 1642–50, decorated after 1655

17, 68 churches was to be decent but simple, and the first Jesuit churches, such as the Gesù in Rome or the Gesù Nuovo in Naples, were initially to have been in stucco and stone only, without marbling, gilding or even frescoes, all of which were lavishly added in the seventeenth century when policy and taste had changed.

In comparison with this austere and heroic phase of reform, the Baroque age was one of fulfilment and enjoyment. It did not produce any figures comparable to the great reforming saints of the sixteenth century, but it was a period in which it seemed that the Church, building on the achievements of the Counter-Reformation, might reassert its position as a temporal as well as a spiritual power. This hope proved illusory, and the efforts of the popes to intervene effectively in European politics were

steadily frustrated by the newly formed centralized states, above all by France, which circumscribed the efforts of Innocent X to take part in the Peace of Westphalia in 1648, resisted all his attempts to interfere in internal affairs and deliberately humiliated his successor Alexander VII into making public and abject apology over a minor diplomatic incident. From this time onwards the papacy ceased to be a major power in European politics.

In the 1620s and 1630s, however, the general optimism seemed justified. The battle of the White Mountain in 1620, in which the Catholic forces totally defeated an alliance of Protestant princes, assured the Empire as a stronghold of Catholicism; missionary work was carrying the faith to the Far East and to the states of Latin America; and, though the finances of the papacy were never sound, the reforms of the late-sixteenth-century popes had created a temporary feeling of security.

The energy which in the last decades of the sixteenth century had gone into reform was now directed towards celebration. The heroes of the Counter-Reformation were canonized—Borromeo in 1610, Ignatius, Francis Xavier, Philip Neri, Theresa in 1622, Gaetano da Thiene in 1629, and these canonizations were the signal for the building of churches and chapels dedicated to the new saints.

As would be expected this new spirit demanded a new style to express its aspirations. The severe didactic manner of painting advocated in the years of reform gave place to a more joyous, more emotional style in accordance with the new religious mood in which the worship of the Virgin and Child and the saints played a leading part. Apparitions of the Virgin and Child, saints in ecstasy and miraculous events became the stock-in-trade of painters and sculptors,[2] and to represent them they invented new formulas: swirling compositions, warm seductive colouring, figures in strong movement, dramatic gestures, and a whole apparatus of clouds, putti and radiances. The greatest master of this style in Italy was Bernini, whose *Ecstasy of St Theresa* may be taken as symbolizing the new art. Painters such as Giovanni Lanfranco, Pietro da Cortona, or Maratta gave brilliant expression to the same feeling, but the greatest exponent of the style in painting lived and worked outside Italy: Peter Paul Rubens, whose altarpieces for the Jesuits and other religious orders in Antwerp were among the masterpieces of the period.

3
67

If this new art is to be described by a single epithet, it could be called *rhetorical*. Artists aimed at arousing astonishment, at creating strongly emotional effects, at imposing them instantaneously, even abruptly, on their audience, and they directed their appeal not only to the sophisticated Roman ecclesiastics and secular aristocrats but also to the thousands of pilgrims who visited the city.

These aims led them to produce a style which to a northerner, often influenced, though perhaps unconsciously, by traditions of Puritanism, may seem vulgar and even irreligious, but the southern Catholics of the day thought it appropriate that the worship of God and the saints should be accompanied by a splendour at least equal to that demanded by secular princes.

3 *Above left* S. Maria della Vittoria, Cornaro Chapel, *c.* 1644–51, with the *Ecstasy of St Theresa* by Bernini

4 *Left* S. Andrea al Quirinale, Rome, by Bernini, 1658–70, interior of the dome

It would moreover be entirely wrong to suppose that, because this rhetorical art made a direct appeal to the emotions and even to the senses, the artists who produced it were unintellectual. Bernini was a man of wide culture who wrote poetry, produced plays, and composed music; Cortona was a master of architecture as well as of painting, and was a learned theologian; and among the pure architects Francesco Borromini was an enthusiastic archaeologist, Guarino Guarini a professional mathematician, theologian and philosopher, and most of the great architects of the period were well versed in geometry and in the art of engineering.

The salient features of Baroque architecture as it was created in Rome and as it later spread to other areas of Europe may be summarized as follows. Baroque architects preferred curves to straight lines and complex forms to those which were regular and simple. The ideal form of the architects of the Renaissance had been the circle, which is symmetrical about every diameter, and the square and the Greek cross, which are symmetrical about their two principal axes. Baroque architects preferred the oval to the circle because it had greater variety in its changing curvature, and the Latin cross to the Greek; but in each case they liked to introduce variations, combinations of different ovals, or curves to break up the straight lines of the Latin cross.

Even in their simple forms the oval and the Latin cross had one characteristic which appealed to Baroque architects: they implied a feeling of movement on their longer axes, as opposed to the static symmetry of the circle or the Greek cross, and this feeling of movement could be intensified by the variations introduced in their more complex plans. This effect was strengthened owing to the fact that Baroque architects often used incomplete ovals, so that one space leads on into the next. In the vertical the same kind of movement is obtained by continuing the main lines of the lower walls right up to the top of the structure, or by an ingenious repetition of forms, sometimes on a diminishing scale on the interior of a dome.

Baroque architects also sought movement in the actual walls of their buildings. This interest is most clearly displayed in their treatment of façades. Whereas a typical Renaissance façade tends to be more or less in one plane, articulated by pilasters or at most half-columns, Baroque architects liked to treat their façades almost like sculpture, setting columns into the walls, opening them up with niches of varying scales, and finally actually curving the whole surface of the façade, which is sometimes treated almost as a single surface, but is often given the sculptural treatment just described.

In the decoration of the interior again Baroque architects employed a number of methods which were foreign to the spirit of the Renaissance. They often combined in a single whole the three arts of painting, sculpture, and architecture, so that the painting of the altarpiece or on the vault, the sculptured figures of saints or donors contribute as much as the architecture to the whole effect. Further, artists working in one medium often use means proper to others, thus creating an actual fusion of the arts. Architectural members are sometimes replaced by sculpture or are so contorted and decorated that they seem more like

5 *Above right* St Peter's, Rome, interior showing Maderno's nave, 1609–26, and Bernini's baldacchino, begun 1624

6 *Right* S. Carlo alle Quattro Fontane, Rome, façade by Borromini, designed, *c.* 1637, executed 1665 onwards, the upper part finished after Borromini's death

sculpture than supporting elements. Sculptors introduce colour—almost like painters—in the form of illusionist marble inlay, by imitating the texture of velvet or silk, or by creating effects of false perspective. Painters use this last device on a vast scale and set up complete buildings on the ceilings of their churches or the *saloni* in their palaces. Architects execute similar effects of *léger-de-main* in three dimensions, producing, for instance, arcades which appear twice their actual length. All these devices contribute, by their element of surprise, to the shock-effects sought by Baroque architects.

The effects of surprise were heightened by carefully controlled light, either directed to highlight some particular feature, or to shine on a fresco or a relief from a concealed source, thus producing an unexplained and dramatic effect.

Other devices are equally 'theatrical'. A favourite method was to spread an action across the whole space of a church; for instance, a martyrdom may be depicted over the altar and the saint may be shown being received in Heaven in a fresco on the vault.

Baroque architects often heightened the striking impression created by their churches by the use of elaborate ornament and rich materials. This is often quoted as the first and chief feature of Baroque architecture, but it is important to remember that it is not to be found in by any means all Baroque works. Some of the most accomplished architects used the simplest materials—brick and stucco—and obtained their effects solely by the ingenuity of their architectural forms.

Symbolism of a complicated kind is often used in the decoration and even the planning of Baroque churches. The attributes of the particular saint to whom the church is dedicated may be included in stucco or painted panels or even worked into the architectural plan, and there are often allusions to the idea that a church was the modern equivalent of the Temple of Solomon. In plan the architect may use a triangle as a symbol for the Trinity, or the six-pointed star of David for wisdom, and in one case a design is known to have been based on the bees in the arms of Urban VIII.

Finally most Baroque architects liked to work on a big scale.

7 *Opposite* S. Ignazio, Rome, frescoes on the vault of the nave by Andrea Pozzo, 1691–94

8 *Below* The colonnade of St Peter's, by Bernini, begun 1656

This is not generally true of the first generation of Roman Baroque architects, and the palaces of the Seicento are rarely as big as, say, the Palazzo Farnese, but Bernini, in the Piazza of St Peter's and in his unexecuted design for the Louvre, gave an idea of the feeling for the colossal which was to be characteristic of the great monastic buildings and palaces erected north of the Alps. This love for a large scale also manifested itself in an interest in town-planning, and Roman Baroque architects produced some of the most celebrated examples of this art, beginning with the Piazza of St Peter's, and including the Piazza del Popolo and the Spanish Steps, and their example was imitated in many other cities in Italy and in other countries. To cope with the articulation of these vast buildings architects adopted the use of a giant Order, embracing two, sometimes three, storeys of a building, a device which had been rediscovered in the sixteenth century but not used extensively till the Baroque period.

This is an example of an important general fact about Roman Baroque architecture. Although it is a fundamentally new and original style, many of the elements which go to compose it had been invented in the previous century. Michelangelo and Palladio had used giant Orders; Peruzzi and Vignola had experimented with oval ground plans; Raphael, Peruzzi and Giulio Romano, and many of the later Mannerists had created *trompe l'oeil* effects in their frescoes; Raphael and Pordonone had hinted at the device of extending the action over the whole space of a chapel; Bramante had constructed false-perspective colonnades in three dimensions; but these artists had used such devices separately and usually in a discreet manner. It was left to the Baroque to combine them into wholes bolder and more

dramatic than anything created in the sixteenth century. Those who condemn the Baroque would call them melodramatic and theatrical, but for the particular purpose envisaged by Baroque architects they were perfectly suitable.

If later sixteenth-century architecture was one source for the methods of Roman Baroque architects, another was the architecture of classical antiquity.[3] This may seem surprising in view of the accusations made by supporters of the Classical schools of architecture over more than two centuries that the architects of the Baroque broke every rule laid down by Vitruvius and every principle implicit in the buildings of Greece and Rome. This problem will be discussed in greater detail in connection with the individual Roman Baroque architects, particularly Borromini, and here it will be enough to state that all the great Baroque architects expressed the greatest admiration for the architecture of Classical Antiquity and that it can be shown that they studied and imitated these works with care and enthusiasm. What distinguished them from their more obviously 'Classical' contemporaries was that they admired and studied a different kind of Ancient architecture and interpreted it in a different manner.

9 *Above* Piranesi's etching of the Piazza del Popolo, showing S. Maria di Montesanto (left) and S. Maria dei Miracoli (right), and the obelisk set up by Sixtus V. The middle street is the Corso, in which is visible the façade of S. Giacomo degli Incurabili; to the left is the Via del Babuino leading to the Piazza di Spagna (see plate 73); on the right is the Via di Ripetta, leading to the port of that name on the Tiber (see plate 71)

10 *Opposite* Turin, S. Lorenzo by Guarino Guarini, 1668–80, interior of the dome

By 1680 what one may call the 'Founding Fathers' of the Baroque—Bernini, Borromini, and Pietro da Cortona—were all dead. They were followed by a generation of less talented architects who, however, succeeded in evolving a kind of moderate Baroque, in which the individual brilliance of the earlier styles was qualified, partly by the influence of French

11 Nymphenburg, the Amalienburg, detail of the ceiling of the Mirror Room, designed by François Cuvilliés, 1734–39

taste, and which was much more acceptable to foreigners. In fact this generation, of which the most important representative was Carlo Fontana, created a style which spread throughout Europe and was employed—with variations naturally—by Juvarra in Piedmont, Fischer von Erlach in Austria, Schlüter in Prussia, Schlaun in Westphalia, Jules Hardouin Mansart in France, and even Vanbrugh in England.

At the same time, however, a more inventive development from Roman Baroque was taking place in Turin, where Guarino Guarini created a highly individual interpretation of Borromini's style, which was carried on in the same district by his follower Bernardo Vittone.

In other parts of Italy the spread of a true form of Baroque architecture was much less considerable than is generally believed. In many areas a strong local tradition inhibited its acceptance. In Venice and in the *terra firma* which it controlled the principles of Palladio, codified by Scamozzi, held sway throughout the seventeenth and eighteenth centuries, and Baldassare Longhena's Salute stands out as an almost isolated

Baroque building. In Florence the followers of Michelangelo, Buontalenti and Cigoli, imposed their style and the Baroque never took root. Milan produced in Ricchino an important forerunner of the Baroque, who probably influenced Borromini, but the later Milanese works in the full Baroque style are pedestrian.

The architecture of southern Italy presents special problems. Naples was hardly affected by the example of Roman Baroque till the early eighteenth century, but architects like Cosimo Fanzago evolved a style which, though it never exploits Roman ideas of planning and spatial invention, shows a feeling for the articulation of the wall in depth and for a particular kind of polychrome decoration which can properly be called Baroque. In the first half of the eighteenth century Naples produced in Ferdinando Sanfelice an architect who understood the principles of Borromini and developed new forms out of them. In Sicily the problem is to some extent similar. Much of Sicilian vernacular, though fine in decorative inventiveness, shows no appreciation of the real aims of Roman Baroque architects and, apart from a few interesting sports such as Angelo Italia, little Sicilian architecture can be called Baroque till the appearance of Rosario Gagliardi and Vaccarini in the middle of the eighteenth century.

It is usual to describe as Baroque the late-seventeenth and early-eighteenth-century architecture of Lecce and the Salento—the 'heel' of Italy—but the term does not apply in any real sense. The architects of this area did not show the slightest interest in Baroque planning or structure, and the effect of their churches depends entirely on rich and elaborate surface decoration, mainly based on motifs invented in the sixteenth century. A phrase like 'stile Salentino' would describe it much more accurately than the generally accepted 'Leccese Baroque'.

In Spain there are a certain number of buildings, notably the three Royal Palaces in Madrid, Aranjuez, and La Granja, which were designed by foreigners in the characteristic Late Baroque style, but the mainstream, which reached its fullest expression in Andalusia, is of a quite different type, characterized by extravagantly broken up architectural forms, mixed with naturalistic statues of ecstatic saints. This style satisfied the emotional needs of the Andalusians, which found—and still find—expression in the great processions of Holy Week in Seville. Some of these Andalusian buildings include decorative motifs taken from northern Mannerist pattern-books, particularly that of the German Wendel Dietterlin, whose type of broken-up pilaster became widely popular under the name of *estipite*. In certain cases, of which the most famous is the sacristy of the Cartuja at Granada, the Mannerist *estipites* take over completely, so that the term 'Baroque' no longer seems an appropriate epithet for them; and this is even truer of the architecture of eighteenth-century Mexico. The term *Churrigueresque* has been suggested for this group, but this has one great disadvantage, namely that the work of the Churriguera family is for the most part conspicuously conservative. We cannot coin a word from the name of the architect who built the sacristy of the Cartuja, because his identity is not known. As will be suggested below in the section dealing with this group of buildings, the term 'Neo-Mannerist' is more precisely descriptive of this style, but is in many respects unsatisfactory.

In Portugal the case is different. There is a vernacular style of altar design which has as much in common with Romanesque forms as with Baroque, but in Lisbon, Oporto, and Braga another style developed in which the architectural forms were

98, 99

115, 116

119, 121

129

133, 136

139, 140

398

395

409, 410

104

based on those of Roman Baroque, interpreted in a highly individual manner. The Portuguese took both these styles with them to their colonies, and in Brazil local architects, of whom 414 the most celebrated, called Aleijadinho ('the Cripple'), was a man of exceptional talent, produced highly original variations on the Portuguese style.

The development and influence of Baroque architecture north of the Alps varied, as might be expected, according to local conditions. In Catholic Austria and South Germany it attained a second brilliant flowering in the first half of the eighteenth century and the great monastery and pilgrimage-churches of this area must count among the finest and most characteristic manifestations of the style. In the Protestant countries of northern Europe the style naturally met with a more limited welcome. In ecclesiastical architecture one can only quote individual Baroque features, such as Wren's west towers of St Paul's in London, but in secular architecture Baroque ideas were more acceptable and were well suited to expressing the power of sovereigns or wealthy individuals. In many cases, however, the Baroque had been filtered through the sieve of French *bon goût* and emerged in a chaster form. The French never accepted the Baroque whole-heartedly, but archi-tects no doubt learned much from the example of Rome. The 145 grand-scale planning of François Mansart's *châteaux* and later 149 the whole conception of Versailles are in line with Baroque ideas, and the last public buildings of Louis XIV's reign, the 178, 168 Invalides, the chapel of Versailles, and the Place Vendôme are even more Baroque in feeling. During the earlier part of Louis XV's reign the demand was for a different kind of building, *hôtels* with small, elegantly decorated rooms as opposed to large public works, and the tradition of monumental architec-ture was temporarily eclipsed. When it reappeared in the middle of the eighteenth century in the generation of Ange-Jacques Gabriel, the Baroque features characteristic of Jules Hardouin 200, 201 Mansart are still visible, but they are expressed in a more severely Classical idiom.

So far the word 'Rococo' has deliberately not been mentioned in this discussion, but when we come to the eighteenth-century buildings of France and South Germany it can no longer be avoided.

Like Baroque the word Rococo has been used in many different senses, but there is general agreement on one funda-mental point: in its origin it was essentially a style of de-coration, more precisely the style which was invented in France for the decoration of private houses and reached its maturity roughly in the period 1725 to 1740. It marked a complete break with the style of the high period of Louis XIV's reign, and 181 even more with that of the Baroque. It is marked by lightness and delicacy; its decorative forms are composed of small, 191 broken curves, executed either in wood or in stucco, floating on the surface of the wall or ceiling, leaving much of it unbroken. Rococo decorators preferred light colours—pinks, pale blues, cool greens, with plenty of white either in the field or in the decoration itself, which is often touched with gold—as opposed to the sombre colours and heavy gilding of the Baroque. Rococo designers eliminate as far as possible the architectural members—columns, pilasters, entablatures—and fuse their decoration into gauze-like patterns over walls and ceilings, which often merge into each other. In its mature form this decoration is often asymmetrical and incorporates the shell as a favourite motif. The term *atectonic* has appropriately been

12 Vienna, the Upper Belvedere by Jean Luca von Hildebrandt, 1721–22, detail of the entrance front

invented to describe this style, as opposed to the Baroque, in which the architectural members, though often distorted in relation to Classical canons, are always fundamental.

The Rococo did not arise suddenly but originated in a type of decoration employed in the rooms decorated for Louis XIV in the last fifteen years of his reign by Jules Hardouin Mansart and his assistants. It was developed by the members of the studio into the style known as *Régence*, which marks a half-way stage between the late Louis XIV rooms and the full Rococo of Pineau or Meissonnier.

Some writers confine the word Rococo to the field of de-coration, but it seems reasonable to extend it to cover certain whole buildings in which the architecture is inseparable from the Rococo decoration, particularly those of Cuvilliés and 11 Dominikus Zimmermann in Germany, where the Rococo 304 enjoyed a great success and produced works of the highest invention and sophistication. The Rococo was also reflected in the arts of furniture and ceramics, and the porcelain of Nymph-enburg and Meissen could be regarded as among the finest

productions of the style. The application of the term can reasonably be extended further to the figurative arts, to include the painting of Watteau and Boucher, the drawings of Cochin and Gabriel de Saint-Aubin, and even the sculpture of J. B. Lemoyne and, in Germany, Ferdinand Tietz and Ignaz Günther.

The problem of Rococo outside France and Germany has never been properly studied. In certain parts of northern Italy, particularly Piedmont and Veneto, there was a direct diffusion of the French style, but the term can be properly applied to the atectonic architecture and decoration of certain Neapolitan artists, particularly the architect Domenico Antonio Vaccaro and the decorative sculptor Giuseppe Sammartino.

So far I have only discussed the senses in which I personally believe the words Baroque and Rococo can most usefully be employed, but something must be said about the origins of the terms and the varying meanings which have been attached to them.[4]

The word Baroque originally meant fantastic or misshapen and it was used in two quite different contexts. The Portuguese used it to describe a natural, irregular pearl, and the Italians applied it to rhetoric, using it to describe a far-fetched or fanciful argument. It was first applied to architecture by French critics of the mid-eighteenth century and, as was the case with Gothic, it was originally used as a term of abuse but stuck as a stylistic description. Francesco Milizia[5] and his Neo-Classical followers in France and Italy used the term to describe the architecture of Borromini and his contemporaries because they regarded it as malformed and as breaking all the laws of Classical architecture. The term continued to be used in this sense till the 1880s, when certain German art-historians began to use it to describe a definite phase in the evolution of architecture.

They were driven to defining this phase by the realization that art after the middle of the sixteenth century did not, as their predecessors believed, simply represent a decadence from Renaissance ideals, but a style with its own principles, quite different from those of the Renaissance itself. These pioneers in the definition of the Baroque—Burckhardt, Lübke, Gurlitt, and above all Wölfflin[6]—applied the term to art in all European countries, roughly from the middle of the sixteenth century to the middle of the eighteenth, but their successors realized that this definition was too wide. Chronologically these later critics—Dvořák and Walter Friedlaender[7]—divided the period into two parts and called the first Mannerism, a word of which the exact application is now subject to much discussion and disagreement. It was originally used to describe painters rather than architects and was applied to the phase after the generation of 1520 (Raphael and the young Michelangelo) but was later extended to cover the architecture of Michelangelo himself and his followers, such as Buontalenti and Tibaldi, as well as that of Giulio Romano and others. At the same time critics came to see that Wölfflin's bold attempt to apply the term Baroque to the art of the whole of Europe in the seventeenth century would not work, and that it was not generally valid for French and Dutch art, which was conditioned by quite different intellectual and political atmospheres. As a result the term came

to be applied in a more restricted sense, though most writers at the present time continue to apply it to the architecture of Apulia and the Spanish colonies—in my opinion wrongly.

Other writers in the 1920s and 1930s held different views of the Baroque. Certain nationalist German writers, such as Hamann[8] for instance, held that it was something fundamentally Germanic and related to Gothic art. One Spanish critic, Eugenio d'Ors,[9] reversed the 'restrictive' tendency of the time and maintained that Baroque was a phase which occurred in all epochs as a reaction from the art of Classical periods towards a style which was lively, vigorous, and irregular. In all he defined twenty-two different Baroque phases in the history of art, from prehistoric times to the architecture of cinemas and hotels of his own day. This application of the word, which makes it practically meaningless, has not been generally accepted, but the term can reasonably be applied by extension to one phase of ancient art, which produced Pergamene sculpture, the Temple of Baalbek, the rock-tombs of Petra, and the cities of Sabratha and Leptis Magna.

The word Rococo was also first used in a derogatory sense.[10] It was coined in the studios of the French Neo-Classical painters of the 1790s to describe the art of the type of which they most strongly disapproved, to which the terms *marquise* and *Pompadour* were applied—unfairly, since the marquise was a keen supporter of the Classical movement inaugurated by her brother, the marquis de Marigny. The word Rococo is probably—though not certainly—derived from *rocaille*, a term used to describe the shell-incrusted rocky surface of artificial grottos, but it has slight echoes of baby-talk in the repetition of the second syllable *ro-co-co*. These overtones would fit with the attitude of superiority which Neo-Classical artists adopted towards the art of the previous generation. French art-historians prefer the phrase 'Louis XV', but this has disadvantages. It emphasizes the French origin of the style, but would be awkward if applied to the German version of the art. Further the various styles current in France during the eighteenth century do not coincide with the political phases. The *Régence* style, which is named after the Regent for Louis XV during the minority (1715–21), in fact originated well before the death of Louis XIV, and the origins of the Rococo go back to before 1721. The discrepancy is even more marked in the later part of the century, because the style called by common consent 'Louis XVI' originated at least two decades before the death of Louis XV. Unfortunately no better stylistic term has so far been suggested for this important phase of French taste.

Some critics have attempted to spread the use of the term Rococo beyond the visual arts. Indeed the plays of Marivaux and the verse of some French poets of the early eighteenth century seem to qualify for inclusion, but when Voltaire is described as a typical *Rokokomensch* the term seems to burst. It could cover some of his verse and the lighter *contes*, but Voltaire, the reformer and fighter for the rights of man, cannot be regarded as Rococo; not that everyone who appreciated the art of the Rococo need have been Rococo in his life. One of its greatest admirers was Frederick the Great, who certainly showed no Rococo delicacy in his conduct of war or politics!

13 *Opposite* Vienna, Karlskirche designed by J. B. Fischer von Erlach, interior of dome, frescoes by J. M. Rottmayr, 1725–30

Part I

Italy

Rome

It has already been said the Baroque was born in Rome, and it is therefore logical to begin any history of the style by a fairly detailed account of the architecture produced there in the seventeenth and early eighteenth centuries.[1]

Introduction

During the years 1575 to 1625 the position of the papacy changed radically.[2] Under Pius IV (1559–65) the Council of Trent held its last and most important session, the decisions of which completed the internal reform of the Church; under his successor, Pius V (1565–72), the victory of Lepanto gave at least a temporary check to the Turks. In fact the two great threats—Protestantism and Islam—had both been contained, and the Church had a breathing-space before starting on its bolder campaign of expansion. Sixtus V (1585–90) restored internal security by destroying the bandits who had made it unsafe to move about the Campagna and even in many of the un-built-up areas of Rome itself. Sixtus was also responsible for laying out the street which still forms one of the axes of the city, running from the Lateran to S. Maria Maggiore and on to the Trinità dei Monti; and which if it had been completed would have run on to the Piazza del Popolo. This road was punctuated by the obelisks which the Romans had brought from Egypt and which Sixtus set up again with inscriptions converting them into monuments to the triumph of the Church. In the same way he restored the columns of Trajan and Marcus Aurelius, but topped them with colossal statues of St Peter and St Paul. Clement VIII (1592–1605) increased the temporal power of the papacy by adding Ferrara to the Papal States in the north of Italy, and gave proof of the new, more liberal atmosphere around the papacy by absolving Henry IV of France on his abjuring Protestantism, in spite of the fact that he was a relapsed heretic—an act of political wisdom which would have been unthinkable in the time of Pius V or even Gregory XIII. During the period in question the finances of the papacy had improved, partly owing to the administrative skill of Sixtus V, partly through the better exploitation of the rich areas belonging to the papacy in the north of Italy, but above all through the increase of the contributions from the Catholic countries of Europe, stimulated by the flow of gold from the Spanish and Portuguese colonies in Central and South America, where the Church played an active part through its missionary activities.

The great missionary bodies were the old orders of Dom-

14 *Above* Palazzo Serlupi, Rome, by Giacomo della Porta, 1585, engraving of the façade

15 *Opposite* Palazzo Aldobrandini-Chigi, Rome, building started about 1590, probably by Giacomo della Porta, continued by Maderno and finished by Felice della Greca

inicans and Franciscans and the new order of the Jesuits. The new orders—the Theatines and Oratorians as well as the Jesuits—received official recognition and attained greater power in the early decades of the seventeenth century. Paul V supported the Jesuits in their old and bitter quarrel with the Dominicans on the question of Grace, and his successor, Gregory XV, who only reigned for two years (1621–23), confirmed this attitude by canonizing their two heroes, St Ignatius and St Francis Xavier.

Therefore when Cardinal Maffeo Barberini was elected pope in 1623, with the name of Urban VIII, the stage was set for a great artistic revival to reflect the new strength of the Church, and Urban was the right man to seize the opportunity. He was a prolific if mediocre poet, was interested in music, and was an enthusiast for the arts of architecture, sculpture, and painting. In Bernini he found exactly the executant that he needed, and his name is connected with almost all the projects sponsored by the pope: the baldacchino and the decoration of the crossing piers in St Peter's, within the same church the pope's own tomb

5, 31

and the monument to Countess Matilda, and the completion of
24 the Palazzo Barberini. The reckless expenditure of Urban and
his nephews—particularly Cardinal Francesco Barberini, one
of the great patrons and collectors of the time—brought
a good deal of odium on the regime and, when in 1644 Urban
died and was succeeded by Cardinal Giambattista Pamphili, as
Innocent X, the whole policy of the papacy in the arts, as well as
in other fields, was reversed. Bernini fell from favour and for a
short time was replaced by Borromini, who was responsible for
the major project of the pontificate—the remodelling of St John
Lateran—and was involved in Innocent's plans for making the
Piazza Navona a monument to his family by building the
37 church of S. Agnese and the adjoining Palazzo Pamphili.
Borromini, however, was temperamentally unable to take

advantage of his opportunity and, even before the death of
Innocent, Bernini had regained papal favour to the extent that
he obtained the commission for the great Fountain of the Four
Rivers in the Piazza Navona, which had been promised to   37
Borromini. With the election of Alexander VII (Chigi) in 1655
Bernini established himself as an even more complete dictator
of the arts than he had been under Urban. All the major
projects of the pontificate—the Cathedra Petri and the pope's   28
tomb in St Peter's, the Piazza in front of the church, and the   8, 21
Scala Regia, the grand entrance to the Vatican—were designed   30
and executed by him. The only important commission which
Alexander gave to another architect was the construction of the
façade of S. Maria della Pace, the church containing his family   60
chapel, which went to Pietro da Cortona.

The popes were responsible for the most important architectural projects of the period, but the new orders played a considerable part.[3] It is true that their principal churches had been built in Rome before the time of Urban VIII—the Gesù was begun by Vignola in 1568, the Oratorians' S. Maria in Vallicella in 1575 and the Theatines' S. Andrea delle Valle in 1591—but much remained to be done. The Jesuits were building a second church, dedicated to S. Ignatius, and the Oratorians added to their church an Oratory, a library, and living quarters for the Fathers, all designed by Borromini.

In the second half of the century Jesuit patronage underwent a fundamental change, partly owing to the policy of the new General, Padre Oliva, who was elected in 1664, with the result that the originally simple and bare Gesù received a rich revetment of fresco and stucco, S. Ignazio was given its dazzling illusionist ceiling fresco by Andrea Pozzo, and the Noviciate church of S. Andrea al Quirinale, built by Bernini between 1658 and 1670, though small, was planned and decorated with the utmost refinement.

Individual members of the papal families and others connected with the Vatican administration contributed to the patronage. The practice of nepotism which had its last flowering at this time meant that vast sums entered the coffers of the more favoured members of the families of Paul V (Borghese), Gregory XV (Ludovisi), Urban VIII (Barberini), Innocent X (Pamphili), and later Clement X (Altieri). Part of these sums was invested in land and many of the great estates—and with them titles—passed from the old Roman families, particularly the Colonna and the Orsini, to the new papal aristocracy; but much was spent on building. Many of the new families rebuilt their family chapels and often embellished the churches in which they stood, and erected magnificent palaces in the heart of Rome and splendid villas in the higher parts of the city or on the Alban Hills, particularly at Frascati.

Rome 1575–1625

The sudden explosion of a brilliant new style of architecture in the years 1625–40 must have seemed the more surprising to contemporary Romans in that the architecture of the previous half-century had been markedly pedestrian.[4] Curiously enough no architect appeared during the period who showed either the individual genius of Caravaggio or the academic perfection of the Carracci and their followers. Michelangelo had died in 1564, and there was no one to carry on his tradition. Unlike his great contemporary Palladio, who left a school and a doctrine which flourished almost unchallenged in the Veneto for two hundred years, Michelangelo's architecture was too individual, too revolutionary to have an immediate effect. One pupil alone, the Sicilian Giacomo del Duca, showed some understanding of it, but he built very little, and Roman patrons preferred the tasteful Classicism of Vignola and, after his death in 1573, had to be satisfied with the mediocrity of Giacomo della Porta, Martino Longhi the Elder, and Domenico Fontana. The last-named was offered incomparable opportunities by Sixtus V in his projects for the rebuilding of Rome, but his talent was limited to the creation of vast, cubical masses of masonry without architectural distinction, as in the Lateran Palace and the wing added by Sixtus to the Vatican. Giacomo della Porta showed greater originality. In S. Andrea della Valle he adapted Vignola's design for the Gesù by slightly heightening the proportions and emphasizing the feeling for the vertical by using clustered pilasters, the lines of which are continued

through a broken entablature and so run right on into the ribs of the vaulting. In the designing of palace façades—for instance the Palazzo Serlupi—he introduced some variety to the form which had been universally accepted since Antonio da Sangallo's Palazzo Farnese by breaking the regular spacing of the windows and so concentrating attention on the centre of the building. He was also responsible for planning—for Cardinal Pietro Aldobrandini, nephew of Clement VIII—the vast Villa Aldobrandini at Frascati, one of the earliest and most splendid of those country retreats which members of the great Roman families built on the northern slopes of the Alban Hills.[5] The villa is heavy and somewhat awkward in design, but the magnificent semi-circle of fountains and statues cut into the hill behind it, which was executed by Carlo Maderno after della Porta's death and perhaps not entirely from his designs, gives some hint of the splendour of the architecture of the next generation.

Most church architects obediently, but timidly, followed the example of Vignola. His plan for the Gesù, with its broad nave, shallow transepts, and multiple side-chapels for the worship of individual saints, was admirably suited to the needs of the Catholic revival and remained canonical for two centuries. The two most important churches based on the Gesù—della Porta's S. Andrea della Valle and Longhi's S. Maria in Vallicella, also called the Chiesa Nuova—have already been mentioned, but della Porta also produced two particularly fine variants of the model on a small scale in S. Maria dei Monti and S. Atanasio dei Greci, the latter for Catholic priests following the Greek rite in preparation for missionary work in the Eastern Mediterranean. Vignola's experiments with oval plans at S. Andrea sulla Via Flaminia and S. Anna dei Palafrenieri were applied on a larger scale and with a slightly greater emphasis on the long axis leading to the high altar by Francesco da Volterra in S. Giacomo degli Incurabili, but no real innovations were introduced in the planning or construction of churches.

With the interior decoration of churches the case is different, and the period saw the introduction of marbling to a hitherto unknown degree. The most spectacular example is the Cappella Sistina, added by Sixtus V to the church of S. Maria Maggiore on the designs of Domenico Fontana. The most important features of this chapel are the tombs of Sixtus himself and Pius V (who made him a cardinal), which consist of large structures

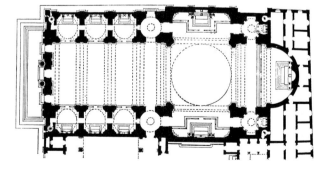

16 *Above* The Gesù, Rome, plan by Vignola, 1568

17 *Opposite* The Gesù, Rome, interior by Vignola. Frescoes by Baciccio, 1674–79, the marbling added in the nineteenth century

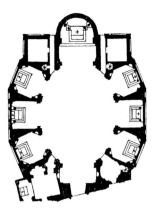

18 *Above* S. Giacomo degli Incurabili, Rome, plan by Francesco da Volterra. Building started in 1590

19 *Below* S. Maria Maggiore, Rome, Cappella Sistina by Domenico Fontana, 1585–90

of coloured marble and columns framing white marble reliefs with scenes illustrating the lives of the two popes. The walls of the chapel are articulated by red marble pilasters with small panels of patterned inlay, and the marbling extends over the whole wall surface, which is enriched with niches containing life-size statues. The decorative scheme is completed by a cycle of ceiling frescoes by a group of minor artists. Paul V added on the opposite side of the church a balancing chapel for his tomb and that of Clement VIII, which is almost identical in design to the Cappella Sistina but even richer in its marble decoration. Smaller family chapels in the same style were built in many Roman churches, one of the most satisfactory being that designed by Giacomo della Porta for the family of Clement VIII in S. Maria sopra Minerva.

The most important architect of the generation before the Baroque, who in many ways prepared the way for it, was Carlo Maderno (1580–1630).[6] Like his uncle, Domenico Fontana, he was born in a village on Lake Lugano, in an area which had for centuries been connected with the great building tradition of Como. During the pontificate of Gregory XIII, probably when he was about twenty, Maderno moved to Rome and joined Fontana's studio. He won the favour of Cardinal Girolamo

Rusticucci, who commissioned him to rebuild the ancient church of S. Susanna. He also came to the notice of Cardinal Camillo Borghese, and when in 1605 the latter became pope, as Paul V, he immediately gave Maderno the most important commission of his career, the completion of St Peter's.

At this time the church was complete as far as the crossing, including the dome, which had been finished by Sixtus V, but it remained to build the eastern arm – liturgically the western, because the church is orientated so that the high altar is at the west end. Ever since Julius II had begun the new St Peter's in 1506 opinions had differed as to whether the church should be in the form of a Greek or a Latin cross with a long nave. Plans for both schemes had been produced, but no decision had been made; now, however, the matter had to be settled. Some maintained that Michelangelo's Greek-cross plan must at all costs be followed, but others argued that his plan did not satisfy

20 *Left* St Peter's, Rome, plan showing the church begun by Bramante, 1506, modified by Michelangelo and completed by Maderno, with the colonnade by Bernini, begun 1656

21 *Below* St Peter's, the dome by Michelangelo, the façade by Maderno and the colonnade by Bernini

22 S. Susanna, Rome, by Carlo Maderno, 1603. Façade

the needs of ecclesiastical ceremonial, because it had no adequate sacristy, few chapels for the worship of individual saints, and no nave, a feature essential to house a large congregation and to give a suitable setting for processions. In the end the party which supported the importance of ecclesiastical demands was victorious over those who argued on aesthetic grounds and Maderno was instructed to add a nave to the church.

After several attempts at a compromise plan which would provide for liturgical needs but preserve the symmetry of the four arms of the church internally, the pope decided to jettison symmetry and to construct the broad nave which exists today. Maderno added two large chapels on either side of the nave and adjacent to the crossing, one for the reservation of the Sacrament and the other for the choir.

The decision to build the nave finally destroyed the possibility of realizing Michelangelo's ideas for the interior; it also created difficult problems for the exterior. Adding the nave meant that from any position near the church Michelangelo's dome would be partly obscured, and a further complication

arose from the project to build twin towers which would have blocked the view of the subsidiary domes built by Vignola. In order to get round the second difficulty, Maderno widened the façade by adding two bays at the ends for the towers. In this way, seen from a distance, the smaller domes would have been visible between the towers. Unfortunately, owing to a structural defect, it proved impossible to build the towers and the church was left with the present long, low front, only relieved by the little structures containing clocks which were added by Giuseppe Valadier nearly two centuries later.

In designing the façade of St Peter's Maderno had to take into account Michelangelo's elevation of the three arms of the church, and he made use of the engravings in which Michelangelo's ideas for the façade of the church were recorded. Michelangelo had intended a portico with two rows of free-standing columns, ten in the back row, four in the front. Maderno abandoned this project because it did not include a loggia from which the pope could give his blessing to the crowds with the dignity required by the new interest in grand ceremonial. At best he could have appeared at a window almost completely obscured by the columns of the portico. Maderno therefore took Michelangelo's portico and, so to speak, squashed it against the wall closing the church. The outer columns of Michelangelo's design are represented by half-columns, and the four middle ones by whole columns, magnificent cylinders of the rough travertine out of which so much of Rome is built.

The addition of the nave and the way in which the façade was adapted to the needs of ceremonial were examples of the new attitude towards ecclesiastical architecture, but they also illustrate the fact that, however much the name of Michelangelo might be revered, his ideas were not regarded as suitable for execution in the new age.

In its way Maderno's façade of S. Susanna (1603) is almost as significant in the history of architecture as his design for St Peter's. It marks the culmination of an important development in the designing of church façades. The façades of most sixteenth-century churches in Rome had followed a simple pattern with two storeys, linked by scrolls, the lower one being broader than the upper to include the aisles. These façades were basically flat – and they were either plain or articulated with very light pilasters. Vignola's projected façade for the Gesù ingeniously enriched this austere and simple scheme by making the façade break forward in two stages. This created an emphasis on the central bay, which was increased by two other devices: the main door was flanked by full columns, and the lines of the central projecting section of the façade were carried up through the whole height of the building and even across the field of the crowning pediment.

Vignola's design was not carried out and the existing façade was erected after his death by Giacomo della Porta. Della Porta followed Vignola's idea of breaking up and enriching the surface of the façade, but he did so in a different way. Whereas in Vignola's scheme the façade breaks forward twice, della Porta's breaks forward, backward, and then forward again; that is to say, Vignola created a steady movement forward towards the centres, but della Porta established a broken movement, forward and then backward.

In the façade of S. Susanna Maderno took up Vignola's scheme and greatly elaborated and enriched it. He makes his façade break forward steadily towards the centre, but he emphasizes the movement by an increase in the plasticity of different sections. On the lower storey the outer wings, which do

23 *Left* Vignola, the unexecuted design for the façade of the Gesù, Rome, from the engraving of 1573

24 *Below* Palazzo Barberini, Rome, the Loggia, begun in 1628 by Maderno, completed by Bernini with the assistance of Borromini

25 *Below left* The Gesù, façade by Giacomo della Porta, finished 1577

not strictly speaking belong to the church, are flat and only articulated with pilaster-bands. The outer bays of the façade of the actual church are given Corinthian pilasters and low reliefs; the next bays are articulated with engaged columns and have heavily pedimented niches with statues; finally the middle section, which contains the door, covered by a segmental pediment, has full columns which support a rather heavy rectilinear pediment. The upper storey is entirely articulated with pilasters, except for the small columns which flank the central window. As in Vignola's Gesù, the lines of the central section are carried up through the crowning pediment, and the whole composition ends with the unusual feature of a balustrade along the top of the pediment. The subtle disposition of Orders and decoration produces an effect of variety and movement unknown in Roman façades of the late sixteenth century.

Maderno also made significant innovations in the designing of palaces. The Palazzo Barberini, planned in 1625 for the family of Urban VIII, is exceptional in being composed of a single block with projecting wings, instead of four blocks round a central court. The explanation is that, unlike most Roman palaces, it was set in a large garden and so could be designed like a villa, opening outwards, instead of being turned defensively

24

inwards. Maderno's model was in fact Peruzzi's Villa Farnesina, built for Agostino Chigi in 1508–11, which had only been imitated in Rome in the intervening 120 years by Giovanni Vasanzio in the Villa Borghese. The triple seven-bay loggia on the west façade – bigger and more spacious than anything of its kind in Rome – opened on to what was originally a garden (the main approach was from the east) and behind it on the ground floor was a covered atrium, consisting of three 'aisles' of seven, five, and three bays respectively and ending in a closed apse, a feature unknown in contemporary architecture, which was much remarked upon at the time as an interesting revival of ancient Roman ideas.

The Palazzo Barberini was too vast a scheme to be much imitated, and the innovations in planning which Maderno introduced in the Palazzo Mattei di Giove were much more influential. The palace was begun in 1598 on a corner site, which enabled Maderno to arrange two entrances, one from each street. The main entrance lies on the axis of the court, which is continued in a garden. The second entrance leads into the portico which runs along the side of the court nearest to the main entrance, and from it the visitor has a view straight on to the main staircase, only, however, up its first flight, because it turns round on a square plan, so that on the first floor it leaves the visitor on the axis of the upper loggia, from which the rooms of the *piano nobile* open. This is an early hint of the vistas which Baroque architects were to use to such effect in the creation of their staircases, most effectively in Germany and Austria in the eighteenth century.

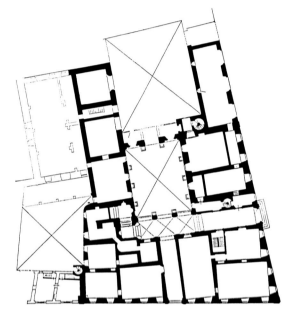

26 *Left* St Peter's, gallery in one of the crossing piers by Bernini, begun 1633

27 *Above* Palazzo Mattei di Giove, Rome, plan by Carlo Maderno, building begun in 1598

28 *Opposite* St Peter's, Cathedra Petri by Bernini, 1657–65

Maderno was much the most inventive architect active in the first thirty years of the seventeenth century, and it was from his shoulders that the great figures of the next generation stepped off, but there were other architects of some importance working in Rome during his lifetime. Paul V employed the Milanese Flaminio Ponzio (*c.* 1560–1613) to extend the Palazzo Borghese and the Quirinal, where he added a wing which included a private chapel decorated by Guido Reni and the huge Sala dei Corazzieri decorated with bold *trompe l'oeil* frescoes by Agostino Tassi and the young Giovanni Lanfranco. Ponzio also built the Cappella Paolina to balance the Cappella Sistina at S. Maria Maggiore. For Cardinal Scipione Borghese he remodelled the church of S. Sebastiano, to which he added a façade of unusual form, with a closed upper storey over an open

three-arched loggia. On his death the pope and the cardinal turned to the mediocre Dutch architect, Jan van Santen, known in Rome as Vasanzio (c. 1550–1621), who completed various buildings left unfinished by Ponzio and also built the Casino in the Villa Borghese.

To the same generation belonged Fausto Rughesi, whose only known work is the façade of S. Maria in Vallicella, the church of the Oratorians (1605), and the mysterious Carlo Lombardo or Lambardi (1554–1620), who was responsible for the façade of S. Francesca Romana (1615), the only Roman building of the period to show the direct influence of Palladio.

Another architect known by only one work in Rome was Rosato Rosati, a Barnabite brother from the Marches, who built the Roman church of his Order, S. Carlo ai Catinari (begun 1611), a spacious building on a near-Greek-cross plan. He left Rome before the church was finished, and the severe but impressive façade was added in 1627 by Giovanni Battista Soria (1581–1651), who represented the most conservative and Classical tendencies of the time. These appear in the front of S. Carlo and also in the façades which he added to two other Roman churches, S. Maria della Vittoria (1625–27) and S. Gregorio Magno, also called S. Gregorio al Celio (1629–33), the latter a grander version of Ponzio's S. Sebastiano.

None of these artists learnt from the novelties which Maderno was introducing into Roman architecture at the time. In the case of Soria his Classicism was probably a conscious reply to the innovations of Maderno, but the other architects just mentioned appear simply to have contined to work in the various conventions current in the late sixteenth century.

This conservative tradition was continued right through the seventeenth century by Giovanni Antonio de' Rossi (1616–95) whose austere churches (S. Maria in Publicolis, S. Maria in Campo Marzio) and palaces (Palazzo Altieri) stand out as altogether exceptional and old-fashioned among the splendidly bold works of the full Baroque which dominated Rome during his lifetime.[7]

Bernini

When Maderno died in 1630, it was clear that there was another architect, of a much younger generation, waiting to step into his shoes, Gianlorenzo Bernini (1598–1680).[8] Even before Maderno's death – perhaps because he was old and ill – several important commissions which he might reasonably have expected to receive as papal architect had gone to Bernini, and after his death the latter rapidly became the favourite of Urban VIII. From this time till his death in 1680 – with one short gap during the first years of Innocent X – his career was one of uniform and ever-growing success.

There is nothing surprising in this fact, as Bernini possessed all the qualities needed for success as an architect at this particular moment. He was a virtuoso and something of a prodigy. By the age of twenty-five he had produced a group of sculptures of which the inventive power and the technical skill had staggered his patron, Cardinal Scipione Borghese, and all the *cognoscenti* of Rome. He had an extraordinary feeling for the dramatic, even the theatrical, in architecture, as well as being a more than competent painter, a poet and a musician. He had a lively mind and was widely read, so that he could converse on equal terms with the intellectuals of his day and was even able to charm Louis XIV and his courtiers on his visit to Paris in 1665. He was also a deeply religious man and a friend of the Jesuits; he practised the exercises of St Ignatius and performed his

religious duties regularly, as we know from the diary of his visit to Paris.

Compared with his spectacular debut in sculpture Bernini's first work in architecture was modest. This was the remodelling of the little church of S. Bibiana (1624), to which he added a portico and a façade. These show some new features in design, such as the insertion of an aedicule in the central section which projects above the side bays, but the architecture has a dryness of treatment surprising in a virtuoso sculptor. At the Palazzo Barberini he modified Maderno's design in execution, but his exact contribution is difficult to isolate. 24

His first real opportunity came when, in the same year that he designed the façade of S. Bibiana, he was commissioned by Urban to decorate the crossing of St Peter's.[9] The scheme was to include a baldacchino over the supposed site of the tomb of St Peter and niches in the piers of the crossing to contain the principal relics of the church. After a series of preliminary projects, in which Borromini certainly played a part, Bernini arrived at the design for the great bronze baldacchino which 31 today dominates the interior of St Peter's. Apart from complicated problems of liturgy and siting – the tomb was not exactly under the centre of the dome – Bernini's main difficulty was to invent a baldacchino which would stand up to the competition of Bramante's vast crossing piers. This he achieved by making the baldacchino out of bronze – taken, incidentally, from the portico of the Pantheon – which made it stand out against the silvery grey of the piers themselves, and, secondly, by adopting twisted or Salomonic columns. These had a symbolical value, because they were copied – with variations – from the twisted columns which had been incorporated into the high altar of Old St Peter's and were supposed to have come from the Temple of Jerusalem. The four colossal columns are decorated with gilt vines with putti climbing in them and support a canopy, also made of bronze but designed to look like a colossal fringe of velvet tassels, decorated alternately with cherubim and the bees of the Barberini arms. The sun, also a favourite device of the family, appears on the entablature over the columns, on which stand four colossal angels who appear actually to be carrying the canopy on garlands of flowers. Behind them four huge volutes rise towards the centre, where they support a cross standing on an orb, the symbol of Christ ruling the world. In its combination of scale and richness of materials, in its dramatic use of colours and contrasts of light and dark, and in its fusion of architecture and sculpture the baldacchino is one of the first – and most remarkable – expressions of the Baroque spirit.

Some of the same qualities appear in the decoration of the piers, which was carried out between 1633 and 1640. The four relics – the lance of St Longinus, the cloth of St Veronica, the head of St Andrew, and a fragment of the True Cross – were themselves kept in chapels dug in the foundations of the piers. At the level of the church were four niches containing the statues of the saints connected with the relics – only St Longinus is by Bernini – and above are galleries in which the relics are displayed on certain days. In the niches which enclose these 26 galleries Bernini incorporated eight of the columns supposed to come from the Temple of Jerusalem, but between these columns he inserted panels of a kind hitherto unknown in architecture or sculpture. Each panel shows an angel carrying the relic and flying against a yellow marble sunset sky with purple marble

29 *Opposite* St Peter's, interior of colonnade by Bernini, begun in 1656

30 Scala Regia, Vatican, by Bernini, 1663–65

clouds. These two colours are carried on through the whole design of the galleries: yellow in the gold of the rays in the half-dome and in the grille over the door, purple in the marble of the balusters of the balcony. Here not only is architecture fused with sculpture, but an element of colour derived from painting is added for good measure.

With the project of placing a baldacchino over the tomb of St Peter was connected the need for a high altar in the apse of the church, and this was to be combined with an appropriate setting for the much-venerated Cathedra Petri which was believed to be the Chair of St Peter but is now known to be the coronation chair of the Emperor Charles the Bald dating from 877. The project was not realized till the years 1657–65, when the newly elected Alexander VII commissioned Bernini to prepare designs. Bernini offered several projects, growing ever larger and bolder, till the grandiose monument which we see today was produced. The chair was enclosed in a huge bronze throne, on the back of which is a relief showing Christ saying to St Peter the words: 'Feed my sheep'. This massive structure is carried by figures more than twice life-size representing the

Four Fathers of the Church. Above is an oval window of golden-yellow glass, with the dove of the Holy Ghost floating in the middle, surrounded by gilt stucco putti and rays which shoot upwards towards the vault and downwards across the pilasters which enclose the whole composition. Here the element of light is added to all the others of which Bernini had made such bold use in the decoration of the crossing.

In the period between the work on the crossing and the creation of the Cathedra Petri Bernini had decorated the piers of the nave of St Peter's with reliefs, so that, with the exception of certain niches still awaiting their statues, the decoration of the interior of the church was complete. Alexander therefore turned his attention to the area in front of the church, which was still without any shape or organization.

At least since the time of Nicholas V (1447–55) the popes had made plans for bringing some order into the zone between St Peter's and the Tiber, and two streets – the Borgo Vecchio and the Borgo Nuovo – had in fact been laid out, but nothing had been done about the area in front of the church, except that Sixtus V had caused Domenico Fontana to erect there the obelisk which had stood in the Circus of Nero, that is to say, just south of St Peter's. This obelisk was to be the focal point of the piazza which Bernini was commissioned by Alexander to build in 1657.[10]

The practical problems which the architect had to solve were complicated and varied. There was first the question of site. The ground sloped down in front of the church, and on the right (east) the old buildings of the Vatican encroached on the area, making it impossible to establish a corridor leading up to the entrance to the Vatican at right angles to the façade of the church. Secondly there were the requirements of ceremonial. The piazza had to be designed so that the maximum number of people could see the pope when he gave his blessing *urbi et orbi,* but he did this from two different points: on some occasions he stood at the Benediction Loggia in the middle of the façade of the church, but on others he appeared at a window in the block of the Vatican built by Sixtus V. Thirdly there was an aesthetic problem. The façade of St Peter's, without the towers that were intended to be added to it, was long and low, and the piazza was intended, if possible, to minimize this effect.

Bernini produced a design which solved all these problems brilliantly. In front of the church he laid out a trapezoidal area defined by two corridors, of which the one on the right, leading to the entrance to the Vatican, just touches the older buildings of the Vatican palace which could not be demolished. In front of this, round the obelisk set up by Sixtus V, he spread out the main colonnade in the form of an oval. The four rows of columns of which the colonnade is composed are so arranged that seen from two points between the obelisk and the fountains they align themselves one behind the other and appear to form a single row.

At the end of the colonnade farthest from the church Bernini left an opening of the same width as that between the two corridors. At a later date he planned to close this with a third arm of the colonnade, so that the whole piazza would have been an enclosed space cut off from the rest of the Borgo, but, although he prepared several schemes for this project, none of them was carried out. The approach to the piazza from the river was ruined in the 1930s by the opening up of the Via della Conciliazione, which completely destroyed this intended effect,

31 *Opposite* St Peter's, Rome, baldacchino by Bernini, begun 1624

although it has the advantage of allowing the visitor to see the dome rising above the church unobscured by the nave.

The colonnade is so planned that, when the pope gives his blessing from the Benediction Loggia in the middle of the façade of the church, he can be seen from everywhere except two small areas to the right and left of the entrance to the two corridors, and by keeping the actual structure low, Bernini also enabled him to be well seen when he gives the blessing from the window in the Vatican Palace. This lowness also serves a purely aesthetic purpose, because the colonnade forms a long horizontal mass which makes the façade of the church itself look higher by comparison.

This effect is intensified by the disposition of the two corridors flanking the space in front of the church, because where these abut on the façade there is a striking contrast between their low pilasters and the giant Order of the church itself. Further Bernini turned to advantage the fact that he could not lay out these corridors as lines at right angles to the façade and produces a 'spreading' effect, similar to that so brilliantly created by Michelangelo at the Capitol, which adds dignity to the building at the end of the composition, the façade of the church.

In addition to forming a prelude to St Peter's, the colonnade had a specific function to perform. Every year, on the feast of Corpus Domini, the Host was carried in procession round the area in front of St Peter's. Till the seventeenth century a temporary structure was built under which the procession passed, with the Host itself carried under a canopy. The colonnade was to form a permanent way for this procession – a purpose which it still serves today. For this reason Bernini made the middle of the three aisles which run between the rows of columns wider than the two outer ones, in order to make a space wide enough for the procession, while the crowd could stand in the outer aisles and in the piazza itself. For the actual form of the colonnade Bernini was probably inspired by reconstructions of an ancient Roman *naumachia,* a circular space enclosed by a colonnade which could be flooded and used for sham sea fights. He also probably had in mind the fact that one of the roads which in ancient times led from the river and passed near the Circus of Nero was known to have been covered, like the great street which survives to this day at Palmyra.

Bernini's colonnade satisfied all the needs discussed above – practical, liturgical, and aesthetic – but for him and his patron Alexander it embodied an idea, a *concetto,* which was for them at least equally important and which the architect himself expressed when he said that its two arms symbolized those of the Church 'which embrace Catholics to reinforce their belief, heretics to re-unite them with the Church, and unbelievers to enlighten them with the true faith'. Such an idea was fundamental to Bernini's conception of the Baroque.

The architecture of the colonnade is surprisingly simple, consisting of an Order of massive Doric columns ending in simple temple fronts with heavy unbroken pediments. Bernini introduced one irregular feature: he evidently felt that the Doric entablature, with its alternation of triglyphs and metopes, would break up the continuity of movement which he sought and he replaced it by an Ionic entablature with a plain

32 *Opposite* Stupinigi, near Turin, by Filippo Juvarra, *salone* with frescoes by Domenico and Giuseppe Valeriani, 1731–33

33 Statue of Constantine by Bernini, Vatican, 1662–68

unbroken frieze. The continuous curve is only broken by the two projecting bays on the cross axis of the piazza, but, as these are without pediments, they scarcely interrupt the movement of the whole colonnade as it swings round towards the church.

The colonnade made a splendid approach not only to St Peter's but also to the entrance to the Vatican, which now came at the end of the right-hand corridor, but, as things stood, this corridor led to a narrow and dark staircase which provided the only access to the main papal apartments. In 1663, on the orders of the pope, Bernini began the construction of a new and grand approach called the Scala Regia. The site available was narrow and irregular, squeezed in on one side by the wall of the Sistine Chapel and on the other by the outer wall of the palace, the two walls being, incidentally, not parallel. Bernini was inspired to a brilliant solution of the problems thus presented. He planned the first flight of the staircase so that it continued the axis of the corridor and at the first landing made it double back on itself, so that it brought the visitor out at the door in the middle of the long wall of the Sala Regia, the principal reception room of the papal apartments. The upper flight of the staircase followed the line of the existing approach, but Bernini showed great ingenuity in exploiting the awkward site to give greater grandeur to the lower flight. He took advantage of the fact that the two walls which enclosed the flight were not parallel and – adapting a device which Borromini had used earlier at the Palazzo Spada (see below, p. 47) – created an effect of false perspective, making the two rows of columns which flank the staircase converge, reducing them in height and lowering the vault as the flight went upwards. In this way he increased the apparent length of the flight, which was limited by the existing landing, but he did not exploit the possibilities of this scheme to the full, as he also sought another effect. The columns stand away from the flanking walls and, if he had wanted to create the maximum lengthening effect, he would have made those at the bottom nearer to the wall than those at the top, so that the angle of convergence would have been greater. In fact he did the opposite and the columns at the bottom of the flight stand further away from the wall than those at the top. His reason for doing this was that it enabled him to create an impressive effect for the visitor approaching along the corridor from the entrance, in the form of a triumphal arch surmounted by the arms of the pope carried by two trumpeting angels. The effect of the staircase is made more dramatic by the insertion of windows at the half-landing and the top of the lower flight, so that the dark tunnel of the vault is interrupted by two patches of light.

The Scala Regia was not only the entrance to the Vatican, it was also the way by which the pope came down to St Peter's on ceremonial occasions. It had therefore to be conveniently linked with the church, and this Bernini achieved quite simply by placing the landing at the bottom of the main flight in direct continuation of the vestibule of the church, thus establishing a right-angled junction between the vestibule and the staircase. The dramatic effect of this junction is heightened by the equestrian statue of the Emperor Constantine which Bernini placed against the wall of the bottom landing, so that it is the first feature to strike anyone approaching from the church to enter the Vatican. The emperor is shown at the moment of seeing the miraculous vision of the Cross, which is in fact attached to the top of the arch facing the papal arms over the entrance to the stairs – a typical application of the Baroque principle of 'extended action'.

This principle is most brilliantly exemplified in two of Bernini's works in ecclesiastical architecture: the Cappella Cornaro and the church of S. Andrea al Quirinale. The Cappella Cornaro, decorated for the Venetian Cardinal Federico Cornaro in the second half of the 1640s, occupies the left transept of the church of S. Maria della Vittoria, which had been rebuilt by Maderno. Its central feature is the group of sculpture representing the vision of St Theresa, probably the most complete expression of mystical ecstasy achieved by a Baroque artist in any medium. The group is set in a niche lit from above by a concealed window – the daylight is now replaced by artificial lighting – enclosed in a projecting aedicule flanked by green marble columns, supporting a richly ornamented entablature and a broken and slightly curved pediment. The entablature is carried round the side walls of the chapel, which contain reliefs showing deceased members of the Cornaro family meditating and disputing. On the vault is a fresco of the Holy Ghost surrounded by angels, painted by Guido Ubaldini, after a drawing by Bernini.

The whole scheme is unified first by the colour which spreads through the marbling, the gilt decoration, and the fresco, and

34 Coloured marble group of members of the Cornaro family by Bernini in the Cornaro Chapel, S. Maria della Vittoria, Rome

secondly by the way the different sections are linked together by the dramatic action: the rays which fall on St Theresa seem to emanate from the Holy Ghost on the vault and, though the members of the Cornaro family in the 'boxes' do not actually look at the miraculous scene, this is clearly the subject of their disputation. The illusionism of the settings in which they are shown is almost frightening. Marble is made to represent red velvet cushions and yellow silk hangings, and the background is a piece of architecture actually carved in relief but in false perspective, which is only normal in painting. The three arts have become inextricably intermingled.

The church of S. Andrea al Quirinale was built for the Noviciate of the Jesuits between 1658 and 1670 and is the most perfect of the three small churches designed by Bernini during the pontificate of Alexander VII.[11] In plan it is a pure oval, with two unusual features: the shorter axis leads to the altar, and the ends of the cross-axis are blocked by solid piers between chapels, instead of being continued, as was the case with earlier oval churches, into the hollow of the chapel. The walls of the central area are panelled with marble of a very delicate pink and articulated with Corinthian pilasters. As in the colonnade of St Peter's the entablature swings round unbroken towards the opening leading to the high altar, where it breaks forward slightly. The martyrdom of St Andrew is depicted in a painting by Giuglielmo Cortese over the altar, strongly lit from a dome which is invisible from the main body of the church, and the figure of the saint, life-size in stucco, floats, in the broken

35 *Right* S. Andrea al Quirinale, Rome by Bernini, 1658–70. Exterior (see plan plate 417)

36 *Below right* Palazzo Flavio Chigi, Rome, by Bernini. Engraving as originally built, begun 1664

pediment over the opening to the chancel, gazing towards the heavenly Host which awaits him, in gilt stucco at the top of the dome, round the edge of the lantern, over which the dove of the Holy Ghost is enclosed in a glory of gilt rays. The main lines of the architecture are again simple, but the effect is one of complete calm and harmony.

35   The exterior is as apparently simple and as subtle as the interior. The oval plan is clearly visible in the cylinder of the central space, surrounded by the ring of chapels, above which rise the bold console buttresses, and the façade reflects these two component elements of the church: the entablature of the central space is carried on over the aedicule which covers the entrance and the line of the chapels in the porch, an oval which echoes that of the chancel in the interior.

Bernini transformed the appearance of the Borgo by creating the Piazza of St Peter's, and he left his mark on other parts of Rome by the fountains and palaces which he built. The *Fontana del Tritone* in front of the Palazzo Barberini is a pure work of 37   sculpture, but in that of the Four Rivers in the Piazza Navona he created a setting of sculpture for the central architectural feature, the obelisk, and produced a monument which dominates the most famous Baroque square in Rome.

Of the two palaces that he built neither survives as he intended it. One, Montecitorio, was finished later by Carlo Fontana, who changed the plans and, as it stands,[12] it is remarkable only for the bold manner in which the architect broke the front into three sections, of which the two outer ones slope back from the central one at a slight angle, and for the original idea of building it on a ground floor composed of rocks. The other, the Palazzo Chigi, was bought in the eighteenth century by the Odescalchi family, who destroyed its carefully thought-out proportions by doubling the length of the façade and adding a second entrance. As originally designed by 36   Bernini it consisted of a central section of seven bays with a rusticated ground floor and above it a giant Order of composite pilasters. This was a novelty in the designing of Roman palaces, which had almost invariably followed the model of the Palazzo Farnese with its rows of pedimented windows.

Bernini applied the same method of composition with even greater effect in the designs which he prepared in 1664–65 for the completion of the Louvre at the request of Louis XIV. His 172   first scheme was a very bold design consisting of two projecting outer wings enclosing a deep concave bay, from the middle of which projected a strong convex section. This was altogether too free for the taste of the French and, after a variant with a 173   single concave central bay, Bernini produced his final design, which consisted of a single colossal rectangular block broken into five sections: two projecting pavilions, articulated by a giant Order, linked by two short wings without any Order to a central pavilion which was given prominence by having engaged columns, whereas the end pavilions only have pilasters. The whole structure was to stand on the rocky base that Bernini had used for Montecitorio, but here it was to be set in a moat. This vast project – perhaps the grandest of all Baroque palace designs – was never even begun, but the design, which was engraved the year Bernini left Paris,[13] was to have an influence

on palace design throughout Europe, from William III's Hampton Court to the eighteenth-century royal palaces in   211, 398 Madrid and Stockholm.

Borromini

The contrast between Bernini and Borromini could hardly be greater.[14] Bernini had all the qualities needed to make a great career; Borromini had none, except a genius for architecture. He was neurotic, difficult, touchy, suffered from something very near persecution mania, and quarrelled with most of his patrons and friends. He never succeeded in gaining the favour of the popes in whose pontificates he lived, except for a short time after the accession of Innocent X, and then only because Bernini was out of favour as a *protégé* of the Barberini. He had a few devoted friends and admirers, of whom the most important was Virgilio Spada, who, as prior of the Oratory of S. Filippo

37 Piranesi's etching of the Piazza Navona, Rome, showing Bernini's
Fountain of the Four Rivers, 1648–51, and the church of S. Agnese, begun
in 1652 by Carlo and Girolamo Rainaldi, continued by Borromini, the
façade modified by Bernini and the dome completed by Carlo Rainaldi

Neri, gave him one of his greatest opportunities and, as adviser
to Innocent X, obtained for him the commission to restore the
church of S. Giovanni in Laterano, his one great public
commission. Of a different kind was Fioravante Martinelli, the
author of one of the most famous guide-books to Rome, who in
his final redaction of this work constantly refers to Borromini
and defends him from the attacks of his critics. But mainly
Borromini worked away from the limelight of papal Rome. His
first patrons were the poor Spanish Discalced Trinitarians of S.
Carlo alle Quattro Fontane, then the Oratorians, a body of men
prominent for their culture and learning, but also for their pious
and simple way of life. The Archiginnasio or University of
Rome and the Collegio di Propaganda Fide were bodies of
importance, but their buildings – though made splendid
aesthetically by Borromini – were nothing, in public esteem,
compared with St Peter's.

As architects the two men were equally different. Bernini was
the master of the Baroque as a combination of all the arts on a
vast scale. Borromini worked with architectural forms alone,
without colour, rich materials, or dramatic lighting. If Bernini's
creations were like operas, Borromini's are like a fugue for
harpsichord, exquisitely thought out and perfect in every detail,
complicated but governed by the most rigid rules.

In his own day – and for nearly three hundred years after his
death – Borromini was accused of being a licentious eccentric,
who debauched architecture by breaking all the rules of the
ancients and working entirely by caprice. In fact nothing could
be more contrary to the truth. He declared that his works were
based on the study of the great works of antiquity, and it can be
shown that this is true. The difference between him and, let us
say, Vignola is that Vignola followed the rules laid down by the
notoriously conservative Vitruvius and chose as his models the
more 'Classical' ancient Roman buildings – the Pantheon, the
Temple of Fortuna Virilis, and so on – whereas Borromini,
although he also appealed to Vitruvius, did so mainly on
technical points and took as his models the more fantastic or
more 'Baroque' works of antiquity, such as Hadrian's Villa, or
the tomb near Capua, known as the Conocchia. It is even
possible that he knew drawings of buildings such as the circular
Temple of Venus at Baalbek, and it is certain that he took as
models reconstructions of buildings of this kind made by the
Milanese architect Giovanni Battista Montano, whose drawings were available at the time in Rome and were engraved
during Borromini's lifetime.

But if he could claim legitimacy, so to speak, for his creations
by an appeal to the ancients, a more important fact is that he
based even his more complicated and fantastic designs on a
strictly controlled geometrical system. He believed that architecture was based on Nature and, though he never explained
what he meant by this, it is probable that his conception of
Nature was close to that of his great contemporary, Galileo,
who wrote that 'the Great book of Nature is written in the
language of mathematics, and its characters are triangles,
circles, and other geometrical figures'. Galileo was much read in
intellectual and artistic circles in Rome in Borromini's time, and

to be erected in Italy in the Gothic style. He arrived in Rome probably at the end of 1618 and was set to work as a stucco-worker under Maderno, who was supervising the decoration of the vestibule of St Peter's. This work brought him into contact for the first time with the architecture of Michelangelo, and we know from his biographers that he took full advantage of this

38 *Left* Palazzo Barberini, Rome. Window next to loggia designed by Borromini *c.* 1630–33; engraving

39 *Below left* St Peter's. Engraving of a window in the attic designed by Maderno

40 *Below* St Peter's. Engraving of windows in the attic designed by Michelangelo

opportunity and studied the apses and dome of the church with passionate interest.

When in 1625 Maderno was commissioned to build the Palazzo Barberini, he took Borromini with him, no longer as a stucco-worker, but as his chief draughtsman, and it is clear that very soon he was allowed a hand in designing certain parts of the palace. The oval staircase in the right-hand wing was certainly planned by Borromini and, although it is basically a variant of an earlier staircase in the Quirinal, it is a remarkable achievement structurally.

Borromini was also responsible for two windows in the bays 38 which link the loggia to the wings of the palace, and these are startlingly novel in conception. The basic idea of the design goes back to Michelangelo's windows in the attic of St Peter's, which 40 have an oval – in some cases enclosing a shell – inserted into the flat hood to the window. Maderno, when he came to build the façade of the church, followed Michelangelo's pattern, but modified it by enclosing the opening in a pediment, thus 39 softening the contrast between the opening and the flat hood which in Michelangelo's design seem almost to press against each other. Borromini made two crucial changes in this design: he ran the lines of the pediment and the opening into a single continuous feature, and he canted the sides of the window, so that they project at 45° to the wall. In this way he established a movement in both the horizontal and the vertical planes through the whole composition. He was to use this motive throughout his life, constantly producing new variations on it, till he gave it its most mature expression in the hood over the door to the Collegio di Propaganda Fide, built in the 1650s. 52 Here the movement is made more subtle and more continuous

there may well be a direct link between his idea of Nature and Borromini's obsession with geometry.

Borromini's real name was Francesco Castello. He was born at Bissone on Lake Lugano in 1599 and came of a family of masons which included Domenico Fontana and Carlo Maderno. At an early age – possibly at nine – he went to Milan, where he would certainly have seen – and may have taken part in – the activities of the great building-yard which was at work on the completion of the cathedral, one of the last great works

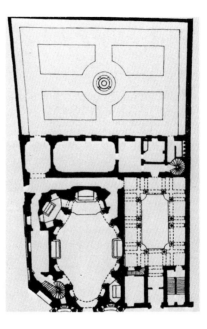

41 *Top left* S. Carlo alle Quattro Fontane, Rome, by Borromini, the cloister, 1634–38

42 *Below left* S. Carlo alle Quattro Fontane by Borromini. Interior of the church, 1638–41

43 *Above* S. Carlo alle Quattro Fontane, plan by Borromini

44 *Opposite* S. Carlo alle Quattro Fontane by Borromini, interior of the dome

owing to the fact that in plan the hood is designed on a concave curve instead of three straight sections at angles of 45° as at the Palazzo Barberini, so that it forms a continuous three-dimensional twist. In this way Borromini converts the feeling of pressure and conflict in Michelangelo's design into a fluent, unbroken Baroque movement.

In 1634 Borromini received his first independent commission for the building of the church and monastery of S. Carlo alle Quattro Fontane, generally known as S. Carlino from its small size. In spite of the extremely awkward and cramped site Borromini produced a completely satisfying solution to the problems presented to him. On the right (west) of the site he inserted a small and simple but ingeniously designed cloister, 41 with its corners cut off by slightly convex bays, and on the left a church which was revolutionary in many respects.

Basically the plan of the church is an oval, which becomes 43 clearly visible in the dome, but a comparison with earlier oval churches, such as S. Giacomo degli Incurabili, shows the 18 ingenuity and liveliness of Borromini's plan. It consists of an oblong central space with the addition of two semi-circular members for the choir and vestibule, and two half-ovals for the main side chapels. In the corners of the church formed in this way Borromini has inserted two smaller chapels, a spiral staircase leading to the campanile, and a passage to the monastery.

The shape of the central space of the church is complex because the bays linking the arches over choir, chapels, and 42 vestibule are neither straight nor simply curved, but consist of

two side bays projecting on concave curves and a straight central bay. This complex plan is simplified at the next level, which consists of four arches and four broad pendentives, and the simplicity is increased in the clear oval of the dome.

In the walls of the church Borromini has introduced a deliberate ambiguity, which enables the two levels to be read differently. The upper level reads clearly as four half-domes separated by pendentives, but below the entablature the eye is first caught by the four 'triptychs' on the diagonals, each defined by four columns and formed by a central bay with door, niche, and statue, flanked by two simpler concave bays with small niches and plain panels over them. This sets up a sort of counterpoint between the two levels of the wall, because the 'triptychs' spread horizontally beyond the limits of the pendentives into the zones below the half-domes.

Free and complex though the plan of the church appears to be, it was actually arrived at by a series of geometrical manipulations which can be traced in Borromini's preliminary drawings.[15] The skeleton of the plan consists of two equilateral 46 triangles (ABC, A′BC) with a common side and two circles inscribed in them. Two further arcs of circles (D, E and D′E′) are drawn with their centres at the apexes of the triangles B and

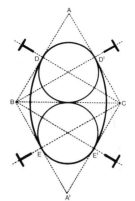

C, and these complete an oval which defines the dome. The apexes of the triangles (A, A′, and B, C) fall at the midpoints of the apses and half-ovals which form the subsidiary elements of the church, and the axes of the small chapels lie along lines which join these apexes to the centres of the circles. In this way the whole plan is evolved from the simple elements of two triangles and two circles.

The dome of the church follows the simple line of the oval as 44 defined in the above scheme, but its decoration is ingenious. It consists of coffering composed of crosses, hexagons, and lozenges, a pattern recorded by Serlio on the basis of the early Christian mosaic in the vault of S. Costanza, but Borromini was the first architect to use it in a fully three-dimensional form and to apply it to a dome instead of a flat ceiling or barrel-vault. It is a typical example of Borromini's basic principle of designing complex forms in simple materials.

The façade of the church was not actually begun till 1665, but 6 there is conclusive evidence to show that from the first Borromini intended it to have a curved plan of the type on which it was finally built. It is therefore one of the earliest, as well as one of the most mature, examples of the fully curved Baroque façade. There is, however, reason to think that the upper storey was not completed according to Borromini's design, and the oval painting carried by angels is quite foreign to his style. It is, incidentally, copied almost exactly from Bernini's high altar at Castel Gandolfo, and it is inconceivable that Borromini, at the end of his life, should have borrowed in this way from his rival.

Borromini's achievement at S. Carlino attracted some attention, not only because of the aesthetic qualities of the design, but because of the attention which the architect had given to practical details and for the relatively low cost of the whole building. As a result he was invited in 1637 by the Oratorians to complete their Roman house by adding to the church an Oratory for musical performances, a library, and accommodation for the Fathers.[16] The most remarkable feature of the whole complex is the façade of the Oratory itself, which, like S. 45, 419 Carlino, is on a curve, but in this case a single, slow curve.

45 *Left* Oratorio di S. Filippo Neri, Rome, by Borromini, the façade, 1637–40, showing also part of Fausto Rughesi's façade of S. Maria in Vallicella (Chiesa Nuova), 1605 (see also engraving on title page)

46 *Top* S. Carlo alle Quattro Fontane, diagram of the plan by Borromini

47 *Opposite* Stupinigi, near Turin, by Filippo Juvarra, 1729–33. Entrance gateway

Borromini was instructed not to use columns, so that the façade would not compete in importance with that of the church, but he turned this limitation to advantage and produced a façade which has the tense quality of a sheet of metal bent under pressure. This effect is heightened by the smoothness of the brick-work, which is composed of very thin bricks with the minimum of mortar between them. On this façade Borromini uses a new form of pediment, a sort of fusion of the straight and curved pediments which Michelangelo had used, one inside the other on the Porta Pia. As in the window of the Palazzo Barberini, Borromini has taken two separate, almost conflicting motifs from Michelangelo and fused them into a single continuous whole.

Borromini's principle of evolving a complex plan on a strict geometrical basis reaches its culmination in the church of S. Ivo. He added the church to the existing court of the Sapienza between 1642 and 1650.[17] As at S. Carlino the plan is composed of equilateral triangles and circles, but here the two triangles interpenetrate to form a six-pointed star – the symbol of wisdom – and a hexagonal central space. Round this space are six bays, three composed of semi-circles drawn on the sides of the hexagon, the other three of a more complex form, including arcs of circles drawn with their centres on the apexes of the triangles. The dome is formed by simply shrinking the ground plan gradually till it reaches the lantern, and the result is a building of extraordinary homogeneity, dominated by the line of the entablature which leads the eye on a continuous movement round the whole space. The recent restoration has brought the church back to its original whiteness, no longer disturbed by the coarse, painted marbling added in the mid-nineteenth century.

Clear though the general articulation of the interior may be it is not as simple as it appears at first sight. The concave bays are slightly more than semicircular, so that the angle formed by the entablature at the point where one bay joins another is slightly less than a right angle and the cornice appears to be pressing into the central space. The wall surfaces are broken up in a variety of different ways: a single tall niche for the high altar, a small niche enclosing double doors and covered by a pediment in the two other concave bays, and a large niche with a gallery over it on the bays which are convex inwards. A string-course dividing the walls into two almost equal parts runs all round the building but is interrupted by the high altar bay. The pilasters are disposed in a complex rhythm: pairs at right angles at the corners where the bays join, further full pilasters in the concave bays, but broken pilasters on each side of the balconies. Further, the broken pilasters are separated from the corner pairs by a gap slightly less wide than the corresponding space in the concave bays.

Even in the interior of the dome there are concealed subtleties. The concave bays are carried up to the lantern without any basic change in their form, by the simple process of reducing their size; but with the bays over the galleries the problem is more complex. At the level of the entablature they are convex inwards, but at the top they have become concave, so that they can be absorbed into the circle round the foot of the lantern, the change being masked by the large window which allows the architect to move from the straight-convex-straight

49

2

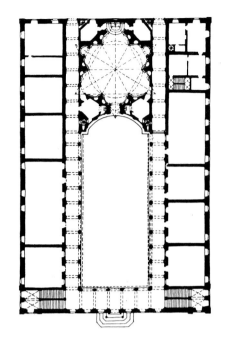

49 Palazzo della Sapienza, Rome, plan showing Borromini's church, begun in 1642, set into the 16th-century university building

plan of the entablature and attic through a zone with three straight elements, of which the central one – the window – masks the change from convex to concave, through being open instead of solid.

The symbolism implied by the star of wisdom in the plan is carried on into the decoration, which includes the cherubim, palm and pomegranates of the Temple of Solomon, and also allusions to the arms of Alexander VII, under whom the decoration was carried out. The same type of symbolism appears on the exterior, one of Borromini's most fantastic inventions, where the spiral ramp above the lantern, like a Mesopotamian ziggurat, was an accepted symbol for the Tower of Wisdom, ending in the Flame of Truth, supporting the Cross on an orb.

Even this apparently wild invention is based on ancient models and a strict observance of geometry. The lantern, with its concave bays separated by coupled columns, is like the Temple of Venus at Baalbek and also one of Montano's reconstructions of ancient buildings, and the plans of the lantern, the stepped roof below it, and the spiral ramp above it were all drawn out with the compasses on simple geometrical principles, as can be seen from the original drawings for some of them, which are still preserved in the Albertina in Vienna.

The lower part of the dome, which looks like a drum, in fact encloses the cupola itself, according to a method of building which Borromini would have seen in sixteenth-century Milanese buildings. In this case it was almost forced on him, because the site was so narrow that he could not include chapels to buttress the dome, the lateral thrust of which is taken by the dead weight of the masonry between the cupola and the cusped exterior.

The same principles of construction and design are to be found in the dome of S. Andrea delle Fratte, built by Borromini between 1654 and 1665. Here again Borromini has started from an ancient model, in this case the Conocchia, an ancient Roman

50

48 *Opposite* Turin, the Superga by Filippo Juvarra, begun 1717. Detail of tower

tomb near Capua, but he has amplified the movement of the original by making the central section curved instead of straight. Beside the dome, which was to have had a lantern with deep re-entrant bays, Borromini set up a campanile which is a remarkable example of the mixture of Classical and unclassical elements in his architecture. The lower stage is a cylinder articulated with Ionic columns, containing alternately open and closed bays, of a type known in ancient Roman bas-reliefs, but this is topped by a structure of concave bays, separated by rectangular piers which merge into winged cherubs. Above this is a crowning feature with a flame-like element enclosing the arms of the patron, the Marchese del Bufalo, and covered by his coronet.

Borromini's last phase is best illustrated by his work on the Collegio di Propaganda Fide, where he built a new chapel – replacing one built by Bernini in the 1630s – and added the façade on the street. In the chapel he developed certain ideas which he had adumbrated in the Oratory, creating a rectangular space with rounded corners, with a low coved vault divided by ribs which cross the space diagonally, leaving a hexagonal panel in the middle, which is filled with a fresco. The façade is yet another instance of Borromini's combination of traditional and novel elements. The columns which surround the windows are of the true Roman Doric Order without bases – a type hardly ever used in Rome in the seventeenth century – but they are disposed at angles which recall Michelangelo's Sforza Chapel rather than any ancient Roman building. Most complex of all is the entrance door. In plan the piers are half-hexagons with slightly curved sides; in elevation they follow Michelangelo's revolutionary pilasters in the Ricetto of the Laurentian Library in Florence in that the 'pilasters' shrink towards the bottom and their capitals are narrower than the shaft, but, unlike Michelangelo's piers, they are canted so that they initiate a movement along a concave line running through the hood of the door, which has the three-dimensional curve described above.

Borromini was much less active in the field of domestic architecture than in church building, but one of his surviving works must be mentioned, the colonnade in the Palazzo Spada. The similarity of the colonnade to Bernini's Scala Regia is immediately striking, but it is now known that Borromini's work was executed in 1652–53, that is to say ten years before the planning of the Vatican staircase, so that he was the innovator in this use of false perspective; but only an innovator in a limited sense, because the idea had been applied in a more restricted way by Bramante in S. Maria presso S. Satiro in Milan, and by Antonio da Sangallo the Younger in the entrance to the Palazzo Farnese more than a century earlier, and further, Borromini probably based his design on one of Montano's drawings of ancient 'temples'. What is surprising, however, is that in Montano's plan, though the columns grow shorter and closer together, there would have been no effect of illusion, because the visitor would have come in at the narrow end of the

51

52

53, 54
30

50 *Opposite* S. Ivo della Sapienza, Rome, by Borromini. Exterior showing the dome and lantern

51 *Top right* S. Andrea delle Fratte, Rome, dome and campanile by Borromini, begun 1654

52 *Right* Collegio di Propaganda Fide, Rome, by Borromini, detail of façade with main door

colonnade and would have been looking, so to speak, down the wrong end of the telescope. It was Borromini's invention to apply the plan to the creation of this peculiarly brilliant effect of deception, which is completely convincing if seen from the door to the library of the palace, the point to which the visitor is automatically led.

In his last years Borromini's illness became more marked. He cut himself off almost completely, even from his friends, and spent all his time shut up in his studio working at plans, which he probably realized would never be executed. At the same time he destroyed many drawings which he had made previously for fear that his rivals might steal them and use them for their own purposes. Finally, in a fit of despair, he tried to kill himself by running himself through with a sword. He lived for seven hours, long enough to dictate to his confessor an account of what had led him to take his life, an account of almost unbelievably calm objectivity. This ability to maintain complete control, even when in the grip of violent emotions – and even pain – has its counterpart in the detachment with which he could control even his most fantastic ideas in architecture. In his life he may have lost the battle between emotions and reason, but in his art he attained a supreme synthesis of the two conflicting factors.

53 *Above* Palazzo Spada, Rome, false perspective colonnade by Borromini, 1652–53

54 *Right* Palazzo Spada, by Borromini, plan of the false perspective colonnade

Pietro da Cortona

The third of the creators of Baroque architecture, Pietro Berettini (1596–1669), usually called Pietro da Cortona from his birthplace, was in the first place a painter, who actually built relatively little in comparison with his two great contemporaries, but he created an individual style, quite distinct from those of Bernini and Borromini.[18]

In his native town he may have become aware of architecture through his uncle Filippo, whose only surviving building, a palace in Cortona, shows a sensitive use of rustication, which is in a certain way related to Cortona's own mature work; but at a very early age he went to Florence and in 1612 or 1613 to Rome. During these early years he studied painting under two very undistinguished painters, Andrea Commodi and Baccio Ciarpi, and there is no evidence to show how or from whom he obtained his training in architecture. In Florence he studied Michelangelo's architecture, particularly the Ricetto of the Laurenziana, of which echoes are to be found in his mature works, and probably also the works of Florentine architects of the next generation, particularly Buontalenti and Cigoli. In Rome he made drawings of ancient buildings; but he does not seem to have learnt much from the architects active in Rome during his youth.

The influence of ancient architecture is particularly apparent in the buildings which he included in his paintings – though it is antiquity seen through the eyes of Raphael – but that is perhaps natural, since they usually represent Classical subjects and it was no doubt by design that Cortona chose a severe Doric Order for the temple in the *Age of Bronze* in the Pitti to suggest not only antiquity in a general sense but specifically an early stage in the history of man.

In the buildings which he actually realized in brick and stone his style is much freer and, given the mystery of his training in architecture, it is surprising to find that from the beginning it is both mature and original.

The date of his earliest building, the Vigna Sacchetti, now destroyed, is not known, but it is generally thought to have been designed before 1630. It is remarkably bold in design for its

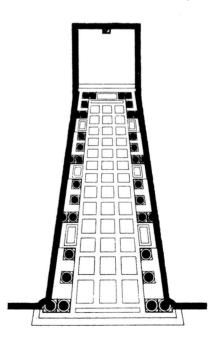

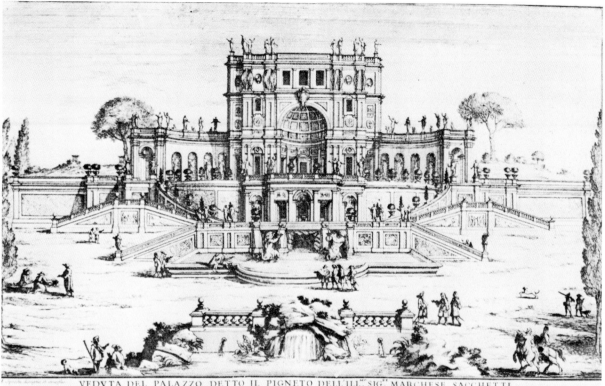

VEDVTA DEL PALAZZO DETTO IL PIGNETO DELL'ILL.^{mo} SIG.^{re} MARCHESE SACCHETTI
FVORI DI PORTA ANGELICA HOGGI IN PARTE DIRVTO
Architettura del Caualier Pietro Berettini da Cortona

55 The Vigna Sacchetti, Rome, (destroyed) by Pietro da Cortona (from an engraving), probably designed before 1630

55   date. The central block with the large niche is derived from Bramante's Nicchione di Belvedere, but the addition of the curving wings was quite new. The open loggias at the ends of the building are of a type unknown in Roman architecture of the period, though the apses cut off by colonnades incorporate ideas which Cortona could have learnt from Palladio's book on ancient baths. The Vigna is important as being probably the earliest instance of a curved façade produced in Rome, though the idea had been hinted at by Antonio da Sangallo the Younger in the Porta Santo Spirito and the bank of the same name. It is also interesting to notice that Cortona has already evolved the particular form of curve which he was to use in all his later works, with a straight section in the middle and fairly sharp curves at the ends, as opposed to the steady slow curve used by Borromini.

420   His only other work in secular architecture was the door at the end of the terrace on the north side of the Palazzo Barberini. Originally this stood in the wall which separated the stable court from the terrace, so that the pediment would have stood out against the sky, an arrangement which would have given emphasis to its unusual form, which is Cortona's version of the double pediment used by Borromini in the façade of the Oratory and elsewhere. The door itself has the kind of refined rustication, with a small layer projecting beyond the main front surface, which was to be typical of Cortona's work and which may owe something to the palace built by his uncle in Cortona. In the windows which flank the door the architect again produces a variant of a theme used by Borromini, in this case the window on the Palazzo Barberini itself; but the curved element enclosing the Barberini bee is somewhat feeble in design. Much more typical of Cortona's style are the consoles supported by guttae on which the windows stand.

In 1634 Cortona, who had been elected president (*Principe*) of the Academy of St Luke, was given permission to restore the crypt of the little church of S. Martina, near the Forum, which belonged to the Academy, in order to erect there his own tomb. While the necessary excavations were being made, the body of S. Martina was discovered and, as relics were highly revered during this phase of the Counter-Reformation, the pope decided that something grander than the proposed restoration was demanded. The pope's nephew, Cardinal Francesco Barberini, undertook to finance not only the restoration of the crypt but also the construction above it of a church to be dedicated to St Luke and to contain over the high altar the canvas of St Luke painting the Virgin, then thought to be from the hand of Raphael himself, which had been presented to the Academy by an earlier president.

Cortona had already been involved in an earlier project for a church on the same site, which was to have been circular in form and was probably destined to be a mausoleum for the family of Pope Gregory XV (Ludovisi). It is significant for the sources of Cortona's style that this design was directly based on one of Buontalenti's projects for the Cappella dei Principi, which was being built on to S. Lorenzo when Cortona was in Florence as a boy. When Cardinal Francesco Barberini took over the project, the circular plan was abandoned in favour of a Greek cross, but there is some evidence from the surviving drawings

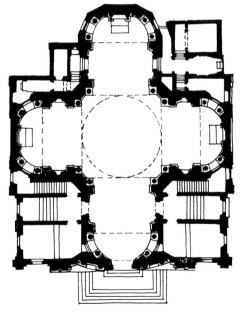

56 *Top left* SS. Luca e Martina, Rome, exterior by Pietro da Cortona, begun 1635

57 *Left* SS. Luca e Martina, plan by Pietro da Cortona

58 *Above* SS. Luca e Martina, interior showing dome

that at this stage it was still planned to make the church a mausoleum, now for the Cardinal and perhaps other members of his family.

The church was long in building – the decoration was still being carried out in the last decades of the century – but it is certain that the foundations, including those of the façade, were complete by 1635. This is important, because it shows that Cortona had proposed a curved façade by this date, which is earlier than the first datable scheme for S. Carlino, though it must be remembered that Borromini may have been planning the façade of the church from the time that he was first commissioned to build the monastery, that is to say, 1634. However, the question of actual priority is not fundamental, because it is clear that various architects were playing with the idea at the same time.

59 *Left* SS. Luca e Martina, interior, begun 1635. Stucco decoration finished by Ciro Ferri after Cortona's death

60 *Below* S. Maria della Pace, Rome, façade, by Pietro da Cortona, 1656–57

56   Cortona's façade reveals many of his characteristics as an architect. The central bay is planned on the curve that he had used in the Vigna Sacchetti but inverted, that is to say, convex as opposed to concave. Further it is framed with two rectangular blocks which seem almost to squeeze it in on both sides. Cortona intended to build two further bays outside these blocks, sloping back from the line of the façade, which would have given the whole building more normal proportions and would have relaxed the somewhat over-compact impression which the façade gives in its present form. The façade was not finished till after Cortona's death, and the group of sculpture which crowns it is almost certainly not from his design. It has even been suggested that he may have intended to finish the front with a broad pediment, and this may well be correct.

    The character of the façade depends in great part on the almost sculptural manner in which the actual surface is treated. In the middle section coupled columns are set into the wall, according to the formula invented by Michelangelo in the Ricetto of the Laurenziana, but here the columns are spaced out and separated by projecting blocks, carved with reliefs. This arrangement intensifies the effect of pressure which appears in the design of the whole façade. Vertically the two storeys of the façade are united by the strong lines of the columns, even though these are interrupted by the clearly defined entablature; but there are equally clear horizontal links formed by the string-courses which seem to be carried on behind the columns and one element of which is brought forward into the pediment over the door. The monumental quality of the whole front is emphasized by the fact that it is constructed in the rough, tawny travertine which was Cortona's favourite material.

57   In plan the upper church of SS. Luca e Martina is almost a Greek cross – though the nave and choir are slightly longer than the transepts – but the ends of all the elements are rounded off in the same curve that Cortona had used at the Vigna Sacchetti, though the middle section is much shorter. What is remarkable

59 about the interior is the treatment of the walls. The Order is a rather heavy Roman Ionic, that is to say, the form with the volutes projecting at 45°. Round the apse the articulation con-sists of pairs of columns set back under an entablature, as on the façade, but without the intervening blocks. These sections are joined to the crossing by piers articulated with pilasters and with broken pilasters in the corners of the re-entrant bays. For the actual crossing Cortona returns to full columns, this time standing free. The result is an elaborate system of layering the walls. At the back is the wall behind the inset columns; then comes a layer formed by the entablature over these columns; and in front of that the plane formed by the entablature over the pilaster piers. The arrangement is complicated by the fact that the back plane, which seems to vanish in the pilaster piers, reappears in the bays between these piers. This method of articulation, combined with the fact that the whole church is in white stucco, gives a strongly sculptural character to the interior, different from the rich, coloured effects achieved by Bernini and the purely architectural conceptions of Borromini. The decoration of the half-domes at the ends of the four members of the church is also composed of heavy, almost sculptural, features: powerful ribs, decorated with bands of laurel leaves, which rise between windows flanked by consoles and covered by broken pediments enclosing round niches.

    The treatment of the dome is also unusual, with ribs cutting 58

across a field decorated with coffers of unusual shape. They
have semi-circular breaks in the middle of the sides, forming a
pattern like the Late-Gothic panel used by Andrea Pisano on
the doors of the Baptistery at Florence. This dome is often
quoted as the first instance of the combination of the two
methods of decorating a dome, the Gothic with ribs, and the
Classical with coffering; but in fact the decoration in SS. Luca e
Martina probably dates from after Cortona's death and is due
to his follower, Ciro Ferri, in which case the method of
decoration in question had already been used by Bernini in his
two churches at Castel Gandolfo and Ariccia.

The lower church, containing the tomb of S. Martina, is
treated in the same manner as the façade of the church, with
closely packed panels and inset columns, but the walls are
composed of rich marbles of different colours, cut so that the
veining forms symmetrical patterns in each panel. The dome of
the upper church shows externally a number of Michelangelesque features, such as the heavy triglyphs with guttae
which support the ribs, and the Ionic volute motif from the
Porta Pia. The design of Cortona's only other dome, that of S.
Carlo al Corso, built from 1668 onwards, is much simpler and is
composed of columns set back, like those in the interior of SS.
Luca e Martina. The same severe simplicity – though combined
with the use of rich marbles – appears in Cortona's other late
architectural work the Cappella Gavotti in S. Nicola da
Tolentino.

In 1656 Cortona was commissioned by Alexander VII to
complete the church of S. Maria della Pace, which contained his
family chapel decorated by Raphael, by reconstructing the
dome and adding a façade.[19] The problem of the façade was
complicated by the fact that the church was flanked by two
narrow streets which ran from it at different angles, and that on
the right the apse of S. Maria dell'Anima impinged on the site
and was only separated from the church by the narrower of the
two streets. The situation was further complicated by what can
only be described as a traffic problem. The church was a
fashionable one – and became more so when its patron became
pope – and the streets that led to it were so narrow that it was
impossible to turn a coach in any of them. Indeed the street to
the right of the church was too narrow to admit a coach at all,
and that on the left, though it was wider, did not admit of two
coaches passing. This disposition gave rise to a series of difficult
situations and the street was declared 'one way' – perhaps one
of the first instances of this procedure in history. In order to
solve this problem Cortona planned in front of the church a
piazza large enough to allow a coach to be turned – and this
involved a considerable space – and at the same time he created
a façade for the church which is one of the most ingenious and –
in the good sense of the word – theatrical of Baroque constructions. The authorities of the church were able to acquire
and pull down two or three houses opposite the church, and this
enabled Cortona to lay out his square in the form of a
quadrilateral with not quite parallel ends. He then spread his
design for the façade of the church over the whole of the largest
side of the quadrilateral. At ground level he built two small
wings, one of which contained an opening for the right-hand
street, and above these wings he made two quadrant bays,
which formed a wide concave setting for the façade itself. The
upper half of this is articulated on the same principles as at SS.
Luca e Martina, but at the lower level Cortona added a portico
which projects in a half-oval, making a strong contrast to the
upper concave bay. The play of curves is far more emphatic

61 S. Maria in Via Lata, Rome, façade, by Pietro da Cortona, 1658–62

than in his earlier church, and the façade offers great possibilities for effects of light and shade. In the treatment of the
upper part of the façade the architect used one device which is,
as far as I know, unique. He cut the travertine, as he had done
with the marble in the lower church of S. Martina, so that the
graining forms symmetrical patterns in the two main panels of
the façade, producing a very curious decorative effect.

Cortona's last architectural work was the façade and vestibule which he added to the church of S. Maria in Via Lata. The
church was built over an early Christian chapel which was
supposed to incorporate the house where St Paul had been
imprisoned when he came to Rome, and in the seventeenth
century this shrine came to be an object of such veneration that
in 1658 Cortona was commissioned to restore it and make it
safely accessible to the faithful. He carried out the work in such
a way as to preserve as much as possible of the original crypt –
much more than in the lower church of S. Martina – and
contented himself with breaking down one wall to make
circulation possible and adding a few decorative features. The
work is an interesting example of the Baroque interest in the
Early Church, and it was carried out with unusual respect for
the interests of archaeology. The restoration of the Constantin-
ian Baptistery of the Lateran, carried out on the orders of
Urban VIII some years earlier, had been much more drastic and
had destroyed much archaeological evidence.

The church of S. Maria in Via Lata itself had been restored
many times, last of all in the mid seventeenth century, but its
entrance front was still unfinished. Between 1658 and 1662
Cortona added to it a vestibule, with a room above it, and built
the façade. The problem here was dominated by the fact that
the church faced on to the Corso, the main arterial road of
ancient Rome, which had never been widened. This meant that
the façade would normally be seen in sharp foreshortening.
Cortona could have got over the difficulty by curving the
façade, but the space available to him was limited, and he
probably felt that a curved façade would not have fitted with

the mile-and-a-half-long row of straight-fronted palaces which flanked the Corso. (The church of S. Marcello, nearly opposite to S. Maria in Via Lata, has a curved façade, but it is set back in a little piazza.) He therefore chose a quite different method and, by opening up the two storeys of the façade, created a beautifully calculated effect of light solids against dark voids. The arrangement of the façade with a room over the vestibule goes back to earlier examples, such as Flaminio Ponzio's S. Sebastiano and Bernini's S. Bibiana, but in the former the upper storey is completely closed, and in the latter, though the central bay is open, there is no deliberately worked out pattern of light and shade. Cortona emphasizes this effect by having pairs of free-standing columns standing out against the darkness of the portico on each storey. The planar effect of the actual building is severe, but variety is added by the richness of the capitals and entablatures and by the unusual arrangement of the upper pediment, in which Cortona inserts an arch protruding into the field of the pediment and so forcing the entablature – or rather the frieze and cornice – to break upwards and follow the curve of the arch. There were ancient precedents for this practice, of which one certainly known to Cortona was the Triumphal Arch at Orange, which had been studied since the late fifteenth century and in which a similar arrangement is found on the ends of the structure.

62 *Below* S. Maria in Campitelli, Rome, by Carlo Rainaldi, façade, 1663–67

63 *Top right* SS. Vincenzo e Anastasio, Rome, façade, by Martino Longhi, the Younger, 1646–50

In the vestibule the free-standing columns are repeated against the wall of the church itself, and the two rows support a barrel-vault with octagonal coffering. The ends are semicircular, and a curious feature of the design is that the coffered vault appears to be carried on behind the apses, an effect of ambiguity unusual in Baroque architecture and more typical of sixteenth-century ingenuity.

Rome: The last phase

Roman architecture of the mid-seventeenth century was dominated by the three great figures of Bernini, Borromini and Pietro da Cortona, but there were other architects active at the same period who attained a certain celebrity, though none showed the inventiveness of the three masters.

Martino Longhi (or Lunghi) the Younger (1620–60), grandson of the sixteenth-century architect of the same name, added the impressive front to the church of SS. Vincenzo e Anastasio near the Trevi Fountain in the years 1646–50.[20] In its use of heavy full columns under a severe entablature it is reminiscent of Pietro da Cortona, but it is original in the spacing of the columns: on the lower storey the side-bays are composed of two widely spaced columns (the outer ones are not visible in the reproduction on plate 63) while the door is flanked by pairs of columns close together, with the entablature broken forward over each of them. This progression, combined with the double curved pediment over the door, strongly emphasizes the central bay of the composition. In the upper storey the six inner columns of the lower stage are repeated to form a single bay flanked by triple columns, an arrangement which creates a lively counterpoint between the two storeys.

Carlo Rainaldi (1611–91) is chiefly famous for building the church of S. Maria in Campitelli (1660–67).[21] The church is a strange mixture of Baroque features and elements which come from late sixteenth-century traditions. The façade has a richness of movement due to the breaking of the entablature, but this movement is discontinuous – forwards and backwards – as in Giacomo della Porta's façade of the Gesù, and the aedicules which the architect introduced in the central bay, while they

63

62

64 Palazzo Colonna, Rome, the *salone*, built by Antonio del Grande, 1654–65. Frescoes by Giovanni Coli and Filippo Gherardi, 1675–78

emphasize this section, seem almost detached from the rest of the façade. In fact they derive from a north-Italian, sixteenth-century tradition, as it appeared, for instance, in Tibaldi's S. Fedele in Milan. The effect of the interior is made dramatic by the use of tall columns standing free of the walls, but the plan is somewhat untidily composed of a succession of square, rectangular, and semi-circular spaces which are not clearly defined in themselves and do not flow smoothly one into the other.

Rainaldi also remodelled the apse of S. Maria Maggiore, after a project by Bernini had been rejected, and was involved in the planning and construction of the twin churches on the Piazza del Popolo – S. Maria di Monte Santo and S. Maria dei Miracoli – begun in 1662, though Bernini played some part in the final design of Monte Santo. In both these projects Rainaldi's style is more sophisticated and more Classical than in S. Maria in Campitelli, as is exemplified in the use of free-standing porticoes, a very unusual feature in Rome at this date.

In secular architecture the most important contributions were made by Antonio del Grande (active 1647–71), an assis-

tant of Borromini, who has not received the attention that he deserves.[22] His most spectacular work is the gallery of the Palazzo Colonna, begun in 1654 but only finished in the late 1670s, when the vault was frescoed by Giovanni Battista Coli and Filippo Gherardi, with assistance from Giovanni Paolo Schor in the decorative parts. The result is one of the most splendid decorative ensembles of the Roman Baroque. The plan of the gallery is unusual in that it is laid out in three sections with two square anterooms, one at each end of the main hall, connected with it by openings flanked by free-standing columns, an arrangement which influenced Jules Hardouin Mansart in his design of the Galerie des Glaces at Versailles and Fischer von Erlach in the Hofbibliothek at Vienna.

Antonio del Grande was also responsible for a new type of entrance to palaces, much grander than was normal in earlier generations, which took account of the fact that coaches had become the normal means of transport for the rich and that they were cumbersome and difficult to turn. In the wing added to the Palazzo Doria-Pamphili facing on to the Piazza del Collegio Romano (1659–61) he arranged a spacious vestibule into which a coach could be driven, so that the visitor could alight under cover and would find himself facing up the staircase which runs parallel to the façade of the palace. It is possible that he took the idea from Borromini, who planned such a vestibule in his unexcecuted projects for the Palazzo Carpegna near the Fontana di Trevi and the Palazzo Pamphili on the Piazza Navona, but del Grande seems to have been the first architect actually to put into execution this plan, which was to be widely imitated and developed in other parts of Italy and in Central Europe.

In the last twenty years of the seventeenth century Roman architects were sharply divided into two distinct, even opposing, parties. One group, which included the architect and painter Antonio Gherardi and the Jesuit Andrea Pozzo, developed the ideas of the 'Founding Fathers' in a bold and unusual manner. The other, led by Carlo Fontana, produced the new moderate style – the 'International Late Baroque' – which was to have a wide influence outside as well as inside Italy.

Gherardi's originality appears in two chapels which he built in Roman churches, the Cappella Avila in S. Maria in Trastevere (before 1686), and the Cappella di S. Cecilia in S. Carlo ai Catinari (1691). The earlier chapel is the more dramatic, particularly in the audacious treatment of the lantern. This is composed of a cylindrical outer shell and an inner ring of Ionic columns supported by stucco angels floating against a feigned balustrade which runs round the actual cupola. Gherardi in fact combines Bernini's use of concealed light with his fusion of sculpture and architecture and carries the effect to a new point of ingenuity. The lower part of the chapel, on the other hand, is composed of architectural features more in the spirit of Borromini, though the altar, which consists of a false-perspective colonnade in coloured marbles, includes elements borrowed from both Borromini and Bernini. The Cappella di S. Cecilia is more completely Berninesque, with angels drawing aside stucco curtains from the window, and a vista through the oval cut-off dome, on which sit trumpeting angels, to a rectangular chamber – lit by a concealed window – which has on its ceiling the dove of the Holy Ghost in a radiance of white stucco rays surrounded by a floral wreath.

Andrea Pozzo, usually known as Padre Pozzo, though in fact

65 *Below* S. Maria in Trastevere, Rome, Cappella Avila, by Antonio Gherardi, before 1686

66 *Right* S. Ignazio, Rome, the altar of S. Luigi Gonzaga by Andrea Pozzo, *c.* 1700, from an engraving

he remained all his life a lay-brother, was not strictly speaking an architect, but the two volumes of his *Perspectiva Pictorum et Architectorum,* published in 1693 and 1698, exercised a wide influence on architects throughout Europe (translations were printed in English, German and Flemish, and a manuscript version exists in Chinese). In addition to diagrams showing how the Orders should be drawn in perspective, the treatise contains designs for altars, tabernacles and temporary structures for *feste,* designed on complex curvilinear plans and composed of architectural features broken up with the greatest freedom, in a spirit akin to that of Antonio Gherardi.

His most important works were executed for the two principal Jesuit churches in Rome: in the Gesù he made the altar of S. Ignatius in the left transept – one of the richest altars in Rome – and in S. Ignazio he painted the apse, dome and nave vault with frescoes illustrating the missionary work stimulated by St Ignatius in all parts of the world (1685–94). In 1702 Pozzo was called to Vienna, where he decorated the Jesuit church, now the University Church, and painted the vast ceiling of the *salone* in the Liechtenstein Summer Palace (1704–07). He died in Vienna in 1709, and his work was to have a widespread influence on Austrian architects and decorators.

7, 66

Pozzo's ceiling-fresco in S. Ignazio was the culmination of a long development in the decoration of Roman church interiors. In the late sixteenth century some churches were left – and were probably meant to be left – with almost no decoration beyond bands of stucco ornament on the ribs of the vault. The Gesù was originally entirely without frescoes and, though the intentions of the Jesuits are not exactly recorded in this case, such simplicity would have been entirely in keeping with their severity in the early years of the company's existence. Where frescoes were commissioned, they were usually confined to small fields within stucco frames, though exceptions occur, for instance in the apse of S. Spirito in Sassia, where a large fresco by Jacopo Zucchi, representing Pentecost, fills the whole apse, or in S. Silvestro al Quirinale, where the Alberti family executed a complete series of *quadratura* or false architectural perspective frescoes on the vault of the choir.[23]

This type of illusionism had been more extensively used in secular buildings, and the most ingenious devices of deception and the confusion of real and painted spaces had been invented by artists such as Salviati in the *salone* of the Palazzo Farnese or Vasari in the Sala dei Cento Giorni in the Cancelleria.

In the ceiling of the gallery of the Palazzo Farnese Carracci

and his pupils created a new kind of illusionist effect, based on an appearance of logic and avoiding the deliberately puzzling and ambiguous effects created by Salviati and his followers. The skeleton of the design is composed of feigned stucco herms and atlantes supporting an imaginary entablature against which stand pictures in gilt frames, while the centre of the vault is covered by further paintings supposedly carried on the fictive entablature. In the corners of the ceiling the eye is allowed to pass through to the sky over balustrades on which stand putti.

Some of the followers of the Carracci rejected the illusionism implicit in the Galleria Farnese, and when in 1613 Guido Reni came to paint the *Aurora* on the ceiling of a room in the Casino attached to the palace of Scipione Borghese, now the Palazzo Rospigliosi, he deliberately executed it as a *quadro riportato*, that is to say, like an easel painting inserted in a stucco frame in the ceiling, without any attempt at illusion, and Domenichino used the same method in his frescoes in the vault of the choir in S. Andrea della Valle, though there the effect is more complex, as the decoration involves a series of scenes, not a single composition.

Generally speaking, however, *quadratura* painting gained in popularity during this period, and in 1621–23 Guercino created his most revolutionary piece of illusionism in the *Aurora* on the ceiling of a room in the Casino Ludovisi, where the whole ceiling is replaced by an illusionist rendering of architecture, landscape, figures and sky. In church decoration the crucial step was taken by Giovanni Lanfranco in the dome of S. Andrea della Valle, in which he revived the complete illusionism employed by Correggio in his two domes in the cathedral and the church of S. Giovanni at Parma – an invention that had not been followed up in the sixteenth century and was a complete novelty in Rome.

67   Even bolder, however, was Cortona's ceiling in the *salone* of the Palazzo Barberini (1633–39). Basically the principle of the illusion is the same as in the Galleria Farnese, but the effect is much bolder because the centre of the space created by the imaginary entablature is supposed to be opened out and the eye passes through to the sky, in which float innumerable figures grouped round the three bees of the Barberini arms and forming a vast and complicated allegory – devised by the Barberini court poet, Francesco Bracciolini – in honour of Urban as pope, symbol of the church triumphant and the instrument of Divine Providence. This central composition is surrounded by four other scenes in the cove of the ceiling, the figures of which burst out beyond the limits of their frames and spread over the imaginary entablature, almost joining the actors in the central scene. Never was the Baroque love of illusionism and allegorical adulation combined in a more striking and yet convincing whole.

Cortona's later decorations are less spectacular but no less successful. In 1640 he was called to Florence to decorate the ceilings of five rooms in the Palazzo Pitti. Here he evolved a new type of decorative scheme, which combined illusionist paint-

67 *Opposite* Palazzo Barberini, Rome, frescoed ceiling of the *salone* by Pietro da Cortona, 1633–39

68 *Top right* The Gesù, Rome, vault of the nave with decoration by Baciccio, 1674–79

69 *Right* Gesù e Maria, Rome, by Carlo Rainaldi, interior, begun before 1675, with tombs of the Bolognetti family

70 *Top* S. Marcello, Rome, façade, built by Carlo Fontana, 1682–83

71 *Above* The Port of the Ripetta, Rome; engraving showing steps by Alessandro Specchi, 1704; above them, the façade of S. Girolamo degli Schiavoni by Martino Longhi the Elder, 1588–90; to the right, the end of the Palazzo Borghese with the loggia added in 1612–14

ings with stucco, including life-size figures in the round, a scheme which was to be imitated in France by Charles Le Brun in the Galerie d'Apollon of the Louvre and the Grand Apparte- 166 ment at Versailles. From Florence Cortona went for a short time to Venice, and this visit had an influence on his last ecclesiastical decorative work in Rome, the vault of the Chiesa Nuova (1663–64), of which he had earlier frescoed the dome and apse in a convention based on Lanfranco's dome at S. Andrea della Valle, which had become the accepted idiom for the decoration of Roman churches. In the nave, however, he set the fresco in a massive architectural frame, carried by stucco angels which stand against heavy coffering – composed of hexagons and lozenges – which emulates the richness of the carved and gilt wooden ceilings which he had seen in Venice. The ceiling decoration also includes another innovation. Up to this time frescoes on the vaults of churches had been confined to a single bay and had been separated by the ribs of the vault. In this case the fresco covers three out of five bays of the nave, and the ribs of the vault disappear behind it.

In the decoration of the nave vault of the Gesù, executed a 68 decade later (1674–79) by Giovanni Battista Gaulli, called Baciccio (1639–1709), the artist combined the methods used by Cortona in the Chiesa Nuova and the Palazzo Barberini ceiling, covering the whole nave with a single fresco framed in stucco, but allowing the figures in the painting to burst out over the frame. This device is particularly effective in dramatizing the theme of the fresco, which is the Glorification of the Name of Jesus, before which vices and heresies flee, tumbling almost literally into the church below.

In the ceiling of S. Ignazio Pozzo dispenses with stucco and 7 covers the whole enormous vault with fresco. It is the boldest and grandest example of *quadratura*, combined with Cortona's daring arrangement of figures plunging over the fictive architecture. The effect is breath-taking, provided one stands exactly at the right point in the church, which is indicated by a marble plaque in the pavement. One of the disadvantages of this type of illusionist fresco is that from all other points it makes nonsense!

While this exuberant tradition of fresco and stucco decoration was developing, architects were also exploiting the possibilities of marble revetment for chapels and even whole churches. Bernini had indicated the possibilities of the material in the Cappella Cornaro and in S. Andrea al Quirinale, and other architects rapidly followed his lead, and produced even richer effects of marbling. For instance, the decoration of the choir of S. Caterina da Siena (a Magnanapoli), which was mainly executed before 1667, has a rich surface of red marble broken by high reliefs in white marble by Melchiorre Caffà, and the whole interior of the Gesù e Maria was converted by Carlo 69 Rainaldi into a marble mausoleum for the Bolognetti family (before 1675). A much more restrained and Classical style of marbling was employed in the Cappella Spada in the Chiesa Nuova, and the Cappella Cibò in S. Maria del Popolo, both by Carlo Fontana (1634–1714), the leader of the group opposed to the extremes of Late Baroque represented by the architects discussed above.[24]

Fontana was an architect of a type very different from the masters of the High Roman Baroque. He was trained in the studio of Bernini, whose building works he supervised for many years, but he did not inherit any of his master's imaginative power. Of his few executed works the most important was the façade of the church of S. Marcello (1682–83), which was to be a 70 model followed by architects all over Europe and was far more

popular than any of those built by Borromini, Bernini, or
Cortona. The façade is concave, but it is based on a continuous
curve, much less rich than Borromini's façade of S. Carlino, but
more widely acceptable because of its simplicity. The surfaces
are clearly defined and there is no counterpoint or subtle
breaking up of masses. It was in fact exactly what was needed by
a public sated with the imaginative splendour of the architects
of the previous generation, and it established Fontana as a safe
man, who knew how to adapt his style to his clients. Within a
few years of Bernini's death he had established what was to be
for a generation the most sought-after studio in Rome, from
which designs and advice were sent out to all parts of
Europe. The efficient organization of his studio is attested by
the drawings which survive, mainly in the Royal Library at
Windsor Castle, which cover all aspects of his architectural
activities, from fortifications to drainage in civil architecture,
and from the design for a candlestick to one for a grand church
in the ecclesiastical field.

In the first half of the eighteenth century there were still
marked differences between various groups of architects, but
there was more gradation of views.[25]

Curiously enough one of Fontana's pupils, Alessandro Specchi (1668–1729), was among those who carried on the Baroque
tradition most boldly, and his steps on the Ripetta (1704), the
port on the Tiber in front of the church of S. Girolamo degli
Schiavoni, destroyed in the late nineteenth century but known
from engravings, were among the freest and most imaginative
inventions of the period, akin in their double-S curves to the
staircases of Buontalenti in Florence or Guarini in Piedmont.
Specchi also produced a project for the Spanish Steps, but his

design was rejected in favour of one by Francesco de Sanctis
(1693–1740; the steps were executed in 1723–25), which, though
one of the most popular sights in Rome, is much more loosely
designed than Specchi's Ripetta – or for that matter than the
staircases of Guarini before him or the Neapolitan Ferdinando
Sanfelice in his own time (cf. below, pp. 88–89).

There was in fact an infusion of southern blood into Roman
architecture at this period. Filippo Juvarra, who spent some
years in Rome before settling in Turin, was a Sicilian, as also
was Filippo Raguzzini (active 1727–71), who built the ingeniously curved façades of S. Maria della Quercia and S.
Gallicano, but is principally remembered for the lively piazza
in front of S. Ignazio (1727–28), with the curved houses and
diagonal streets, almost like a stage-set. Gabriele Valvassori

72 *Below* S. Maria Maddalena, Rome, niche on the façade attributed to
Giuseppe Sardi

73 *Right* The Spanish Steps, Rome, by Francesco de Sanctis, 1723–25.
Above them, the façade of the Trinità dei Monti, late 16th century

74 *Below right* Piazza di S. Ignazio, Rome, by Filippo Raguzzini, 1727–28

75 *Above* Palazzo della Consulta, Rome, by Ferdinando Fuga, façade,
1732–33

76 *Opposite* Fontana di Trevi, Rome, by Nicola Salvi, 1732–45

(1683–1761), a Roman by birth, was less inventive in planning
than Raguzzini, but in his façade of the Palazzo Doria-
Pamphili facing the Corso (1731–34) the windows have hoods
of a Borrominesque type, and the four galleries which he
constructed over the loggie of the court, decorated with frescoes
by Aureliano Milani, are even richer variations of the Galleria
Colonna. They are in fact one of the last examples of that
combination of painting, stucco and gilding – to which in this
case are added mirrors – typical of late-Roman Baroque
architecture. Even more fantastic than Valvassori's windows
are the niche-heads on the façade of S. Maria Maddalena
(1733), generally but uncertainly ascribed to Giuseppe Sardi
(1680–1753), in which the free adaptation of Borrominesque
forms is combined with the use of inverted half-pediments, a
device invented by Buontalenti but used later by Bernini in the
Cappella della Pietà in St Peter's. Equally free and ingenious are
the stucco fountains and doors in the court and vestibule of the
Palazzo del Grillo, by a hitherto unidentified architect.

The buildings of Raguzzini, Valvassori and Sardi have often
been described as Rococo, but they have nothing in common
with true Rococo. The term *barocchetto* has recently been
invented for them, and there is much to be said for it, since it
implies that they belong to the Baroque, but the diminutive
suggests the rather light and gay quality which distinguishes
them from Roman architecture of the seventeenth century.

Between the *barocchetto* and the consciously anti-Baroque
school of Galilei stand three 'middle of the way' architects who
have been little studied: Carlo de Dominicis (active 1721–40),
Domenico Gregorini (c. 1700–77) and Pietro Passalacqua (d.
1748). The first is responsible for the oval church of SS. Celso e
Giuliano (1733–36), and the two latter remodelled the basilica
of S. Croce in Gerusalemme (1744), to which they added an
oval vestibule, enclosed in an unusual curved façade. Passalac-

qua also built the small oratory of the Annunziata, near the
hospital of S. Spirito in Sassia, and Gregorini that of S. Maria
in Via. These architects employ the oval plan which had become
accepted since the mid-seventeenth century, but they do so in a
timid way, without any of the boldness of Borromini. Their
decorative vocabulary is also lacking in vitality compared with
Valvassori. They do not actually imitate Carlo Fontana, but
their architecture has a cautiousness which brings them very
close to him in spirit.

With the election of the Florentine Cardinal Lorenzo Corsini
as Pope Clement XII in 1730 official taste in Rome moved
sharply towards Classicism. The period was dominated by the
two Florentine architects whom Clement called to Rome:
Alessandro Galilei (1691–1736), and Ferdinando Fuga
(1699–1781), to whom must be added the Roman Nicola Salvi,
author of the Fontana di Trevi (1697–1751).

The most important event of the pontificate was the competition for the façade of S. Giovanni in Laterano, opened by
Clement in 1732. Borromini had made designs for this, but they
had not been carried out, and the first church in Christendom
remained without a façade of any sort. All the architects in
Rome sent in designs, which ranged from the Baroque fantasies
of Pozzo and Raguzzini to the subdued grandeur of Galilei's
project. It was typical of Clement's taste that Galilei's design
was chosen, but it can be argued that it was the only one of those
submitted which showed a real sense of the monumentality
needed in a façade on such a vast scale, which was to be seen at a
distance by those entering Rome along the Via Appia, across
the open space which lay to the east of the church. The façade
contains echoes of Michelangelo's Capitoline palaces and of
Bernini's unexecuted design for the front of St Peter's, but it has
many personal and original elements, such as the central
crowning feature and the introduction of pairs of columns and
pilasters to emphasize the main breaks in the façade. It is one of
the great monuments of Classical taste of early eighteenth-
century Rome, but it is still within the Baroque idiom in its
scale, in the use of the giant Order, and in the large statues
which crown it and stand out against the sky, like those of
Bernini on the colonnade of St Peter's.

Galilei was also commissioned to add a façade to his national
church, S. Giovanni dei Fiorentini (1734). Here he adopted the
traditional Roman façade, but the unusual width of the church
enabled him to introduce a strong emphasis on the horizontal,
which is heightened by the almost unbroken line of the entablature and the repetition of paired columns. The contrast
between this classicized front and that of, say, SS. Vincenzo e
Anastasio is too obvious to need underlining.

The third work built by Galilei for Clement was his family
chapel in S. Giovanni in Laterano (1732–35). This is the
architect's most explicitly Classical work. In plan it is square,
with arms that are hardly more than shallow straight-ended
niches. The floor is composed of radiating sections, and the
vaults are decorated with severe hexagonal coffering. It is
symptomatic of Clement's taste that he took for the principal
feature of his own tomb in the chapel a famous porphyry
sarcophagus and four ancient columns, also of porphyry, which
had stood for centuries in the portico of the Pantheon.

Fuga remained closer to the true Baroque than Galilei.[26] His
two principal palace façades, the Consulta (1732–33) and the
Cenci-Bolognetti, opposite the Gesù, are both variants on
Bernini's Palazzo Chigi, but with the emphasis on the central
section removed in favour of a more regular – and more

monotonous – repetition of units. In both palaces the side sections are of the same height as the central bay; the pilasters of this section are repeated at the ends of the façade and are echoed in the pilaster-bands which articulate the intervening sections of the front. Further, in the Consulta the architect has inserted a large mezzanine over the ground floor, which makes the two storeys of almost equal height, and has emphasized this feature by articulating the lower storey as well as the upper with pilasters. This 'regularized' variant of Bernini's design was to be much more widely imitated than the original. In the courtyard of the Consulta Fuga inserted a staircase with the flights rising towards the centre, a sort of inversion of a type which he may have seen in the palaces of Ferdinando Sanfelice when he visited Naples shortly before 1727 (cf. below, p.88). In the Palazzo Corsini, which he built for Clement XII round the nucleus of a palace which had belonged to Queen Christina of Sweden, he created a staircase on a much grander scale, approached by a three-aisled entrance leading to an octagonal vestibule, the staircase itself occupying a block between two courts from which it receives light on both sides. The conception is splendidly Baroque, but the dryness of the mouldings and the decorative detail betray the influence of the increasingly Classical taste of the period. 121

Fuga's earliest Roman church, S. Maria dell'Orazione e della Morte (1732–37), is a competent exercise in the same idiom as de Dominici's SS. Celso e Giuliano. In the later church of S. Apollinare (1745–48) he returned to a much more conventional plan – a single nave with side-chapels and a dome over the choir – and the same dry decorative detail which he used at the Palazzo Corsini.

His most important – and his most difficult – commission was the construction of the façade of S. Maria Maggiore, one of the oldest and most venerated of the Roman basilicas. Basically Fuga used the traditional Roman church façade, with the upper storey narrower than the lower, but he adapted the design to suit the particular conditions with which he was faced. The church was unusually wide, with five doors, a fact which led 78 Fuga to make his façade of five and three bays, instead of the usual arrangement with three bays below and one above. This increase in width of the façade helped Fuga to solve another of the problems with which he was faced, namely the fact that the façade of the church was not free-standing, but was enclosed between two high wings containing the College of Canons attached to the church, which would have crushed a façade of the normal Roman type. A further problem which faced the architect was that, as at St Peter's, the façade had to include a benediction loggia and a vestibule for pilgrims. This gave him the opportunity of opening up the structure, and this he did with the utmost ingenuity, choosing his elements carefully, so as to produce the greatest effect of variety in building up the triangular design of the façade. On the lower storey the openings are all flat-headed, with a segmental pediment over the central bay and straight pediments over the two outer bays. The upper storey has arched openings, which echo the curve of the central pediment of the lower storey, while the pediment of the middle bay picks up those of the side bays to right and left of the

77 *Above left* S. Giovanni in Laterano, Rome, façade, by Alessandro Galilei, 1733–36

78 *Left* S. Maria Maggiore, Rome, façade, by Ferdinando Fuga, 1741–43

lower storey. The crowning feature and the statues on the
balustrade echo – somewhat feebly – those on Galilei's façade
of the Lateran.

In 1751 Fuga was called to Naples by Charles III, together
with Luigi Vanvitelli, whose one important work in Rome had
been the restoration of S. Maria degli Angeli, the church which
Michelangelo had created for Pius IV in the ruins of the Baths
of Diocletian. Their works in Naples will be discussed below, in
the chapter dealing with Southern Italy.

The most famous monument of Late Baroque architecture in
Rome is the Fontana di Trevi, finally realized by Nicola Salvi in
the years 1732–45, after more than a century of abortive
attempts to give monumental form to one of the most important sources of water supply in Rome.[27] The structure is the
largest and most ambitious of all Roman fountains, with a
grand façade covering the palace behind the fountain, including
as its central feature a niche set in a sort of triumphal arch. This
niche frames a statue of Neptune guiding a team of sea-horses
and tritons which charge over a zone composed of architecturally formed fountains dissolving into rocks carved into naturalistic foliage. Trevi was the last and most ebullient expression of
the Romans' love of fountains, which was an expression of the
vital part which the supply of water played in the very existence
of the city; but up to this time Roman fountains had been more
modest in scale and more architectural in conception. Artificial
rocks had been used in the fountains which decorated the villas
of Frascati and Tivoli, but they had been stylized. It was an
innovation to use rocks in a fountain which stood in the middle
of the city, and an even bolder one to make the rocks so
naturalistic that they almost looked as though they had been
brought down from the Apennines. The idea was to catch on,
and Salvi is indirectly responsible not only for the fountains of
Caserta and the new settings given to those of Versailles by
Hubert Robert for Louis XVI, but for all those which sprawl
across the squares of modern capitals, not only in Europe but in
North and South America and many other parts of the world.

The Baroque died in Rome under the impulse of the Classical
revival inaugurated by the circle of artists round Cardinal
Alessandro Albani. Paradoxically, however, the architect
whom the Cardinal chose to build the villa to contain his
collection of ancient works of art was Carlo Marchionni
(1702–86), a feeble representative of the late phase of Roman
Baroque architecture, and it is only in the decoration of the
interior and in the various pavilions in the garden that the new
Classical taste appears. But before the Classical revival took
complete hold of Roman architecture one great masterpiece
was created: Giovanni Battista Piranesi's chapel for the Priory
of the Knights of Malta on the Aventine. This chapel defies
classification. It is composed of elements taken from ancient
art – both Roman and Etruscan – transmuted by a feverish
imagination into a picturesque whole which has no parallel in
earlier architecture.[28]

Rome was the artistic centre of Italy and indeed of the world
during the Baroque period, but as what we nowadays call 'Italy'
was a conglomeration of separate states jealous of their
independence and proud of their own traditions, political and
artistic, it is not surprising to find that Baroque art developed
different characteristics in different areas. In some centres, such
as Turin, the style was directly and powerfully influenced by
Rome, but in Venice, whose architects had always shown great
independence, there was little contact with Rome, and in

79 S. Maria del Priorato, Rome, by Piranesi, façade, begun 1764

Apulia and Sicily the discoveries of Roman architects were
hardly taken into account till well into the eighteenth century
and then only in one or two of the larger cities. The following
sections will be devoted to studying the local varieties of
architecture during the period and to examining how far they
can properly be described as Baroque.

Northern Italy

Piedmont

While Rome was passing through this uninventive phase in the last decade of the seventeenth century and the first part of the eighteenth century a remarkable architectural movement was growing up in Turin. The opportunity for the creation of this school was provided by the ambitions of the house of Savoy, which between the middle of the sixteenth and the middle of the eighteenth centuries grew from a minor duchy into the most powerful state in Northern Italy and a force in European politics.[1]

After the peace of Cateau-Cambrésis in 1559, which restored to Savoy the territories she had been forced to cede to France, the duke, Emmanuel Philibert, abandoned the old capital of Chambéry and made Turin his centre of government. By a mixture of adroit diplomacy and some fighting he and his successors strengthened the position of Savoy in Italy to the extent that in the early eighteenth century the house of Savoy rose to royal estate, first for a short time as kings of Sicily (from 1712 to 1720), and then from 1720 onwards as kings of Sardinia.

Naturally the heads of the house of Savoy felt the need to make Turin a capital worthy of their new power and in fact during the two centuries in question they planned and carried out one of the most impressive schemes of urban development produced in the Baroque era.

The scheme began modestly. In 1577 Pellegrino Tibaldi, who had built the church of S. Fedele in Milan (begun 1569), was called to Turin to design the church of SS. Martiri, dedicated to the patron saints of the city, but a much more important phase was opened in 1584, when the Umbrian Ascanio Vittozzi (c.1539–1615) was offered the post of official architect to the duke, Charles Emmanuel, and began the systematic layout of the city. He preserved the grid-plan which had survived since Roman times, but along the old streets he built palaces on a regular pattern, over porticoes, imitating the arrangement known in many North Italian towns, such as Bologna. In addition he laid out the large Piazza Castello, designed on the same pattern, round the mediaeval castle of the Savoys, later known as the Palazzo Madama. The scheme was extended in the early seventeenth century by Carlo di Castellamonte, who built the Piazza S. Carlo, south of the Piazza Castello, with twin churches flanking the opening at the south end of the square. This arrangement immediately brings to mind the two churches on the Piazza del Popolo in Rome, but in fact the Piedmontese example is earlier than the Roman, since the two churches were built in 1619 and 1639 respectively, though their façades were not added till much later. Vittozzi and his immediate successors established a scheme for the building of Turin which has been followed ever since, and even the additions of the 1930s and the reconstructions after the Second World War conformed to it.

Vittozzi was also an architect of some inventive power in the designing of churches. The Santuario di Vicoforte near Mondoví is a bold oval structure of such large scale that the dome was not built till the mid-eighteenth century. The SS. Trinità in Turin (begun in 1598) was of an ingenious tri-lobed plan appropriate to its dedication.

During the first half of the seventeenth century Savoy was involved in internal dissensions and unsuccessful foreign wars, but peace and order were re-established by Charles Emmanuel

II (1638–75), and it was during his reign that the most brilliant phase of Turinese architecture began with the arrival of Guarino Guarini (1624–83), one of the most inventive architects of the period and the only one who really understood the true novelties of Borromini's work and was able to develop them into an original style of his own.[2]

Guarini was born in Modena and at the age of fifteen entered the Theatine order. He was trained in theology, philosophy and mathematics, and his writings on these subjects fill many folio volumes. It is not known exactly how or when he became interested in architecture, but it is clear that during his training in the Theatine house in Rome from 1639 to 1647 he must have studied the work of Borromini. In 1647 he was transferred to Modena, but in 1660 he moved to Messina, where he supplied designs for the church of the Padri Somaschi and the façade of the Theatine church of SS. Annunziata. On his journey south probably he would have passed through Rome and so would have had the opportunity of seeing Borromini's works of the 1650s. In 1662 he was sent to Paris to design the Theatine church there, called Sainte Anne-la-Royale. None of these early buildings survives; of the churches in Messina, that of the Padri Somaschi was never erected and the SS. Annunziata was destroyed in the earthquake of 1909, and of Sainte Anne-la-Royale only a small part was built and that was destroyed in the nineteenth century. Fortunately, however, the designs of all of them are preserved in the engravings in Guarini's *Architettura Civile* published in 1686 and again, in enlarged form, by his pupil Bernardo Vittone in 1737. He made designs for two other churches for towns outside Italy, S. Maria Oettingen in Prague, and the Divina Provvidenza in Lisbon, both of which are recorded in engravings, but it is not known whether the churches were actually built or whether he visited the cities in question. In 1666 Guarini was transferred to Turin, where he spent the remainder of his life and built the only two ecclesiastical works which survive, the Theatine church of S. Lorenzo and the Cappella della SS. Sindone, attached to the Cathedral.

If we examine the designs of his churches, whether in the actual buildings or the engravings, certain features appear which are common to all of them: first and foremost a love of complex ground plans and a new type of dome structure. In the plans Guarini was evidently inspired by the works of Borromini which he saw in Rome, but he developed the possibilities of complex designs much more fully than his predecessor. His plans are sometimes circular, sometimes polygonal with 6, 8, or 10 sides. In other cases they are based on more traditional forms

80 Lisbon, S. Maria della Provvidenza (destroyed), plan by Guarino Guarini, from an engraving

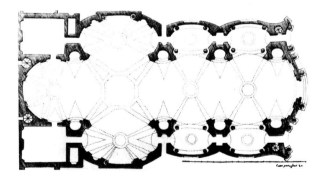

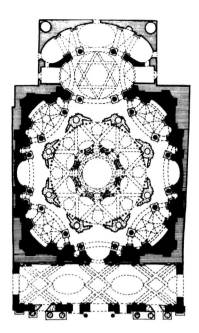

81 *Above left* Paris, Sainte Anne-la-Royale, by Guarino Guarini, begun 1662, destroyed in the early 19th century, section, from an engraving

82 *Above* Turin, S. Lorenzo, plan by Guarino Guarini, 1668–80

83 *Below* S. Lorenzo by Guarino Guarini, interior

– a Greek or Latin cross – but Guarini never fails to introduce some variations into the scheme: the bays will be octagonal or oval, or they will overlap, so that one flows into another. His dome structures can be most conveniently discussed in connection with his two surviving churches, but even in some of the earliest – Sainte Anne-la-Royale and the Padri Somaschi – he already made ingenious use of his method of replacing the solid cupola by interlocking ribs. This enabled him to build up his churches to a great height and with changing shapes for each unit. In Sainte Anne, for instance, the stages of the dome read circular – hexagonal – circular, creating a structure that externally is almost like a pagoda.

Guarini also invented new forms for individual architectural features. For instance, he seems to have invented the kidney-shaped window, and in Sainte Anne-la-Royale he introduced a doubled Serliana, the bottom of which has the same form as the top, but inverted, so that the window is symmetrical about the horizontal as well as on the vertical axis. In the Divina Provvidenza for Lisbon, which is composed of interlocking oval spaces forming a sort of Latin cross, the nave walls are articulated with Salomonic pilasters. This particularly curious device does not seem to have been repeated either by Guarini or his successors, but the kidney-shaped window enjoyed a great success with the Central European architects of the eighteenth century, who produced many ingenious variations on it.

Fortunately Guarini's most important ecclesiastical buildings in Turin have survived – though S. Lorenzo lacks its façade – and they give a very complete idea of his skill and originality. S. Lorenzo was built between 1668 and 1680. Its plan is basically an octagon, to which is added a small oval choir with its short axis leading to the altar; but within this simple scheme Guarini has contrived an almost incredible number of variations. All the sides of the octagonal centre space are slightly convex inwards and all, except the entrance bay, have Serlian arches, leading to the choir 'transept', and to the chapels on the diagonal axes, which are of unusual shape, being enclosed between two arcs of circles. Above this lower arcaded zone is another, much simpler, composed of alternating arches and broad pendentives which support the dome. The Serlian theme is continued into this zone in the form of windows in the lunettes between the pendentives. Above this intermediate zone rises the dome, composed, as in Guarini's earlier churches, of ribs crossing each other so as to form the network visible in plate 10, and leaving an octagonal space in the centre. On this octagon is erected a lantern which is covered by a small dome, also constructed of ribs. There are pentagonal openings in the solid part of the main dome, above the oval windows which light it. As a result of these windows, the Serlian windows below them and the rectangular openings in the lantern, the whole upper part of the church is flooded with light, in contrast to the lower zone, which only receives light from small windows in the vaults of the chapels and the choir. The choir itself is oval in plan, but its vaulting conceals this fact because it consists of a circular ribbed dome, like the main dome in small but with six instead of eight points, the end section being vaulted with ribs touching this dome. Beyond the choir and separated from it by yet another Serlian arch is a further oval space containing the high altar.

The effect of varied movement in the lower zone is of extreme subtlety. The bays on the cross-axis are on a simple convex curve, but the altars which stand in them – and seem to grow out

of them – are more complex. Their outer sections consist of narrow bays composed of a solid wall, curved and projecting almost at right angles to the wall; these are followed by free-standing columns, the entablatures above which make the beginnings of a concave curve. This, however, is not continued and the middle of the altar is composed of a shallow niche covered by an arch in a single plane. This niche is articulated with pilasters, in front of which are free-standing, life-size statues representing the Madonna del Carmine and S. Gaetano of Thiene. This ingenious mixture of curved and flat planes suggests that Guarini had seen and understood Borromini's tombs in the Lateran or in S. Giovanni dei Fiorentini, and he adopts from them some of the Michelangelesque ideas which they incorporated.

A further subtle difference is introduced between the bays on the main axes and those on the diagonals. Both sets are convex but, whereas the bays on the main axes have a steady, slow curve, those on the diagonals spring from the walls in sharp curves, almost orthogonal to the walls themselves, which are abruptly interrupted by a straight section in the middle.

In addition the side element of the Serliana – composed of a flat trabeation joining a pilaster to a column – is repeated in the side walls of the chapels on the corners of the octagon of which the plan of the church is composed.

The exterior of S. Lorenzo cannot be fairly judged in the absence of the façade, but the dome stands up in a series of concave bays in two tiers, topped by the small cupola of the lantern, providing a pagoda-like structure much imitated by Guarini's followers in Piedmont.

Guarini's other surviving work of ecclesiastical architecture, the Cappella della SS. Sindone, was built to enshrine the Holy Shroud, a relic which belonged to the house of Savoy and was regarded by them with great veneration, in spite of the fact that its authenticity had been officially denied by the Church in the later Middle Ages.

The chapel was begun in 1657 by Amadeo di Castellamonte, son of Carlo, but when Guarini was called in in 1668, he so completely transformed the design that it can be considered as essentially his invention. The placing of the chapel presented problems, because, although it was to form part of the Cathedral, it had also to communicate with the Royal Palace. The solution was to set it to the east of the high altar and above the level of the church, so that it should be at the height of the state apartments on the first floor of the palace. Castellamonte chose a circle for its basic plan, dividing it into three sections of 120° each, which enabled him to place one door on the main axis of the Cathedral leading to the palace, and two more openings giving access to flights of steps running from the transepts, parallel with the choir. Guarini was compelled to take over this basic plan, as the walls had already risen to a considerable height when he was put in charge of the building, and he emphasized the tri-partite plan – possibly an allusion to the Trinity – by establishing three vestibules for the three entrances. The vestibule leading to the palace is cut off by a door, but the full circles of the others are visible, joining the chapel to the

84 *Left* S. Lorenzo, interior of dome

85 *Opposite* Turin, Cathedral, interior of the dome of the Cappella della SS. Sindone, begun by Amadeo de Castellamonte in 1657, completed by Guarini between 1668 and 1690

steps leading from the church itself. The circumferences of these circles are divided into three parts, each consisting of an opening flanked by two free-standing columns, the openings leading to the chapel, to the steps, and to a sacristy. Between these sections are columns which are linked above by ribs forming an equilateral triangle on the dome, which, however, is so low that it almost looks like a flat ceiling.

The height and articulation of the lower zone of the chapel had been established before Guarini's arrival, since Castellamonte had constructed an Order of Corinthian pilasters supporting an entablature running right round the chapel, but Guarini enriched this effect by inserting a smaller Order to carry the galleries over the vestibules, and he continued the entablature of this Order round the whole chapel, interrupting it by arched niches between the pilasters of the main Order. Above this zone the design is entirely Guarini's. He gave a grander scale to Castellamonte's design by uniting the bays of the lower zone in pairs, over which he constructed a sort of low pediment composed of shell-forms reminiscent of Buontalenti's decorative motives, and over them a single arch rising up to the spring of the dome and enclosing an upright oval window. Between these arches are broad pendentives, not unlike those in
83 S. Lorenzo, but decorated, like the fields of the arches between them, with a low-relief pattern of stars and hexagons.

Above this zone rises a tall drum, lit by large round-headed windows which alternate with niches, and the design culminates
85 in a dome of extraordinary fantasy, peculiar even for Guarini. This is formed by a series of layers, each composed of flattened arches, containing windows divided in the middle by a short vertical strut. In the lowest layer the ends of the flattened arch rest on the tops of the arched windows of the drum; in the next layer they rest on the tops of the lowest arches, and this process is repeated six times. At each stage the flat arches project further into the central space, so that at the top they shrink to the size of the ring supporting the lantern, which in its turn is composed of ribs lying in an almost horizontal plane, leaving triangular openings lit from above by windows in the outer shell of the lantern. In this way – as at S. Lorenzo, but in a more complicated manner – the whole dome is transfused with light, while the lower part of the chapel is in relative darkness.

The use of material and the treatment of detail in the chapel are superb. There is no colour, except for the gilded galleries, and the whole chapel is constructed of grey marbles of varying tones, very dark, in fact nearly black, in the bottom zone and lighter in the cupola itself. The pattern of the floor, which is also made of marbles of different greys, is based on panels of dark grey marble radiating from the centre of the chapel. Half of these run unbroken to the outer circumference of the chapel, but the remainder are interrupted by further panels, the sides of which are also on radii of the circle but are broken at the corners by slight, almost rectangular, cut-out elements. Each panel has a brass star inlaid in its centre, and the effect is almost of a series of starred panels suspended on ribbons from the middle of the chapel.

The floors of the vestibules are even more complex. In the centre of each is a many-pointed sun enclosed in a circle, from which rays extend outwards in alternately long and short triangular groups. On the outer circumference of the circle are little equilateral triangles in bronze and chevrons in the lighter marble. These leave spaces which are basically diamond-shaped, but Guarini was not content to leave them in their simple forms, and he elongated them by cutting out a small

triangle at each end of their longer axis. In order to fit the elongated shape of these diamond panels he gives the brass stars with which they are inlaid an elongated form by extending the rays on the long axis of the diamond. As a final piece of sophistication the sun in the middle of the floor, which at first sight one would guess to have sixteen points, in fact has fifteen, five corresponding to each of the three sections into which the vestibule is divided. The tri-partite scheme is carried on into the minutest detail.

The flights of stairs leading from the transepts of the Cathedral to the chapel are composed of steps curved in a form deriving from Michelangelo's steps in the Ricetto of the Laurenziana in Florence, a form much imitated by his Florentine followers, particularly Buontalenti. They are approached through two tall doors of black marble with ornaments in the style of the same architect. Externally the dome of the chapel presents an exotic effect, since the low, ribbed windows of the dome, topped by a tall thin spire, combine to produce an almost Chinese effect – an impression probably not consciously intended by the architect.

Guarini also built or enlarged several palaces for the duke of Savoy and members of his family. He added a wing to the country palace of Racconigi and began the Collegio dei Nobili, which was left unfinished, but much his most remarkable work in this field was the palace begun in 1679 for Emmanuel Philibert, Prince of Carignano, the head of a cadet branch of the Savoys. This also was left unfinished and disastrously completed in the late nineteenth century, but the main wing facing the piazza is as Guarini intended it. It is a magnificently   86
mouvementé design, with straight wings separated by a deep concavity which is interrupted by a strongly convex bay in the middle. The play of curves is strengthened by the sharp hollow of the half-domed niche over the main door, covered by a pediment straight in elevation but curved in ground plan.

The contrast of concave and convex forms is close in feeling to Borromini, but the most exact parallel is with Bernini's first –   172
and rejected – design for the Louvre, which Guarini must have known from drawings, perhaps transmitted from Paris to the court of Turin through the dowager duchess of Savoy, Madama Reale, who was an aunt of Louis XIV. Guarini has, however, modified Bernini's design in several important respects. Whereas the latter conceived his façade as consisting of a single Order standing on a rusticated basement, Guarini gives equal importance to the two storeys of his palace, each of which is articulated with an Order, a sort of Tuscan below and Corinthian above. But the character of the Palazzo Carignano depends essentially on the fact that it is conceived and executed in brick, a material widely used in Piedmont since ancient Roman times. Guarini was evidently influenced by this local tradition, but his moulded brick ornament derives more obviously from Borromini's use of the same material in the Oratory, S. Andrea delle Fratte or S.   45
Maria dei Sette Dolori. But even Borromini never conceived any decoration in brick as bold as the broken double-curved pediments over the windows or the 'winged' motifs repeated in the ornament of the pilasters on the Palazzo Carignano.

During his lifetime Guarini published a treatise on fortification (1676) and one on the measurement of buildings (1674), but his main treatise on architecture remained unpublished and did not see the light till 1737 under the title *Architettura Civile*, though the engravings of his principal churches had appeared in 1686. It is interesting to note that the treatise is the only work of the kind produced by an Italian Baroque architect.

It covers a vast range of subjects, but the most important parts deal with the application of geometry to architecture, from orthogonal projection to stereotomy or the cutting of stones to fit complicated vaults. From the historical point of view the most interesting fact about the treatise is that Guarini puts up a vigorous defence of Gothic architecture, the principles of which he analyses with considerable insight.

He begins by making the bold assertion that, as in all other subjects, it was foolish to become a slave to the Ancients, and that it is possible to correct their rules, in order to produce buildings which will please 'reasonable judgement and a judicious eye', and on this principle it is permissible to study the architecture of the Middle Ages. He points out that the qualities of Gothic architecture are exactly the opposite of those governing ancient Roman architecture: the latter aims at being and appearing solid, the former at appearing frail but being in fact very strong. In a passage too long to quote in full he praises the boldness of their structure in building, 'a tall steeple supported stably on thin columns, Orders which bend outwards beyond

the feet [of the columns], which hang in the air without any column to support them', and he goes on to talk about the open-work towers and tall windows and their manner of vaulting 'which pleased many'.[3]

This reference to their vaulting helps to explain one important fact about Guarini's architecture, namely that his ribbed domes are closely reminiscent of certain European works of the Middle Ages, but even more exactly of a type of Islamic dome-structure in Spain, for instance in the Mosque of Cordova and one in Toledo, now the church of Cristo de la Luz. How he could have known these works is uncertain. If he went to Lisbon, he may have travelled through Spain and seen examples of the type, or he may have seen drawings of them brought by other architects from Spain, perhaps at an earlier date, because they were certainly known to Leonardo, who drew one on a sheet of studies now at Windsor. Whatever the solution, the connection is too precise to be accidental. As would be expected, Guarini did not copy his models slavishly, because in the examples in Spain which might have been known to him the ribs stand against and support a solid dome; Guarini gave them a new meaning by opening up the spaces between the ribs, so that the light can stream through them.

86 Turin, façade of the Palazzo Carignano by Guarino Guarini, begun 1679

When Guarini died in 1683 there were several competent architects working in Turin, but the next three decades form a period of relative inactivity. When, however, Victor Amadeus II became king, first of Sicily (1712) and then of Sardinia (1720), he needed an artist who worked in the grand manner to carry out his projects. He was lucky in his choice of Filippo Juvarra (1678–1736), a Sicilian whom he had met in Messina on his only visit to the island as king in 1714.[4] Juvarra had been trained in Rome, mainly in the studio of Carlo Fontana, and he succeeded his master in the role of adviser to those concerned with major building projects all over Europe. In Italy he made designs for palaces at Lucca, Mantua, Como, Bergamo, and other smaller towns; he sent plans to the Landgraf of Hessen-Cassel; he spent two years in Lisbon working for the king of Portugal, visiting Paris and London on his return journey, and in 1735 he was called to Spain to provide plans for the Royal Palaces.

His most important works, however, were built in or near Turin for Victor Amadeus. In some of these his Roman training is much in evidence as, for instance, in the façade of S. Cristina (1715–28), which is an adaptation of Fontana's S. Marcello. Juvarra modified Fontana's design in several ways: he simplified the architectural forms by leaving out the pediment and aedicule which tend to break up S. Marcello, and replaced them by a lively group of figure sculpture, adding a row of flaming candelabra as the sky-line.

The church of S. Filippo Neri was a much more important

87   Turin, exterior of the Superga by Filippo Juvarra, 1717–31

become king of Sicily, and it was certainly conceived as a monument to the glory of the house of Savoy.

It stands magnificently on a steep hill, more than 1300 feet [87] above the city. Baroque architects and patrons had an eye for a site, and Juvarra designed his church to tell at a distance. He adapted the model of S. Agnese in Piazza Navona to suit a free- [37] standing building, but it is worth noticing that the complex tops [48] to the towers are closer to Borromini's original design, known from a drawing, than to the tamer version actually built. These towers are of a type frequently used at almost the same date in South Germany and Austria, and this has led to a suggestion of direct influence from the north, but it seems more likely that both the Turinese and the northern architects based their designs on the same Roman model.

undertaking. Juvarra was called in by the Oratorians in 1714, when the church begun by Guarini and continued by Michele Garovo had collapsed. Juvarra does not seem to have taken any account of the earlier scheme, but created a completely new church with a simple but spacious nave, side-chapels and a deep choir. The design is in a sense an enlargement of Borromini's Roman Oratory, but its rounded corners, each broken by a door, a niche and a window, one above the other, are more like his Re Magi. For the walls over the side-chapels of the nave the architect used a complicated variant of Guarini's kidney-shaped windows, the only trace in the church of the influence of Juvarra's great predecessor.

Juvarra's later church of the Carmine (1732–35) also consists of a single nave, but it is much taller in proportion than S. Filippo Neri, owing to the insertion of an attic between the main entablature and the spring of the vault. The church contains one great novelty: it is built in the form of a wall-pillar church, with the walls separating the chapels carried the full height of the nave, allowing for high galleries over the chapels. Further Juvarra has abandoned the entablature which invariably ran over the arches leading to the chapels in earlier Italian churches and replaced it by sculptured groups, producing an effect reminiscent of a cut-out on a stage-set – and it must be remembered that Juvarra had been active as a stage designer during his years in Rome. Finally he pierced the vaults of the chapels with openings through which light comes from the tall windows above.

The wall-pillar church is an essentially northern Late-Gothic form (cf. below, p.222) and the Carmine is one of the very rare examples of influence from countries north of the Alps on Italian architecture of the post-Renaissance period. The presence of this Gothic element may at first sight suggest that Juvarra was influenced by Guarini's enthusiasm for mediaeval architecture, but in fact his approach is entirely different: he adopted a particular kind of Late-Gothic plan and he showed no interest at all in the ribbing of Gothic vaults which intrigued Guarini.

Juvarra's reputation rests, however, on three major works in or near Turin: the Superga, the Palazzo Madama, and the palace at Stupinigi.

The Superga is said, not very convincingly, to have been built on the spot from which Victor Amadeus II and Prince Eugene of Savoy – who was in command of his army in the campaign of 1706 against the French – surveyed the enemy's troops before the victory which forced the French to raise the siege of Turin. It was in any case begun in 1717, a few years after the duke had

88 *Top left* Turin, façade of the Palazzo Madama by Filippo Juvarra, 1718–21

89 *Above* Palazzo Madama, staircase by Filippo Juvarra

90 *Top* Stupinigi, near Turin, by Filippo Juvarra, 1729–33, aerial view

91 *Above* Palazzo Madama, engraving of the complete project

Seen from a distance the church produces a magnificent effect. The dome stands up strongly, the portico seems boldly designed, and the towers give proper support visually to the central part of the building; but closer inspection reveals certain weaknesses. The portico with its unusual proportions – it is almost square in plan – seems too thin to form a base for the cupola, and there is a lack of continuity between the portico, the cylindrical wall which encloses the body of the church, and the rectangular section which contains the transepts. The interior also shows a certain indecision. The four arches of the main openings are each in a single plane, but the walls and the arches leading to the chapels on the diagonals are curved, while the entablature which supports the drum of the dome forms a continuous circle, thus creating an awkward relation between the lower and upper sections of the church. We look in vain in Juvarra's churches for the careful use of material and the attention to detail which characterized those of Guarini. Here we find only stucco, competently but rather coarsely moulded

and not designed to cling to the form of the structure, as would have been the case with Borromini or Guarini.

The Palazzo Madama consists of an irregular quadrilateral block, dating mainly from the fourteenth century, which originally had four round towers at the corners. In 1718 Madama Reale, the widow of Victor Amadeus I, commissioned Juvarra to plan a complete reconstruction of the castle. Of this scheme only the wing containing the grand staircase was carried out, and this was designed to be the central element in a much larger 91 façade of nineteen bays, with taller pavilions at the ends.

Compared with Guarini's Palazzo Carignano the Palazzo 86 Madama strikes a severe note. It is designed entirely in terms of planes and straight lines. The façade is divided into three equal 88 parts of three bays each, articulated by a tall Corinthian Order, which encloses the *piano nobile* and a mezzanine and stands on a rusticated ground floor, as in Bernini's third Louvre design, 173 though the round-headed windows on the *piano nobile* and the trophy-reliefs on the central piers have a slightly French flavour. Juvarra has emphasized the central section by making it break forward and giving it free-standing columns instead of the pilasters which articulate the wings.

The staircase itself, which fills the whole of the pavilion, is of 89 a grandeur hitherto unknown in Italy and perhaps only excelled by the Escalier des Ambassadeurs at Versailles. It may in fact 176 derive from France, because its plan with two symmetrical flights, each doubling back on itself, seems to have been invented by Louis Le Vau in one of his projects for the Louvre. This was never carried out, but the design seems to have been widely known outside France, presumably through copies after the drawings. Carlo Fontana planned to use it in the Granary which he built for Clement XI near the Baths of Diocletian, but the project remained on the drawing-board and the first staircase of this type actually to be built appears to be Fischer von Erlach's at Klesheim for the Archbishop of Salzburg, which was begun in 1700, though examples of half the plan, that is to say, a single staircase doubling back under a barrel-vault covering both flights, had been built in Italy, for instance by Borromini and Longhena.

Though the design of the staircase may derive from France, the treatment of its individual features, such as the balustrade and the stucco decoration of the walls and the vault, is completely Italian. The top landing is broken into a complex – and curiously enough not quite symmetrical – series of curves; the massive scrolls and masks at the half-landing twist slightly out of the plane of the balustrade, as if to guide the visitor on his way. In detail these piers and the stucco decoration generally are Roman in feeling and recall the forms of Pietro da Cortona.

The Palazzo Madama is a typical example of the workings of the Late International Baroque: a French plan, known in Rome and Vienna, is treated in a manner which derives from Roman Baroque; and on the exterior French elements in the windows and the reliefs are worked into a whole which is directly inspired by Bernini.

By contrast Stupinigi (begun 1729) seems entirely un-French, Piedmontese and highly personal to Juvarra. It was nominally conceived as a hunting lodge and is still called the *Palazzina di Caccia,* but in its scale and its position, some six miles outside the city, the parallel with Versailles is obvious; but only in function, not in form. Stupinigi is laid out on a basis of wings radiating from a central block, two of which are bent round, so 90, 92 that they eventually form a hexagonal court with smaller wings projecting from two of its corners. The idea of a building

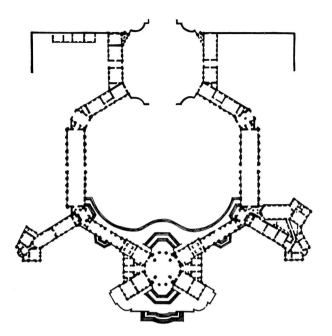

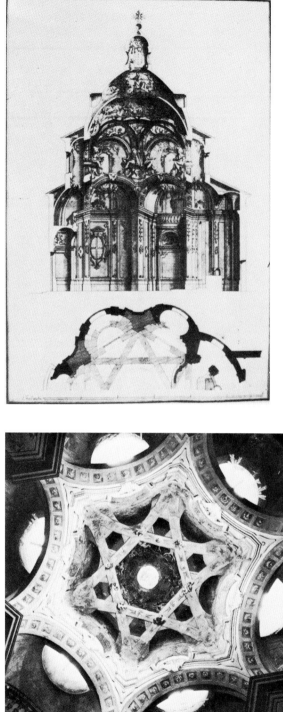

with radiating wings is almost certainly derived from an un-executed plan for a villa by Carlo Fontana – which seems also to have been known to Fischer von Erlach – but the idea of extending the wings to enclose a forecourt is Juvarra's. This arrangement creates a magnificent approach to the central block, which is distinguished from the other sections by being taller and curved both in plan and in roofline. This block contains the great *salone,* a room unlike the festival halls usual in Italian palaces. It is in many ways more like a church than a ball-room, and in fact its design is very close indeed to some of the projects for rebuilding the Cathedral of Turin which Juvarra produced at about the same time. In plan it consists of an octagonal central space, covered by a saucer-dome supported on four free-standing piers, round which are grouped two larger and two smaller apses. Its height is unexpectedly great in relation to the ground which it covers. This has the practical advantage that it allows the architect to introduce galleries for orchestras or spectators, but it increases the church-like effect of the whole room. The lines of balconies, pediments, and frames are broken into free Baroque curves, and the ensemble is completed by frescoes which have a touch of the Rococo in their light and gay colours, but which are conceived in terms of heavy figures, still Baroque in feeling.

Juvarra's conception of architecture was basically different from that of Guarini and he seemed for a moment to have eclipsed the latter, but Guarini's ideas were taken up and developed by his true successor, Bernardo Vittone (1702–70).[5] Except for a few years of training in Rome, Vittone spent the whole of his life in Piedmont, building churches for monasteries or parishes all over the province, often in small and relatively unimportant places. His studies in Rome no doubt gave him a good conventional training in architecture, but much more important for the formation of his style was the fact that he was entrusted by the Theatines with the editing of Guarini's treatise. Vittone himself wrote two treatises of immense length, the *Istruzzioni elementari* (1760) and the *Istruzzioni diverse* (1766), as well as a mass of notes which have never been fully studied.

92 *Top left* Stupinigi, plan by Filippo Juvarra

93 *Top right* Sanctuary of Vallinotto, by Bernardo Vittone, 1738–39, section and plan

94 *Above* Sanctuary of Vallinotto, interior of dome

His earliest documented work, the little Sanctuary standing alone beside a farm at Vallinotto, near Carignano, which was built in 1738–39, shows him already master of a highly sophisticated architectural idiom. In plan the church is a hexagon with six nearly semi-circular chapels, in three of which convex *coretti* have been inserted at the level of the entablature. The bay containing the altar is open and joined to a semi-circular retro-choir by a screen of columns reminiscent of Palladio. The arrangement of the dome is of hitherto unknown complexity. From the six main piers of the church spring ribs which form a network like that in Guarini's S. Lorenzo, but above this are two frescoed shells, the lower without windows but with a wide opening in the centre leading through to the outer shell, which is lit by concealed windows and a small lantern. This scheme is based on the by now generally accepted idea of concealed lighting, but no Roman architect had used it in this particular form, and Vittone's model was certainly J. H. Mansart's church of the Invalides, which he could have known through engravings. In the zone linking the church with the dome Vittone has followed Juvarra's lead at the Carmine and has eliminated the straight entablature over the chapel arches. In a preliminary design recorded in an engraving he followed Juvarra's scheme exactly, making arches support groups of sculpture standing out against the space over the chapels, but in the executed building he partly closed the zone over the arches, piercing it with round-headed openings. He broke through the vaults of the chapels, as Juvarra had done at the Carmine, and the openings thus created, combined with those in the lower ribbed dome, enable the spectator to look through from one space to another – sometimes to the inner dome, sometimes to the outer, or in the central opening to one superimposed on the other – in a manner far more complex than occurs in any church by Guarini.

Vittone's basic architectural ideas are fully developed at Vallinotto, and most of the later centralized churches only show variations on them. S. Chiara at Brà, for instance, differs in that the dome is constructed in the traditional manner with ribs against a closed shell, but Vittone cuts trefoil openings in its surface, which allow the spectator's view to pass through to figures of angels painted on the outer shell just behind the openings. S. Chiara differs from Vallinotto in being taller and in having four chapels instead of six. In both these features it comes close to Juvarra's *salone* at Stupinigi, and so the church-like *salone* may have been an influence on the designing of an actual church.

In one group of buildings – the chapel of the Albergo di Carità at Carignano (1744) and the church of S. Maria in Piazza in Turin (1751–54) – Vittone introduces another novelty by inserting in the pendentives of the dome half-cylindrical hollow bays which he continues up into the zone of the drum. This ingenious device links the two zones together effectively, but is visually awkward.

The exteriors of Vittone's churches are the exact expression of their internal structure. Each zone is clearly visible, the result being a pagoda-like structure, basically like Guarini's S. Lorenzo; but Vittone follows the internal structure more closely than his master, who at S. Lorenzo makes the interior and exterior surfaces curve in opposite directions. With Vittone the external bays follow the internal exactly, all convex at Vallinotto or S. Chiara, all concave at Grignasco, where the exterior has a firmness which reminds one that ultimately Vittone is the spiritual heir to Borromini.

While Vittone was creating his fantastic structures for the churches and monasteries of Piedmont, the art of the court of Turin was developing in a quite different direction, towards a Rococo which is closer to French decoration of the time than anything else to be found in Italy. This is apparent in a series of small rooms in the Palazzo Reale designed by Benedetto Alfieri (1700–67), who succeeded Juvarra as official architect to the king. These rooms are among the most delicate examples of an art much favoured in the courts of Italy and to be found in the royal or ducal palaces in many Italian towns. Only Rome set her face firmly against this light-hearted style, and the suite of rooms on the top floor of the Palazzo Barberini appears to be an almost unique example of the style in the city.

Genoa, Lombardy and Emilia

In the other parts of North Italy the Baroque did not take root and flourish as it did in Piedmont, but all the major towns from Genoa to Venice produced individual works of interest.

Genoa had seen a great wave of expansion and building in the second half of the sixteenth century.[6] The Strada Nuova, now the Via Garibaldi, was laid out and flanked by a series of the most splendid palaces to be found in any European city. The most inventive architect of the period was Galeazzo Alessi (1512–72), who created a type of palace and villa ideally suited to the difficult sites of the city, which continued to be used for a century and a half after his death. In the early seventeenth century the tradition was carried on by Bartolomeo Bianco (before 1590–1657), who in the University produced one of the few purely Baroque buildings in Genoa. It owes much to the Palazzo Doria-Tursi, now the Municipio, one of the most advanced Genoese palaces of the sixteenth century, which was built by two associates of Alessi – Domenico and Giovanni Ponzello – and probably owes much to his inspiration. In the Palazzo Doria-Tursi the architects had taken advantage brilliantly of the steeply sloping site on which the palaces of the Strada Nuova are built to create a succession of spaces at different levels, leading from the vestibule at street level to the main arcaded court one stage higher, through a grand Imperial staircase to the upper floors and to a garden at a higher level at the back of the palace. Bianco followed this pattern, but modified it by making the staircase carry on up to the terraced third floor and by extending the loggia on the ground floor of the main court round the vestibule, thus fusing the two principal sections of the building into a single whole more completely than had been done in the earlier palace.

Genoese palaces of the later seventeenth and eighteenth centuries are notable for the lavish decoration which they received at the hands of a series of virtuoso *quadratura* fresco painters, among whom the most important were Domenico Piola and Lorenzo de Ferrari, who were responsible for the decoration of the great rooms in the Palazzo Bianco (destroyed during the Second World War), the Palazzo Rosso, the Palazzo Carega-Cataldi, and many others. About 1780, however, that is to say, at a time when the Baroque had been superseded by some form of Classical revival in almost all parts of Italy, Genoa produced one remarkable architect in the old style, Gregorio Petondi, who laid out the Via Nuovissima, now called the Via Cairoli, a worthy extension of the Strada Nuova, and remodelled the Palazzo Balbi. The latter had been begun in the sixteenth century on a site on the Via Cairoli, but was extended by the acquisition of a site at the back facing on the Via Lomellini, which ran at a lower level. Petondi seized upon

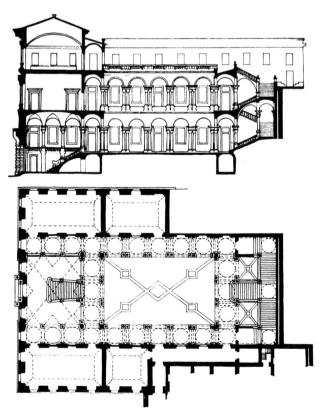

this typically Genoese problem to create a brilliantly designed double staircase, so that from the Via Cairoli the visitor can go up, past a mezzanine floor, to the *piano nobile,* or down to the apartments on the ground floor on Via Lomellini – an ingenious variation on the disposition used by Hildebrandt in the Upper Belvedere in Vienna of which Petondi no doubt knew the plans. 97 271

Lombardy, and particularly the area round Lake Como, had produced a great line of architects and masons in the later Middle Ages, which continued through the fifteenth and six-teenth centuries, but towards the end of the period the men of real ability – Domenico Fontana, Carlo Maderno, and Borro-mini – tended to leave their native towns and seek their fortunes in Rome, and the two great reformers and builders, St Charles Borromeo and his nephew, Cardinal Federico Borromeo, relied mainly on architects imported from elsewhere, such as Pelleg-rino Pellegrini Tibaldi from Bologna. The one great exception was Francesco Maria Ricchino (1583–1658), who was born and died in Milan and apparently never left Lombardy, except for a short visit to Rome when he was sent by Cardinal Federico Borromeo to complete his training, probably in the very first years of the seventeenth century.[7] The evidence of his surviving works suggests that he studied the buildings of Vignola and his successors, and that he probably saw the façade of S. Susanna, but he also learnt much more from the architects of his native

95 *Top left* Genoa, the University by Bartolomeo Bianco, designed 1630, the court

96 *Left* Genoa, the University, plan and section

97 *Above* Genoa, staircase in the Palazzo Balbi by Gregorio Petondi, 1780

city, particularly from his master Lorenzo Binago (1554–1628) and from Tibaldi. He was deeply influenced by the ideas of his patron Federico Borromeo, and his churches are the clearest reflection of the Cardinal's ideals in ecclesiastical architecture.

In the church of S. Alessandro, Milan (begun 1601), Binago had evolved an ingenious combination of centralized and longitudinal planning by using a series of square spaces, each covered by a dome, to form a Greek cross, but adding a square choir and a semi-circular apse, which created an emphasis on the long axis. In his earliest church, S. Giuseppe (1607–30), Ricchino uses the same method in a very simplied form, and the church consists essentially of a square domed nave followed by a smaller choir of identical shape. To both elements are added very shallow rectangular chapels, so that they become almost Greek crosses. This method of designing was never taken up in Rome, but it was used in the eighteenth century by Giovanni Domenico Vaccaro in Naples, and by Johann Michael Fischer in Bavaria, though it is difficult to say whether there is a direct connection. In his plans for other churches Ricchino was more adventurous and created ingenious combinations of squares and Greek crosses, as well as experimenting with oval elements.

The exterior of S. Giuseppe is highly original, because Ricchino has applied a typical Roman façade to the drum of the octagonal dome over the nave of the church, one side of which forms the central section of the façade itself. This combination

98 *Right* Milan, exterior of S. Giuseppe by Francesco Maria Ricchino, 1607–30

99 *Below* Milan, façade of the Collegio Elvetico by Francesco Maria Ricchino, begun 1627

of the two forms creates a new kind of variety in the relation of the façade to the body of the church. The scheme may have influenced Borromini, who would certainly have seen the church in building during his early years in Milan.

Ricchino, who was employed on work at the cathedral of Milan from 1603 onwards and was in charge of it from 1631 to 1638, produced many designs for the façade. Some of these are composed of a combination of Tibaldesque motifs,[8] but one of them, dating from 1606, has a movement forward in steps emphasized by full columns, which shows that the architect had learnt a lesson from Maderno, in particular from S. Susanna. In the façade which he added to the Collegio Elvetico (begun 1627), however, he made a much more revolutionary move and designed the central part of the building on a concave curve – at least seven years before Borromini and Cortona applied the same method to the façades of S. Carlino and SS. Luca e Martina. It is difficult to decide whether or not they knew his design. Borromini had left Milan by 1618, and Cortona never visited the city; on the other hand it is quite possible that the former had kept up a connection with Ricchino, who might have sent a drawing to Rome.

99

Ricchino was also an accomplished designer of palaces. In the Palazzo Annoni he used a single repeated arch for the loggias of the cortile, but in the Palazzo Durini (1648) and the Brera he followed Tibaldi's Collegio Borromeo at Pavia and created a magnificent effect with a series of Serlian arches. He actually worked at the Collegio Borromeo, which he extended by adding at the back two wings with colonnades in the style used earlier by Fulvio Mangone at the Collegio Elvetico, which was ultimately inspired by Palladio.

One other monument built near Milan during Ricchino's lifetime must be mentioned, namely the Sacro Monte at Varese, designed by Giuseppe Bernasconi (begun 1604), with fourteen chapels, all different in design and showing an extraordinary variety of circular, oval, square, and polygonal forms.

During the latter half of the seventeenth century little building was carried out in Milan, but in the first half of the eighteenth century there was a revival which produced a number of impressive, if not very original, palaces. The Roman-born architect Giovanni Ruggeri (d. before 1743) built the Palazzo Cusani, the façade of which, dating from 1715, has windows and a balcony of bold Borrominesque curves. Bartolomeo Bolla, a Milanese by birth and training, was responsible for the Palazzo Arese, now Litta (1743–60), notable for its impressive door flanked by huge Atlantes, a formula much used in Genoese palaces – as well as by Puget on the Hôtel-de-Ville of Toulon – but which goes back to Leone Leoni's Palazzo degli Omenoni (c.1573) in Milan itself. The aristocracy of Milan also built numerous villas, of which one of the most impressive is Ruggeri's Villa Visconti at Brignano.

In the principal cities along the Po Valley building activity of the same kind occurred in the eighteenth century, but the architects were competent rather than original. Typical of them were Gianantonio Veneroni of Pavia, whose Palazzo Mezzabarba (1728–30) shows a knowledge of the forms of doors and windows evolved by the Roman successors of Borromini, and Antonio Arrighi, who built the grandiose staircase in the Palazzo Dati (1769) at Cremona. Similar examples could be quoted in most other towns in the Po Valley. Even in much smaller places, such as Sabbioneta, an occasional detail of great charm – and originality – may suddenly appear, such as the door to a former Convent, now the Municipal hospital.

There also arose a local form of Rococo, more closely allied in form to contemporary work in Naples than to anything produced in France. The architects who developed this style were specialists in the designing of staircases, of which brilliant examples are to be found in the Palazzo Crivelli, Milan (architect and date unknown), the Palazzo Albertoni-Arrigoni at Crema, attributed to Giuseppe Cozzi, and the Palazzo Stanga at Cremona, designed by the owner, who was a competent amateur architect. Mantua has several small palaces with windows and doors in full Rococo style, but neither their date nor their authors seem to be known.

It might be expected that Bologna would have produced a great architectural movement complementary to its flourishing school of painting in the seventeenth and early eighteenth centuries, but this is not the case. The academic tradition of the city in the arts would clearly not have been congenial to a flowering of the Baroque, but even the most successful architect of the period, Carlo Francesco Dotti (1670–1759), never rose above mediocrity.[9] His contemporaries, Giovanni Battista Piacentini and Francesco Maria Angelini (1680–1731), produced impressive variants of the grand Baroque staircase in the Palazzo Ruini-Ranuzzi, now the Palace of Justice (1695), and the Palazzo Montanari.[10]

The main contribution of Bologna to architecture was, however, made in an indirect way, through the art of stage-design, which reached its highest point in the work of the Galli-Bibiena family, Ferdinando (1657–1743), his brother Francesco (1659–1731), and his two sons, Giuseppe (1696–1757) and Antonio (1700–74).[11] The art of *quadratura* or the painting of *trompe l'oeil* architectural perspectives had been a speciality of

100 Ferdinando Galli Bibiena, drawing of a stage design. *London, British Museum*

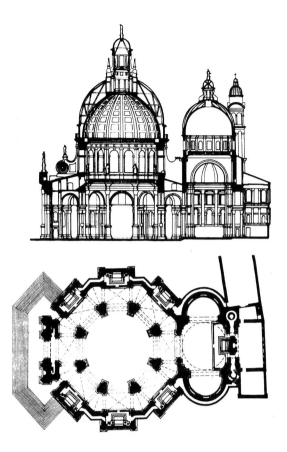

101 *Above* Venice, S. Maria della Salute by Baldassare Longhena, plan and section, begun 1631

102 *Above right* Sabbioneta, Cathedral, the dome of the Chapel of the Sacrament by Antonio Galli Bibiena, *c.* 1770

103 *Opposite* S. Maria della Salute, exterior detail showing scrolls

Bolognese painters since the last years of the sixteenth century and had reached an astonishing point of virtuosity in the hands of Angelo Michele Colonna (1600–87) and Agostino Mitelli (1609–60), who worked in collaboration, and this art was now applied with brilliant results to the designing of stage-sets. The Bibiena family set a fashion which spread all over Europe, and they themselves held posts in Vienna, Dresden, Berlin, and Mannheim, as well as Parma and other Italian cities.

Some members of the family also erected real buildings. Francesco built the celebrated Teatro Farnese at Parma (1720; destroyed during the Second World War), and Antonio the smaller but beautiful municipal theatre at Bologna (1750). Antonio was also active in ecclesiastical architecture. He added the chapel of the Sacrament to the Immaculata at Sabbioneta and built the parish church at Villa Pasquali nearby. These two buildings are notable for the extraordinary decoration of the domes, which consists of an open network of stucco standing out against the outer shell, which is painted sky-blue and brilliantly lit by concealed windows, almost like the pierced decoration in some Islamic domes. A variant of this unusual design was used by the unknown architect of the Palazzo Gangi at Palermo.

Venice

The ghosts of Palladio and Scamozzi hung so heavily over Venice in the seventeenth and eighteenth centuries that they prevented Venetian architects – and Venetian patrons – from developing a full Baroque style. Architects of the period in Venice and on the *terra firma* continued to imitate the models created in the sixteenth century, mainly those of Palladio, but they sometimes used forms current in the generation before him, for instance for churches the Greek cross in a square, which was popular in the first half of the sixteenth century.[12]

The single exception to the general rule was Baldassare Longhena (1598–1682) who, in the church of S. Maria della Salute, produced one of the masterpieces of Baroque architecture.[13] Longhena was trained in the studio of Scamozzi, and his early works, such as the Palazzo Giustiniani-Lolin (probably designed in 1627) or Palazzo Widman (*c.* 1630), are markedly conservative, even going back to early Cinquecento types rather than to the more fully developed models of Sansovino or Sanmicheli, or those of his own master. Longhena's great opportunity came, however, when in 1631, at the age of 33, he was commissioned by the Senate to build the Salute in fulfilment of a vow made to the Virgin during the plague of 1630.

The plan of the church, which is basically octagonal, may have been inspired by the sixteenth-century churches of this form which abound in Lombardy, but Longhena has transformed his model by surrounding it with an ambulatory and adding to it a choir of novel design, consisting of a bay with an apse at each end, closed by an arch which covers the high altar and leads to the *coro* or monks' choir. These units are bound together by a careful control of light: the main space is strongly

100

102

101

105

104 *Above* Canaletto, *View of S. Maria della Salute*, Venice. *Windsor Castle, Royal Collection*

105 *Right* S. Maria della Salute, interior

lit by the windows in the dome; the choir is much darker, lit from above, and the *coro* is slightly lighter, with windows in the walls. The result is a succession of light and dark spaces, the effect of which is intensified by the four free-standing columns which flank the high altar and stand out against the lighter *coro* in a manner reminiscent of Palladio's designs at S. Giorgio and the Redentore.

104   For the external appearance of the church Longhena drew extensively on Antonio da Sangallo the Younger's design for S. Giovanni dei Fiorentini – recorded in engravings in Labacco's

103 *Architettura* – particularly for the huge scrolls which support the dome and which are the dominating feature of the Salute as seen from a distance across the Grand Canal. Longhena has altered his model in several significant ways. He made the whole building simpler by changing the plan from a sixteen-sided polygon to an octagon, thus reducing the number of scrolls to eight, and at the same time he increased the size of the scrolls, thus making the general effect more powerful and less fussy than the sixteenth-century model. In Sangallo's design each of the sixteen facets of the building is decorated with a single tabernacle, except for the entrance, which has a façade covering three bays. Longhena, on the other hand, established a sort of crescendo by varying the decoration on the outside of the chapels. Those on the cross-axis of the church have single

106 Venice, interior of the Gesuati by Giorgio Massari, c. 1736

107 Venice, façade of S. Maria degli Scalzi by Giuseppe Sardi, 1683–89

pilasters at the corners, whereas those on the diagonals, flanking the entrance, have four pilasters, the outer ones being supported by half-pilasters, and in addition three niches with statues. These lead up to the climax of the entrance façade, which is not only broader than the chapels, but is boldly articulated with full columns which enclose two rows of niches, again with statues. This façade is topped by a balustrade on which stand five statues, as opposed to the three on the pediments of the chapels. This building up of architectural and sculptural decoration towards the central feature is reminiscent of Maderno's method on the façade of S. Susanna, but it is here applied to a more complex structure in three dimensions. The combination of sculpture and architecture is typically Venetian and can be seen as an extension of the system used by Sansovino in the Library, and by Scarpagnino on the façade of the Scuola di S. Rocco. Moreover, it was to remain one of the hall-marks of Venetian Baroque throughout the seventeenth and early eighteenth centuries. Longhena used it again in similar form on the façade of S. Giustina, now deprived of its pediment, but in his S. Maria dei Derelitti or dell'Ospedaletto the sculpture takes over completely and the architectural elements almost disappear. The lower storey is composed of an Ionic Order, of which the square piers are covered with high reliefs of lions' masks and bunches of fruit; the upper storey has an Order of Atlantes, and the attic is covered with shields and other decorative elements. The same method is applied by Giuseppe Sardi on the façade of S. Maria del Giglio (or S. Maria Zobenigo; 1678–83) and at the

107   Scalzi (1683–89), by Alessandro Tremignon at S. Moisè (1668),

and by Domenico Rosso at S. Stae (after 1709), though in these cases the architectural frame-work is more clearly in evidence than in the Ospedaletto. In Giovanni Battista Fattoretto's façade of the Gesuiti (1715) the architecture reasserts its position fully and the front builds up in a series of whole columns, breaking forward and backward in a manner reminiscent of certain Sicilian façades, such as Andrea Palma's on   132
the cathedral at Syracuse or Rosario Gagliardi's S. Giorgio at   133
Ragusa Ibla. It is characteristic of these Venetian façades that, even when the architects make great play with sculpture, it is never fused with the architecture, as it is with Bernini, but retains its independent existence.

The Venetian architects of the seventeenth and eighteenth centuries use a variety of forms in their façades. At the Ospedaletto, S. Maria Zobenigo, and S. Moisè the front consists of two storeys of equal width, topped by an attic, but at S. Stae the two storeys are united by a giant Order in the manner of Palladio, and at the Scalzi Sardi uses the Roman type, with a wider lower storey, though the proportions are heavier than would be normal in a Roman church.

The interior architecture of Venetian churches continued throughout the seventeenth and eighteenth centuries to be simple and designed in Palladian terms, as for instance in the Gesuati (c. 1736) by Giorgio Massari, which, however, shows a   106
trace of influence from Longhena in the placing of the high altar against the arch leading to the well-lit *coro*. The only exception   108
is the Gesuiti, where the architect, Domenico Rossi, has indulged in an outburst of inlaid-marble decoration which has

hardly any parallels north of Naples. It is true that, compared with the southern examples, the effect is relatively simple, because the pattern of the inlay is broader and less complicated, and because the colours are limited to grey-green and white, but the impression is still one of great richness, reaching a climax in the choir, where the four full columns are decorated with the inlay.

Domestic architecture in Venice was conservative throughout the period under consideration. The palace plan established by the middle of the sixteenth century continued to be used till the end of the eighteenth. These palaces are designed round a long vestibule on the ground floor running right through the building from the middle of the canal façade. From this vestibule a staircase leads to the *salone* on the *piano nobile*, followed by a gallery running right over the vestibule to the canal and flanked by suites of smaller rooms overlooking the side-canals or streets. The disadvantage of this plan is that the

108 *Right* Venice, high altar of the Gesuiti by Domenico Rossi, 1715–29

109 *Below* Venice, façade of the Palazzo Rezzonico by Baldassare Longhena, *c.* 1667. Top floor added by Giorgio Massari, 1752–56

gallery, being only lit at one end, is apt to be dark, but the *salone*, lit on three sides, makes a magnificent approach to the *piano nobile*.

The façades follow the pattern laid down by Sansovino and Sanmicheli in the mid sixteenth century – which itself was based on late-mediaeval models – with a central section, usually of three bays, on each floor, corresponding to the vestibule and gallery, flanked by windows for the smaller rooms. In the Palazzo Rezzonico and the Palazzo Pesaro Longhena did little more than enrich the detail by the addition of rustication and a slightly increased use of sculpture, reminiscent of his treatment of church façades.

The staircase formed an important feature of most Venetian palaces. In the seventeenth and eighteenth centuries it usually followed the pattern of a single flight doubling back on itself,

110 *Below* Palazzo Rezzonico, the ball-room, frescoed by G. B. Crosato, with architectural *quadratura* probably by Agostino Mengozzi Colonna, *c.* 1750

111 *Below right* Venice, S. Giorgio Maggiore, the staircase by Baldassare Longhena, 1643–45

the two flights being covered by a single vault and not being separated from each other by a wall as in Central Italian sixteenth-century staircases. Some of the finest examples of this type of staircase by Longhena can be found in ecclesiastical buildings, the Seminario Patriarcale and the Convent of SS. Giovanni e Paolo, and it was also for a religious body that he designed his most remarkable creation in this field, the staircase at S. Giorgio Maggiore (1643–45). This is of the Imperial form, dividing into two branches at the first landing and following round the walls enclosing the whole staircase. This type of staircase was invented in Spain in the middle of the sixteenth century – the earliest surviving example is in the Alcazar at Toledo – and had been used in Genoa in the Palazzo Doria-Tursi and the University, but Longhena gives it a breadth and an openness lacking in the Genoese examples, where the site is cramped owing to the rising ground at the end of the site. It is the first grand and spacious Italian staircase and a direct predecessor to the Escalier des Ambassadeurs at Versailles.

In the eighteenth century palace façades were influenced by the Palladian revival created by architects such as Giorgio Massari, but at the same time the interior decoration remained extremely rich. The ceilings were embellished with stuccoes and

frescoes, from the hand of Tiepolo and his contemporaries, as in the *salone* of the Palazzo Rezzonico. In certain of these rooms, for instance in the *salone* of the Palazzo Widman, the architectural features are reduced to insignificance, and are replaced by a play of stucco or fresco decoration. In smaller, more intimate rooms a real Rococo style appears. Sometimes, as in the Ridotto Venier, the whole ceiling is covered by a wave of stucco curtains or clouds which completely obscure the boundaries of the space, and in others – particularly in some of the smaller rooms in the Palazzo Ducale – the walls are lightly decorated with touches of stucco thrown on the wall and modelled with the spatula, almost like South Bavarian Rococo decoration. Perhaps the most exquisite example of the style is the series of mezzanine rooms in the Palazzo Foscarini, in which the ceiling has gilt Rococo curls cutting across a sky against which fly birds, and the walls are decorated with *chinoiserie* panels painted in gold on a ground composed of white tiles, which give a peculiar luminosity to the whole room. This playful and elegant type of Rococo was even better suited to the decoration of country houses than to palaces, and

112 Venice, Palazzo Foscarini, room on the mezzanine floor

exquisite examples of it can be found in many villas on the *terra firma*.

As might be expected, the Baroque took even less hold on Vicenza than on Venice, and the tradition of Palladio and Scamozzi continued to dominate the architecture of the town. Curiously enough, however, in the eighteenth century a certain number of church façades were built on a Roman pattern (S. Vincenzo, S. Gaetano, S. Marco degli Scalzi), but they are of no quality.

The South

As has been pointed out in the Introduction, architecture in Florence was hardly touched by the Baroque.[1] It has been argued elsewhere that Gherardo Silvani's façade to S. Gaetano is Baroque, but it is entirely flat and its decoration is taken directly from Buontalenti. The Cappella Feroni in the SS. Annunziata – built on the design of Il Volterrano and decorated by Foggini – qualifies better, but it is really a work of sculpture, an art in which the Florentines were much more influenced by the Baroque than in architecture. The church of S. Giuseppe, near S. Croce, by Giacinto Manni, shows some awareness of Roman Baroque methods of design, but the only works of architecture executed in a true Baroque manner in Florence were done by an artist who, though Tuscan by birth, was purely Roman by training – Pietro da Cortona's decorations in the rooms on the *piano nobile* in the Palazzo Pitti. In these rooms the artist created a new manner of combining stucco and fresco which was to have a considerable influence outside Italy, particularly in France; but it is typical of the atmosphere in Florence that his bold and highly original project for extending the Pitti Palace itself was rejected in favour of one by a local architect which simply repeated the Quattrocento pattern to an almost intolerable length.

In other parts of Italy, such as the Marches, Umbria, or the Abruzzi, there was little building activity of interest during the seventeenth and early eighteenth centuries, though almost every village church was at least renovated in a vernacular Baroque style; and the other centres in which real and individual Baroque styles were produced are to be found in the South, above all in Naples and Sicily.

Naples

The circumstances in which the Baroque developed in Naples were very different from those which prevailed in other Italian cities.[2] In Rome everything depended on the papacy; in Turin architects satisfied the ambitions of the house of Savoy; in Venice they followed the dictates of the Senate or, to a lesser extent, the religious orders and the wealthy citizens. During the greater part of the period in question Naples was simply a province of Spain, governed – often very badly – from Madrid through the intermediary of a viceroy, who was generally more occupied with defending the coast against the attacks of pirates and areas inland against the activities of bandits than in embellishing the city. On the other hand, as the viceregal court was developed and the nobility were tempted more and more to abandon their estates and spend the greater part of their time dancing attendance on the viceroy, the need for new or at least redecorated palaces increased and many Neapolitan nobles spent far more than they could afford on creating a fine setting for their lives in the city. It was, however, above all the Church that fostered the outburst of building activity that took place in the seventeenth century and the first half of the eighteenth century. Neapolitans were famous for their piety – or superstition – and they spent enormous sums on building churches and chapels, as well as endowing masses for the repose of their souls. Further, many fathers found it more economical to put their daughters into a convent than to pay a dowry for them, and on each such occasion a substantial gift accompanied the novice and went into the coffers of the convent. In size and wealth the religious houses in Naples far surpassed those of all other Italian cities. Certain areas of the town were almost entirely given over to convents and monasteries, and, as they housed only a fraction of the population that the area would have accommodated, their existence and continual expansion led to the appalling overcrowding of the city which was a perpetual source of worry to the authorities.

When Alfonso of Aragon captured Naples in 1442, he determined to establish the new Renaissance style to replace the Gothic favoured by the Angevins and, in order to do this, he invited a number of distinguished Tuscan architects to come to Naples and design the palaces, villas, and churches with which he intended to enrich his new capital. In so doing he established a practice which prevailed for a long time in Naples, and it was not till the early seventeenth century that a style of architecture arose which could properly be called Neapolitan. The last foreign invasion was constituted by three major architects: Domenico Fontana, who escaped to Naples from Rome after the death of his patron, Sixtus V, and built the palace of the viceroy; the Florentine Giovanni Antonio Dosio, who laid out the great cloister in the Certosa of S. Martino, and the Jesuit Father Giuseppe Valeriano, who built the principal church of his order in Naples, the Gesù Nuovo, which, however, owes most of its present magnificence to the rich marble and fresco decoration added to it – in a spirit quite contrary to Valeriano's desire for simplicity – in the seventeenth and eighteenth centuries. It is curious to notice that during the fifteenth and sixteenth centuries all the visiting architects came from Central or Northern Italy and that, in spite of the fact that Naples was under the dominion of Spain, there is hardly any trace of Spanish influence in the development of architecture, either at this time or during the Baroque period.

The first architect to stand out as having created an identifiably Neapolitan style is Fabrizio Grimaldi (1543–1613), who in his churches, such as S. Maria degli Angeli a Pizzofalcone (begun 1600), established a model for spacious Latin-cross churches articulated internally with elaborately clustered pilasters, which was to be followed in Naples for more than a century.

The creator of Neapolitan Baroque architecture was Cosimo Fanzago (1591–1678), who was born near Bergamo but came to Naples at the age of seventeen and became in the fullest sense of the word naturalized. He was trained as a marble-worker, and his greatest achievements are in the decoration of churches and chapels rather than in planning, but in his particular field he had no rival.

Southern Italy and Sicily were rich in coloured marbles, and Fanzago took advantage of this fact to create some of the most resplendent decorative effects in occidental architecture. Curiously enough the possibilities of using coloured marbles for the decoration of churches were first exploited in Central Italy, in Rome and also in Florence, where it can be regarded as a sort of extension of the local art of inlaying furniture with the semi-precious *pietre dure*. It seems to have been introduced into Naples by Domenico Fontana and by the Florentine sculptor Michelangelo Naccherino (1550–1622), who established a successful workshop for decorative marbling in the city; but it was left for Fanzago to exploit the full possibilities of the medium. This he did in a series of chapels, in which the most elaborate patterns of coloured marbles, some abstract, some imitating flowers, are combined with white marble decoration in relief, based on the forms invented by Buontalenti which Naccherino had brought to Naples.

In the Certosa of S. Martino, where he worked for more than thirty years, Fanzago deployed his art to the fullest extent. In the cloister – which he completed to the designs of Dosio, but adding his own decorative detail – he developed his Buontalentesque vocabulary to a new point of complexity, particularly in the doors, in which he combined figure sculpture, which he executed himself, with decorative and architectural detail, some quite naturalistic, like the swags of hanging fruit, some more ambiguous, like the cartouches over the doors, which are apparently intended to look like grotesque masks. In the church, of which the choir had already been decorated before he took over, he produced a wonderful harmony of colour effects, dominated by yellows, warm browns, and dull reds, which continue the tones of the frescoes which Lanfranco, Ribera, and others painted on the vault in the spandrels and beside the windows. The marbling spreads not only over the walls and pilasters but across the whole floor – brilliantly restored in the 1960s – so that the visitor is enveloped in gay and rich colours, strengthened by the sun which streams in through the windows. The marbling is entirely executed in flat inlay, except for the huge rosettes on the piers separating the chapels, which are in dark grey, almost black marble, the carving of which is perhaps the most remarkable example of Fanzago's virtuosity.

As a pure architect Fanzago was less inventive than as a decorative sculptor. His church plans are conventional, and he showed a preference for the simple Greek cross, which had

113 Naples, Certosa di S. Martino, the cloister begun by G. A. Dosio, *c.* 1600. Completed and decorated by Cosimo Fanzago, 1623–29

completely gone out of fashion in Rome. It is only in his façades that he shows real originality. In several of these he was faced with the problem – common in Neapolitan churches – of having the nave at a higher level than the street on which the church faced, and in two churches, S. Giuseppe a Pontecorvo and S. Maria della Sapienza, he solved this ingeniously by placing the

114 *Top left* Certosa di S. Martino, doors in the cloister, by Cosimo Fanzago, before 1631; busts added in the 1640s

115 *Above* Naples, Palazzo di Donn' Anna by Cosimo Fanzago, built 1642–44, but left unfinished; from an 18th-century engraving

116 *Top right* Certosa di S. Martino, interior of the church by Cosimo Fanzago, finished before 1656

117 *Right* Naples, façade of S. Maria della Sapienza by Cosimo Fanzago, 1638–41

steps in two flights behind the façade, at S. Giuseppe running round the walls of a vestibule, and at the Sapienza parallel with the façade.   117

His most remarkable building, however, is the huge Palazzo Donn 'Anna built in 1642–44 for the Spanish viceroy, the duke of Medina, and his wife, who was heiress to the vast wealth of the Carafa family. It is a large block composed of three wings round a narrow court, on a rock projecting into the sea below the heights of Posillipo, to the west of Naples. The palace was never finished and has suffered from neglect over the last three centuries, but an engraving made in the 1760s gives an idea of it when its main outlines were clearer than they are now. It was planned to be approached from the sea, and the viceregal barge would have tied up under a triple arcade on the east side, like that visible on the main façade but one floor lower. The triple arcade was the outstanding feature of the design and was repeated on three floors on each façade. The main front is broken by recessed bays on the top floor, and the corners are cut off and given different treatment on each floor – a flat panel on the ground floor, a semi-circular bay on the first, and a   115

118 *Left* Naples, detail of the high altar of S. Domenico Maggiore by Cosimo Fanzago, *c.* 1650

119 *Below left* Naples, staircase in the Palazzo Bartolomeo di Maio by Ferdinando Sanfelice

120 *Below* Naples, vault of the church of Villanova by Ferdinando Sanfelice

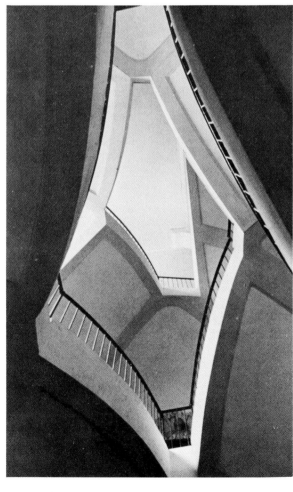

rectilinear recess on the second, an arrangement which produces sharp variations in depth, the effect of which is heightened by the variations in the treatment of the surfaces of the different floors – a feature which is unfortunately not indicated in the engraving.

Among Fanzago's contemporaries were several architects who were competent but uninventive, and the only individual work to stand out from their productions is the grand staircase added to the viceregal palace about 1650, almost certainly by Francesco Antonio Picchiatti, which, like Longhena's staircase at S. Giorgio Maggiore, is based on Spanish royal models. It is, however, wider and more spacious than the earlier examples, running through seven instead of the usual five bays. It never received the intended decoration, and the marbling that we see today was added after the palace was damaged by fire in 1837.

In the last decades of the seventeenth and the first of the eighteenth centuries there was a revival of a monumental style with Dionisio Lazzari (1617–89), Arcangelo Guglielmelli (active 1674–1717), and Giovanni Battista Nauclerio (active 1676–c.1740), whose churches, articulated internally with full columns, have an almost Roman grandeur, but at the same time the decorative tendencies of Fanzago were continued in the brilliant marbling of Bartolomeo and Pietro Ghetti and the almost Rococo stonework of Giovanni Battista Nauclerio and his brother Muzio.

The first half of the eighteenth century saw the rise of two architects of real distinction: Ferdinando Sanfelice (1675–1748), and Domenico Antonio Vaccaro (1681–1745).

As an inventor of new forms, both in planning and in structure, Sanfelice stands out as the most original architect of the Neapolitan Baroque. His greatest achievements lie in the designing of churches on unusual ground plans and the building of palaces with dramatic and ingeniously disposed staircases.

It is recorded that he made several designs for churches in the shape of a star, a form unknown in Italy but used occasionally by Central European architects. They were in fact rejected in favour of simpler designs, but he actually built a library of this form in the monastery of S. Giovanni a Carbonara, which was destroyed in the nineteenth century, and two hexagonal churches by him survive, one at Villanova, on the top of Posillipo, the other in a palace belonging to his wife's family, the Ravaschieri, at Roccapiemonte. The latter is very simple in design, but the former has alternately flat and rounded bays – three of which contain doors leading to the street, the sacristy and the monastic buildings – and the central space is composed of six broad and simply designed ribs meeting in a six-lobed panel of stucco round the symbol of the Trinity in glory.

120

Sanfelice came of an important and wealthy Neapolitan family and built for himself a large palace (Palazzo Sanfelice) – in fact one of the largest eighteenth-century Neapolitan palaces. It is designed round two courts, with a façade of eleven bays, broken by three slightly projecting sections, the outer two containing the monumental entrances flanked by caryatids, which lead to the two courts. The right-hand court is closed at the end opposite the entrance by a grand open staircase. In plan it is a variant of the Imperial staircase, differing from the normal type in that it starts with two flights running parallel with the façade, which turn in and round till they meet again and are continued in a single flight in the middle bay. This plan has the advantage of leaving the central bay open to form a vista, usually through to a garden, but in this case to a sort of grotto, because the ground rises steeply and the garden is at the level of

418

121 Naples, staircase in the Palazzo Serra di Cassano by Ferdinando Sanfelice, 1720-38

the first floor. In the placing of the staircase and in its general plan Sanfelice seems to have had in mind Genoese models, such as Bianco's University, but the effect is far more dramatic, because whereas in the Genoese palace the staircase is hidden behind the double loggias of the court, here it opens straight on to the court itself. Added to this, Sanfelice has made the staircase not merely open but with the upper stages transparent, so that the visitor looks through to the back and is aware of the pattern made by the superimposition of the openings in the front and back walls, which slope in opposite directions, following the lines of the flights. Open staircases had been a feature of Neapolitan architecture since the sixteenth century, but they had never been given such prominence before or been treated in such a complex manner.

The other court of the palace has the form of a rectangle with the corners cut off, and ends with an equally ingenious staircase. Unlike the one in the right-hand court, this is completely closed and consists of two spirals which touch each other and have common lozenge-shaped landings at ground and first-floor levels. The design is almost certainly based on a mediaeval type, of which an early sixteenth-century example is in the Burg at Graz and may have been known to Sanfelice, since he was in contact with Austria through the imperial viceroys.

Sanfelice designed many closed staircases on unusual plans, of which a particularly beautiful example is that in the Palazzo Bartolomeo di Maio, in the form of a lozenge of which the sides 119 are all convex inwards, producing an extraordinary effect of movement and tension.

121 Sanfelice's most magnificent staircase is in the Palazzo Serra di Cassano. The palace is built on a large open site, and Sanfelice was free to design on a grand scale. The main entrance – now alas! closed – is on the east and leads into an octagonal court, at the end of which stands the huge arched entrance to the staircase chamber. The staircase itself is on a completely novel plan, in two halves, in the middle of which are semi-circular landings, which form a pair of bastions facing the visitor as he approaches the staircase. The two flights meet at a bridge in front of the door to the main apartments of the palace – a form reminiscent of Fischer von Erlach's staircase in 257 the Winter Palace of Prince Eugene in Vienna (1695), of which Sanfelice may have seen drawings or the original, if, as is possible, he actually visited Vienna. Most of Sanfelice's staircases are in simple materials – brick and stucco, or the rough porous stone of Pozzuoli – but at the Palazzo Serra he has played a more elaborate game. The staircase itself is in a rough dark-grey volcanic stone, but the detail – which is ultimately Fanzaghesque in derivation – stands out against it in a fine, creamy marble.

All his life Sanfelice was active in designing the temporary structures which the Neapolitans loved to erect on any important occasion – a wedding, a birth or a funeral, or the feast day of S. Gennaro, the patron saint of Naples. Generally

122 Calvizzano, near Naples, S. Maria delle Grazie by Domenico Antonio Vaccaro, interior of dome, probably dating from the 1730s

these were altars set up in the street, in which the fact of working in wood and plaster instead of solid materials allowed the architect to indulge in liberties of design which he never took in his permanent buildings; but on really important occasions, for instance the birth of Charles III's first son, the whole piazza in front of the Palazzo Reale was enclosed in a vast hemicycle of arcades with booths and shops, in the middle of which stood a tall tower, almost like a pagoda.

If Sanfelice was essentially an inventor of architectural forms, Vaccaro was the continuer of the decorative tradition established by Fanzago. It is true that, when he had a free hand in planning a church, he showed considerable skill, as, for instance, in the Concezione a Montecalvario (1718–24), which is composed of an elongated octagon, surrounded by chapels forming an ambulatory, or in S. Michele, which consists of a series of square elements, but his real talent was for decorative effects, whether in stucco, marble, or maiolica tiles. His skill in fusing architecture and decoration is shown in the Concezione, where, in addition to designing the building, he planned the stucco and painted the altarpieces, producing a whole which bears the marks of his personality in every detail.

Perhaps his most striking work is at S. Maria delle Grazie at Calvizzano, a few miles north of Naples, where he added choir and transepts to an already existing nave. Here he created a spacious and luminous structure, evenly and strongly lit and painted white. The most remarkable feature, however, is the dome. In this he eliminated all the structural lines – such as the 122 join of drum and cupola – and swathed the whole surface in a sort of stucco awning, which opens at the top on to a cloud-flecked sky around the lantern, thus producing an effect which can properly be called Rococo.

In his treatment of inlaid marble altars and altar-rails Vaccaro is even more explicitly Rococo. He started from the forms established by Fanzago and his followers, but he eliminates, as far as possible, all architectural features. The firmly articulated divisions and clearly defined scrolls of Fanzago are dissolved in *rocaille* panels and curved elements more like branches than architectural members – an effect underlined by the addition of putti among them. The altars, which with Fanzago were always in one plane, now swing in a curve behind the *mensa*, which is itself often supported by a sort of sarcophagus-urn with a curved silhouette. The marble inlay itself is given a new liveliness by the introduction of high-relief sculpture in white marble, consisting partly of decorative motifs, but also of full-relief putti who cling to the ends of the altars. The tops of the altar-rails – which from the functional point of view 123 should be flat – are often broken by curves or ornaments. The most fantastic example of this method of designing is to be seen in the altar-rails in the church at S. Martino, probably by Giuseppe Sammartino (1720–93), a follower of Vaccaro, where the cartouches on the top of the rails – of a richly Rococo form – contain panels of lapis lazuli, onyx, agate, and other semi-precious stones.

Vaccaro did not, however, depend entirely on the use of rich materials, and his most enchanting decorative scheme is the cloister in the wealthy convent of S. Chiara. This is laid out with pergolas supported on octagonal piers in coloured maiolica, on 124 which are depicted twining clusters of vine which fuse with the real vines stretching over the walks. Between the piers are benches, also of maiolica, with scenes taken from engravings by Callot and other purely secular sources, and at one of the points where the walks cross is a fountain, on the bottom of which

123 *Above* Naples, Certosa di S. Martino, altar-rails, probably designed by Giuseppe Sammartino, *c.* 1760

124 *Left* Naples, S. Chiara, maiolica cloister by Domenico Antonio Vaccaro, 1739–42

125 *Opposite* Caserta, staircase in the Royal Palace by Luigi Vanvitelli

1781), and Luigi Vanvitelli (1700–71). Fuga was a Florentine by birth, and Vanvitelli was the son of a Dutch painter called van Wittel, but both had been trained in Rome, where they represented the classicizing tendency fostered by Clement XII. They brought with them a style completely foreign to the traditions of Naples and, though they left their mark on the city by the sheer bulk of their buildings, their style was never assimilated by local architects, who continued to work in the manner of Vaccaro or Sanfelice till the full Classical revival set in during the first decades of the nineteenth century.[3]

Fuga designed several palaces for Neapolitan families, of which the two most important, built for the Giordano and Aquiro di Caramanico familes, stand side by side in the Via Medina, looking like Roman intruders; but his most important commission was the construction of the Albergo dei Poveri, a vast poor-house, in which Charles III planned to house the many beggars for which Naples was notorious. The building, more than 400 yards long, was never finished and lacks the church which was to have been the centre of the complex, with arms radiating to all parts of it, but as it stands it is a long bleak front, almost unbroken, except for a slightly projecting central pavilion with steps in front of it. The problem of organizing

swim fantastically shaped and coloured fish, again in maiolica. The whole is a pure Rococo dream.

In 1751 Charles III, who had become king of the two Sicilies when the Bourbons were restored to Naples in 1734, decided on a vast plan of public works and summoned to Naples for this purpose two foreign architects, Ferdinando Fuga (1699–

126 *Above* Caserta, Royal Palace by Luigi Vanvitelli, entrance front
designed 1751

127 *Opposite* Palermo, S. Caterina, altar of St Catherine

such a huge front was a difficult one, but it must be said that
Fuga made very little attempt to solve it.

126   Scale was also a difficult problem at Caserta, the palace
which Vanvitelli built about fifteen miles north of Naples to
house the king and his by now endless train of courtiers. It
consists of a rectangle, about 200 by 150 yards, divided into
four courts by wings which cross at the centre of the whole
building. Vanvitelli makes little use of Baroque devices to break
up the monotony of the façades, though greater variety would
have been introduced if the pavilions planned at the four
corners had been built; but in the designing of the central
feature of the interior he shows a real sense of dramatic
planning. The king – or any distinguished visitor – would have
driven into the palace along its main axis till he arrived at the
point where the two inner wings meet. There he would have got
out of his coach in a monumentally designed vestibule, from
which he would have had views into all the four courts of the
palace, and a grand vista leading to the park with its mile-long
fountains running down one of the foothills of the Apennines.
125   To his right he would have seen the grand staircase, designed,
like everything else at Caserta, on a vast scale, and simple but
rich in its decoration – rich in that it is entirely constructed of
marble, but simple in its severe lines and subdued colours. At
the top of the staircase, over the vestibule, was an octagonal
arcaded space, which gave access to the chapel and the apart-

ments of the king and queen. The chapel is clearly inspired by
that of Versailles, and indeed the taste of Louis XIV is evident
in the planning of the staircase and, even more conspicuously,
in the simple rectilinear design of the marbling. The conception
is Baroque, but the detail shows how far Vanvitelli was committed to the cause of Classicism.

Most of Vanvitelli's energies were absorbed in the building of
Caserta, but he also executed some work in Naples itself. He
remodelled one or two palaces which are of no great interest,
but he is responsible for two churches of considerable merit.
The better known is the Annunziata, which was built to replace
a church burnt down in 1757, and is a magnificent and clearly
designed Latin-cross building, with full columns supporting a
flat entablature – perhaps Vanvitelli's most explicitly Neo-
Classical design – but the smaller oval church, designed for the
Padri Missionari of S. Vincent de Paul, is a very successful
synthesis of a Baroque ground plan and classicizing detail.

Sicily
For almost the whole of the Baroque period Sicily, like Naples,
was governed by a Spanish viceroy, but, as in Naples, Spanish
influence was of no effect in the arts. More surprisingly, the
connection with Naples was also negligible in the field of
architecture.[4] This is no doubt partly due to the traditional
hositility and mutual scorn which exists between Sicilians and
Neapolitans, but it seems also that, when Sicilians needed
stimulus from outside the island, they turned to the real centre
of Baroque, Rome, rather than to Naples. It is, however, above
all important to notice that Sicilian architecture of the seventeenth and eighteenth centuries, generally speaking, was

remarkably independent and developed its own style to satisfy the needs of its patrons.

These needs were conditioned by circumstances in many ways similar to those which prevailed in Naples: the development of an elaborate viceregal court and the increasing wealth of the Church. Palermo, as the capital and the seat of the viceroy, was more in contact with what the Sicilians scornfully call *il Continente* than other towns in the island, and Roman influence is apparent in a few – not very interesting – buildings dating from the last decades of the seventeenth century. A much more lively style was introduced by Giovanni Biagio Amico (1684–1754), who appears to have absorbed the ideas of Borromini directly and interpreted them with typically Sicilian vigour.

128 *Below* Bagheria, Villa Valguarnera by Tommaso Napoli, built between 1709 and 1739

129 *Top right* Palermo, S. Francesco Saverio by Angelo Italia, detail of the interior, built between 1684 and 1710

130 *Right* Palermo, S. Zita, wall decoration in the Cappella del Rosario, begun about 1650

Even more remarkable is Angelo Italia (1628–1700), who produced not only the beautifully harmonious façade of the church at Palma di Montechiaro on the south coast of the island, but also the revolutionary design for S. Francesco Saverio in 129 Palermo, built on a centralized plan with hexagonal chapels on the diagonal axis, which run through two storeys and open on to the central space, an example of the carrying on of one space into another, which can only be paralleled in the churches of the Piedmontese Vittone, an architect two generations younger than Italia.

The Sicilian nobles, whose life was centred on the court of the viceroy, enlarged and redecorated many of their palaces in Palermo, but they rarely built them entirely *de novo*, and the result is often architecturally an unsatisfying compromise.

Fortunately, however, they also felt the need to build villas outside the city, to which they could retreat in the summer months – having abandoned their estates even more completely than their opposite numbers in Naples – and in these villas their architects had a free hand and produced designs of great originality. The most celebrated is the Villa Palagonia at Bagheria, more on account of its grotesque garden sculptures, added by the eccentric son of the original builder, than for its architectural qualities, but the neighbouring Villa Valguarnera, built by the same architect, Tommaso Napoli, between 1709 and 1739, retains its original character more completely and is among the finest manifestations of the real Sicilian Baroque, with a double staircase in the form of contrasting curves, nestling into the deep curve of the façade. The effect is partially marred by the covered entrance at the top of the steps, added in the nineteenth century. Many other villas of the same type are to be found on the Piana dei Colli to the west of Palermo.

The one technique in which the architects of Palermo – and

also of Messina – were directly influenced by Neapolitan architects was in the use of coloured marble inlay. The work of this kind in Messina was destroyed in the earthquake of 1908, but Palermo still has three churches – S. Caterina, the Immaculata Concezione, and the Jesuit Casa Professa – and innumerable chapels covered with a luxuriant marble decoration, exceeding in richness and complexity even the work of Vaccaro and his school in Naples. Long before the Neapolitans, the architects of Palermo began to introduce white marble figures and decorative features in high relief, for instance in the Cappella del Rosario in S. Zita, which dates from about 1650. The workmanship required for this extremely difficult type of marble cutting is still to be found in Sicily, and the Casa Professa, which was badly damaged by a bomb in 1943, has been restored so skilfully that it is almost impossible to tell new from old.

Technical skill of the same order was shown by Giacomo Serpotta (1656–1732) and his son Procopio in the stucco decoration with which they ornamented a series of oratories belonging to Palermitan confraternities.[5] The decoration consists of a flutter of draperies, putti, and swags of fruit round and over the architectural features, such as pilasters and windows.

131 *Below* Palermo, S. Zita, Oratorio del Rosario by Giacomo Serpotta. Stucco relief of the *Battle of Lepanto*, 1685–88

the floor is a maiolica map of the sky, and the ceiling has a double vault, the inner one standing out dark against the outer painted shell, like Antonio Bibiena's domes at Sabbioneta and Vi'lla Pasquali.   102

The Palazzo Gangi ballroom was the last example of the gaiety which inspired the architecture of Palermo for a century and a half. The influence of the French enlightenment began to penetrate Palermitan society, and with it came a change of taste. The architects of Palermo produced an attractive variant of the French style current in the last years of the reign of Louis XV, ingeniously adapted to the coarser building materials of the island. Full Neo-Classicism, partly derived from English, partly from French sources, took over in the very last years of the century.

In the south-east of the island Syracuse produced a quite different type of building. The most characteristic is a series of elegant palaces in a rather simple Baroque idiom, which owe much of their charm to the fine white stone of which they are built. A particularly fine example is the Palazzo Beneventano del Bosco, built by Luciano Alì (begun 1779). In a very different style is the façade added to the Cathedral – basically a Greek temple of the fifth century BC – by Andrea Palma in   132 1728. In plan this façade is designed entirely in planes parallel to the wall of the church, but its progression of columns, standing free from the wall, produces an effect of movement which is fully Baroque. It also incorporates one feature which is typical of Sicilian architecture: it is a belfry as well as a façade. In fact it is almost square in plan, and the upper storey encloses a large bell-chamber opened by broad arches on the sides as well as on the front. This particular type of belfry-façade was developed by Rosario Gagliardi, the most original architect of the period in Sicily. He was born in Syracuse and worked over the whole south-east area, which was called the Val di Noto. His most impressive works are the churches of S. Giorgio (1744)   133 and S. Giuseppe at Ragusa Ibla, where he combines the piling up of free-standing columns with a slightly convex central bay. In these churches the emphasis on the tower-like character of the structure is greater than in Palma's façade at Syracuse, as they consist of three full storeys. In S. Giorgio the structure ends with a square dome, double-curved in profile, but at S. Giuseppe the bells are hung in three arches in a thin wall, an arrangement which goes back to the Middle Ages and was widely used in Sicily in the Baroque age.

Noto, between Syracuse and Ragusa, is the most famous Baroque town in Sicily, mainly because of the fact that, when the old town was destroyed in the earthquake of 1693, which devastated the whole south-east of the island, the city council, guided by a learned and authoritarian landowner, Giovanni Battista Landolini, decided to rebuild it on a new site, about ten miles to the south of the old one, and as a result they were able to create a complete Baroque town, laid out on a regular grid-system and all built within half a century in an almost uniform style. The charm of the town is greatly enhanced by being built in an exceptionally beautiful yellow stone, which gives a golden glow to the palaces and churches, but the architecture itself is not outstanding. Gagliardi built two churches – S. Domenico and S. Teresa – but they are much less distinguished than his work at Ragusa; and the Cathedral has a fine façade of later date (c. 1770), slightly French in flavour. The most attractive feature of the palaces is the series of balconies, carried on   134 grotesque figures or animals, projecting like Gothic gargoyles from the wall and supported in their turn by grotesque masks

132 *Above* Syracuse, façade of the Cathedral by Andrea Palma, begun in 1728, also showing the colonnade of the 5th-century BC Greek temple round which the Cathedral was built

133 *Opposite* Ragusa Ibla, façade of S. Giorgio by Rosario Gagliardi, built 1744

In certain cases, for instance in the Oratory of S. Zita, the artists introduced not only figures modelled with a high degree of naturalism, but scenes composed of minute figures in settings
131   which may include not only buildings but also ships and other paraphernalia. In this they were following a local tradition which goes back to the early sixteenth century, when Antonello Gagini applied the same technique in marble in the decoration of the apse and in the holy-water stoups of Palermo Cathedral.

Many palaces in Palermo were also redecorated in the eighteenth century, and in the ballroom of the Palazzo Gangi – known to many through having been used for the filming of the ball scene in the *Gattopardo* ('The Leopard') – an unknown architect produced one of the most brilliant manifestations of Italian Rococo. Walls, looking-glasses, shutters, chairs and sofas are all decorated with the most delicate gilt Rococo curls;

and cherubs' heads wrapped in deeply cut acanthus leaves. The cherubs' heads and the foliage are Baroque in feeling, but the general character of the 'gargoyles' – particularly when they take on the form of animals – is almost mediaeval. In fact the tradition of such balconies goes back, in Southern Italy at least, to the late sixteenth century, and the example on the façade of S. Croce at Lecce in Apulia, which probably dates from that period, includes eagles, dragons, and lions which could be paralleled in the doors of Romanesque churches in many parts of Southern Italy and Sicily. As will be seen in plate 134, the actual architecture of these palaces, particularly the windows, is archaic for the mid-eighteenth century and is reminiscent of late-sixteenth-century Florentine buildings. The Baroque elements in these palaces are therefore very slight.

Richly carved, somewhat provincial decoration, rather like that of the palaces of Noto, is to be found on many of the palaces of Catania, the most important centre of Baroque architecture on the east coast, which was largely rebuilt after the earthquake of 1693. The windows of the Palazzo Biscari by Francesco Battaglia, which are typical of this group, defy stylistic classification. They are Baroque in the richness and the depth of the carving, but the architectural members have been completely eliminated. This feature would ally them to the Rococo, but they lack the lightness and delicacy essential to this style, and, unlike Vaccaro and Sammartino in Naples, the designers did not employ any of the decorative motifs associated with the Rococo. For want of any better term, their style could perhaps be described as Catanian Vernacular, a phrase which would distinguish it from both the true Baroque and the Rococo and bring it closer to what I want to call the *Stile Salentino* in Lecce. In contrast to the external decoration of the Palazzo Biscari, the *salone* within is a magnificent example of full Rococo, marked by a free use of almost liquid stucco, reminiscent of the decoration to be found in South Bavarian Rococo churches.

There was, however, another much more sophisticated school of architecture active at the same time in Catania, of which the leader was Giovanni Battista Vaccarini (1702–68), who was born in Palermo but sent to Rome for training in the early 1720s.[6] He returned to Catania about 1730 and immediately became the dominant force in local architecture. His first commission was to complete the Municipio, begun in the local style in 1695. He imposed his new manner most obviously in the central bay, in which the jambs of the doors are canted, and the movement which this establishes is carried on through the outer section of the curved balcony into the lines of the windows above. This treatment of a single feature shows a real understanding of the methods of Roman Baroque architects, particularly of Borromini and the more enterprising architects of the early-eighteenth century, rather than of Carlo Fontana and his school, and the same knowledge is implicit in the designs of Vaccarini's churches. In S. Giuliano he follows the oval design of S. Maria di Montesanto, and in S. Agata the Greek cross of S. Agnese a Piazza Navona, modified by the introduction of galleries with curved screens – a favourite feature in Catania – supported by three-cusped arches. In the exteriors of these churches he shows great originality. On top of the oval dome of S. Giuliano he set an open belvedere, a common feature in Sicilian – and Neapolitan – religious houses, designed to enable the nuns or monks to take the air on hot summer evenings. Usually these belvederes were placed over some part of the monastic buildings, and it must be admitted that Vaccarini's

134 *Opposite* Noto, balcony of the Palazzo Villadorata

135 *Above* Catania, windows in the Palazzo Biscari built by Francesco Battaglia before 1730

136 *Overleaf left* Catania, S. Agata by Giovanni Battista Vaccarini, 1748–67

137 *Overleaf right* G. B. Tiepolo, the *Feast of Antony and Cleopatra*, Palazzo Labia, Venice

solution is novel rather than successful. The exterior of S. Agata, on the other hand, is a masterly interpretation of Borrominesque ideas. The façade consists of a single storey, with a high attic, crowned with statues and urns, planned in three concave bays, which form a contrast to the lower storey of which the outer bays are convex. In this arrangement Vaccarini is basically following the example of S. Carlino, but he also introduces non-Borrominesque elements: the 'fringe' which runs across the façade below the balconies to the windows is derived from Bernini's Baldacchino, and the capitals of the pilasters, which are composed of palm-leaves, lilies and crowns, are taken from a plate in Guarini's treatise. Both these features

are treated with great sharpness, made possible by the fine-grained brown stone of Catania. Unlike most Roman churches S. Agata is free-standing and designed to be seen from all four sides. The lower structure leads up to the octagonal drum and the dome, which is strongly defined by curiously heavy, rounded ribs.

The innovations of Vaccarini were taken up by Stefano Ittar, a Tuscan architect who settled in Catania in 1765 and built a number of fine churches, of which the most interesting are S. Placido (finished in 1769) and the Collegiata (*c.* 1768). In the former Ittar follows Vaccarini in his use of contrasting curves, but in the latter the treatment is a little more restrained and the façade is planned on a series of curves, all concave. The detail also is a little more chaste, in accordance with the growing tendency towards Classicism, which was felt in Catania as much as in Palermo.

138 *Opposite* Palermo, S. Caterina, detail of marble inlay

139 *Below* Lecce, the church of S. Croce (begun in the late 16th century and finished in 1646) and the Celestine convent attached to it (second half of the 17th century, probably by Giuseppe Zimbalo)

Lecce and Apulia

The problem of stylistic terminology becomes particularly acute in the case of Apulia. The phrase *Barocco Leccese* appears in every Italian text-book on architecture, and the concept is to be found in most English works that mention the architecture of the seventeenth and eighteenth centuries in Southern Italy, but it can be argued that there is not a single building in Lecce or the surrounding district – the Salento – which can properly be described as Baroque.[7]

The churches of Lecce – and they are typical of the whole area – have almost no features in common with those of the Roman Baroque. In plan they are generally rectangular or in the form of a Latin cross, without any of the sophisticated adjustments which true Baroque architects applied to these forms. In a very few cases their designers venture on an oval or an elongated octagon, but they do so without extracting from these forms any of the liveliness which they take on in the hands of even a minor follower of Borromini. Their façades are flat, and Leccese architects do not seem even to have apprehended the innovations of Maderno. It is no chance that, when an eighteenth-century architect simply applied the decorative sculpture of the period to the Romanesque front of SS. Niccolò e

140 *Top* Lecce, detail of the façade of S. Angelo

141 *Above* Martina Franca, detail of windows and balconies, Palazzo Mattolese

Cataldo, he produced a façade which, apart from the twelfth-century door, could pass as a typical product of the period. Even the Romanesque rose-window does not disturb the effect, because the motif was frequently used in the Salento in the seventeenth and eighteenth centuries.

The charm of Leccese churches lies in their sculptural decoration, but even this has little to do with the Baroque. Its character is partly dictated by the qualities of the local stone, which is soft and easy to carve when quarried, but hardens after a short time when exposed to the atmosphere. It therefore allowed – one might almost say encouraged – architects to let their sculptor-assistants loose on the decoration of their buildings, and both the façades and the altarpieces of the churches show a richness and gaiety of decoration which have perhaps no parallel, save in Sicily. The decorative motifs employed are, however, mainly derived from a sixteenth-century vocabulary which had been long out of date in Rome or even Naples. The explanation probably lies in the fact that Apulia was a very remote province, forming part of the kingdom of Naples but cut off from its capital by the mountains, and separated politically from other provinces in the north, with which it might have communicated by sea. Leccese architects must, therefore, have relied primarily on decorative engravings or pattern-books, and it seems that they continued to use those published in the late-sixteenth or seventeenth centuries long after they had been abandoned elsewhere.

The most famous building in Lecce is the church of S. Croce and the attached Celestine convent, and it illustrates most of the features of the local architecture. The lower half of the façade was probably decorated in the last years of the sixteenth and the first years of the seventeenth centuries, and the upper half is dated 1646; but the archaic elements are startling. The rose-window is a direct imitation of the Romanesque type mentioned above in connection with SS. Niccolò e Cataldo, and the supports of the balcony – mentioned in relation to the architecture of Noto – have equally strong mediaeval features. The columns of the lower floor have the weightiness of those to be found in a Norman cathedral, and those above, decorated with low-relief carvings and encircled with bands of lotus-leaves are of a type which would be conceivable in North Italy in the early sixteenth century but had long passed out of fashion.

The façade of the monastery dates from the second half of the seventeenth century – it is probably by Giuseppe Zimbalo – but it has few affinities with the Baroque. It is true that the broken and curved pediments derive ultimately from Borromini, but they are thinned by being seen through engravings. The little motifs in the corners of each rusticated bay have also a feature very typical of Leccese decoration and quite antithetical to the Baroque: they look as though they had been cut out of plywood with a fret-saw.

There is in fact only one building in Lecce that conforms in any fundamental way to the principles of the Baroque, namely the façade of S. Matteo, and that, as has been pointed out by local historians, stands out as a freak in the architecture of the town. The church is said to have been built by a local architect called Achille Carducci between 1667 and 1690, but it is not certain that he was responsible for the façade, added in 1700, which is entirely different stylistically from the interior. One has the impression that the façade was built by an architect who had seen real Baroque works – perhaps the churches of Gagliardi in Sicily – and had attempted, not altogether successfully, to imitate them.

The above analysis is not intended to denigrate Leccese architecture of the seventeenth and eighteenth centuries, but only to show that it cannot properly be included in the category of the Baroque. Its charms are undeniable. The sculptural decoration is lively in conception, rich in detail – often symbolical and allusive – beautiful in colour, and skilful in execution, except where the human figure is involved, but the architecture would be better classified – as has been suggested in the introduction of this section – under some term such as *Stile Salentino* rather than as a subdivision of the Baroque.

If there is no real Baroque architecture in Apulia, there is a small group of Rococo buildings of a sophistication unexpected in such a remote area. Apart from one or two churches, for instance one at Muro Leccese, the buildings in question are all to be found in the town of Martina Franca, between Taranto and Bari, outside the area dominated by the Leccese style. The town has been since the Middle Ages the centre of a flourishing wine trade and, though it was for a time under the domination of the Grimaldi family, it has a long tradition of democratic government and evenly distributed wealth. This is at once apparent from the fact that, apart from the ducal palace, which is of little interest architecturally, the town is composed of small *palazzi*, which are simply town houses of anything between three and seven bays, built on the street without a courtyard, all white-washed and decorated with extremely fine Rococo doors and windows, deeply cut in a warm, dark-brown stone. The main church, dedicated to S. Martino, is by an otherwise unrecorded architect called Giovanni Mariani, who may also have built the church at Muro Leccese, but is certainly not the author of the Rococo palaces, many of which have almost identical details and appear to be by a single hand. We are, therefore, faced with the unusual problem of an isolated group of buildings in a remote part of Apulia, having nothing in common with the style of neighbouring towns, and yet highly sophisticated in style and skilful in execution, designed by an architect who is unknown and whose work is not found elsewhere. Was he a talented local craftsman, working on the basis of engravings which he obtained from some major centre – perhaps Naples – but if so, what are the engravings? Or was he a foreigner trained in one of these major centres? If so, we are compelled to ask which centre, because his work is unlike anything to be found in Naples or Rome, or even Palermo. Only a search of the town archives could provide the solution – and it is quite likely that these are incomplete, in which case the mystery will remain.

141

Baroque architecture reached maturity in Rome and northern Italy and these areas were to provide the main sources from which it spread to the other parts of Europe. The process of diffusion varied in different countries but certain common features appear in almost all areas.

The fame of Rome as the artistic centre of the world exercised a fascination in all countries outside Italy and aroused a desire to emulate the art which she had created or was creating; but other non-artistic factors also played an important part in the spread of the Baroque style. The links were often dynastic or political. In France an Italian queen and later an Italian first minister fostered the growth of a taste for the Baroque: in Bavaria, a Savoyard electress encouraged a connection established through the proximity of the area round the Italian lakes which produced the excellent masons who for generations had migrated to Southern Germany and Austria. In Salzburg the taste of a series of archbishops encouraged more sophisticated architects from Italy to settle in their city, and towards the end of the seventeenth century the emperor and the members of the imperial court succeeded in attracting to Vienna artists of considerable distinction, including Fra Andrea Pozzo.

Ecclesiastical links were also important, especially those established by the Jesuits, who insisted that all building schemes, from whatever part of Europe, should be submitted to Rome for approval, and the central organization in Rome did not hesitate to make criticisms or, if necessary, to supply alternative plans.

In addition to the migration of artists from Italy, there was a movement in the opposite direction. It was the ambition of every young artist working north of the Alps – whether architect, sculptor or painter – to visit Rome and to study there the great works of the past and those which were being executed in his own day, and contemporary biographers always note – almost apologetically – the cases of artists who failed to achieve this ambition. At the end of the seventeenth century and during the first years of the eighteenth the studio of Carlo Fontana was, as has already been said, a centre of training to which all young architects sought admission. But for those who could not make the journey there were other means of getting acquainted with what was taking place in Rome. Travelling artists often brought home drawings of what they had seen in Italy, and from the end of the seventeenth century there was a regular output of engravings reproducing the work of the major Roman masters. In the early volumes such as Falda's *Nuovo Teatro delle Fabbriche . . . . di Roma* (1665) the engravings only give general views of the buildings in question, but Ferrerio's *Palazzi di Roma* includes accurate ground-plans and elevations. In the eighteenth century the position grew even better and the two volumes of engravings of Borromini's two major works – S. Ivo and the Oratory of S. Filippo Neri – published in 1720 and 1725, and three volumes of Rossi's *Studio d'Architettura Civile* (1702–21) provided reliable measured drawings not only of whole buildings but of details such as doors, windows, balustrades and fireplaces. These books played a vital part in making the vocabulary of the Roman Baroque accessible to architects all over Europe – and even farther afield in the Spanish and Portuguese colonies of Central and South America. In the following chapters the dissemination of the Baroque, the modifications which it underwent in the different areas, and the varied forms – sometimes highly fantastic – which it took on will be studied in detail.

France – the first country to be considered – presents a special case. It had gone through the process of Italianization earlier and more thoroughly than any other European country – with the possible exception of Spain – and it had created its own synthesis of Italian and northern elements so as to establish a genuine Renaissance style of its own. Its commercial and political links with Italy were close and continuous – though not always friendly – and it was, so to speak, on familiar terms with Rome culturally: it could take what it wanted and reject what it felt was alien to its own clearly defined and proudly held principles. It was able to absorb Italian innovations gradually, because its artistic tradition did not suffer the total interruption which befell Central Europe as a result of the Thirty Years War, and by the early years of Louis XIV's personal reign felt sufficient self-confidence to reject Bernini and commit the completion of the Louvre to French architects.

Part II

France

Introduction

The French, in their flirtation with the sensuous forms and emotive devices characteristic of the Roman Baroque, were cavalier from the outset and, though they never decisively rejected such forms, it may be said that Bernini's visit to Paris in 1665 was the occasion for the opposition to Italian influence to rally its forces in favour of rational French Classicism. Yet who were the French in this connection: the king with his Spanish mother, Italian grandmother and Italian mentor; the great ecclesiastics who had encouraged the Flamboyant style of the late Middle Ages; the great nobility who had commissioned the anti-Classical, non-intellectual Mannerism of the late French Renaissance; the *bourgeoisie* who had not hitherto been considered representative of France in matters of patronage? If the attitudes of the *bourgeoisie* were now to be of predominant significance it was because their power, consolidated through Richelieu's policy of reducing the feudal nobility, though momentarily eclipsed by Mazarin's promotion of his compatriots, was to be the foundation of Colbert's state. Formed though he may have been in the Italianate court of Mazarin, Colbert, like Richelieu, saw the importance for French prestige of French preeminence in art and to him the prime sources of authority were reason and discipline – qualities he looked for in vain in the Roman tradition of Bernini. Though it has little to do with Roman Baroque, it is certainly not insignificant that the essentially flamboyant, anti-Classical, Rococo began to emerge during the decline of Louis XIV following the demise of Colbert and the weakening of ministerial authority under his successors – when the king took a more personal initiative.

Louis XIII and Richelieu

It is hardly an exaggeration to say that under Richelieu – when French Classicism was brought to maturity in their various fields by Descartes, Pascal, Corneille, Poussin, Claude Lorrain, Philippe de Champaigne, Mansart, Lemercier – every important private commission came from the *bourgeoisie* or the new *noblesse de robe* to which the most successful members of the middle class were being promoted.[1] Hard working and serious, committed to *ordre, raison, mesure* – ready to agree with La Bruyère that 'entre le bon sens et le bon goût il y a la différence de la cause à un effet'[2] – this class provided not only the private patrons but such men as the financier and administrator Sublet de Noyers, who – supported if not schooled by his cousins the Fréarts – seems to have acted as Richelieu's chief adviser on artistic matters before he became secretary of state for war in 1636 and long before he acquired the dormant office of Surintendant des Bâtiments in 1638.

In the preface to the *Parallèle de l'architecture antique et de la moderne,* a seminal work of academic French Classical theory published in 1650, Fréart de Chambray described Sublet, to whom it was dedicated, as 'the true author', and the 'Maecenas of the century'.[3] In this role he promoted the completion of the court of the Louvre and the decoration of the Grande Galerie linking it with the Tuileries, both as a palace for the king and a centre for the arts which would rank as the greatest modern monument in Europe. To this end, especially for the decoration of the Grande Galerie but possibly even to form an academy, he recalled Poussin to France, inviting Duquesnoy to accompany him – a somewhat chauvinistic policy soon expanded, probably at the instigation of Mazarin, into one of outright rivalry with Rome involving the attempt to attract leading Italian artists including Guercino, Cortona and Algardi – if not yet Bernini – as well.

It is necessary to consider the patronage, private and public, of Sublet and the Fréarts, for they were involved in the purification of the French tradition from the excesses of the du Cerceau period – to which the Flemish were now addicted – and the protection of that tradition from the licence of the contemporary Roman Baroque. In the capacities of artistic adviser to Richelieu and private patron, respectively, Sublet was associated with Jacques Lemercier and the Jesuit brother Etienne Martellange who, at least from the academic point of view of the author of the *Parallèle,* were the two leading Classicists to emerge in France after Salomon de Brosse. Both had been in

Rome during the formative years of the Baroque but neither was seduced by its licentiousness; on the contrary, searching for an alternative to the florid sixteenth-century French forms, especially in ecclesiastical architecture, each went back to post-Tridentine Roman models and introduced them to France stripped of any suggestion of Mannerism.

Architecte du Roi soon after his return from Rome in 1614, ten years later Premier Architecte charged with completing the Louvre, and Richelieu's architect, Lemercier was supported if not promoted by Sublet[4] and the considerable reputation which he enjoyed throughout the seventeenth and eighteenth centuries was based on precisely those qualities which the author of the *Parallèle* most consistently praises – regularity and sobriety above all.[5] Indeed it is necessary to look briefly at

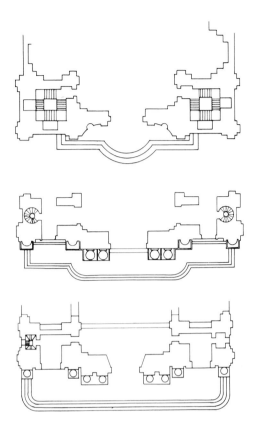

421

Lemercier's work because the related work of Martellange was seen at the time, and was meant to be seen, as a manifesto of the ideals of Sublet's circle, as much anti-Baroque as anti-Mannerist.

Lemercier's first major ecclesiastical exercise, and his first important work not constrained by existing building, was the chapel of the Sorbonne – according to Sauval the only building commissioned by Richelieu that was regular both inside and out, demonstrating comprehension of the rules of Classical architecture. The plan, which dates from 1629, is close to that of Rosato Rosati's S. Carlo ai Catinari in Rome and Lemercier's recollection of the unusual articulation of S. Carlo's cupola – arched windows separated by clustered pilasters – which was not actually executed until after he left Rome, suggests that he

had been associated with Rosati's studio.[6] For the main front Lemercier adopted the standard Roman form with an upper storey narrower than the lower and though he retained Rosati's spacing of the Order, with less height he was able to reduce the number of decorative elements, clarifying the composition and allowing less interference with the horizontals. This first major French attempt to revise the Roman form of church façade in accordance with academic principles has not generally been enthusiastically received. The spacing of the Order, the size and shape of the openings and the attempt to add movement by varying the plasticity of the lower Order – whether considered as a staid reflection or an academic correction of Maderno's Santa Susanna – have usually been criticised and Lemercier himself took the opportunities given him by the Cardinal at Richelieu and Rueil to attend to these matters, regularizing and clarifying still further essentially the same *ordonnance*.[7] Lemercier's greatest success, however, was the most original feature of his Sorbonne composition – the north façade with its magnificent portico providing access to the college court. Treated in the grandest manner, according to Blondel, this façade was more regular than that of any other sacred monument in Paris: ' . . . nous ne pouvons trop en recommander l'examen à nos Elèves'.

Before Lemercier's work at the Sorbonne, the regularization of the Roman form of church façade had been experimented with several times by Martellange – notably in projects for Le Puy in 1605, Avignon in 1617, Vienne in 1623 and Blois in 1624.[8] In the Jesuit Noviciate in Paris, commissioned by Sublet in 1630, Martellange perfected these experiments after experience of Lemercier's work – elevations of the Sorbonne dated

142

1630 survive amongst his papers.[9] Like Lemercier, Martellange went back to the Roman school of Giacomo della Porta, flourishing at the turn of the century when Martellange himself was in Rome. His precise model was S. Maria dei Monti but he adopted the Doric and Ionic Orders instead of the Corinthian and Composite, revising the proportions accordingly, and while retaining all the elements of della Porta's façade he pursued the ideals of clarity and regularity even further than his Roman or French mentors – subjecting all the details to the clearly sustained horizontals of the entablatures (like both della Porta and Lemercier), of the socle upon which the upper Order rests (like Lemercier) and of the string-courses aligned with the entablatures of the central openings which bind the outer bays and consoles to the central section. Martellange expressly sought an undertaking from the Jesuit authorities that he would

144 *Below* Château of Blois, vault of the staircase in the Orléans Wing by François Mansart, 1635–38

145 *Right* Château of Blois, drawing of a project for reconstruction by François Mansart, 1635. *Paris, Bibliothèque Nationale*

not be obliged to follow the orders of any Jesuit father but it is hard to believe that his patrons, Sublet and the Fréarts, were not closely involved with the design – as they themselves claimed. They were certainly delighted with the finished building, to which Poussin contributed an altarpiece, and in his *Parallèle* Chambray boasts that 'cette église est estimée la plus régulière de Paris, et quoy qu'elle ne soit pas chargée de tant d'ornemens que quelques autres, elle paroist néantmoins fort belle aux yeux des intelligens tout y estant fait avec une entente extraordinaire'. Academic critics from Sauval in the seventeenth century to Blondel in the eighteenth agree and according to Chantelou even Bernini considered the Noviciate 'l'unique pièce achevée qu'il eût vue à Paris'.[10]

As a manifesto of academic Classical principles the Noviciate

was a response to the design lately adopted by the Jesuits for the façade of their Maison Professe in Paris, now St Paul-St Louis. The commission for the church had originally been given to Martellange and his plans of 1625 incorporated a great niche in the façade[11] which, rather than anticipating High Baroque developments, recalled the Nicchione of the Vatican Belvedere – or Collin's portal to the stables at Fontainebleau. Flanked by an *ordonnance* derived from de Brosse's nearby church of St Gervais, this great niche might well have appealed to Martellange as a dramatic accent of less doubtful licence than de Brosse's heavy segmental pediment, with its strange recession reminiscent of the mannered composition of St Etienne-du-Mont. Similarly the complete reliance on architectural members – the Orders themselves and the pedimented doors, windows and niches – and the sparing use of sculpture only in association with the architectural members, seem to testify to a rejection of the excesses of the late French Renaissance. Yet Martellange's façade, at least as depicted by the foundation medal, is not without a suggestion of the gaucheness present in much of his work before his association with the circle of Sublet.

Apparently for lack of sumptuousness, rather than for any

143

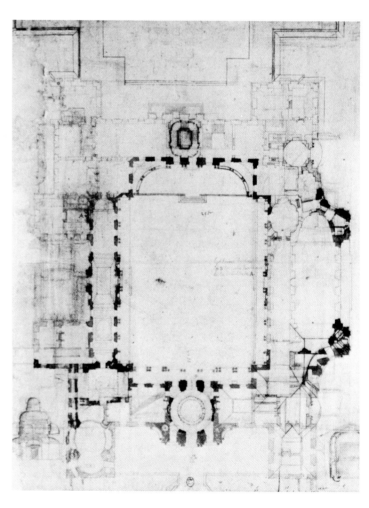

gaucheness, Martellange's façade design was rejected and work began on the façade early in 1629 to a new design by Père François Derand. Derand also referred to St Gervais but instead of the single plane with the entablature breaking forward over the columns, free-standing Orders and minimal carved ornament of de Brosse's composition, Derand broke the central bay forward, increasing the plasticity of his Order from half-colümns on the side bays to three-quarter ones in the centre – in the manner of Maderno – and applied ornament liberally – in the manner of his Flemish contemporaries. Martellange bitterly criticized this new project: apart from purely practical considerations he condemned not only the profusion of carved ornament in Derand's project but the Roman Baroque conception of movement as well. Though Derand was not supplanted this attack was not without its effect and the variation in the plasticity of the Order was suppressed. But in attracting the attention and the support of Sublet and his cousins in this dispute Martellange had the last word. In his journal on 19 October 1665 Chantelou reported that in connection with St Paul-St Louis he had told the Jesuits that they had allowed Derand and his Flemish cronies, whom they took to be oracles in architecture, to spoil their church by covering its façade with 'vilains ornements'. The Jesuits responded that connoisseurs were rare and it was necessary to please the multitude – moreover Richelieu had found their church beautiful. Chantelou replied that the cardinal had been a very great minister but had known little about architecture and that the advantage of consulting connoisseurs was well borne out by the Noviciate which, they were forced to agree, had received universal approbation.[12]

While Sublet and his circle, including Lemercier and Martellange who knew early Baroque Rome, were bent on purifying the French Classical tradition by rejecting both Mannerist and Baroque techniques and promoting an academicism based on the revision of late sixteenth-century Italian forms, François Mansart, who had never been to Rome, was perfecting the work of his French predecessors and invigorating the native tradition by drawing upon much the same sources as those used by the Roman Baroque masters themselves.[13] In the first decade of Richelieu's ministry he had inherited the mantle of Salomon de Brosse who, rejecting the essentially decorative Mannerism associated with the circle of the du Cerceau in which he had been trained, revived the logical and coherent approach to *ordonnance* evolved by the mid-sixteenth-century masters, Lescot and de l'Orme. Continuing de Brosse's experiments under the patronage of members of the *noblesse de robe,* in 1635 in his plans for the reconstruction of the Château of Blois commissioned by the king's brother Gaston d'Orléans, Mansart gave the fullest expression to the qualities generally associated with the French Classical spirit of the seventeenth century – clarity combined with subtlety, restraint with richness, obedience to a strict code of rules coupled with flexibility within them, and concentration by the elimination of inessentials. Yet in a way utterly characteristic of François Mansart, great individualist that he was, these plans for Blois also reveal an interest in forms and techniques which were soon to become hallmarks of the Roman High Baroque.

The principle of varying the plasticity of the Order in concert with variations in the plane of the wall, exploited so brilliantly by Maderno at S. Susanna and thereafter a characteristic Roman High Baroque way of producing movement in a façade, was by no means new to France. Lescot and de l'Orme had seen

in it the key to the solution of the basic French problem of binding *pavillons* and *corps-de-logis* together into a consistent whole, at once effecting transition from one mass to another in the interest of unity and expressing distinction between the masses in the interest of variety – a problem which little concerned the Italians, with their preference for homogeneous masses, until they began to experiment with the centralization of their church façades in the late-sixteenth century. This approach to *ordonnance*, further developed by Salomon de Brosse to ensure the subordination of all the parts in a hierarchically ordered whole, was fundamental to François Mansart's conception of scale and monumentality. At Blois, where the site was irregular and the internal requirements more complex than any faced by de Brosse, Mansart showed extraordinary virtuosity in varying the expression of the strictly correct Orders to achieve clarity in the definition of the parts within a completely consistent whole and to provide the energy which infuses the scheme with vitality. Thus, while Mansart's

146 *Below* Paris, Hôtel Lambert, begun by Louis Le Vau in 1640, engraving of a section

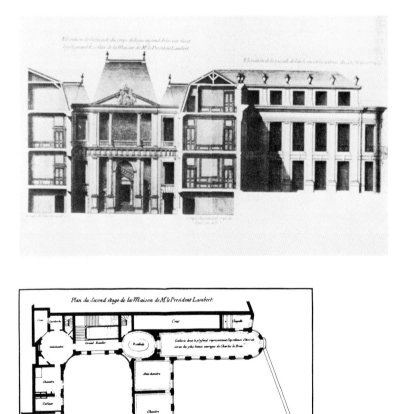

147 *Above* Hôtel Lambert, engraving of the plan of the principal floor

work at Blois might in this respect be compared with contemporary developments in the Roman school of Maderno, its significance lies more properly in the context of specifically French developments.

Likewise it is unlikely that direct influence from contemporary Rome would explain the appearance in Mansart's Blois project of other forms and devices popular with Baroque masters: the curved façades, the variety of interior shapes, the vertical perspectives, the dramatic vistas. Quadrants at the head of a court were familiar enough in France and already present in Mansart's earlier Hôtel de l'Aubespine and Château de Berny, but the semi-oval external walls of Blois were possibly suggested by the work of Giovanni Battista Montano whose influence on Mansart was already apparent in the altar of St Martin-des-Champs. The oval chapel was closely related to Mansart's earlier plans for the church of the Visitation in Paris which itself derives from sixteenth-century French sources and Montano. The entrance pavilion with its cut-off dome surmounted by a drum and a second dome with the lantern was based on earlier experiments at the Visitation involving the contrast of illuminated and shaded forms, but the principal staircase, in which the quite dramatic lighting from diagonally placed sources concealed from the main flight by the first floor gallery, has no precise precedent. The great interior *enfilades* derive from the French tradition, but Mansart showed his originality with the landscaping, an exercise in urbanism on a monumental scale anticipated only at Balleroy, in which the *château* itself was to operate as the climax of converging open vistas in the manner hardly more spectacularly developed later by Le Nôtre.

Many of the same techniques appealed to the bold imagination of Mansart's younger rival, Louis Le Vau, most of whose major works belong to the period of Mazarin. Evolving the plan of the Parisian *hôtel* side by side with Mansart in the last seven or eight years of Richelieu, Le Vau's combination of convenient distribution with vigorous forms can best be seen in the *hôtel* he built from 1640 onwards at the end of the Ile St Louis for the ostentatious financier J. B. Lambert: the curved court façade – the incoherent, essentially decorative *ordonnance* which has more to do with 'du Cerceau' Mannerism than with mature Classicism – the variety of interior spaces including oval vestibules, and above all the theatrical staircase contrived to double back on itself to produce the maximum effect on the visitor ascending through narrow dark flights on to a wide, bright landing commanding an extensive vista through vestibules and gallery up the river beyond. And it was his capacity for good theatre which was to be the making of Louis Le Vau in the period of Mazarin, the opening of which coincided with the completion of the Hôtel Lambert.

146, 147

148 *Opposite* Vaux-le-Vicomte, *château* by Le Vau, gardens by André Le Nôtre, 1657–61

Mazarin and the minority of Louis XIV

With Sublet's discomfiture in 1643 after the deaths of Richelieu and Louis XIII, and the accession to power of Mazarin – the Italian adventurer, *protégé* of those scions of the Roman Baroque era the Colonna, the Sacchetti and the Barberini, agent of Richelieu, confidant of the queen – the pattern of patronage radically altered.[14] Mazarin replaced Sublet with the ineffectual Le Camus and he himself set the style for the next twenty years. Lemercier went on working at the Louvre as Premier Architecte but was soon eclipsed by the more versatile, less fastidious Le Vau in the service of Mazarin's richest and most ostentatious ministers. Poussin had already returned to Rome. Chambray accompanied his cousin into exile and devoted himself to the task of setting down the ideals of his administration in his *Parallèle* which, significantly enough, was published in 1650 at the moment during the Fronde when Mazarin's political demise seemed imminent.

Mazarin, as already suggested, may well have been responsible for the broadening of Sublet's policy of cultural chauvinism by including the leading Italian masters in the royal invitation to France. In 1644 he took this up again and tried to persuade Bernini to come to Paris to transform the Hôtel Tubeuf, which he had leased at the end of the previous year, into a *palazzo*. He failed. Overlooking the Premier Architecte, he turned to François Mansart whose reputation as a transformer of town houses in particular was hardly yet rivalled, even by that of Le Vau, and who was far the most imaginative – if not Baroque – of any of the then established architects. Their relationship, complicated by Mansart's attitude to his patron during the Fronde, proved to be unhappy and Mansart was never again employed by the cardinal but he does seem to have been responsible for the principal extensions to the Hôtel Tubeuf including superimposed galleries to the west of the garden. Early in 1646 Giovanni Francesco Romanelli – pupil of Pietro da Cortona and *protégé* of Francesco Barberini who had just fled from the persecution of Innocent X to Mazarin's protection in Paris – was engaged to decorate the upper gallery. In doing so he introduced Paris to the approach of his master, then working on the Pitti Palace in Florence, based on a combination of luxuriant white and gold stucco work with simulated easel pictures and dominated by great illusionist scenes of heaven.

151

Ceilings incorporating illusionist panels in steep perspective were not new to France – Primaticcio and Niccolò dell'Abbate had introduced such panels, varied in shape and richly framed, for the Galerie d'Ulysse at Fontainebleau and they had decorated the ceiling of the chapel of the Hôtel de Guise with a single unified composition of semi-illusionism. The second school of Fontainebleau had largely ignored this approach and it was not until the later years of Richelieu that Simon Vouet took it up on his return to Paris, further developing it in the light of his experience of later sixteenth-century and contemporary interiors in Italy. Amongst his earliest works of this type was the gallery of the Château de Chilly, about 1631, where the scheme as a whole followed the precedent set by Primaticcio and Niccolò.[15] However the overall effect of the heavy network of stucco ornament must have been closer to Veronese and the principal frescoes, depicting the rising of the sun and of the moon, were indebted to the great contemporary treatments of similar subjects by Guido Reni and Guercino – Guido for

individual motifs, Guercino for the conception *di sotto in sù*.

Vouet's most important opportunities were provided in the late 1630s and the 1640s by the queen mother, in works now vanished, and by the Chancellor Séguier who, *protégé* of Richelieu and one of the chief paladins of Mazarin's era, was shortly to be the promoter of Le Brun. The mixture as at Chilly but with more of Veronese in the *di sotto in sù* frescoes is apparent in Séguier's library and gallery, which Vouet decorated in the 1640s, but for the chapel, 1638, he produced a single, unified scheme of consistent illusionism inspired by the Guise chapel.[16] Whereas the latter was dominated by a continuous relief-like frieze of figures, however, Vouet disposed his figures freely behind a balustrade which suggested the termination of the walls and the opening up of the room to the sky. This initiative was not to be followed up in France until Le Brun adopted it for the Salons de la Guerre and de la Paix at Versailles in the 1680s. Contrary to it was the ceiling of the Gallery of the Hôtel de la Vrillière which François Perrier

painted in the late 1640s under the direction of François Mansart. Here the semi-illusionist scenes were viewed through a painted framework of simulated architecture and stucco recalling in many of its details Mansart's treatment of the stone vault above his staircase at Blois.

It is tempting to see Mazarin's choice of Romanelli for the

144

149 *Opposite above* Versailles, garden front built by Le Vau, 1669, enlarged and altered by J. H. Mansart, from 1678

150 *Opposite below* Versailles, Galerie des Glaces by J. H. Mansart and Charles Le Brun, begun 1678

151 *Right* Paris, Palais Mazarin, detail from the vault decoration of the Galerie Mazarine (added by Mansart to the Hôtel Tubeuf) by Francesco Romanelli, 1646–47

152 *Below* Paris, Louvre, vault decoration by Romanelli in the Salle des Saisons, 1655–57

decoration of Mansart's gallery at the Hôtel Tubeuf as a
151 rejection of the work of Mansart and Perrier in favour of the
latest Italian developments and this was doubtless not un-
connected with the rift between Mansart and Mazarin. The
long narrow vault there was hardly suited to a single unified
exercise based upon a fixed viewpoint perspective or to the
highly plastic type of stucco work developed by his master, so
Romanelli divided it into panels and treated them as easel
pictures with relatively simple, interlocking frames, except for
the central panel which shows the 'Fall of the Giants' in clumsy
perspective. This apparently appealed to the queen mother for
though Romanelli returned to Italy on the completion of his
work at the Hôtel Tubeuf in 1648 he was called back in 1655 to
152 decorate her new summer apartment at the Louvre. If the
nature of the field in the Galerie Mazarine seems to have
suggested a modification of the Baroque character of Cortona's
work, the smaller, more compact rooms of the queen mother's
apartment at the Louvre presented no such problem of unity.
With the possibility of a fixed viewpoint in the centre of such
rooms and with the lines of the structure as a framework,
Romanelli could choose either illusionist or non-illusionist
scenes, or both, and indulge in much more of Cortona's rich
variety of forms and contours.

In the years before the Fronde – when the cardinal was active
as a patron of the High Baroque even in Rome, buying the
Palazzo Bentivoglio and commissioning the façade of SS.
Vincenzo e Anastasio from Martino Longhi the younger –
Romanelli's was not the only Italian art of any significance to
dazzle the French. A constant stream of Italian works of all
kinds flowed into the court of Mazarin, who was now an
insatiable collector. A devotee of the stage since his earliest
youth with the Jesuits and later the Barberini, Mazarin promoted Italian operas and ballets at court, and the duke of
Parma, at the queen's behest, sent Giacomo Torelli, one of the
leading stage designers of the day, to mount them.[17] The
extravagant spectacle of his productions – dramatically lit,
using the richest materials, relying on the fusion of the arts for
their sumptuous vistas and fantastic feigned architectural

settings – was not only to be reflected in the great triumphs,
court *fêtes* and *pompes funèbres* throughout the reign but
informed the taste of the young king: the first major result was
the fairy-tale *château* – 'Palais d'Armide' – which emerged from
the king's earliest embellishments at Versailles, with Le Nôtre's
gardens as much the setting for his spectacular *fêtes* as were Le
Brun's interiors the setting for his court; Marly was to be
another. In the short term, however, the ostentation of these
alien court entertainments did a great deal to increase the
bitterness felt by the *bourgeoisie* over the employment of
Italians by Mazarin's régime, and the disaffection of the very
class promoted by Richelieu to the disadvantage of the *noblesse
d'épée* was seen by the latter as the opportunity to reassert itself.
The outbreak of the Fronde in 1648 marked a devastating
reversal of Mazarin's fortunes and temporarily terminated the
development of French Baroque: its most brilliant phase opened
with his final triumph in 1653.

Meanwhile the fortunes of François Mansart too had
suffered a sharp setback when in 1646 the queen mother
replaced him with Lemercier on the commission for the Val-de-
Grâce – which involved not only a major church but a vast
palace in whose plan he took up again his experiments with the   155

153 *Left* Versailles, engraving of the Cour de Marbre built by Philibert Le
Roy and Louis Le Vau, 1624–69

154 *Above* Fresnes by François Mansart, 1644–50, section of the Chapel

155 *Opposite* Paris, Val-de-Grâce, church by François Mansart and
Jacques Lemercier, begun 1645

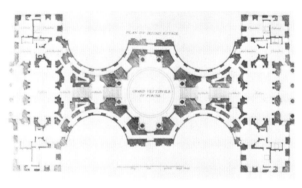

156 *Above* Antoine Le Pautre's design for a *château*, engraving of a general view, 1652

157 *Left* Antoine Le Pautre's design for a *château*, engraving of a plan of the ground and first floors, 1652

158 *Below* Maisons by François Mansart, 1642–46, frontispiece of entrance front of the Château

development of vistas through interrelated spaces of richly varied forms. After the Fronde he had to rely on the patronage of the more fastidious members of the *noblesse de robe*. One such was the secretary of state, Henri de Guénégaud, who gave him the opportunity at Fresnes to carry out a reduced version of his scheme for the church of the Val-de-Grâce. The elaboration of the theme of the assumption of the Virgin, to which the chapel was dedicated, provided a startling anticipation of that dramatic extension through the architectural space of the movement of figures represented in painting and sculpture, which was to be so brilliantly exploited in Bernini's later churches: at Fresnes statues of the apostles were arranged in expressive postures on either side of the empty tomb on the main altar, looking up to a painting of the Virgin ascending in the canopy over the altar, and to God the Father waiting to receive her in the main dome.

Perhaps the most fastidious of all Mansart's patrons was René de Longueil who in 1642 gave him the opportunity at Maisons to build and rebuild in his incessant quest for perfection. The Château is widely considered the principal master-piece of French Classical architecture and in the same way as the architect of the Parthenon envigorated the rigorous system within which he worked by cross-fertilizing it with the Ionic,

154

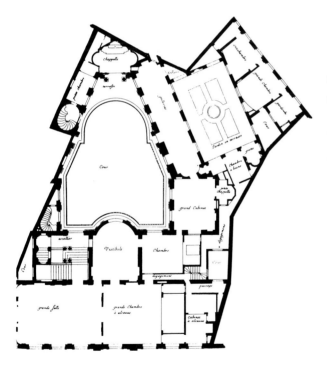

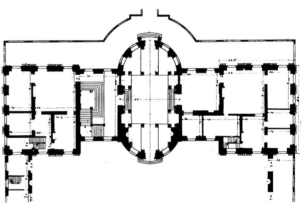

159 *Top* Le Raincy by Louis Le Vau, engraving of the general view, started before 1645

160 *Left* Paris, Hôtel de Beauvais by Antoine Le Pautre, engraving of the plan of the first floor, 1652–55

161 *Above* Le Raincy, engraving of the plan of the ground floor by Louis Le Vau, before 1645

158

François Mansart envigorated the rigorous system of his own time by the restrained use of such Baroque devices as playful sculpture, the subtle variation of the form of the Order in response to the complex projection and recession of planes to produce movement in the façades, and curved façades contrasted in plan with curved interiors. And the Château was the culmination of a vast landscaping exercise dominated by extended open vistas across the fields and the forecourts, past the *communs* whose Orders were proportioned to enhance the apparent size of the Château, and beyond through the terraces patterned to reflect the symmetry and order of the building itself.

Meanwhile, during the Fronde, while Chambray saw his chance to publish Sublet's principles in 1650, Antoine Le Pautre looked for a different outcome to the cardinal's difficulties and dedicated his *Desseins de plusieurs Palais* to Mazarin in 1652. Le Pautre had subscribed to the ideas of the author of the *Parallèle* in his first important work, the austere chapel of Port-Royal, 1646, with its façade recalling the north portico of Lemercier's Sorbonne chapel. His 'plusieurs Palais', on the other hand, show no restraint whatsoever: vast and crushing in scale and weight, powerful in massing, energetic in sculptural detail, drawing the maximum effect from the contrast of concave and convex forms, rich in internal vistas, there is nevertheless a sense of self-conscious Mannerism about most of the plans and in some designs (e.g. the second project), there is a

156, 157

162 *Above* Vaux-le-Vicomte by Louis Le Vau, *salon*

163 *Left* Vaux-le-Vicomte, Chambre du Roi by Louis Le Vau and Charles Le Brun

Mannerist tension between the lucid Palladian plan and the bombastic motifs of the elevation.[18] The only analogy for this sort of thing in France was the work of Louis Le Vau – though, as we shall see, he was unable to handle disparate elements as convincingly as Le Pautre and one has to look to Vanbrugh as Le Pautre's worthiest disciple. The only French artist to share his enthusiasm for atlantes was the Provençal Pierre Puget. A pupil of Pietro da Cortona, after assisting at the Pitti from 1640–43 he spent much time in Toulon where the portal he applied to the Hôtel de Ville in 1656 was supported by powerful figures freer in their modelling and more fluid in their composition than anything yet seen in Paris.

If his book did not succeed in attracting the patronage of Mazarin to its author, a prominent member of the queen mother's circle, Catherine de Beauvais, had from Le Pautre perhaps the most persuasively Baroque *hôtel* ever built in Paris. Its bizarre distribution was in fact dictated by a wildly irregular   160

site, and the curved façades of the court were actually suggested
by existing foundations. But if the boldness of Le Pautre's
response to the challenge is worthy of Borromini, the virtuosity
of his solution to the problem of fitting individually symmetrical rooms into the fabric is perhaps more reminiscent of
Vignola at Caprarola or the Villa Giulia. Like his contemporary altar at St Laurent – with its concave side bays – and
his later façade to the Jesuit church at Lyons – with its Orders
increasing in plasticity in response to the projection of its
central bay – the façade of the Hôtel de Beauvais on the rue St
Antoine – with the contrasting curves of its entrance portal in
particular – acknowledges the influence of contemporary
Rome. From the balcony above the portal, appropriately
enough, Anne of Austria watched the theatrical entry of her son
and daughter-in-law into Paris along a processional way
punctuated with extravagantly sumptuous triumphal arches –
422   of which Le Brun's were the finest – the first of the great series of
spectacles translated for the king from the stage of Torelli to the
streets of his capital and the terraces of his gardens.

On Mazarin's return after the Fronde, Mansart did not
regain official favour. Having been granted the government of
the Château of Vincennes and seeking an architect to transform
it in 1654, Mazarin chose Le Vau from a short list – which
included Mansart and Le Muet – presented to him by his
secretary Colbert.[19] The colossal Order of Le Vau's twin
rectangular blocks is Baroque in scale and weight but hardly
more Baroque in practice than it had been in the hands of
Bullant in the late sixteenth century and his portal is a solid
Classical exercise. On the death of Lemercier in 1654, Le Vau
became Premier Architecte charged with the completion of
the Louvre. Pressing on from 1660 with the continuation of the
south and north wings, begun under Lescot and Lemercier –
adding a weighty frontispiece of colossal Corinthian columns,
borrowed from Bullant at Ecouen, as the south portal – he
remodelled the Petite Galerie after a fire in 1661 and began
planning the important wing which was to close the composition on the east.

Besides these great royal works, it was for Mazarin and the
most powerful members of his regime that Le Vau produced his
most spectacular works. For the Secretary of State Hugues
de Lionne, he built one of the most important *hôtels* in Paris at
the end of the period – with a theatrical staircase approached on
the long axis of the vestibule through a triple arched opening.
Above all he built the *châteaux* of Le Raincy and Vaux-le-
Vicomte and transformed Meudon for the Intendant des Finances Bordier and the joint Surintendants des Finances Fouquet and Servien respectively. Of these the first, built just before
159, 161   the Fronde, was Le Raincy. Here he demonstrated his skill in
internal distribution to meet new standards of comfort and
convenience and made his first experiments with Baroque
massing by introducing a great oval central pavilion which
dominated the composition and projected the main reception
rooms into the garden but disrupted the plan and interrupted

164 *Top right* Paris, Collège des Quatre Nations (now Institut de France),
begun 1662 by Louis Le Vau

165 *Centre right* Paris, Hôtel Lambert, Galerie d'Hercule by Louis Le Vau
and Charles Le Brun, begun *c.* 1650

166 *Right* Paris, Louvre, Galerie d'Apollon by Louis Le Vau and Charles
Le Brun, 1661–63

the inconsistently articulated façades on both sides with its curved projections. At Meudon, after the Fronde, he modified this device, curving only the corners of the pavilion on either side of a flat frontispiece which was bound to the *corps-de-logis* by continuous superimposed Orders. At Vaux (1657) – his most brilliant plan from the point of view of convenience – the central pavilion containing the oval salon projects only on the garden façade but with its curvature emphasized by a huge dome and again with no consistent use of the Orders it is hardly less disruptive than at Le Raincy. On the court side concave walls provide a one-storey link across the *corps-de-logis* between the central and intermediate pavilions on the doubled sides.

Influential as the approach to planning developed in these works was to be, their composition reveals Le Vau's failure to understand Baroque techniques, in particular to control the movement introduced into façades by curvature or to produce it by varying the plasticity of a consistent Order; indeed given his vigorous approach to massing his free use of the Orders – essentially decorative in the tradition associated with the du Cerceau rather than architectonic – actually inhibited the production of the dramatic climax which was the principal aim of Baroque composition. In his work for the executors of Mazarin's will, the Collège des Quatre Nations, begun in 1662, this is particularly apparent. The domed church flanked with quadrant wings, combining motifs from Pietro da Cortona and Borromini, presents a dramatically effective ensemble but the interpolation of superimposed Orders on the quadrants between the colossal Order of the sides and the centre again disrupts the unity of the composition and prevents that powerful centralizing effect achieved in the Roman models.

Le Vau's project for the completion of the Louvre – under execution in 1663 – was Baroque in scale and, part of a truly monumental scheme embracing the Collège des Quatre Nations, seems to demonstrate a greater understanding of the need for a consistent articulation than any of Le Vau's earlier works: the Order of colossal Corinthian columns applied rather awkwardly as the frontispiece of his extended south wing in 1660, and reflected on the other side of the river by the Collège, was spread over the entire eastern façade, including the side pavilions and the vigorously projecting central pavilion containing yet another vast oval salon. As Le Vau had realized twenty years earlier at the Hôtel Lambert the strength of a colossal Order was required when a building was to be viewed from afar but still there was no attempt to vary its plasticity, to harness the power of the massing, express the distinction between the *corps-de-logis* and the pavilions and to provide the sort of variety within an overall unity of which François Mansart was such a master.

At Vaux, of course, the building – with all its faults – is by no means the whole story. Set in Le Nôtre's splendid garden – based on the principle, already developed by François Mansart at Blois and Maisons, of placing the *château* at the climax of the extended open vistas to which vast tracts of the landscape were subjected – and decorated with Le Brun's sumptuous ceilings of painting and stucco above tiers of richly framed panels of painted arabesques, it was the most startling ensemble of the day.

Le Vau had employed Romanelli at Le Raincy but he first worked with Le Brun about 1650 – shortly after Le Brun's return from Rome – on the Hôtel Lambert gallery.[20] There, faced like Romanelli in the Galerie Mazarine with a long, low, narrow vault, Le Brun divided the field with painted architect-

ure – resting on the continuous cornice of the real Order framing the entrance – and, more imaginatively than Romanelli, he simulated the sky at the ends as the scene for suitable mythologies and suspended feigned tapestries as *velaria* – like Raphael at the Farnesina – across the central sections. At Vaux, on the other hand – after Romanelli had confirmed Cortona's approach in the popularity of the court with his work for the queen mother – Le Brun drew upon his first-hand experience of the great rooms at the Pitti. Above similar rich white and gold stucco coves dominated by winged non-illusionist figures of Fame supporting *trompe-l'oeil* medallions and panels whose frames curl into volutes to ease the transition from wall to cove, he opened illusionist scenes like Cortona – and Romanelli. Exuberant as it was and Baroque in the combination of the arts, Cortona's work at the Pitti carefully observed the inviolability of the frames and, establishing decisive contrasts in the white and gold stucco work, ensured that each element of the design was self-contained. It was on precisely this principle, and with decreasing importance placed on the profusion of stucco motifs and illusionism, that Le Brun forged for Louis XIV the style of decoration which, first expressed on a royal scale in 1663 on the vault of the Galerie d'Apollon at the Louvre – where height and breadth permitted a much more stunning variety of shapes and depth of relief than in the Galerie Mazarine or that in the Hôtel Lambert – was to reach its apotheosis in the Grands Appartements at Versailles – 'Baroque tamed by the French Classical spirit'.

The influence of Mazarin's taste survived his death. It is apparent not only in the designs approved by Colbert for the Collège des Quatre Nations but also in the choice of Guarino Guarini as the architect for the other building provided for in the cardinal's will, Sainte Anne-la-Royale. This was to be the church of the Theatine order, which Mazarin had introduced to France in 1644, and had it been completed it would have been the only unequivocally Baroque building in Paris. For this very reason it fell victim, before it was far advanced, to the change of artistic climate following Bernini's unsuccessful visit to France. This in fact followed a severe reversal of Le Vau's own fortunes; indeed, the chief legacies of the Baroque era of Mazarin – briskly terminated not by the king's assumption of personal power but by the dismissal and arrest of Fouquet organized by Colbert after the great *fête* which launched Vaux – were the interiors of Le Brun and the gardens of Le Nôtre. For while Le Brun and Le Nôtre brought to the era of Colbert precisely that combination of sumptuousness and order which the prestige and power of the new monarchy required, Le Vau emerged from his discomfiture only by changing his style.

167 *Opposite* Versailles, Salon de la Guerre by J. H. Mansart, Coysevox and Le Brun, begun 1678

168 *Overleaf* Versailles, Chapel by J. H. Mansart with paintings by Antoine Coypel and Charles de la Fosse, 1688–1710

Colbert and the maturity of Louis XIV

On 1 January 1664 Mazarin's *protégé*, Colbert, officially assumed the responsibilities of Surintendant des Bâtiments.[21] He was the supreme example of the type of statesman to emerge in France through the policy of promoting the *bourgeoisie* under Richelieu and he began to fill the role which Sublet de Noyers had cast for himself – with the Perraults, of similarly respectable *bourgeois* origins, in place of the Fréarts. Unlike Sublet, however, his conception of 'bon goût' was flexible and responded to extra-artistic considerations. As one contemporary observer put it 'ce n'était pas particulièrement qu'il aimait les artistes et les savants; c'était comme homme d'Etat qu'il les protégeait, parce qu'il avait reconnu que les Beaux-Arts sont seuls capables de former et d'immortaliser les grands Empires'.[22] Thus it is not necessary to see in his first important act as Surintendant – the cessation of work on Le Vau's project for the Louvre and the submission of that project to the criticism of Le Vau's colleagues in both France and Italy[23] – any hostility to the Baroque tendencies in the work of the architect

whose career he had hitherto done much to further – most recently in retaining him for the Collège des Quatre Nations. Rather it was dictated by considerations of prestige and power. The prestige of the Louvre as the principal residence of the greatest king in Europe demanded the greatest architectural talent, and Colbert hoped to commission François Mansart, who had been working on the Louvre for some time; unable to hold Mansart to a specific project, however, he turned to the Italians and attracting Bernini, widely considered the greatest master in Europe, gained the added advantage of despoiling the pope. Hardly less important was Colbert's determination to destroy the power which the Premier Architecte had gained at the expense of the Surintendant des Bâtiments under his weak predecessor, in the interest of centralized control over all the

169 *Below* François Mansart, drawing of a project for the east wing of the Louvre, *c.* 1664 *Paris, Bibliothèque Nationale*

170 *Bottom left* François Mansart, plan of a project for the east wing of the Louvre, 1664 *Paris, Bibliothèque Nationale*

171 *Bottom right* Pietro da Cortona, drawing of a project for the west wing of the Louvre, 1664 *Paris, Musée du Louvre*

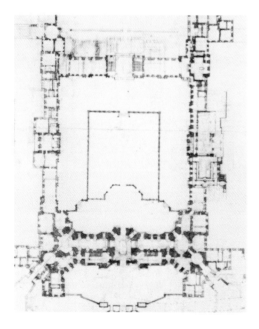

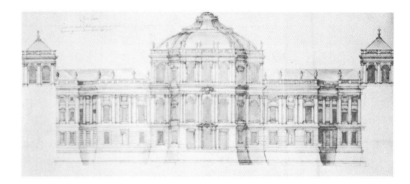

organs of the state – art and artists included. The manoeuvre had considerable artistic consequences however, for from it emerged the hybrid style of the new Louvre and Versailles – Baroque in scale, richness of materials, colour, but regulated in accordance with academic Classical principles, even when relying on the fusion of the arts in interiors – which at once satisfied the king's taste for display, responded to Colbert's

ideal of order, and expressed their common conception of the grandeur of the French monarchy.

From the surviving proposals of Le Vau's colleagues for the east front of the Louvre three different approaches emerge: Le Vau's scheme with a colossal Order rising from the ground was favoured by François Mansart and Pierre Cottard; Lescot's scheme of the interior court with its superimposed Orders, first translated to the exterior by Lemercier ten years earlier, was favoured by Jean Marot; a colonnade supported by a rusticated basement was favoured by Léonor Houdin in a strictly Classical, indeed Bramantesque, interpretation of the traditional French *château* entrance screen dating from 1661, and by Claude Perrault, brother of Colbert's chief *commis* Charles, in a lost project which later testimony claims anticipated the solution ultimately adopted.

169, 170   In an incredibly complex series of drawings – demonstrating precisely that inability, or unwillingness, to bring the creative process to a practical conclusion which made it impossible for Colbert to retain him – François Mansart brought his own style to its apogee.[24] It is not possible, considering them, any longer to speak of Mansart as merely envigorating French Classicism: his ideas for the Louvre are quite distinctly Baroque in their

172 *Top* Bernini, drawing of the first project for the east wing of the Louvre, 1664 (*Sir Anthony Blunt Collection*)

173 *Above* Bernini, engraving of the final project for the east front of the Louvre, 1665

174 *Opposite* Paris, Val-de-Grâce, baldacchino by Gabriel Le Duc, 1664

scale, in the vigour of their massing, in the movement explicit in curved façades and Orders of varied plasticity, in their planning for dramatic vistas through richly diversified room shapes, not only along the principal axes at right angles to one another but along the diagonals as well. Yet there is no specifically Roman importation in all this torrent of invention: on the contrary the colossal Corinthian Order was doubtless suggested by Le Vau's existing work, and the massing of differentiated blocks, the *ordonnance* based on the principle of progression in plasticity, the planning about *enfilades*, were all the essential characteristics of the French tradition which Mansart had inherited from de Brosse, de l'Orme, and Lescot and which he had begun to develop thirty years before he turned his attention to the Louvre.

According to Charles Perrault Colbert admired his brother's

colonnade, but it did not conform to the existing work – one of Colbert's chief concerns – and of those French architects whose designs did so conform none was considered worthy. At first Le Vau's projects were sent to Italy for criticism but then Colbert asked the Italians for original designs: Bernini, Cortona, Rainaldi and the otherwise unknown Candiani responded. Colbert wanted as much of the existing building as possible to be kept, and Cortona and Rainaldi clearly tried to work in what they believed to be the French royal idiom. Rainaldi produced a bizarre composition of pavilions and *corps-de-logis* of exaggerated verticality with a second Order superimposed over the already colossal Corinthian suggested by Le Vau and kiosks bearing vast crowns further superimposed on the pavilions. In several alternative projects Cortona also wrestled unsuccessfully with the alien approach to massing in terms of pavilions and *corps-de-logis* and in one case also strove for verticality by superimposing a second Order over one of colossal Corinthian pilasters. However in his design for the west front, with its concave and convex segments of wall, though retaining a disproportionate central pavilion which seems based on Le Vau's, he reverted to the Roman type of *palazzo* façade developed after Bramante by Sangallo and Michelangelo with its Order raised on a rusticated basement to embrace two storeys below a concealed roof. Bernini on the other hand, though keeping all the existing work, made no concession to its style beyond the adoption of a colossal Corinthian Order. The great central oval pavilion in his first scheme, containing a vast *salon,* was doubtless suggested by Le Vau but in setting it off against concave wings he used one of the most characteristic techniques of the Roman High Baroque and his composition here seems to reflect the plate of the so-called Temple of Honour and Virtue in Jacopo Lauri's *Antiquae urbis splendor*. Indeed Baroque architects like Bernini, generally interested in the plans and forms of ancient buildings rather than their details, were inspired as much by fantastic reconstructions, like those of Montano (or Lauri), as by the actual remains. Moreover Bernini apparently sought to appeal to French taste by referring to the Venetian School – which his comments to his French guide, Chantelou, later indicate he despised: he combined the loggias of Sansovino's Library with the clustered pilasters and half columns of his colossal Order in a scheme which otherwise suggests Michelangelo's Palazzo dei Conservatori.

Whether or not one takes Colbert's praise of Bernini's scheme – 'superbe et magnifique . . . ' – at its face value, his criticisms were concerned with practical considerations of climate, convenience, comfort and security – the darkness of the great central *salon,* the impracticability of flat roofs in Paris, the concealment which would-be assassins might find amongst the arcades – and betray no overt objections to Bernini's style. However, he did find the crowned oval extraordinary, and perhaps even deformed, and he did require that the king's palace should be, and should appear to be, overwhelmingly strong. For that, he stressed, it was not necessary to construct a fortress but simply to ensure that the entries could not easily be approached and that the structure 'imprime le respect dans l'esprit des peuples et leur laisse quelque impression de sa force'.[25]

Angry though he was, Bernini responded with an enlarged second project of three floors, the upper two articulated with a colossal Order resting on a rusticated basement – as in Michelangelo's Palazzo dei Senatori – in which the oval central

pavilion is suppressed in favour of a great curved central block concentric with the rest of the façade, offering arcaded galleries only on the upper two floors. Though this too was open to practical criticism it appealed to the king, and Bernini was invited to Paris to sort out the difficulties on the spot. Given a quasi-royal progress through France and received by Chantelou near Paris he spent the summer and early autumn of 1665 transforming this second project into the definitive one. The *ordonnance* and basic divisions of the three-storey façade remained but with the curves and the external loggias removed this certainly satisfied Colbert's requirement of apparent strength. Colbert had more difficulty however in concentrating Bernini's attention on the internal requirements of the palace and little success at all in persuading him to renounce the extravagance of refacing the existing buildings. Though contrary to French tradition the scheme was adopted and Bernini was pressed to remain in France to execute it, despite the fact that with his arrogance and rudeness he disparaged his French colleagues, openly insulted Charles Perrault and exasperated Colbert himself – for he retained the king's admiration.

After the laying of the foundation stone on 17 October 1665 and Bernini's departure, work on the foundations proceeded slowly and over the next year the French opposition mobilized itself. Charles Perrault took every opportunity to play upon Colbert's own misgivings about the cost and impracticability of Bernini's project and though both Le Vau and Mansart were asked for new projects Colbert, wishing to retain the king's commitment to his Paris residence, apparently felt it unwise to counteract his master's enthusiasm for Bernini's scheme. In April 1667, however, preoccupied with the augmentation of Versailles the king was finally persuaded to abandon Bernini's plans, and a commission composed of Le Vau, Le Brun and Claude Perrault was set up to complete the Louvre. A year later Colbert himself explained to Chantelou that Bernini's project, 'quoique beau et noble', was so ill-conceived in so far as the comfort of the king was concerned that after the expense of 10 million *livres* on it His Majesty would be as cramped as ever; he, Colbert, had insisted that the king's apartment could properly be sited only in the south wing, where it was, 'mais que le Cavalier n'avait point entré là-dedans, et ne voulait faire les choses qu'à sa fantaisie'.[26]

Apart from the foundations for his Louvre scheme, the only tangible result of Bernini's visit was the splendid bust of the king which he carved while in Paris – even the equestrian statue ordered at that time was out of fashion when it ultimately reached Versailles in 1685. Yet his work was certainly not without influence. Before and after his visit various church fittings throughout France were modelled on his baldacchino of St Peter's. The most notable, perhaps, is the high altar of the Val-de-Grâce designed by Le Duc in 1664. When the drawings for it were shown to Bernini in Paris his reaction was one of disparagement but his revisions were not followed. Of more fundamental importance, however, were his Louvre projects themselves. If the third project for the east front, which was engraved, is submitted to the criticism spelt out in the mid-eighteenth century by J. F. Blondel the result is very close to the scheme actually adopted for the south front and its expression in terms of the colonnade of the east front.[27] Thus the executed projects for the Louvre may be seen as academic Classical revisions of Bernini's Roman Baroque composition and the Louvre façades, together with the garden façade of Versailles –

the design for which must be viewed in the light of developments at the Louvre – provided four generations of royal academicians with their principal models for monumental architecture.

According to the register of the deliberations of Colbert's commission, kept by Charles Perrault, it was Colbert's order that Le Vau, Le Brun and Claude Perrault should work on the project in common so that none of them could claim the authorship to the prejudice of the others. However, unable to agree on a single design the commission submitted two 'dont l'un étoit orné d'un Ordre de colonnes formant un perystile ou galerie au-dessus du premier étage et l'autre étoit plus simple et plus uni sans Ordre de colonnes'.[28] According to Charles Perrault the division was between his brother on the one hand and Le Vau and Le Brun on the other. Consistently referring to the scheme with the colonnade as his brother's, he reported that Le Vau was responsible for the one without Orders – which, unlike the colonnade, accorded with the existing south wing – and the surviving drawings include a version of it generally attributed to Le Brun. Perrault also relates that Colbert preferred the scheme without Orders – indeed, it had been Colbert's persistent concern that the new work should accord with the old – but the king chose the colonnade scheme on 13 May 1667.[29]

At first it was intended that the new east wing should be joined to the north and south wings as planned by Le Vau but in June 1668 the project was revised to provide for the doubling of the south wing so that the king, the queen, the royal family and their attendants could be accommodated in the most agreeable part of the *château*. The revised project was criticised, presumably by Charles Perrault whose job it was as *commis* of the Surintendant des Bâtiments to assess projects, and defended by François Le Vau, Louis' brother who had long been called upon to review projects of the Premier Architecte at least twice before; their comments provide the key to the transformation of the Baroque schemes

175 Paris, Louvre, east front (Colonnade) by Claude Perrault, Louis Le Vau and Charles Le Brun, 1667–70

for the Louvre into models of academic French Classicism.[30] François Le Vau's principal aim was to demonstrate that the advantages to be gained by doubling the south wing – 'la commodité ... la beauté et la bienséance' ("comfort, beauty and propriety") – would be worth the expense of time and money involved. To provide all the accommodation needed by the royal family and their attendants in the south wing, Lescot's attic would be replaced with one great storey or two small ones above that of the king, giving the building a height proportioned not only to its length but to its usage; the now necessarily colossal Order would be applied both to the east and the south fronts. Charles Perrault condemned in particular the placing of an obviously habitable storey above that of the king, as contrary to *bienséance*, and the use of a colossal Order, cut by the floor it should have been supporting, as irrational. François Le Vau replied that *bienséance* equally required a second storey for the Enfants de France and that the proportions of the façade as a whole required an Order of great weight and majesty.

Whatever the role of Louis Le Vau in the evolution of the 1667 project for the Louvre, François Le Vau's involvement in the revision of that project went further than mere advocacy. In so far as his defence specifically deals with the east wing it is closely related to a project published over his own name, in which the revised end pavilions are almost direct quotations of the *corps-de-logis* of Pietro da Cortona's west front and this design marks the transition from the project of 1667 to the executed one.[31] The latter followed François Le Vau's approach for the side pavilions, doubling the side pilasters, but the simplified central pavilion was also derived from Cortona's 'quarto disegno'; there was to be only one attic storey above the king's floor but, as in François Le Vau's project, the Order embracing both these storeys was greater than that of the 1667 colonnade; the medallions of Lescot, used in the 1667 project above the first-floor windows, were kept instead of the rectangular panels which Le Vau borrowed from Cortona for the blind attic of his east façade.

The general disposition of a rusticated basement supporting an Order before the *piano nobile* with an attic above the Order and the specific use of rectangular panels above the first-floor windows provide an intriguing link between François Le Vau's project for the Louvre and the scheme devised at much the same time – probably in the spring of 1668 – for the new garden range at Versailles. If one were to search for a French precedent for the Roman approach to *ordonnance* which the king was known to prefer after the visit of Bernini – as the office of the Premier Architecte presumably did when planning the enlargement of Versailles early in 1668 – one could hardly do better than Salomon de Brosse's Palais des Etats at Rennes – itself derived from the Roman tradition of Bramante through Primaticcio's Aile de la Belle Cheminée at Fontainebleau – which includes even the deep central recession in the first floor, so important to the new work at Versailles. One need only replace de Brosse's high roof with an attic above the Order and add rectangular panels above the windows of the *piano nobile* to have all the essentials of the Versailles scheme.

The discussion between the architects concerned and the officials in the Surintendance about the revision of the 1667 Louvre project shows that the transformation of the Roman forms of Bernini and Cortona into the principal models of later French Classical architecture was directed in accordance with basic academic principles – *bienséance* or *convenance* above all, and *vraisemblance* – and this was clearly Claude Perrault's

176 Versailles, engraving of the Escalier des Ambassadeurs by Louis Le
Vau and Charles Le Brun, begun in 1671

role.[32] Charles Perrault's objections to the projected
heightening of the south wing were precisely those Claude
raised against the proposal to complete the Cour carrée by
substituting a full Order for Lescot's attic: that it was contrary
to *convenance* to raise a habitable storey of equal magnificence
over that of the king and that the height of a building should not
necessarily be proportioned to its length. Moreover the
colonnade, compared by Perrault to the peristyle of an antique
temple, is strictly Roman in the detail of its Order and Claude
was the one member of the Commission with pronounced
archaeological leanings.

As Colbert's principal advisers on architectural theory the
Perraults would have played a role similar to that of the Fréarts
under Sublet, and Charles Perrault, like Chambray, wrote a
Parallèle of the 'Ancients' and 'Moderns'. The similarity stops
there for, whereas Chambray preached the need to return to the
ancient Classical authorities and learn again to apply their ideas
in all their purity, Perrault dared to suggest that blind adulation
of the Antique was irrational and that his own contemporaries
had made great advances on it. Chambray's views reflect
those of Sublet but Sublet's policy was to provide an authoritative French school of art: Perrault's views reflect the conclusion
which Colbert drew logically enough from the same policy. If
Colbert's conception of state order required rules for the arts,
his conception of French prestige required that those rules
should be French and, therefore, modern. Thus, ironic as it may
seem that an independent-minded critical spirit should be
brought to the service of the authoritarian state, it is clear that
the very idea of an absolute standard of beauty, embodied in the
Antique, had to be challenged if an authoritative French
standard was to be set up – that Claude Perrault in his
ordonnance had to demonstrate that beauty was relative if he
was to clear the way for the acceptance of a definitive French
schedule of proportions.

Most of the inconsistencies in the alignment of the leading
figures of the period can, in fact, be explained in terms of
expediency. Charles Perrault well illustrated the anomaly of Le
Brun's position as champion of the Ancients, for instance, when
praising him in *Les Hommes Illustres* as the greatest of the
Moderns. The hero of the Ancients, Poussin, had failed to

provide a model in the Grande Galerie of the Louvre for the
type of decoration which the courts of Mazarin and Louis XIV
required, and Raphael, at the Farnesina and Villa Madama,
was hardly an adequate alternative; but in taking Cortona as
his model Le Brun was more successful than almost any other
French artist in using Baroque devices. For in Cortona's work
he found an inspiration· well attuned to his native ability to
handle vast compositions in a free and lively manner, to cover
vast spaces with a vigorous but coherent fusion of the arts, and
however sincere his admiration for Poussin and Raphael there
is more than a trace of personal ambition, of concession to the
régime of Colbert, in his dogmatic stand for the Ancients in
theory – reflected in his practice as a not always happy constraint on his native talents. By the same token the anti-
academic stance of Mignard, who supplanted Le Brun under
Louvois, can similarly be fully explained only in terms of
personal rivalry. For his part, Claude Perrault – the Modern –
was in practice inspired by the Antique and drew directly upon
his study of it in the transformation of the Baroque projects for
the Louvre to meet the needs of the king and Colbert, yet he
discussed the proposals of his colleagues not primarily in the
habitual terms of the proportions and details of the Orders but
of *vraisemblance* and *convenance* – of what was true, or at least
apparently true, to physical realities and of what was appropriate for modern usage, in particular the usage of the king of
France. And though submission to the rules of proportion in
architecture was obviously a fundamental condition of Colbert's rational order for the arts, it was above all their conformity to the rules of *convenance*, reflecting the hierarchical order
of the French monarchy, which gave the Colonnade and the
garden façade of Versailles their authoritativeness.

The new work at Versailles enveloping the original *château* of
Louis XIII was underway by autumn of 1668 and, halted in
1669 when a more radical rebuilding exercise was briefly
entertained, completed in 1671. The façade was altered for the
insertion of the Galerie des Glaces and addition of the vast
north and south wings by J.H. Mansart in 1678. Though Colbert
and his assistants ensured that the king received a building of
high quality – in its original form – inevitably it was outshone
by the splendour of the gardens and interior decorations which
preoccupied the king as the setting for his court. Unequalled in
extent and variety though they were, Le Nôtre's gardens were
based on the principles he had applied at Vaux and the
Tuileries and which François Mansart had evolved at Blois and
Maisons. The interiors, executed by Le Brun between 1671 and
1686, are based on a similar combination of the arts as those at
Vaux and the Galerie d'Apollon in the Louvre but the high
relief stucco work, especially the figural element, is reduced, the
integrity of the painted zones is never violated, and though
illusionist panels generally occupied the centres of the ceilings
and in the corners of the greater rooms glimpses of the sky are
revealed beyond balustrades with spectators, non-illusionist
panels play an increasingly important role. The walls are now
covered with velvet or encrusted with marbles, richly coloured
and varied in regular geometrical patterns rather than panels in
several tiers painted with arabesques as at Vaux. The rooms are
rectangular in the main, as Colbert had rejected 'les figures
rondes' in his criticism of Le Vau's 1669 scheme for the
complete rebuilding of the Château. As usual in France a
continuous Classical cornice marks the junction of wall and
ceiling and in the principal spaces – for instance the Escalier des
Ambassadeurs or the Galerie des Glaces – a full Order was

177

176

177 Versailles, Salon de Diane by Le Vau, Le Brun and his pupils, showing Bernini's bust of Louis XIV

150   adopted. An Order was not in itself unfamiliar in French interiors since the work of Lemercier at the Louvre under Sublet but now, executed in the richest marbles and gilt bronze, combined with sculpture and painting – in which illusionism plays an important role in the Escalier des Ambassadeurs – it was an essential element of the final permutation of Le Brun's approach to the fusion of the arts which began with his experience of Cortona and Romanelli nearly forty years before.

The clear lines of the Louvre colonnade and the garden façade at Versailles – the sustained horizontals of a strong basement surmounted by a faithfully observed Order and often a balustrade masking the roof – were to be the hallmarks of French Classical architecture from the later 1660s onwards. Yet many of the principal royal works of Jules Hardouin Mansart show less restrained Baroque devices – presumably to satisfy the king.[33] His models were occasionally contemporary Italian works but more often those of his French predecessors. Thus on the one hand the relationship between the Galerie des Glaces and the Salons de la Guerre and de la Paix must be compared to that between the Salone and Galleria of the slightly earlier Palazzo Colonna in Rome. On the other hand the curved façades of the twin stable blocks at Versailles (1679) into which all the elements were bound by a consistent articulation of the utmost simplicity, might be taken as revisions of Le Vau's Collège des Quatre Nations. So too might the Dôme des   164

179 Invalides, as originally planned in 1679 with detached quadrant
178 arcades. The church itself was directly derived from François Mansart's designs for the Bourbon chapel of St Denis, its High Renaissance plan crowned by a cut-off dome with vertical perspective and dramatic lighting, and its façade subjected to a climactic movement by the breaking forward of its super-imposed Orders with the plane of the wall in progressive stages, the upper Order one step behind the lower in achieving full plasticity. The great rusticated Orangery at Versailles, 1681, retains something of the vitality and Baroque boldness of scale which Le Pautre borrowed from Le Vau, without the manner-isms of either. The colouristic effects of Le Vau's Trianon de Porcelaine were consciously emulated in the Trianon de Marbre (1687) which replaced it – a unique example of such rich external revetment in France. And Marly (1679) – where the principal pavilion was placed at the head of a great pool flanked by small guest pavilions in serried ranks – recalled Torelli in its theatrical perspectives, its painted architecture and sculpture: indeed it crystallized something of the fantasy of the first Versailles during one of the king's great early *fêtes*.

178 *Below* Paris, Invalides, exterior of the Eglise du Dôme by J. H. Mansart, 1680–91

179 *Below right* J. H. Mansart, engraving of the project for the completion of the Invalides

180 *Opposite* Nancy, Place Stanislas. Gilded iron grilles by Emmanuel Héré, 1752–55

The decline of Louis XIV, the Regency and Louis XV

Colbert died in 1683, and the discretion with which that great minister guided the king's absolutism was wanting in his successor Louvois. Staggering under the burden of Louis XIV's conception of his monarchy, following the extravagant ex-pansion of Versailles, France was reduced by the severe reverses in the almost ceaseless, and now increasingly futile, war waged to further that conception to an equally ceaseless threat of bankruptcy. Yet in the brief moment of peace following the Treaty of Ryswick in 1697 the last monumental projects of the reign – the Place Vendôme, the decoration of the Dôme des Invalides, the Chapel at Versailles, the high altar of Notre-Dame – conceived and even begun much earlier, were completed. Mansart's ability to appease the king's taste for the Baroque without breaking the bounds of academic Classical discipline is revealed in each of them.

The Place Vendôme and the earlier Place des Victoires, conforming to the now canonical Roman *ordonnance* in the Louvre version with a colossal Order proportioned to an ex-tensive open space, were to be held up by the Academy as the models for the French Classical square. Despite the reticence of their *ordonnance* these royal squares were essentially exercises in scenic architecture, designed first and foremost to glorify the king whose statue they framed, inviting comparison with such Roman Baroque conceptions as the Piazza of St Peter's rather than the essentially practical Place Royale of Henry IV. The great ecclesastical projects brought to completion in this per-

iod are also essentially Baroque conceptions subjected to the discipline of academic Classical principles. The *ordonnance* of the Louvre colonnade was translated to the interior of the chapel at Versailles to provide the great height needed for the provision of the king's tribune on the level of the *grands appartements* – ironically enough producing an almost Gothic sense of verticality which was further developed in a Baroque way by Coypel in his great *quadratura* ceiling. To the Dôme des Invalides also was now added a quite Italianate richness in the gilt trophies on the exterior of the dome, in the sumptuous colossal Order and vigorous relief panels of the interior and above all in the high altar, with its black Salomonic columns, based on Bernini's composition in St Peter's. This same approach was adopted for the new altar erected in Notre-Dame in response to the king's determination to fulfill his father's vow.

After the completion of these great works for Louis XIV, and with the construction of the Château-Neuf for the Dauphin at Meudon, crown patronage virtually ceased until the maturity of Louis XV, but the monumental tradition was kept alive by the king's architects in the service of the intendants of several French provinces, the Bourbons in Spain and the princely and ecclesiastical courts of north-eastern France and western Germany. The two leaders here were Mansart's chief collaborator and successor, Robert de Cotte, whose own share of the responsibility for the late works of Louis XIV in Paris is great, and their younger assistant Germain Boffrand.[34]

An independent spirit working for an independent court, Boffrand went back to the French masters of the mid seventeenth century and to Bernini's projects for the Louvre, to borrow some of the basic Baroque devices which had been rejected by academic French Classicism. Thus for the duke of Lorraine's palace at Lunéville, 1702–06, modelled on Le Vau's Versailles, he drew the vast plan together in the middle by reviving the massive portico of unfluted Corinthian columns which Le Vau had incorporated in the south front of the Louvre and which Colbert had prevented him from extending around the east front. In his first project, 1711, for the duke's retreat at La Malgrange he used the same Order to bind the great projecting central pavilion containing a vast oval salon into the composition, expressing the distinction between the pavilions and the *corps-de-logis* by confining the Order to the latter – as pilasters on the sides and columns only in the centre.

Despite its rejection by the Crown, the projecting oval salon providing the climax to the principal *enfilade* was Le Vau's chief contribution to the development of the French *château* in the late seventeenth and eighteenth centuries. Like many of his contemporaries and successors – such as Bullet at Champs at the beginning of the century and Ange-Jacques Gabriel at St Hubert over fifty years later – Robert de Cotte incorporated such a projecting central salon in his great schemes at the end of the War of the Spanish Succession in 1714, for the king of Spain, the electors of Bavaria and Cologne, and, in 1723 in competition with Boffrand, for the prince-bishop of Würzburg. Emulating Versailles in ideal plans for all these at first, he modified that ideal to accommodate existing building at Schleissheim and Bonn or in accordance with the equally grandiose ideal set by the Escorial in Spain. At Schleissheim he introduced diagonal axes by inserting circular rooms in the corners of the

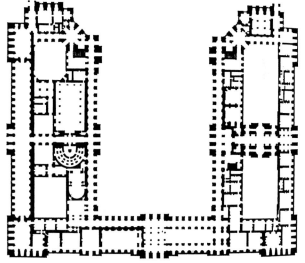

181 *Opposite* Paris, Hôtel de Soubise, Salon Ovale by Germain Boffrand, with paintings by Charles Natoire, 1735

182 *Top* Germain Boffrand, engraving of the second project for La Malgrange, Nancy, *c.* 1712

183 *Centre* Lunéville, exterior of the *château* by Germain Boffrand, 1703–23

184 *Bottom* Robert de Cotte, plan for the first project for the Neues Schloss, Schleissheim, *c.* 1714

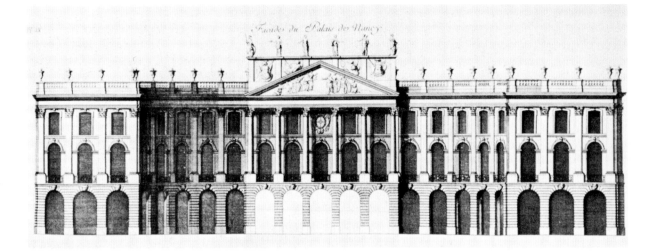

185 Nancy, engraving of the façade of the Ducal Palace by Germain Boffrand

wings flanking the *cour d'honneur* – a device which reveals his knowledge of François Mansart's plans for the Louvre. Preferring the Roman *ordonnance* of the Colonnade or Versailles for most of these projects, he revived the 'incorrect' expression of the Order in terms of the half columns of Bernini's third project for the Louvre in the plans for Buenretiro near Madrid and later actually applied such an Order to the river front of the palace which he built for the prince-bishop of Strasbourg from 1720 onwards.

Boffrand showed an even more pervasive interest in Bernini's projects for the Louvre in a second idea for La Malgrange. A virtuoso exercise in planning, Baroque in its conception of unity, it is dominated by a rotunda expanding the great curved central pavilion of Bernini's first project but instead of setting this off against concave wings, like Bernini, he made it the pivot for four diagonal wings as Fischer von Erlach had done for Count Althan *c.* 1693. A colossal Order rising from the ground, as in the Louvre projects of both Bernini and Le Vau, was used around the rotunda and before the façades closing the triangles between the divergent wings. The entrance was placed in one of these and the vista down the main axis – inviting a progression from the vestibule and gallery inserted into the first triangle through the great circular central space, to the heart-shaped staircase and oval salon of the second triangle – would have been incredibly rich. In his last important work for the duke of Lorraine, the 'Louvre' of Nancy, Boffrand used the broad concave recession of Bernini's first and second projects to frame a vast temple front motif but instead of a colossal Order resting on the ground this time he introduced the *ordonnance* of the Colonnade, as expressed in the great royal squares of Jules Hardouin, to Nancy. The local architect Héré, like most of his contemporaries working on civic schemes in provincial capitals in the first half of the eighteenth century, followed that example for his Place Royale in Nancy. Even the interpolation of playful Rococo iron work, seductive as it is, does not deny the essentially Classical academicism of the *ordonnance* nor the Baroque grandeur of the conception which embraced three linked squares.

Splendid as the late works of Louis XIV and those planned by his architects for foreign princes were – or would have been had they all been realized – the most significant contribution of the period of his decline was the development of the non-monumental, anti-architectural mode of interior decoration which produced the Rococo. In this mode the Orders had no place – or they were invaded, eaten away and undermined by naturalistic or stylized floral motifs in a mockery of their claim to express the forces implicit in structure. Moreover the strict geometrical division of traditional French revetment was also abandoned in favour of irregular and increasingly sensuous mouldings which actually invaded the field they surrounded, breaking down the distinction between frame and framed.

The first steps on the path which was to lead to this new decorative style were taken in the office of the Premier Architecte at Versailles in the last decade of the seventeenth century – doubtless under the direction of Jules Hardouin himself though the responsibility is sometimes credited, unconvincingly, to his draughtsman Pierre Le Pautre.[35] With the disappearance of Colbert Le Brun's influence was undermined by Louvois and in any case the Italianate grandeur which he had done more than anyone else to translate into French, using the most sumptuous materials, could no longer be afforded. Besides, in 1686 Le Brun had finished the Grande Galerie – and with it the Grands Appartements – and the king's attention turned to the development of a style more fitted for personal apartments. This culminated in the decoration of rooms for his granddaughter-in-law, the duchesse de Bourgogne, in 1698 where, His Majesty decreed, 'il faut qu'il y ait de la jeunesse mêlée dans ce que l'on fera.'[36]

A new suite of rooms decorated for the king following the death of the queen in 1684, was given wood panelling, still in superimposed tiers of regular geometric shapes, painted white and gold throughout; tall mirrors, some reaching to the cornices, were placed over mantelpieces, instead of paintings; windows were elongated and sometimes arched. The same desire for relative simplicity, lightness and clarity, the same tendency to develop vertical accents, characterized the decoration of the more private rooms at Versailles and a new suite at Trianon (1686–91), the increasingly elongated, but still geo-

186 *Opposite* Nancy, grille in the gardens of the Place Royale (Place Stanislas) by Emmanuel Héré, 1752–55

187 Studio of J. H. Mansart, engraving of a project for an overmantel, 1699

metrical, panelling being subjected to an Order in the *parade* rooms at Trianon.

In work for the Crown painted arabesques, which had formerly decorated the rectangular panels of most French interiors, as at Vaux, were now used only in intimate rooms. Here and in the main rooms of private houses, where marble and bronze were not appropriate and painted vaults were rare, Bérain and later Claude III Audran developed this type of decoration from the example of Le Brun – an interlinking of the band-work popular with the Northern Mannerists and the acanthus tendrils of the *grotteschi* of the followers of Raphael introduced into France by the first School of Fontainebleau, in which figural elements like herms or sphinxes grow from the foliage to support medallions, simulated relief panels, baldachins etc. Bérain decorated the new, elongated panels of the Dauphin's *cabinet* at Meudon (1699) and his arabesques invaded the field of framed pilaster strips flanking a fashionable tall, arched mirror in a way which anticipated the Rococo. Restrained though it yet was such a violation had hardly been seen in France since the period of Francis I. The apartments installed for the little duchesse de Bourgogne and in the Ménagerie at Versailles in 1698, were decorated by members of Mansart's studio in the same spirit. In one of the rooms the impost, pushed up into an arch by the tall mirror, breaks and curls and from the scrolls carved foliage shoots out to invade the spandrels which themselves are formed into irregular fields separated by a great shell – thus the arabesque work, hitherto painted on the surface of the panels, was now carved and fused with the frame. Moreover a delicate foliage invaded the framed pilasters supporting this arch, denying them any suggestion of strength though they retained Ionic capitals and bases. In 1699 similar tall, arched mirrors surmounted by panels with their frames interrupted by 'C' or 'S' scrolls, masks, shells, etc. and supported by pilaster strips hardly related to an Order, framed

and invaded by band-work or foliage, were installed in the apartments of Marly. And at the very centre of Versailles two years later in the new bedroom installed for the king, which retained a full Composite Order, arabesques invaded the shafts of the Ionic pilasters supporting the tall arched mirrors and the panels of the doors. In the neighbouring Antichambre de l'Oeil-de-Boeuf, with its ravishing frieze of children playing with garlands, the frames of the panels above the windows, mirrors and doors were filled with acanthus scrolls and the still rectangular panels of wainscot and doors were dominated by filigree rosettes, palmettes etc.

From these beginnings the style quickly developed in the panelling of the last important works for the Crown before the king's death in 1715, the furniture of the chapel of Versailles and the Choir of Notre-Dame, but more particularly in the comfortable modern *hôtels* now being built in Paris. In the reception rooms of these essentially private houses, as in the withdrawing rooms, the Orders were not considered *convenables;* though vestigial pilasters, panelled and invaded by arabesques, were occasionally used, in lieu of an effective architectonic structure a symmetrical geometric frame remained the basis of order throughout, even when corners were rounded and cornices reduced to a hollow cove, the upper edge of which broke out into the field of the ceiling. But within this framework the formerly regular pattern of panels and mirrors was first modified by circles and ovals and then dissolved into undulations. Arabesque forms, not only 'C' or 'S' scrolls but herms – usually in the form of 'têtes en espagnolette' – masks, symmetrical *coquilles,* sphinxes etc. and later their more bizarre relatives such as irregular *rocaille* shell-work, dragons and batwings, assumed a more important role not only in framing mirrors, *dessus-de-porte* and the increasingly large panels which filled the wall between the major accents provided by the mirrors, the windows and the doors but even on the upper edge of coves which began to break out into the ceiling. On the sensuously curved base of the organ in the chapel at Versailles (1709–10) the *palmier* – presumably in this context a permutation of the martyr's palm but quickly to become a generally popular motif with Rococo designers – made its first appearance and the figurative reliefs which dominated the choir stalls at Notre-Dame were to be reflected in the cartouche-framed scenes, rimmed with shell or foliage, which were to occupy the centres of many later panels as an alternative to

188 Studio of J. H. Mansart, drawing for a cabinet in the Ménagerie, Versailles, 1698. *Paris, National Archives*

189 Paris, engraving of the Galerie Dorée in the Hôtel de Toulouse by Robert de Cotte and François-Antoine Vassé, 1718–19

190 Paris, engraving of the Galerie d'Enée in the Palais-Royal by Gilles-Marie Oppenord, 1717

rosettes in domestic interiors.

These late ecclesiastical works were carried out under Robert de Cotte but the Premier Architecte and his colleagues in the Bâtiments du Roi, under-employed on royal works, were deeply involved in the private sector. Working here for such important figures as the duc d'Orléans and the comte de Toulouse, who had scarcely dared to leave Versailles until the tragic series of royal deaths in 1711–12 reduced it to a very morbid place indeed, there was scope further to develop the tradition of Le Brun for great interiors where the Orders were required – vestibules, stairwells, galleries, *chambres de parade*, great *salons*, the last represented by the Salon d'Hercule at Versailles. The two principal works of this type, the Galerie Dorée of the Hôtel de Toulouse, carried out under the direction of de Cotte, and the Galerie d'Enée of the Palais-Royal by the Flemish designer Oppenord, who spent much time in Rome and whose principal earlier works in Paris were Baroque altars, offer a particularly instructive comparison. Dominated by a robust fluted Corinthian Order the Galerie d'Enée was no less architectonic than the Galerie des Glaces though the vigorous sculpture with which Oppenord interrupted the entablature and the weighty obelisks with trophies which he applied to the panels between the pilasters were certainly more Baroque than the relief work in the late interiors of Le Brun. There is also an Order and a considerable amount of figure sculpture – relating to the count's two chief concerns, the sea and the chase – in the Galerie Dorée but here de Cotte allowed his sculptor Vassé to treat the shafts of the pilasters as panels decorated with arabesques in the way by now familiar in less important rooms, reducing them to transparent fictions of support, and the rest of the woodwork, especially the frames of the murals between the pilasters, is as sensuous and light-hearted as any of the period which led to the Rococo.

Of de Cotte's associates active in the domestic field in the first

decades of the eighteenth century, Boffrand made several of the most important contributions to the further development of the style. In the salon of the Petit Luxembourg (1710) for instance, he first experimented with the curving of an uninterrupted impost up over the arches of doors, windows and mirrors to form a sort of scalloped valance right round the room at the expense of the tectonic frame. With the rounding of the corners and the reduction of the cornice to a support for an upturned fringe of foliage in the cove of the ceiling, this tended towards the blurring of the structural lines and prepared for that ambivalent relationship between walls and ceiling which was to be the key to his most dazzling interiors. A crucial stage on the way was the circular salon at La Malgrange (1711) where the arched upper windows penetrated the cove and their balconies were supported by figures resting on the imposts of the arched doors and windows below them. The most spectacular examples of the type, perhaps the most ravishing rooms surviving from the period, are the oval salons which he installed for the Prince and Princesse de Soubise in their Paris *hôtel* about 1735. In the upper room walls, spandrels, cove and ceiling are merged in a splendid fusion of the arts: the crucial role is played by vestigial pendentives in undulating frames, containing Natoire's Psyche panels, supported by putti resting on the upper curves of the main wall panels and crowned by stucco cartouches in sprays of foliage linked both across the ceiling to the central rosette by filigree bands and around the cove by a quivering moulding, supporting more putti over more cartouches crowning the arched embrasures of the windows, mirrors and doors.

The incredible fertility of invention which Boffrand displayed in these rooms was disciplined by a strict regularity and each individual element was essentially symmetrical – unless the panels of the doors of the *salon* at La Malgrange were in fact to have been as represented in the engravings of 1745.[37] By the

above all in fantastic ornament engraved as an end in itself. It was his metal-work and the compositions in his books of ornament – 'des Fontaines, des Cascades, des Ruines, des Rocailles et Coquillages, des morceaux d'Architecture qui font des effets bizarres, singuliers et pittoresques, par leurs formes piquantes et extraordinaires, dont souvent aucune partie ne répond à l'autre'[38] – which earned him the reputation of having invented the 'genre pittoresque' but he executed nothing like them in the field of architecture, external or internal, in France and thus – ironically – escaped the severer censures of the mid-century critics. Indeed the projects which he did produce for execution – usually abroad – are hardly Rococo at all. For instance his design for the completion of Saint Sulpice (1726) is certainly Baroque, employing Orders before contrasted concave and convex sections of wall in the manner of Borromini, though the profile of the transept roofs, with their asymmetrical *palmier* finials, anticipated the architectural fantasies of his *Livre d'Ornemens* which, composed of twirling consoles and asymmetrical arches, defy the laws of gravity – and categorization. Equally plastic in treatment, and using asymmetry in a similar way, was the panelling Meissonnier designed for the Maison Bréthous in Bayonne about 1733. In its plasticity as in

194

196

191 *Top* Paris, Petit Luxembourg, salon by G. Boffrand, 1710

192 *Above left* Nancy, engraving of a section through the central salon of the Château de la Malgrange by G. Boffrand, begun 1711

193 *Above right* Nicolas Pineau, drawing of a project for panelling. *Paris, Musée des Arts Décoratifs*

fourth decade of the century, even while he was working on the Hôtel de Soubise, Nicolas Pineau and Juste-Aurèle Meissonnier, experimenting with asymmetry, had produced the 'genre pittoresque', the fully evolved phase of Rococo in France.

Meissonnier – born in Turin of Provençal parents, trained as a goldsmith and considered by most mid-eighteenth-century critics as primarily responsible for the invention of the 'genre pittoresque' – had first experimented with rugous forms and asymmetrical composition in silver and gold then, as Directeur de la Chambre et du Cabinet du Roi from 1726, in decorations for court *fêtes* and ceremonies, occasionally in architecture and

some of its motifs – if not in its irresponsibility – his approach here too is related to the Italian Baroque of Turin. The scheme which Meissonnier produced for the Polish Count Bielenski in 1734, with its *quadratura* ceiling feigning the expansion of the space of the room, might similarly be called Baroque, were it possible to speak of architecture at all in this context of riotously asymmetrical anti-structural and *rocaille* forms.

The genre of fantastic ornament engraved with little thought of practical application had long been well represented in France but in the fourth decade of the eighteenth century the suites published by Meissonnier and his contemporaries, in

195

194 *Above* Juste-Aurèle Meissonnier, engraving of a fantastic design, *c.* 1734

195 *Above right* Juste-Aurèle Meissonnier, engraving of a project for a cabinet for M. Bielenski, 1734

196 *Below right* Juste-Aurèle Meissonnier, drawing of a project for the west front of Saint Sulpice, Paris. *Waddesdon Manor*

particular Jacques de Lajoue, had an unlooked-for consequence. Especially their cartouches – which fused disparate elements often in naturalistic settings and referred back to works of Stefano della Bella from the mid seventeenth century but were essentially asymmetrical like those of Toro in the 1720s and reflected the current mania for shelly and watery forms anticipated in the marine context of the Galerie Dorée and in the engraved work of Oppenord – had an important effect on the design of panelling at the hands of Pineau who, accordingly, was the principal butt of the mid-century anti-Rococo critics' attacks. After a period in Russia Pineau was active in Paris from the early 1730s where his first works were in the context of the essentially linear, surface ornament of the *Régence*. However his style developed under the direct impact of the fourth-decade engravers. He introduced individually asymmetrical elements which were not necessarily balanced by their mirror images in neighbouring panels, as they had generally been hitherto, and he showed a marked preference for fantastic motifs such as serpentine dragons and rich shell work, resorting less and less to the superimposed grotesque motifs popular with the masters of the previous decades. Ultimately he avoided straight lines whenever possible and relied solely on the asymmetrical play of curved frame mouldings meeting in, or focussed upon, highly plastic *rocaille* cartouches.

193

Academic critics had tolerated the Rococo – indeed welcomed it for private rooms – until they saw the 'genre pittoresque' threatening the fundamental principles of Classical art.[39] For the Parisian *hôtel*, both inside and out, far from representing a relaxation of academic discipline, was one of its most characteristic expressions. It was designed to satisfy the standards of comfort and convenience now demanded in private life. Advances in planning were certainly accompanied by the development of the Rococo style of ornament originally invented to make living spaces more agreeable. Stressing the importance of *convenance* in distribution and discounting the value of symmetry in plans – beyond centralization about the major rooms – academic theorists like J. F. Blondel in the middle of the eighteenth century remained proud of the improvement of

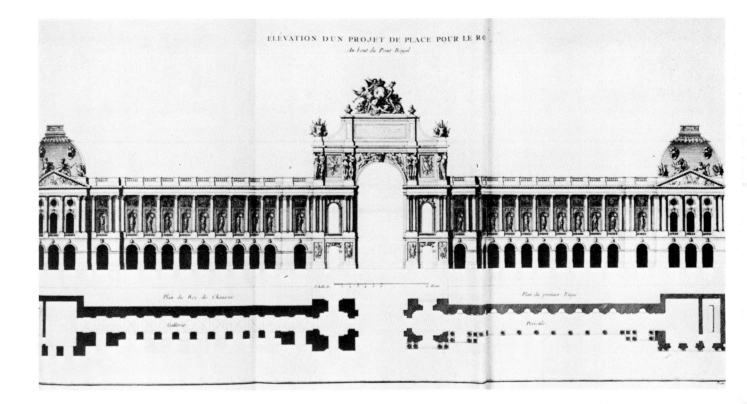

planning because it was regulated, but they came to despise the development of ornament because it was unprincipled and for one to equate the changes in these two fields, to talk of 'Rococo planning', would be misguided. In any case the most important features of the plans of both town and country houses in eighteenth-century France – the convenient arrangement of apartments and the projection of living rooms into the gardens – were the legacies of Le Vau and special features – such as dining rooms, corridors for servants – had been the concern of Jules Hardouin Mansart. Nor was there anything specifically Rococo about the virtuoso planning ability needed by most Parisian architects to satisfy these requirements on irregular sites: that need was dictated by an unflagging will to uphold academic principles and ensure the symmetry of individual rooms, mask oblique junctions, preserve unimpeded the unifying *enfilades* through and across the building – and, as early as 1657, Le Pautre had shown the way. Even a plan as extraordinarily Baroque as Boffrand's Hôtel Amelot conformed to these principles. And the principle of *convenance* which distinguished private from public rooms, dictating where they should be placed, also regulated the *ordonnance* of façades: the Orders were appropriate only for royal or public buildings, private houses should be simple, unostentatious, but conform to the spirit of the appropriate Order in decorative details and proportions. When, as the eighteenth century advanced, Rococo ornament began, tentatively, to spread from the interior to the exterior of buildings it was time to call a halt. For licence permissible in private would certainly corrupt if displayed in public and it was precisely in that type of building upon which it was not appropriate to use the Orders that the danger was at its greatest.

The office of the Bâtiments du Roi had never indulged in the extravagance of the 'genre pittoresque', even when producing for a child king. Ange-Jacques Gabriel went on providing ravishing Rococo designs throughout his career as Premier Architecte, when it was necessary to match existing work, but before the middle of the century the first sign of reaction against the Rococo approach to interior decoration appeared in one of his earliest unconstrained works, the Salon of the Pavillon

199

197

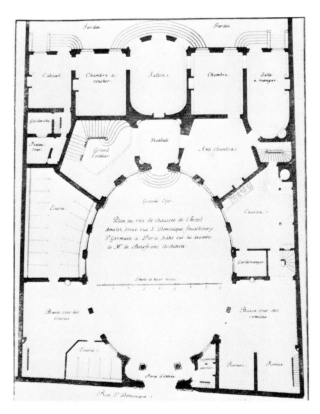

197 *Opposite* Versailles, Cabinet de Musique de Madame Adelaïde by Ange-Jacques Gabriel, executed 1752–53, modified 1767

198 *Top* Claude Aubry, engraving of a project for the Place Louis XV, Paris, 1748

199 *Above* Paris, plan of the Hôtel Amelot de Gournay by Boffrand, 1712

Français in the garden of the Trianon, which was given a full Order.[40]

Gabriel had inherited an unbroken tradition of monumental architecture from his predecessors – his father Jacques V, Robert de Cotte and Jules Hardouin Mansart. Despite the lack of opportunities for great works in the period from the decline of Louis XIV to the maturity of Louis XV, the vitality of that tradition was well illustrated by the enthusiastic response to the competition for a Place Louis XV for Paris in 1748. The entries were mostly modelled on the projects of the French architects of Louis XIV but Boffrand referred to Bernini's first project for the Louvre as he had done nearly half a century earlier for the duc de Lorraine's palace at Nancy. The king ordered Gabriel to draw upon all that was best in the entries and his executed project, while demonstrably satisfying the king's requirements, is a commentary on the Colonnade of the Louvre, more Classical in rejecting the coupled columns yet still Baroque in the scale of the Order and the vigour of the contrast between mass and void. And in the scope of the conception, preserving the vista from the Tuileries to the Champs Elysées on the east-west axis and disposing the twin buildings on either side of a street extending the north-south axis from the river to the climax of

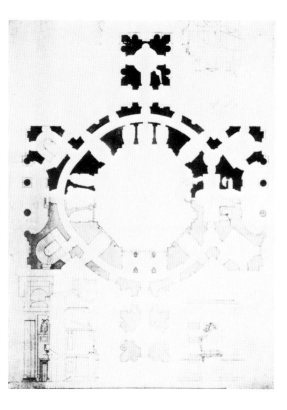

the whole civic scheme in the church of the Madeleine, it was hardly inferior to any of the great Baroque schemes of seventeenth-century Rome.

Elsewhere, when the occasion required, Gabriel did not abstain from specifically Baroque motifs – such as the academically 'incorrect' Order of colossal half-columns which he borrowed from Bernini's third project for the Louvre for the 1759 *grand projet* for Versailles – but the basic attitude of his contemporaries in the Royal Academy of Architecture is better illustrated by his revision in 1754 of a project by the Danish architect Eigtwedt for a great church commissioned by Frederick V for Copenhagen. In two projects, the first keeping to the executed foundations, Gabriel went back to Eigtwedt's principal source, Juvarra's Superga, and then further back to Juvarra's own principal source, S. Agnese. In his second project he

gave the façade a great concave recession, as at S. Agnesè, only to annihilate the movement latent in the device by clamping the great temple front of Juvarra's Superga across it. For both projects he clearly recalled the dome of the Superga but with reference back to St Peter's he reversed the essentially Baroque process by which the mass and weight of cupolas had been progressively reduced with the heightening and lightening of the drum. Eigtwedt had taken this to an extreme and Gabriel not only revised the relative heights of dome and drum but enlarged the piers between the openings in the latter into blind bays to give more weight. In his first project he recessed the entablature above the windows like Juvarra, associating the Order with the blind bays. In the second project, on the contrary, the Order *in antis* belongs to the window bays, and the plane of the great piers is now the most forward one of the drum. The motif of columns *in antis* here may come from Cortona's dome of S. Carlo al Corso but it also appears in Rainaldi's towers at S. Agnese – which both Juvarra and Gabriel recalled. There is a piquancy about this precise quotation from S. Agnese because Gabriel's project is clearly a correction of the approach to design expounded in such works as S. Agnese by High Baroque architects – the influence of whom was considered so dangerous by the theorists of academic French Classicism.

200 *Above left* A. J. Gabriel, drawing of the second project for the Frederikskirke, Copenhagen, elevation and section. *Copenhagen, Royal Archives*

201 *Above* A. J. Gabriel, plan for the second project for the Frederikskirke, Copenhagen. *Copenhagen, Royal Archives*

Part III

Flanders, England and Holland

Flanders

In the first half of the sixteenth century, owing to a series of dynastic marriages and inheritances, the Low Countries, which correspond to modern Belgium and Holland, became part of the vast empire of Charles V. When he abdicated in 1555 he handed them over to his son Philip II to whom he also gave the kingdom of Spain, and from that time onwards they were governed from Madrid. The Reformation had made great progress in the Low Countries and several of the most important cities, including Antwerp, the greatest port of northern Europe, became largely converted to the new faith. Philip was determined to destroy the heresy and sent the duke of Alba to exterminate or convert its adherents. After years of civil war the northern provinces of Holland and Zeeland seceded and established a separate predominantly Protestant state, under the rule of William of Orange, which was eventually recognized by Spain at the treaty of Münster in 1648. Antwerp had meanwhile been reconverted to Catholicism and remained under Spanish rule, but the northern states held the mouth of the Scheldt and were thus able to block its access to the sea, with disastrous effects on its trade. It remained however the richest city of the southern or Spanish Netherlands and a great centre for intellectual and religious activities.

The ideas of Italian Renaissance architects penetrated into the Netherlands in much the same way as in other countries north of the Alps, that is to say, by the spread of Italianate decorative motifs which were applied to buildings in the Gothic style; but there was one exception to the rule: the palace erected in Brussels about 1550, probably by Sebastian van Noyen (c. 1493–1557), for the great statesman Antoine Perrenot, Bishop of Arras, later known as Cardinal Granvelle, who had spent many years in Rome. The palace, which is an adaptation of Antonio da Sangallo's two lower storeys of the court in the Palazzo Farnese, with the half-columns replaced by pilasters, is one of the few works built north of the Alps which show a real understanding of the principles of Roman High Renaissance architecture.[1]

By comparison the Town Hall at Antwerp, executed and probably designed by Cornelis Floris (1514–75), though it is one of the most impressive sixteenth-century Flemish buildings, looks provincial. It is articulated with the correct Orders – though not very correctly designed – but they are applied to a façade which rises in the middle to a tall gable, almost like a truncated belfry. Floris' influence, however, was mainly as a

decorator, and he evolved a type of grotesques – partly derived from Italy and partly based on the interpretation given to the genre by the artists of the School of Fontainebleau – which spread over the whole of northern Europe, including Holland, England, North Germany, and Scandinavia. Half a generation later the style was amplified by Hans Vredeman de Vries (1527-after 1604), whose architectural and decorative engravings were also widely studied.

During the religious struggles of the later sixteenth century building naturally fell into abeyance, but under the Regency of the Archduke Albert of Austria and his wife Isabella, daughter of Philip II of Spain, and particularly during the Twelve Year Truce (1609–21), a revival took place in the economy of the country which allowed a sudden flowering in intellectual, religious, and artistic fields. This flowering was led by the Jesuits, who were active in all these areas. Their enthusiastic combating of heresy was accompanied by the creation of a system of education far superior to any that existed in Flanders at the time, and they were responsible for a high percentage of the most important buildings put up during the seventeenth century.

The greatest individual exponent of this movement was Rubens, but in architecture a number of figures appeared who combined elements of early seventeenth-century Italian styles – not always very fully digested – with features, particularly in planning, which were still derived from mediaeval traditions, which survived so late in Flanders that the choir of St Jacques at Antwerp was finished in 1656 in the Gothic style and immediately furnished with choir-stalls and pulpit which were fully Baroque.

The first Flemish architect to import new ideas from Italy was Wensel Cobergher (c. 1560–1634), originally trained as a painter, who spent some twenty-four years in Naples and Rome, returning in 1604 to Antwerp, which was the great centre not only of commerce, but also of artistic activity in Flanders. His church of the Carmelites in Brussels (1607) is a competent version of contemporary Roman models, but when he attempted to use more complicated plans, as at Notre-Dame de Montaigu (1604) which is built on a heptagonal plan to symbolize the Seven Sorrows of the Virgin, it was clear that he could not work out a harmonious solution to the geometrical problems involved. His church of the Augustinians at Antwerp (finished in 1618) is important as an early example in Flanders of a nave-arcade supported by Tuscan columns, a form which was often to be repeated by later architects.

Like Cobergher his brother-in-law, Jacob Francart

(1583–1651), was trained in Italy as a painter and returned to Flanders in about 1608. Here he soon devoted his attention to architecture. In 1616 he published a short treatise, the *Premier Livre d'Architecture,* dedicated to the archduke, whose service he had entered. It contains a series of engravings mainly of architectural details, such as windows and doors, with a curious mixture of Italian and local features, which were to exercise considerable influence on later architecture in Flanders.

In his earliest church, built for the Jesuits in Brussels (1616–21), he follows Cobergher's scheme in the interior, though with taller arches and lunette windows, but both here and in the later church of the Béguinage at Malines he makes an innovation in the design of the façade by dividing the lower storey into five bays – three of which are continued into the second storey – and then adding an attic, which creates an effect of height quite foreign to Roman church façades of the period. This pattern was followed, with the omission of the extra side-bays, by Guillaume Hesius (1617–90) in the Jesuit church at Louvain (1650–60), remarkable for the richness of its carved decoration, both in the interior and on the façade.

206

The most important Flemish architect of the first half of the seventeenth century was Pierre Huyssens (1577–1637). Unlike Cobergher and Francart he was not trained in Italy, though he spent two years in Rome when he was a man of fifty. One of his most ambitious churches is that of Notre-Dame (begun 1629) built for the Abbey of St Pierre at Ghent, which is unusual in having a domed Greek-cross section as a nave, followed by a long choir flanked by aisles. The arrangement brings the dome very near to the west end of the church, so that it is seen in direct relation to the façade. In order to give it adequate support visually, Huyssens designed the façade with unusually wide proportions: a five-bay lower storey and a rather low upper storey – without attic – which allows a full view of the drum and cupola.

Huyssens's most important works, however, were executed for the Jesuit Order, which he joined at the age of twenty and for which he built churches at Antwerp, Bruges, and Namur. His enthusiasm for architecture was so great that it actually got him

202 *Below left* Antwerp, façade of the Jesuit church by Huyssens and Rubens, begun 1613

203 *Above* Antwerp, Jesuit church, interior in a painting by W. von Ehrenberg. *Brussels, Musée des Beaux-Arts*

204 *Opposite* Antwerp, Rubens' house, courtyard and loggia, designed by the artist

into trouble with his superiors, who ordered him to be transferred to a house where no building was taking place, presumably so that he might devote himself wholly to his religious duties. In the churches at Bruges (1619) and Namur (1621) Huyssens follows the pattern set by Francart at the Béguinage at Malines, except that in the former the façade is much lower and almost conforms to Roman models in its proportions. The interior of St Loup at Namur is unusually rich in the treatment of the surface; the columns are banded, the arches are interrupted by raised voussoirs, and the barrel-vault – itself a novelty in Flanders – is covered with cartouches and acanthus decoration carved in relief on the stone.

In spite of the fact that it was gutted by fire in 1737, the Jesuit church at Antwerp stands apart as the most splendid of all seventeenth-century churches in Flanders, partly in the richness of its materials and decoration, but also in the originality of its design. In plan it is a simple basilica, with apses at the ends of the nave and aisles, but in elevation it is unique among Flemish churches of the period in having two superimposed arcades of equal size, the upper of which covers a gallery. As in many Jesuit churches, these galleries were to accommodate students attending the college, and somewhat similar solutions to this problem are to be found in many West and South German Jesuit churches of the sixteenth century, though none of them has the elegance and lightness of the Antwerp church.

203

The façade is unusual in its rich, carved decoration and its broad proportions. The general disposition with five bays, three wide and two narrow, on the lower storey is not unlike Francart's Béguinage church, but the storeys are kept lower, and the width of the whole is increased by the addition of two squat towers, set slightly back from the façade itself. The basic plan of the façade is related to that of Maderno's S. Susanna in that it breaks forward in three steps towards the centre, but the

202

6

effect is made more complex – and perhaps less clear – than in the Roman church by the fact that the architect breaks the entablature over each column or pilaster and does not follow Maderno's method of increasing the plasticity of the Order from pilasters to half-columns and columns as he approaches the centre. The corners of the main façade are treated in an unusual manner, with a full column coupled with a pilaster. The combination of columns and pilasters has some parallels in Italian sixteenth-century buildings, such as Antonio da Sangallo the Elder's church of S. Biagio at Montepulciano, but there the arrangement is reversed and the pilaster comes – probably more logically – at the corner, outside the column.

The exact share of Huyssens in the designing and building of the Jesuit church at Antwerp is difficult to determine. The church was actually begun in 1613, but before that date a number of projects had been submitted, some of a rather fanciful type, but these had been rejected. The moving spirit in the whole scheme was Father François Aguilon, then rector of the college, who had an enthusiastic interest in architecture and may have contributed to the working-out of the plan, but the name of Huyssens appears in the document of the college with the title *architectus* and there can be little doubt that he was in charge of the buildings. It must be remembered, however, that Rubens, who was a close friend of the Jesuits, was responsible for the paintings which decorated the church – of which all but three altarpieces were destroyed in the fire of 1737 – and is known to have played a part in the designing of certain architectural features.

Rubens spent the years 1600 to 1608 in Italy and was in Rome for the first two and most of the last three years of this period, which overlapped the visits of Cobergher and Francart. He would therefore have seen much the same monuments as his two compatriots, but he was – as would be expected – far more sensitive to what he saw and interpreted it in a much more imaginative way.

Rubens was not a practising architect and the only occasion when he directed an actual structure in brick and stone was when he added a wing and a loggia to his own house, which still stands in Antwerp, heavily restored but recorded in seventeenth-century engravings. On the other hand it is clear from the buildings which appear in his paintings that he was much interested in architecture, and his designs for the title-pages of books and, above all, for the temporary structures put up in 1635 for the entry of the Archduke Albert and the Archduchess-Infanta Isabella into Antwerp (engraved in the volume called *Pompa Introitus*) give evidence of real originality.

While Rubens was in Italy he devoted much time to studying ancient Roman statues – and making drawings of them – and it is safe to assume that he looked attentively at the remains of ancient buildings. There is apparently only one case in which he introduced an identifiable monument into one of his paintings – the circular building in the background of the sketch for the S. Ildefonso altarpiece in the Hermitage is taken from the so-called Carceri near Capua – but he often drew on sixteenth-century authorities, such as Serlio and Montano, for the ancient monuments which he included in the settings of his paintings. He also frequently used Salomonic columns, which he saw in St Peter's many years before Bernini employed them in the baldacchino.

He studied the works and designs of sixteenth-century architects. A plate in Serlio supplied him with the design for the loggia in his garden, and the heavily rusticated columns in

many of his paintings probably go back to the same source, though Rubens could have seen actual examples of the device in the works of Giulio Romano in Mantua and elsewhere. Sometimes he used buildings which were being worked on while he was in Rome, such as Maderno's aisles to St Peter's, the unusual arches of which occur in one of his sketches for tapestries.

The most remarkable feature about Rubens's use of Italian architecture, however, is the degree to which he drew on Michelangelo, above all from the late Roman works. For instance, the base which Michelangelo designed for the statue of Marcus Aurelius on the Capitol reappears in the pedestal supporting the Virgin or allegorical figures in several of Rubens's compositions, and the type of door, with the upper corners cut off diagonally, which Michelangelo invented for the Porta Pia, was used by Rubens not only in many paintings, but in the gate leading to the garden of his own house. He was also clearly fascinated by Michelangelo's combination of curved and straight pediments in the Porta Pia. He took the elements apart and put them together in new combinations – with the

205 Rubens, drawing for the high altar in the Jesuit church, Antwerp. *Vienna, Albertina*

204

206 Louvain, former Jesuit church (now St Michel), top of the façade, by Hesius; 1650–60

207 Brussels, façades of houses on the Grand' Place, after 1695

curved element outside the straight, sometimes adding volutes at each end of it. In an unexecuted design for the high altar of the Jesuit church he not only used Salomonic columns and a broken pediment, but the curved elements of the pediment form S-curves, a device hinted at in the attic windows of the Porta Pia but not generally used till it was popularized by Andrea Pozzo in the late seventeenth century. In fact Rubens did to Michelangelo what no Italian architect did before Borromini: he absorbed the most revolutionary features of his late works and transformed them into something new and highly personal.

In the works referred to above Rubens was moving towards a personal syle which could be called Baroque *avant la lettre*, but in some of the designs for the title pages he was even bolder and introduced curved forms which are in advance of anything being produced in Italy at the time.

Unfortunately his example was not followed and, generally speaking, Flemish architecture of the second half of the seventeenth century is of little interest. The most distinguished building was Hesius' Jesuit church at Louvain, of which the façade has already been mentioned, but of which the interior is also impressive for its lofty proportions – due to the insertion of an attic over the entablature – and for the high quality of its carved stone decoration. Hesius' rival, Luc Fayd'herbe (1617–97), was essentially a sculptor, and his Thurn and Taxis Chapel in Notre-Dame-du-Sablon in Brussels is notable for both its figure sculpture and its decorative detail, but his two excursions into real architecture – the priory church of Liliendael and Notre-Dame d'Hanswyck, both at Malines – were clumsy in design and so unstable in structure that another architect had to be called in to save them from collapsing.

The strangest phenomenon was the rebuilding of the Grand' Place at Brussels after its destruction in the bombardment by the French in 1695. The Guild Houses, which filled three sides of it – the fourth being occupied by the Late Gothic Town Hall – were such symbols of the city's status that they were rebuilt in

forms which were basically those of the original sixteenth-century houses, with the addition of certain details of figure-sculpture and ornament in a more up-to-date style. This strange manifestation of conscious conservatism, even of archaism, was the swan-song of Flemish Baroque architecture.

But is Baroque the right word? In the case of Rubens, as has been said above, there are many features of his architectural designs which reveal him as a forerunner of the Baroque, but in a sense it could be said that he was never really put to the test, because he never designed and executed a complete building. His contemporaries did, and if their works are examined on the basis of a comparison with contemporary buildings in Rome, it is difficult to escape the conclusion that they will be found wanting. These architects showed no feeling for spatial invention and were only at home with traditional late-mediaeval plans; when they experimented with more complex forms, the results were disastrous. They showed some skill in handling the Roman Baroque form of church façade and created a local variant with an extra storey in the middle section, and they enlivened the surface of these façades with vigorous – if somewhat coarse – sculpture; but it cannot be said that they made any real contribution to the main development of Baroque architecture.

England

The Baroque style is primarily identified with absolute monarchy in politics and with Roman Catholicism in religion. England was solidly Protestant throughout the period, and the Catholic faith of Charles I's and Charles II's queens and of James II was entirely local in effect. Moreover, during the seventeenth century the English monarchy changed from absolute authority by Divine Right to power maintained by the will of Parliament and an unwritten constitution. The social climate was thus very different from that of those areas – especially papal Rome – on which the definition of the style is based. Other factors were temperament – the English distaste for extremes – and the English Channel, which has always provided both a measure of insulation from European ideas and a means of seeing clearly and selectively what the Continent has to offer. The English Baroque was, like the English Renaissance before it, an amalgam of ideas adapted from Italy, France and the Netherlands to the conditions, beliefs and tastes of English society.[1]

Both political and artistic ideals changed rapidly during the period, which may be divided into three phases. The first began with the Restoration of Charles II to the throne in 1660 after Cromwell's short-lived republic and ended with the Glorious (and bloodless) Revolution of 1688 in which James II was succeeded by his nephew and son-in-law, William III, and his daughter Mary, as joint constitutional monarchs responsible to Parliament and people. Subsequently artistic initiative passed from the monarch to noblemen and *nouveau riche* commoners, and in the decades either side of 1700 a number of great Baroque houses were built for prominent Whigs, members of the party which accomplished the Revolution of 1688 and secured the succession not of James II's Catholic son but of the Protestant Queen Anne (1702) and George I (1714).[2] These two phases overlapped with a third, which comprised the mature and late work of Sir Christopher Wren between *c.* 1680 and *c.* 1710.

While some seventeenth-century patrons and architects had personal knowledge of European architecture, travel was not essential for the absorption of current ideas. Of the principal English Baroque architects only Thomas Archer (*c.* 1668–1743) visited Italy; James Gibbs (1682–1754) reached London in 1709 by way of Carlo Fontana's studio and soon recognized that Baroque was not the school of the morrow;[3] Wren (1632–1723) only reached the Ile-de-France; Hugh May (1622–84) visited Holland and probably France; Sir John Vanbrugh (1664–1726) stayed in the latter country mainly as a political prisoner; Nicholas Hawksmoor (1661–1736) did not travel, and his extensive knowledge of recent and ancient building was derived entirely from books and engravings. Indeed by making available to architects disposed to use them a wide range of visual sources, developments in reproductive engraving were the biggest single factor in the establishment of the English Baroque style.

It was only necessary for English architects and patrons to be open to influence from abroad, and this disposition is more evident by contrast with the situation after about 1715, the year of Colen Campbell's neo-Palladian manifesto in the first volume of *Vitruvius Britannicus, or the British Architect;*[4] while the plates of his elegant publication represented a mixture of current styles, his title alluded to, and his introduction emphasized the veneration due to the work of the first English Palladian, Inigo Jones, in contrast to the excesses of Bernini, Borromini and Fontana. In his *Letter Concerning Design* circulated in manuscript about 1712,[5] the 3rd earl of Shaftesbury had predicted the emergence of a new national style, without defining it except negatively as anti-French, anti-Wren and anti-Baroque. Politically the reaction from contemporary Europe received impetus from the union of England and Scotland in 1707 and from growing disenchantment soon afterwards with British involvement under Marlborough in the European war. *Vitruvius Britannicus* showed positively a direction and a range of visual references for the national style, and made of the English Baroque period an interlude between the era of Jones and that of his revival.

When Jones visited Rome in 1614 he annotated the accounts of ancient buildings in his copy of Palladio's *Quattro Libri dell' Architettura,* and his taste in both painting and architecture stopped short of late Mannerism and the art of the Carracci and Maderno. As architect and artistic adviser to Charles I from 1625 he found much in common with that monarch's taste for Renaissance art.[6] The Whitehall Banqueting House, his first mature work (1619–22), owes more to Palladio and indeed to a building like Peruzzi's Farnesina of the early sixteenth century than to contemporary architecture, much as both the art collections and the cultural ideals of Charles's court were modelled on those of High Renaissance princes. In the 1630s

208 Greenwich Hospital, seen from the river terrace, by Wren, begun 1698. The blocks nearer the river were designed by Webb, 1663–69

Jones's colossal portico at the west end of old St Paul's Cathedral looked back directly and uncompromisingly to ancient models (especially the Temple of Venus and Rome) and not at all to Carlo Maderno's new façade of St Peter's which he must have noticed while in Rome. His project of c. 1638 for a new Whitehall Palace, and later ones by his pupil John Webb (1611–72), are based on the additive repetition of small units which would have been tedious and lacking in monumentality.[7] The apparent simplicity of his buildings conceals a complexity largely metaphysical and conceptual, concerned with numerical harmonies and symbolisms. There was, however, another side to Jones's artistic activity: in stage design he used machinery as well as painting and lighting to produce illusions and transformations, and in comparison with other Baroque designers he was limited only by the smallness of English court stages.[8]

Thus in 1642, when the outbreak of the Civil War interrupted normal court life, the most modern architecture in the country was stylistically about a century behind central and northern Italy. By 1649 Webb conceived an unexecuted design for Durham House in the Strand in terms of greater mass, larger unit scale and the use of a giant Order. He first put them into execution about 1654 in adding a giant portico to The Vyne (Hampshire), where the order is a kind of primitive Corinthian (without cauls) which reflects his and Jones's concern with Vitruvius and the origins of architecture. Shortly after the Restoration Webb was summoned from retirement to design a new palace for Charles II at Greenwich, and in the only range built he used his new formal language to greater effect. As the only English architect of his time who was both talented and professionally trained, he produced a design of distinction, grandeur and meticulous finish. Although the vocabulary of detail is derived from Palladio, both the scale and the overall effect of the elevation relate unmistakeably to designs and influences nearer Webb's own time. The use of a giant Order in the centre and end sections with astylar intermediate sections devoid of continuous verticals, makes a façade which is read in five larger units rather than in twenty-three bays. There is no visible basement, the bases of the Order being at ground level; this emphasizes the massiveness of the building, a feeling which is reinforced by the large attics over the end sections. (In fact these are too emphatic, being intended to be seen in relation both to an identical range across the court and to the central range which was to be surmounted by a larger attic with a central dome.)

In exile Charles II had seen, in Paris and The Hague, contemporary architecture and decoration on a grand scale, including the Huis ten Bosch and recent work in the Louvre. His own taste in the arts was broader and more worldly than his father's, and his expenditure, especially on architecture, was considerable in spite of chronic financial difficulties. Had he been richer, his court would have come closer in atmosphere and achievement, if not to that of the Baroque popes, at least to those of his cousins Louis XIV and the Medici grand dukes of Tuscany. While his first Surveyor was Sir John Denham, artistically a nonentity, the cynicism of this appointment from expediency is moderated by his employment of both Webb and Hugh May, and by his early recognition of the talents of Sir Christopher Wren.[9] Greenwich was abandoned about 1669 in a general retrenchment in the years after the Great Fire of London, and Charles seems then also to have given up hope of a new Palace of Whitehall, for which one of Webb's later drawings is dated 1661. The extent of the king's personal concern

208

with Whitehall is shown by the incident in 1664 when he drew a plan of the proposed palace for the diarist John Evelyn; Wren appears to have been involved in that scheme,[10] although he held no official position in the King's Works until 1669 when he succeeded Denham over the heads of Webb and May, and though he carried out no large-scale secular works until the

209 Windsor Castle, St George's Hall by May, 1682–84, decorated by Antonio Verrio (destroyed)

1680s. Moreover in 1673 Charles appointed May, already since 1668 comptroller and thus second in command of the works, to the separate post of surveyor at Windsor Castle, where over a decade he created a Baroque palace of striking interior richness, illusionism and, in some parts, formal ingenuity.

In the absence of drawings and personal records Hugh May remains a mysterious though not an indistinct character.[11] He learned painting from Sir Peter Lely as well as acquiring elsewhere an exact knowledge of architectural design and practice. As servant to the 2nd duke of Buckingham before the Restoration he visited Holland more than once, and in the early 1660s with the design of Eltham Lodge, Woolwich, he introduced to England a kind of domestic Classicism which is specifically Dutch in its application of a giant pilaster frontispiece of stone or stucco to a brick elevation, and more loosely and indirectly indebted to Palladian models. Significantly, whereas in his Dutch prototypes such as the Mauritshuis, the Order stands on a basement half-storey, in May's houses the bases are at ground level as in Webb's Greenwich building. At Eltham also May experimented on a small scale with the spatial possibilities of the staircase. At the second landing it divides into two flights; one leads directly to the main upper floor while the other leads to a large half-landing from which small flights ascend to the main level.

210A

May's most important work was at Windsor Castle, where he remodelled the upper ward and built new ranges of state rooms for the king and queen, each approached by its own staircase;

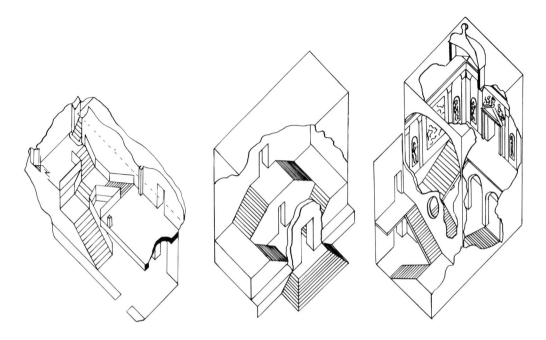

210 A Eltham Lodge, staircase by May, 1663–64
    B Windsor Castle, King's Staircase, by May, 1675–79 (destroyed)
    C Windsor Castle, Queen's Staircase, by May, 1675–79 (destroyed)

most of this work disappeared in the making of the present state apartments. His treatment of the exteriors involved the insertion of deep round-headed windows which emphasized the massiveness of the walls, provided a pattern of darkly shadowed recesses, and gave the castle a neo-Norman air that was appreciated in the next generation by Vanbrugh and Hawksmoor. In the state rooms he supervised a team of artists and craftsmen including the decorative painter Antonio Verrio and the carver Grinling Gibbons. The illusionism of Windsor, in which ceiling after ceiling opened into a painted sky, was closer to Italian models, which May is unlikely to have seen, than to French ones. The two biggest and grandest rooms, in which walls as well as ceiling were painted in *trompe-l'oeil,* were the Chapel and St George's Hall. The whole decoration of the Hall was based on the Order of the Garter, and the dominant colours were the silver, blue and crimson of the Garter costume. In the Chapel carving was added to painting, and an illusionist tableau of the Last Supper in a fictive niche was painted behind the altar.[12]

The King's Staircase, which consisted of symmetrical diverging lower flights with converging ones above, suggests that May knew of the staircases of Le Vau, such as the Escalier des Ambassadeurs at Versailles (begun 1671) or that in an unexecuted design for the Louvre (1667). The Queen's Staircase was more complex: three consecutive flights rose around a square cage articulated by a fictive architecture of pilasters with statues in niches and bas reliefs. In the wall above the middle flight a window looked into a further staircase, also painted in *trompe-l'oeil.* The compound of real and illusionist spaces in the main staircase was top-lit by a wooden lantern resting on pendentives. Both staircases were destroyed before 1800 and their spatial effect, the loss of which is the most regrettable in all May's work, can only be imagined from plans and descriptions.

The great stair built by Wren at the south end of the Whitehall Banqueting House in 1686 and destroyed by fire in 1698 was an unpainted version of the Queen's Staircase; it provided for the only time in its history a worthy entry to Jones's great room.

Wren's only comparable work in the fusion of painting, sculpture and architecture was designed after May's death: the Catholic chapel built at Whitehall for James II in 1685–86 and also destroyed in 1698. Evelyn's famous diary entry in December 1686 describes the painting of Verrio, the carving of Gibbons and Quellin in the great marble altar screen, the rich vestments and the Italian music with an equal mixture of artistic enthusiasm and religious outrage. Wren was not by nature a decorator, and considered architecture a sterner, more abstracted and less transitory affair. Neither his sympathy with European Baroque nor its influence on him was constant, although, as his style passed from the equivalent of the early Renaissance to that of his contemporary Carlo Fontana, his later work in general is more justifiably identified as Baroque.

Until his thirtieth year Sir Christopher Wren's career was that of a post-Baconian sceptical scientist especially interested in geometry and astronomy.[13] Yet from childhood he drew and made models, and the wide interests of his father, who had been dean of Windsor, included building if not architecture. When in an unsuccessful attempt to engage him in the fortification of Tangier in 1661 Charles II offered Wren the reversion of the surveyorship, the king was perhaps aware of the young geometrician's true potentialities. By 1665, with university buildings to his credit and the future of St Paul's on his mind, Wren was involved enough in architecture to spend some months in France; with introductions to François Mansart and Bernini, the experiencing of modern architecture at first hand was probably the primary purpose of his visit. The destruction of London in the Great Fire a few months after his return gave him unique opportunities and the surveyorship in 1669 sealed his career. Through the work of the next four decades and his fragmentary writings run the threads of a belief in the rational beauty of mathematical absolutes and an equal concern for the visual effect of architecture.[14] This duality is part of the general

England 151

seventeenth-century dilemma between Classical and Baroque, but in Wren the varying balance produced on occasion works in which the solid geometry of architecture is especially apparent.

212   The exterior of St Paul's (begun 1675) is visually striking as well as intellectually powerful, but not emotionally exciting: Wren distrusted 'Fancy' or imagination, which 'blinds the Judgement'. His use of relief, of the giant Order, of illusion, and in his later years of plasticity of modelling, show a familiarity with European architecture and at times a sympathy beyond the limits of his first-hand knowledge. St Paul's is modelled, grooved, textured and enlivened with naturalistic carving in a manner that is French rather than Baroque. In the transept ends, however, in about 1680, Wren's favourite device of a decorative frieze at the level of the capitals is continued without a break into pilasters enriched with similar relief, so that individual parts of the elevation and distinctions between them are blurred and the eye is encouraged to read the whole unit as

215 indivisible. In the towers (after 1704), as in some of the later steeples of his post-Fire churches (especially St Vedast, 1694–97), the Borrominesque play of concave and convex is the more remarkable in that his sources were confined to engravings. Characteristically, however, some apparent curves in the western towers are composed of short straight lines, and the design was evolved deliberately as a foil to the dome. Wren often cheated the eye: at Hampton Court (begun 1689), as earlier in his most Classical building, Trinity College Library, Cambridge (1676–84), internal convenience required the principal floor inside to be lower than the apparent external storey-division, and in both buildings the difference is concealed behind the filled-in tympana of the cloister arches. St Paul's has

214 an outer dome of leaded timber tall enough to ride over the whole City, and a considerably lower inner one of masonry concordant with the dimensions of the crossing; a hidden intermediate brickwork cone supports the lantern. By raising the aisle walls through two storeys Wren screened both the basilican clerestory and his buttressing system; the screen walls, which contain niches instead of windows, make a visual mass adequate for the dome above them, and also disguise the relation in scale between exterior and interior. Characteristically again the screens contribute structurally to the abutment of the dome. By adding projecting chapels at the west end and making a corresponding extra large western bay within, Wren managed to combine the long Latin-cross nave of his brief with the impression of a nave and choir each of three bays and thus of a symmetrical, though longitudinal, building with a central domed space.[15]

Wren's constant aesthetic problem was to reconcile the absolute scale of parts to whole in a building with the relative scale of man. The Great Model for St Paul's (1673–74) was rejected on religious grounds, as too far in plan from the mediaeval tradition of Latin-cross cathedrals, too close in design to St Peter's in Rome and such intermediate designs as Mansart's project for a Bourbon mausoleum (which Wren may have seen in Paris), and also on practical grounds because a structure consisting mainly of a dome could not be completed in instalments. The High Renaissance purity of the Great Model is on a Baroque scale: the first horizontal moulding would have been above eye level and the second one over twelve feet from the street. In the 1680s, at Chelsea Hospital and the unfinished palace at Winchester, Wren failed to integrate the domestic scale of the fenestration with the giant-Order frontispieces called for by the size of the layout. At Hampton Court, where

he settled for two adjacent wings giving the illusion of a palace approaching Versailles in extent, he was finally able to assimilate the language of Bernini's last design for the Louvre which he had seen and 'would have given my skin for' in 1665. But formal invention was limited by William and Mary's desire for an economical and speedy English Versailles, and Hampton Court depends largely, like its prototype, on area and decoration to convey the greatness of monarchy. In the Fountain Court the upper windows are framed by the lion-skins of 211 Hercules, with whom William III identified himself more consistently than did his French cousin; although he was the first constitutional king of England William understood and accepted the function of monarchy and the rôle of the arts in its support.

In 1698 Whitehall Palace burned down leaving little besides Jones's Banqueting House. Wren produced on paper schemes in which the giant Order is used so liberally that the scale of Jones's building is sacrificed to it, and the many varied blocks are interesting both individually and in their interrelation.[16] In the sailors' hospital at Greenwich (founded by William and Mary in 1694 to outshine Charles II's Chelsea for soldiers) Wren was obliged to incorporate another building by Jones, the Queen's House, as well as Webb's unfinished palace. In thus designing a building without a middle he nevertheless succeeded in a combination of scales, a variety of masses and, in the Painted Hall decorated by Sir James Thornhill (1708–12), the 216 finest successor to May's Windsor interiors. In the side courts there is much firmer evidence for the free participation of Hawksmoor, Wren's assistant, than in the towers of St Paul's or the designs for Whitehall or Hampton Court.

Thornhill's ceiling honours not the monarch but Britannia, and at the Revolution of 1688 the artistic prerogatives of monarchy were already passing with the political prerogatives of power to the Whig nobility. In 1687 the 4th earl (1st duke) of Devonshire began to rebuild Chatsworth. His architect was William Talman (1650–1719), who had probably been a pupil

211 Hampton Court Palace, the Fountain Court, by Wren, 1689–92

was overtaken as a result of changes both in the politics and in the economy of England; the vogue for ceiling painting had temporarily displaced plasterwork in great houses, while the architectural innovations of Chatsworth were widely appreciated and adapted.

The three most important successors to Chatsworth were Hawksmoor's Easton Neston (Northamptonshire), Vanbrugh's and Hawksmoor's Castle Howard (Yorkshire), and Archer's Heythrop. The last of these (begun *c.* 1706) was built for the duke of Shrewsbury, who had lived in Rome; only the exterior of the main block survives. Archer crowned the Italianate silhouette and giant Order with an entablature of Bernin-

218

212 *Left* London, St Paul's Cathedral by Wren, from the south-east, 1675–1710

213 *Below* St Paul's, detail of the Phoenix at the south transept end by Caius Gabriel Cibber, 1699. The Phoenix symbolizes rebuilding after the Great Fire of 1666

214 *Bottom* St Paul's, section and plan

215 *Opposite* St Paul's, the north-west tower

of May and who, like Webb at Greenwich, divided his elevation into masses rather than separate bays; the unusual even number of bays eliminates a central division.[17] In contrast to the high pitched roofs of previous great houses Chatsworth, designed two years before Hampton Court, has the silhouette of the Italian *palazzo*; it is hardly accidental that Devonshire was one of the group which invited William and Mary to the throne. In interior decoration also, although it was not the first private house to have illusionist decorative painting, Chatsworth assumed royal standards, and the chapel is a scaled-down version of May's at Windsor. As the timing of Talman's work at Thoresby is uncertain – it was burned down on completion and rebuilt – the south range of Chatsworth may be his first major work. He is not known to have travelled, but he had considerable knowledge of French and Dutch architecture, and developed an interest, inherited from May and ultimately from France, in the use of oval rooms. Talman built up a considerable country house practice in the 1690s, often using his own team of craftsmen as May and, in France, Le Vau had done. However, his arrogance gradually lost him commissions including the completion of Chatsworth. By 1700 the court style which early in the century had led the country at some distance

224

219

216 *Top* Greenwich Hospital, the Painted Hall by Wren, begun 1698, decorated by Thornhill, 1708–12

217 *Above* Kimbolton Castle by Vanbrugh, 1708–10, the east front, portico by Alessandro Galilei, 1719

esque proportions, while much of the detail was derived from Roman Baroque originals, through the first volume of Rossi's *Studio d'Architettura Civile* (1702–21) rather than directly.[18] Nevertheless Archer's literal use of contemporary sources was exceptional, and in the garden pavilion at Wrest Park he provides a text-book example of a building whose appearance changes from different angles. Its plan is a circle within a hexagon, and alternate faces present a concave and convex aspect. In his two London churches, St Paul, Deptford (1712–30) and St John, Smith Square (1713–29, twice burnt out but restored in 1968 to its original appearance) he used full columns to dramatize his interiors. The exteriors again show a geometrical sympathy with architects such as Fischer von Erlach, although the vocabulary of detail derives mainly from Wren and Vanbrugh (for example cannon balls on the exterior of St John). Archer also carried out, and modified, a design for the south front of Wentworth Castle made by the Huguenot Jean Bodt.[19] Bodt, who worked mainly in Berlin, was one of several foreign architects who visited England in the late-seventeenth or early-eighteenth century, including Daniel Marot, who made designs for William and Mary.[20] Fischer von Erlach, who intended to come in 1704–5, and Juvarra, who

came in 1720, were perhaps attracted by the completion of St
Paul's. Alessandro Galilei was in England in 1714–19, made
designs for a royal palace and for churches, but carried out only
one building, the Doric east portico at Vanbrugh's Kimbolton
Castle (1719).[21] Like his later façade to the Lateran in Rome,
Galilei's structure overtops the building behind it.

Foreign craftsmen were adaptable to the English situation: in
the early-eighteenth century they included many plasterers who
worked in buildings which cannot themselves be called either
Baroque or, in the 1730s, Rococo. One of the finest as well as
most interesting is the hall at Moor Park, Herts. Sir James
Thornhill's enlargement of the Caroline house for the *nouveau
riche* Benjamin Styles (*c.* 1725–28) included a new stone exterior
with a giant portico and the decoration of the interior. After
legal disputes in 1728 and 1730 between Thornhill and Styles
the latter employed Venetian painters to redecorate the interior; in the hall new canvases by Jacopo Amigoni were
inserted into Thornhill's scheme of painting and plaster relief.[22]
Such plasterwork may properly be called Rococo, but in
England, as in Ireland where many plasterers worked in the
eighteenth century, the term applies to details rather than to
ensembles.[23] The style continued until the advent of neo-

218 *Top* Easton Neston by Hawksmoor, completed 1702, west front

219 *Above* Chatsworth, the south front by Talman, 1687–89

220 *Below* London, St John, Smith Square, by Archer, 1713–29.

221 *Bottom* London, St Mary Woolnoth by Hawksmoor, 1716–27, interior

222 *Right* Wrest Park, the pavilion by Archer

Classical decoration about 1760, and the 'Chinese Room' at   221
Claydon is actually after 1769.

The two greatest wholly Baroque English architects, Hawksmoor and Vanbrugh, were contrasting and complementary
figures. Hawksmoor was a pupil of Wren and, next to Webb,
the best trained professional of his century.[24] By about 1690 he
was undertaking commissions of his own while continuing to
assist his master in the Royal Works and at Greenwich and St
Paul's. By 1699 he had formed an unofficial partnership with
Vanbrugh, a soldier and writer of comedies with no experience
in architecture but with boundless imagination and the determination to succeed which underlies the professionalism of his
later years. Initially Vanbrugh needed not only Hawksmoor's
knowledge, experience and draughtsmanship but, to a very
large extent, his style.[25]

Hawksmoor's design for Christ's Hospital Writing School of
1692 shows a preoccupation with bare surfaces, large masses
and round arches which derives rather from Wren's remarks
about the geometrical basis of his art than from his practice.
The exterior of Easton Neston (*c.* 1695–1702), however, com-   218
bines the silhouette of Chatsworth, the texture of Wren, and
Hawksmoor's personal preference for closely spaced giant
pilasters along the main fronts. Inside the house, changes of
room height and orientation offer a sequence of spatial sur-
prises, culminating in the staircase, nearly half the length and   228
the full height of the house and at right angles to the upper and
lower galleries which it connects. The dimensions of the steps

223 *Opposite* Blenheim Palace, the saloon, *c.* 1720

enforce on the visitor a very slow pace, and the great end window illuminates the stair as one faces inwards but in the reverse direction presents an almost tangible glare.

Hawksmoor's greatest opportunity coincided with the greatest project for public architecture of the early eighteenth century, the Commission of 1711 for building the Fifty New Churches in London and the suburbs. The inspiration of these buildings was partly political, and their grandeur and prominent siting were monuments to the Tory government of 1710–14 and to Queen Anne as well as to the High Church party within the Church of England. As one of two permanent surveyors to the Commission Hawksmoor saw the execution of six of his designs, or half the number of churches actually built. (Two others were by Archer.) All six are planned on axes intersecting at right angles, with various combinations of cruciform, square and rectangular shapes. At St George-in-the-East, which was burnt out in 1941 and rebuilt in a different internal form, the

224 *Opposite top* Chatsworth, from the north-west, by Talman and others, 1687–1702

225 *Opposite bottom* Vienna, garden façade of the Upper Belvedere by Hildebrandt, 1721–22

226 *Above left* Moor Park enlarged by Thornhill, *c.* 1725–28, the hall with paintings by Jacopo Amigoni, *c.* 1730

227 *Above right* Claydon House, the 'Chinese Room' decorated by Luke Lightfoot(?), 1769

228 *Right* Easton Neston by Hawksmoor, *c.* 1695–1702, the staircase

main space consisted of a vaulted Greek cross within a square, with flat ceilings in the corners; to this were added what Hawksmoor called 'wings' at the west, containing a gallery, and at the east containing the pulpit and opening into an apse. Since the gallery continued along the north and south sides of the main space there was considerable ambiguity between the formal and functional basis of the plan; this is a feature of all Hawksmoor's churches which he exploited to induce feelings of awe in the beholder. Even in St Mary Woolnoth the logic of the plan (a square within a square) was originally complicated by the presence of galleries on three sides. Later, in the circular Mausoleum at Castle Howard (begun 1729) Hawksmoor used indirect lighting and such irrational elements as full columns partly embedded in the wall to achieve an unnerving effect. In his church exteriors he developed both the bold use of plain prismatic surfaces and arcades to recall the gravity of Ancient

221

229 *Right* London, St George-in-the-East by Hawksmoor, 1714–29

230 *Below* Castle Howard by Vanbrugh and Hawksmoor, from the north as intended (engraving 1725), built 1700–1712 without the forecourt and west wing.

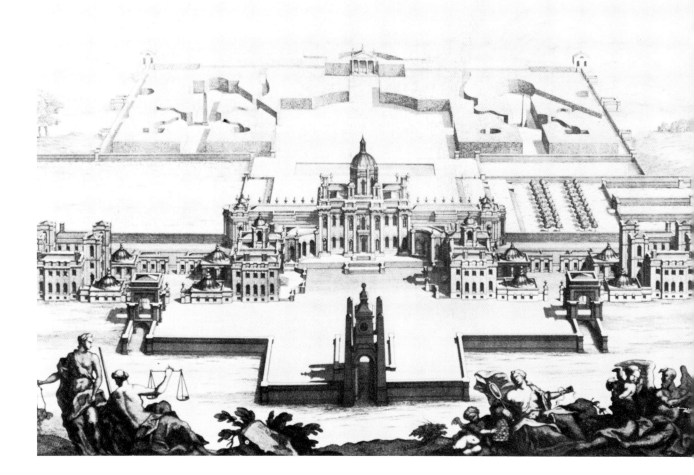

Rome (which he never saw) and an individual vocabulary of plastic forms rich in evocative quotations from Antique, Mannerist and even Gothic detail. The octagonal lantern of St George-in-the-East re-interprets in straight lines the lanterns of Borromini, as well as the shape of certain mediaeval English ones, while the draped finials derive from Roman cylindrical altars. The multiple mouldings, exaggerated keystones and ear-like projections of the side doorcases derive, complex in allusion but simplified in cutting, from the Michelangelesque tradition of architectural metaphor.

At Castle Howard (1700–12) and Blenheim (1705–25) Hawksmoor assisted Vanbrugh as draughtsman, detailer and administrator; in both exteriors Wren's French-inspired surface found its final expression. Castle Howard was built for the Whig 3rd earl of Carlisle, who left politics to develop, as a moral duty, forestry, agriculture and state living on his Yorkshire estates. It was intended to eclipse Chatsworth in the approp-

231 *Left* Grimsthorpe Castle, the hall by Vanbrugh, 1723–26

232 *Below* Blenheim Palace, by Vanbrugh and Hawksmoor, north front, 1705–16

233 Blenheim Palace, the hall, 1705–10

dimensional modelling both in main masses and in Hawksmoor's details; in all this, and in such eccentricities as the broken and stepped-back pediment over the entrance, it sustains comparison, in the international phase of Baroque, with major works of Fischer von Erlach and Juvarra.   *232*

Blenheim became involved, still unroofed, in the Marlboroughs' temporary disfavour in the last years of Queen Anne, and in 1716 Vanbrugh resigned in disagreement with the duchess; Hawksmoor was solely responsible (1722–25) for the Long Library or gallery on the west side and some of the state rooms on the south front. The hall ceiling was painted by Thornhill and the Saloon, with more than a glance at the   *223* exterior architecture, by Louis Laguerre.

One source of Blenheim's exuberant skyline is the neo-mediaevalism of Shakespeare's England.[27] By 1708 Vanbrugh had taken this revival of a revival a stage further, in remodelling Kimbolton Castle in what he called 'the Castle air'; ten years   *217* later he was building for his own use a more explicit Castle, small but tall and towered, at Greenwich, and designing in Seaton Delaval (1720–28) a house much smaller than Blenheim, more concentrated in its romantic variety of masses and turrets, in which plain surfaces and Italian Renaissance window detail replace the liberal use of the giant Order and rich texture. The appearance from 1715 of Campbell's three *Vitruvius Britannicus* volumes and Leoni's translation of Palladio made positive what had been the negative image of Shaftesbury's predicted national style and put the Baroque, which had owed its existence to the enthusiasm of individual architects and patrons, out of fashion.[28] Increasing although highly personal use was made of Palladio both by Hawksmoor and by Vanbrugh, who had for long held the *Quattro Libri* in authority. In the hall at Grimsthorpe (1723–26) in which the blind arcade motif of the   *231* side walls is transformed into double open screens at the ends, Vanbrugh demonstrated with remarkable economy and imagination the justice of his belief that he could have supplied Shaftesbury's prescription had Campbell not forestalled him.

230 riation of the court style; Vanbrugh raised the hall into a tall dome, opened arches between the hall and its flanking staircases, and engaged the Venetian Giovanni Antonio Pellegrini to paint, and the Italian stuccoists Bagutti and Plura to model, in strictly limited fields. He exploited the corridor, a rather new feature of house design, for its perspective chiaroscuro. Castle Howard in consequence combines decoration and architecture with more emphasis on the latter than in Talman's and May's painted interiors.

Blenheim Palace, the nation's gift to the victorious duke of Marlborough, is a peculiarly English Baroque monument: both Marlborough and his chosen architect considered it an impersonal commemoration of the deed, not the doer.[26] In finishing it after Marlborough's death in 1722, however, his widow altered its meaning to a personal monument to the duke. Blenheim inevitably became the focus of attacks, from Shaftesbury onwards, on what soon came to be considered a foreign style. Its imagery is that of Versailles and its language is one of complex rhythms and textures, large scale and rich three-

Holland

The political separation of the Netherlands from Flanders, although not ratified until the Peace of Münster (1648), was effectively recognized by the twelve-year truce of 1609. Thereafter the United Provinces, with the Princes of Orange as hereditary Stadholders, were both independent of Spanish rule and, although predominantly Protestant, unusually open for the seventeenth century to religious toleration. Many Dutch artists visited Rome, but in both theory and practice their borrowings from Italy were selective.[1] As a young painter about 1630 Rembrandt professed to be able to see enough Italian art at home and too busy to travel, a contention which is supported by his subsequent understanding of, and adaptations from, Renaissance art. Jacob van Campen (1595–1657) went to Rome, an undistinguished painter, and turned to architecture. Like Inigo Jones he seems to have looked in Italy at Renaissance rather than contemporary buildings. His domestic work of the 1630s, such as the Mauritshuis in The Hague, owes more to France in the use of pilasters and a high-hipped roof than it does to Palladio and Scamozzi in details, but van Campen's generation was the first in Holland to appreciate Renaissance architecture three-dimensionally rather than as the application of pseudo-antique detail to individual façades. In the former Town Hall of Amsterdam (now Royal Palace), begun 1648, van Campen fused the direct and indirect (via France) influence of Italy to produce classical rhythm, restraint and purity of line and detail, but on an overwhelming scale. The Town Hall can be called Baroque in its scale and also in the complex relation of the themes and forms of its decoration both to the mercantile prestige of the city in a Europe pacified at Münster (in the year of its foundation) and to the various formal encounters between the individual and the civic body.[2]

234 Town Hall of Amsterdam (now Royal Palace), begun 1648, van

Dutch architects experimented with centralized churches both for their geometry and for their compactness in accommodating a congregation, but as settings for the severity of Calvinist workshop their interiors (e.g. van Campen's New Church, Haarlem in the 1640s) are simple and sparsely decorated.[3] The Huis ten Bosch outside The Hague, begun in 1645 by van Campen's pupil Pieter Post for the Stadholder, encloses a cruciform domed hall and is perhaps distantly related to Palladio's Villa Rotonda; after 1649, however, the hall was entirely decorated by Jacob Jordaens and other Flemish and Dutch painters as a memorial to Prince Frederick Henry, in a decorative scheme which is unparalleled in the Netherlands either in its illusionism or in its courtly programme. Other 'palaces' were merely substantial town or country houses.[4]

In the later seventeenth century public buildings reflected the grandeur of the Amsterdam Town Hall and the taste and the technique developed there for sculptural decoration, rhetorical in intention and often brilliant in execution, that directly influenced English art in particular. Louis XIV's revocation of the Edict of Nantes in 1685 drove many Huguenot craftsmen from France; of those who settled in Holland the most important was Daniel Marot (1661–1752) who became architect to William III of Orange and England. Marot was above all a designer of ornament, and on the strength of his use of French detail his architecture is called Baroque by the Dutch.[5] Ironically, the nation which had resisted French territorial ambition in the 1670s became at the end of the century, culturally speaking, a French province.

234 Amsterdam, Royal Palace (former Town Hall) by Jacob van Campen, begun 1648

NORTH SEA

BALTIC

Danzig

Hamburg

Lüneburg

Bremen

Clemenswerth

Elbe

Celle

Hanover
Brunswick
Salzdahlum

Berlin
Brandenburg
Potsdam

Warsaw

Vistula

Rüschhaus
Münster

Magdeburg

Weser

Ems

Nordkirchen

Rhine

Lodz

Düsseldorf
Benrath

Cassel

Leipzig

Wahlstatt

Breslau

Oder

Cologne
Brühl
Bonn

Elbe

Dresden
Pillnitz

Coblenz

Fulda

Osek
Ploskovice
Gabel

Smiřice

Liblice

Ostrava

Mainz
Frankfurt

Main

Trier

Darmstadt
Holzkirchen

Werneck
Banz

Eger
Carlsbad

Vierzehnheiligen
Kappel
Waldsassen

Břevnov

Prague

Karlskrone

Würzburg
Ebrach

Bamberg
Pommersfelden

Bayreuth
Gössweinstein

Mariánský Týnec

Obořiště

Sedlec

Mannheim
Heidelberg

Schöntal

Nuremberg
Ansbach

Amberg

Kladruby

Pilsen

Nicov

Opařany

Želiv

Žďár
Křtiny

FRANCE

Speyer

Bruchsal

Brno
Austerlitz

Rajhrad

Carlsruhe
Rastatt

Schönenberg
Ludwigsburg
Ellwangen

Freystadt

Regensburg
Straubing

Frain

Altenburg

Göllersdorf

Stuttgart

Neresheim

Eichstätt

Weltenburg

Zwettl

Dürnstein

Klosterneuburg
Schlosshof

Strasbourg

Rhine

Dillingen

Danube

Ingolstadt

Rohr
Aufhausen

Osterhofen
Aldersbach
Fürstenzell

Passau

Gottweig
Herzogenburg

St Pölten

Ulm
Günzburg

Freising

Linz

Melk

Zwiefalten

Wiblingen

Augsburg

Altomünster
Schleissheim

St Florian

Obermarchtal
Steinhausen

Fürstenfelt

Munich

Stadl-Paura

Garsten
Schlierbach

St Peter
Freiburg

Siessen

Ottobeuren
Weingarten

Rottenbuch
Kempten

Landsberg

Wessobrunn
Wies

Rott am Inn
Diessen

Salzburg

Spital am Pyhrn
Admont

Mariazell

St Blasien
Basel

Neu-Birnau
Weissenau

Benediktbeuern
Ettal
Tegernsee

L. Constance

St Gallen

VORARLBERG

Garmisch

Inn

Weizberg
Graz

Danube

Budapest

Ráckeve

Einsiedeln

Innsbruck

SWITZERLAND
GRAUBÜNDEN

St Veit am Vogau

L. Balaton

L. Como

Como

ITALY

Milan

Venice

Map of Central Europe

| 0 | 20 | 40 | 60 | 80 | 100 miles |
| 0 | 20 | 40 | 60 | 80 | 100 | 120 | 140 | 160 km |

Part IV

Central and Eastern Europe

Introduction

The present division of Europe into an East and West, virtually coinciding with the division between peoples of Mediterranean or German, and Slav or Magyar stock has helped to efface the memory of an earlier Europe in which there was an equally important distinction between North and South, deriving from acceptance or repudiation of the Reformation. Central Europe in the sixteenth century embraced both these divisions. Its territories comprised the innumerable sovereign states of Germany and autonomous cantons of Switzerland – variously Catholic, Lutheran or Calvinist – on the one hand, and on the other the Slavonic and Magyar lands of Poland, Bohemia, and Hungary, whose common feature was that each had an elective monarchy. Presiding by ancient right over the Germanic parts of this territory (save the Swiss cantons, whose *de facto* independence had been recognized in 1499) was the emperor, heir to the hybrid Carolingian claim to be both successor to the emperors of Rome and elected head of their Germanic supplanters. Since 1438 this title had been held continuously by the Habsburg dynasty, which with time also succeeded in converting its originally elective rule over Bohemia and Hungary into a permanency, like that over the Empire itself.[1]

In the seventeenth century an attempt was made to challenge this Habsburg claim to automatic succession to the Empire. In 1619 one of the seven electors – four sovereign princes and three sovereign archbishops – then entitled to elect the emperor, the ruler of the Palatine Frederick V, attempted to thwart the candidature of Archduke Ferdinand, whilst engineering his own election as king of Bohemia by its largely Protestant nobility. The archduke defeated these manoeuvres, being crowned as the Emperor Ferdinand II at Frankfurt and wresting back Bohemia from Frederick after the Battle of the White Mountain (1620). Ferdinand, who had already embarked on the extirpation of Protestantism from his original archduchy of Styria, followed up this victory with the ruthless dispossession of all the Protestant-inclined nobility in Bohemia and Moravia, and the substitution of a new, Catholic and loyal nobility in its stead. Alarmed both for their religion and for their independence, the Protestant sovereigns of Germany had banded together in self-defence. Denmark, Sweden, Spain and France entered the fray, and the Thirty Years War was set on its bloody and destructive course.

The Thirty Years War had a catastrophic effect upon the arts in Germany. There was not only the destruction, depopulation and diversion of resources from patronage to warfare, but the havoc wrought upon civil life, and upon the life of the guilds in particular. The exacerbation of the antagonism between Catholic and Protestant, which had already dealt a blow to the reciprocity of guild life at the Reformation, combined with the hazards of travel to make impossible the old system of learning through *Wanderschaft* (going as a journeyman from city to city, wherever there was work). The fortunate practitioners of more transportable skills like painting or sculpture were sometimes able to work abroad, in Italy (like Carl Loth in Venice, or Heinrich Schönfeld in Naples) or in the Netherlands (where Joachim von Sandrart settled after living in Rome). Those who might have wished to practise building or the building-related arts, like stucco-work or fresco-painting (with the exception of *quadraturisti* like the Schors and Haffners) had no such traditions of travel or acceptance abroad to fall back on.

Stucco and fresco were anyway, as their names suggest, Italian imports, and they were associated with a mode of architecture that was itself of Italian origin. The prestige of Italian Renaissance architecture had already led to the direct employment of Italians at various places in Central Europe.[2] Trading relations between the Free Cities of the Empire and Italy were close (whence the Fondaco dei Tedeschi in Venice and the early receptivity to Italian forms in Augsburg, Nuremberg, and Cologne) and intermarriage between the sovereigns of Central Europe and the princely houses of Italy was not infrequent. Hence the marriage of Matthias Corvinus, king of Hungary, and Beatrice of Aragon-Naples (1476) helped to promote the remarkably early erection of buildings by Italians in the purest Florentine Quattrocento style in Buda and Visegrád. The enthusiastic reception given to Italian art and artists in Hungary was exceptional, and was anyway cut short by the loss of the central part of the country to the Turks for a century and a half after 1541, but isolated monuments elsewhere resulted from similar invitations to Italian craftsmen. In Poland King Sigismund I, who had spent his early life at the Hungarian court, and whose second wife was to be Bona Sforza, invited Bartolomeo Berrecci from Florence in 1516 to build a mausoleum to his first wife beside Cracow Cathedral (1519–33). In Bavaria, immediately after being deeply impressed by a state

235 *Overleaf left* Munich, Ahnengalerie in the Residence, wall decoration designed by Effner, ceiling by Cuvilliés, 1726–30

236 *Overleaf right* Melk, *loges* inserted in the abbey church (built by Jakob Prandtauer 1702–14) by Beduzzi in the nave gallery

visit to his Gonzaga relatives in Mantua (1536), Duke Ludwig X built a new palace within the city of Landshut directly inspired by what he had seen, and with the aid of builders sent from Mantua (1537–43).In Bohemia, Benedict Ried's idiosyncratic adoption (via Hungary) of Renaissance detail on the Vladislav Hall (*c.* 1500) was followed after his death by the Emperor Ferdinand I's invitation to Comasque masons to build the Belvedere overlooking the Castle at Prague (1534–41).

Here, for the first time, we encounter a major work of architecture (significantly indebted to Serlio's treatise) erected by the migrant Italians who were to be instrumental in popularizing Renaissance forms and techniques throughout southern Central Europe, and who were to make up for the lack of native artists caused by the breakdown of the guild system during the Thirty Years War.[3] These Comasques came from a small group of villages round Lake Como, in which there was a long tradition of adopting masonry as a profession and of using this skill to migrate and find a living away from a barely cultivable homeland, whilst returning there when possible to marry or to retire. Though several of them learnt to practise other arts, particularly that of fresco (and, indeed, their ability to provide a team of craftsmen was one of the factors in their success), their main skills were as masons and stonemasons, from which stemmed their quite novel specialization – stucco-work. The particular asset of this skill was that, being a new art, not merely did its practitioners face no native competitors, but it also lay outside the traditional demarcations and regulations of the local guilds. Revived in direct imitation of such Roman work as that found in the Golden House of Nero, it was at first the preserve of artists like Perino del Vaga, Giovanni da Udine and Federico Brandani. It was the Comasques who, by the latter part of the sixteenth century, were combining the practice of stucco-work with their jobs as masons, a combination of activities subsequently adopted to a greater or lesser extent by the later clans of peripatetic masons, the Graubündeners and the Vorarlbergers.

The Comasques migrated not only northwards; the Rovio branch of the Carlones flourished as painters and sculptors in

237 *Opposite* Stadl-Paura, Church of the Trinity by Johann Michael Prunner, 1714–25

238 *Below* Vienna, grille by Arnold and Konrad Küffner to the Upper Belvedere built by Hildebrandt, 1721–22

Genoa, whilst the building trade at Rome recruited heavily from Como. Several achieved the status of architects, notably the Fontanas, Carlo Maderno and Borromini. North of the Alps, though none but Santini Aichel achieved such artistic stature, more probably found employment. There they benefited from the innate prestige of Italian architecture, and from their mastery of the unfamiliar techniques of stucco and the bastion method of fortification. The political state of Germany, and the inevitable slowness of the native guild system in adjusting to a new architectural mode that placed a strong reliance on plaster vaults and mouldings in place of the Gothic reliance on stonemasonry, weakened native competition. (This was not the case with roof-carpentry, where there was no such break with tradition, so that Germans continued to surpass – according to Boffrand – even the French.) Finally, the *Welsche*, as they were called (the word originally just meant foreigners, but came to be restricted to Italians) helped one another through their intense clannishness, which at times threatened to exclude Germans from employment in their own country. Thus the same names – e.g. Carlone, Spazio, d'Allio, or Castelli – constantly recur, even over several centuries, whilst intermarriage maintained solidarity. This was in no way different from the dynastic tendencies prevailing amongst German craftsmen, but whereas these dominated a single city or locality, the Comasques were usually mobile, moving and inviting their compatriots to any place where work was to be found. It was no accident that, when the Italians began to be displaced from the southern Empire towards the end of the seventeenth century, it was by Germans with similar roots in remote village communities, and similar mobility.

The Empire had one distinguishing characteristic that made this kind of mobility particularly valuable; it was composed of innumerable sovereign entities – *reichsfreie* (Imperial Free) territories, ranging from those ruled by dukes and margraves, prince-bishops and prince-abbots, to Imperial Free Cities, and to some lands no bigger than a manor ruled by *reichsfreie* counts or knights. None but the largest states amongst these – Austria, Bavaria, Prussia, or Saxony – could provide assured and continued employment for architects, and even in these much depended upon the personal proclivities of the prince – there were no great opportunities under Frederick William I of

239 Würzburg, pilgrimage-church of the Käppele by Neumann 1748ff.

Prussia, or Maria Theresa of Austria. The Imperial Free Cities, which had accounted for some of the finest Late Gothic and Early Renaissance architecture, never recovered sufficiently from the shift in oriental trade from the Mediterranean to the Atlantic seaboard, or from the Thirty Years War, to become a significant source of patronage. The lesser *reichsfreie* nobles, who were concentrated in Swabia, Franconia and in the Rhineland, where no one dynasty had succeeded in establishing itself as a successor to the Carolingian dukedoms – rarely had the resources to build. This still left the major sovereign princes, both lay and ecclesiastical, and in the Catholic south, the greater abbeys, whether *reichsfrei,* or just rich with the accumulated land of almost a millennium of mortmain. The artist could go from one to another of these patrons, as each rebuilt or redecorated, and from each he could enjoy protection, and exemption from the control of the guilds – from the

240 *Right* Nymphenburg (Munich), stucco group of Diana by E. Verhelst, between 1734 and 1739 on the Amalienburg

241 *Below* Augsburg, Schäzler Palace, *Festsaal*, panelling by P. Verhelst, frescoes by Gregorio Guglielmi, 1765–70

sovereign entities, because they could confer *Hoffreiheit* (freedom of the court), which meant that the artist remained subject to their jurisdiction alone; and at monasteries that were not sovereign, because they were situated in the countryside, outside the effective writ of the guilds.

The impulse to rebuild or to build from scratch was felt by almost every one of these sovereigns in the seventeenth and eighteenth centuries; partly because of the need to repair the ravages of the Thirty Years War and under the spur of emulation and modernity, and partly from the demonic pleasure of planning and building – what the Schönborn family, who were particularly afflicted with it, familiarly referred to as their *Bauwurmb*. But there were also more specific reasons. In the case of the lay and episcopal princes, one of these is commonly described as the desire to create miniature Versailles. This is a partial truth, in that Versailles was then the epitome of French architecture, and it was to France and to French architects that most German princes turned for inspiration and advice. But the inspiration as often came from other French palaces like Marly or the Trianon, and actual attempts to create from nothing a new complex to house a whole court, and to include formal grounds and a planned city were rare – Rastatt, Carlsruhe, and Ludwigsburg are however examples – and, as demonstrated by the fate of Fischer von Erlach's original design for Schönbrunn, the concept was rejected by Louis XIV's real rival, the emperor.

What the German princes were most eager to do was to come down from their mediaeval castle-eyries to build in the plain – the Residenz at Landshut is the earliest instance of this and that at Würzburg one of the latest – and to build in a form that took account of the new ceremoniousness of court life; a ceremoniousness which, despite the French word *etiquette* first used in Germany to describe it, emanated from Burgundy via the Spanish Habsburgs rather than from France. Court etiquette centred upon two things, the reception of distinguished guests and attendance upon the person of the prince. The great halls and ceremonial staircases, in whose design the prince himself was sometimes involved, served as a worthy frame for the one, whilst the subtly graded succession of rooms forming an apartment calibrated the other. In one instance, the *Reiche Zimmer* of the Munich Residenz, the planning and decoration of the rooms expressed the latent claim on the part of their occupant to promotion from electoral to imperial status.

The rebuilding of monasteries was partly governed by similar considerations, and partly by changes in the mode of living of the monks and their superiors.[4] On the one hand monks, on the model of the friars, now required individual cells in place of the former communal dorters, and also expected the provision of a separate set of common rooms, centring on two refectories, one for summer and the other for winter use; on the other much more lavish provision had to be made for guests, and for the abbot or prior in his role as ruler and host. This provision was partly practical, but it was also strongly representational: the lavish scale and decoration of the *Fürsten-* or *Kaiserzimmer* expressed a monastery's submission to, yet also its worthiness to receive, its ultimate overlord. This was generally balanced by equal expense lavished on the church and the library, whose decoration often betrays the fact that they were not merely undertaken *ad maiorem gloriam Dei*, but also in celebration of the monastery's and the order's century-old services to Christian religion and learning. Monasteries were also generally the custodians of the major pilgrimage-places, which benefited from a startling revival of popularity in the seventeenth and

eighteenth centuries. Again, rebuilding was not merely undertaken to house the shrine or image more worthily, and to accommodate the increased numbers of the faithful, but also to enhance the prestige of the pilgrimage and augment the number of pilgrims.

It is important that by far the greater number of rebuilt and remodelled churches in the Catholic parts of the Empire after the Thirty Years War were executed for the monastic orders, whether directly for themselves, generally as the culmination of the entire reconstruction of an abbey or priory, or as the churches of pilgrimages administered by them. On the one hand it was easier to set about the reconstruction or total internal transformation of these churches, set in the middle of the countryside, because there were no complications arising from family chapels decorated with altars and tombs as each family saw fit. Old altars could be ruthlessly discarded, and everything – frescoes, stucco, sculpture, altars, pulpit, confessionals, and even apostle-light sconces – could be renewed, to partake in an overall programme of decoration and meaning. For on the other hand, the older monastic orders, set in the country, and recruited largely from the middling ranks of rural towns, found it easy to slip back into the kind of piety and learning that had prevailed before the upheavals of the Reformation. There was thus a revival of symbolic thought, manifested not only in the number of churches on symbolic plans that were designed in the Baroque period, but also in the motives behind the total reconstruction or internal redecoration of the rest. Churches were seen metaphorically as embodiments of the Church, and after their transformation were therefore invoked in countless sermons as the Bride of Christ, the New Jerusalem.[5] This justification for adornment and renewal chimed with the desire to redecorate or rebuild in the new style, that sprang both from the revived prosperity of the monasteries after the religious wars were at last over, and from the desire to celebrate the new-found security of Catholicism from attacks either by the Protestants or the Turks. And whilst the Catholic parts of the Empire, in the frescoes and furnishings of their churches, and in the churches themselves, celebrated the very things that had provoked the Protestants into schism – the Virgin and the cult of saints, pilgrimages, monasticism, the Real Presence, the sacrament of confession – the Protestants sought to evolve an architecture that was specifically Reformed. These efforts, which were codified in two treatises by Leonhard Christian Sturm (1669–1719) in 1712 and 1718, were rewarded with a triumphant conclusion in Bähr's Frauenkirche at Dresden (1726–43).

These two kinds of patron, the lay and the ecclesiastical (prince-bishops built as laymen, on account of their aristocratic birth and sovereign status, whatever their personal piety), held out two distinct forms of architectural career. Princes needed above all architects who could plan complex sets of apartments, design showpieces like the ceremonial staircases and great halls, and also little pavilions and hermitages intended for less formal moments, men who could coordinate the work of the multitude of craftsmen – joiners, woodcarvers, gilders, stuccadors, painters etc. – required to fit out their interiors. Since most princes

242 *Opposite* Würzburg, Neumünster, façade probably designed by Johann Dientzenhofer, 1712–16. One of the most strictly Italianate works in Franconia, based on a knowledge of Carlo Fontana's façade of S. Marcello (plate 70)

had voyaged and pretended to some competence in architecture themselves, it was desirable for their architects also to be travelled men with whom they could converse, so the latter tended to be gentlemen-amateurs, Frenchmen (who received a kind of automatic patent of nobility in Germany), or officers trained as military engineers. Ecclesiastical patrons by contrast needed men who could manipulate space and light to produce the most striking and effective church interiors, men whose craft training would have familiarized them with the techniques of vault-construction, and who had the entrepreneurial skills to supervise the erection of vast monastic ranges out of the simple materials of brick and plaster. The dichotomy should not, however, be exaggerated – Neumann, for instance, triumphantly bestrode both spheres of activity (working in the main for a prince-bishop with a keen interest in the building of churches) – but, just as there were architects like Cuvilliés or Pöppelmann who never carried through a whole church, there were others like Johann Michael Fischer and Dominikus Zimmermann in Bavaria, or Prandtauer and Munggenast in Austria, who were never invited to build palaces. Decorative artists were less compartmentalized in their activity, but even amongst these it should be remembered that there was an almost complete separation between the carvers of church furnishings, like pulpits and choir-stalls, who were often lay-brothers, and the makers of palatial *boiseries,* and that certain stuccadors, like the elder Feichtmayrs, operated in an almost exclusively ecclesiastical context.

For the craft mason, though many of his ecclesiastical clients lay outside the sphere of guild control, it was nonetheless necessary to have gone through the guild system of training, which meant spending four years as an apprentice, at the end of which he was *freigesprochen,* supplied with a passport, and obliged to travel abroad as a journeyman on his *Wanderschaft.* To become an independent master, he had first to have supervised the execution of a building as a *Polier,* and then to gain admittance to the guild of a particular town by the presentation of a masterpiece and the payment of a fine. Not till then could he work on his own account, though many journeymen did so illegally as *Pfuscher.* Most guilds were by this time exclusive and nepotic, so that even for the most talented, marriage to the daughter, or more usually the widow, of an established master, which brought with it citizenship of the town concerned, was the usual means of entry. By contrast with this largely practical training, the architects who designed palaces had generally acquired their knowledge of architecture from travel, books and engravings. Military engineer-architects had in addition a useful knowledge of mathematics and geometry (as did some painter-architects from their familiarity with perspective and *quadratura* – which Padre Pozzo suggested was sufficient to qualify anyone as an architect) and some practical knowledge of building and surveying through learning the art of fortification.

The result of these distinctions in social origin and training between the architects of churches and those of palaces is that there is thus not only a stylistic division between the Protestant North – orientated more towards the Netherlands and France, and mostly preoccupied with secular architecture and the peculiar problem of formulating a specifically 'Protestant' form of church architecture – and the Catholic South, but also within the South itself, two distinct strands of development that fertilized one another, but remained essentially distinct.

Because of the diversity of developments involved it is difficult to provide a satisfying definition of the Baroque in Central Europe, and even harder to try to define Rococo architecture as a distinct tectonic phenomenon, rather than as a modification of the Baroque, characterized or induced by the use of a form of decoration chiefly associated with the type of ornament known as *rocaille* (an ambiguous shelly substance).[6] As in England the use of the word Baroque is rendered problematic by the fact that the term Renaissance is not wholly appropriate to what went before, whilst in Central European church architecture there is anyway no clear demarcation between the two. Moreover, because of the Thirty Years War, the natural time-lag in assimilating developments in Italy was accentuated, both by the absence of any significant building activity during the war, and by the dominance after it of the itinerant Italians practising what might be described as provincial Renaissance survival architecture (even if incorporating certain features that may be regarded as Baroque).

Baroque architecture in Central Europe may be said to begin with the displacement of these itinerant Italians; on one level, in the capitals, by architects directly familiar with developments in Rome, and on the craft level by Germans themselves, migrating to areas with a dearth of trained builders. Those with first-hand experience of Rome included both native architects – Wolf Casper von Klengel (1630–91) in Saxony, Hermann Korb (1656–1735) in Brunswick, Johann Bernhard Fischer von Erlach (1656–1723) and Jean Luca von Hildebrandt (1668–1745) in Austria, Andreas Schlüter (*c.* 1663–1714) in Prussia, and Cosmas Damian Asam (1686–1739) and Egid Quirin Asam (1692–1750) in Bavaria – and foreigners, like the Italians Domenico Martinelli and Domenico Egidio Rossi (from Lucca and Fano respectively) in Austria, and the Burgundian Jean-Baptiste Mathey in Bohemia. It is striking how many of these were artists rather than architects by training. The German craft builders who emigrated from their homelands included the Bavarians who went to Bohemia and the Upper Palatinate – amongst them the Dientzenhofers – the Tyroleans who repopulated Lower Austria – notably Prandtauer and Munggenast – and the itinerant Vorarlberger masons and Wessobrunner stuccadors, who took on the Comasques and Graubündeners at their own level in Switzerland and Swabia. At the same time the kind of uncritical admiration of all things Italian revealed in Prince Eusebius von Liechtenstein's 'Treatise on Building' (*c.* 1678), and in the Electress Henriette Adelaide's dismissal of Germans as 'più idioti nell' edificare', which had licensed the employment of Italians however mediocre, gave way to a more discriminating desire for designs from the leading architects in Italy. Guarini produced designs for the Theatine Church in Prague, and it was hoped that he would do the same for Munich (though in the event Henriette Adelaide contented herself with the uninspiring Agostino Barelli); whilst Carlo Fontana was asked to produce designs for Fulda, for palaces in Prague for Counts Martinitz and Sternberg, and for a country seat for Prince Johann Adam von Liechtenstein. That virtually none of these designs was realized – any more than plans supplied by de Cotte or Boffrand in the eighteenth century, when France was setting the tone for palace architecture, were executed – was

243 *Opposite* Bad Wurzach, staircase of the Residence built by an unknown architect for Truchsess Ernst Jakob von Waldburg-Zeil-Wurzach, 1723–28

almost inevitable in view of the architects' unfamiliarity with their client's requirements. The next best thing was therefore to bear off one's own architect from Rome – as Archbishop Waldstein did with Mathey, or Count Kaunitz did with Domenico Martinelli – or to employ someone like Fischer von Erlach or Hildebrandt who could claim to have worked under Bernini or Fontana.

Three amongst this first generation of Baroque architects were also sculptors (Fischer von Erlach, Schlüter and E. Q. Asam), and three were painters by training (D. E. Rossi, J. B. Mathey, and C. D. Asam). Domenico Martinelli came to architecture via the study of geometry and mathematics, whilst Klengel – foreshadowing the trend in the eighteenth century – was a military engineer. The preponderance of artists helps to account for the important role in Central European architecture played by the associated arts, though this was also a reflection of the wishes of the patrons. The architecture of this first generation (with which the Asams must be reckoned, though they were younger, because in Bavaria the Graubündeners kept their hold longer – first through Max Emanuel's favour, and then through his prolonged exile) is naturally characterized by a strong Italian, and particularly Berninian, flavour.

It was not until the Treaty of Rastatt had ended the War of the Spanish Succession in 1714, bringing peace to the Empire, and allowing Max Emanuel and his brother Joseph Clemens back to their electorates of Bavaria and Cologne, that the already prevalent admiration of things French blossomed in a remarkable series of palaces and pavilions built by the sovereign princes of the Empire in the French mode – some to plans sent from France, some with French architects or *dessinateurs,* almost all using French craftsmen and furnishings, and with French garden layouts. Church architecture in the Southern Empire was touched by these influences, mainly in the field of ornament, which evolved from heavily plastic figurative cartouche and acanthus ornament (the latter itself once inspired by French engravings), through ribbonwork and the so-called *Régence* – chiefly inspired by the engravings of Bérain and Audran – to *rocaille,* a fusion of the new shell-based and asymmetrical French ornament of the 1730s with surviving indigenous strains of the asymmetrical cartouche tradition. France had however nothing to offer – with the possible exception of the Church of the Invalides and the Versailles Court Chapel – in the way of strictly architectural models for churches in Germany. Here the picture is one of indigenous architects emancipating themselves from adherence to foreign prototypes, and reinvigorating the native tradition with a new feeling for fluid space – as exemplified in the churches of J. M. Fischer, K. I. Dientzenhofer, and Balthasar Neumann – and for the integration of architecture and decoration – supremely in the churches of Dominikus Zimmermann.

Moreover, just as in the field of ecclesiastical architecture there were kinds of structure whose development as special types was virtually peculiar to the Empire – pilgrimage-churches and monastic libraries – so in secular architecture there were features that preoccupied architects to a degree unknown in Italy or France – notably the ceremonial staircase, which called forth their best from Fischer von Erlach, Hildebrandt and Neumann, and even resulted in anonymous works of distinction like the staircase of the Waldburg Schloss at Bad Wurzach (*c.* 1725).

243

When the second generation of architects in the Catholic parts of the Empire died – K.I. Dientzenhofer in 1751, Neumann in 1753, J. M. Fischer and D. Zimmermann in 1766, Cuvilliés in 1768, and J.C. Schlaun in 1773 – the creative *élan* went out of architecture in the regions in which they operated, as it had already done in Austria by the accession of Maria Theresa. Neumann's son, Franz Ignaz, was a brilliant engineer like his father, but he was refused the opportunity of completing his father's church of Neresheim on account both of his youth and of his desire to execute the vaults as his father had planned them – a revealing failure of confidence on the part of the abbey. The sons of Fischer von Erlach and Cuvilliés – Josef Emanuel and François the Younger – were both competent architects and accomplished draughtsmen, but both came under the influence of the French academic tradition, and did not develop their fathers' achievements. In the event it was French *émigré* architects, who had never lost their foothold in the courts of the Rhineland, who superseded the already moribund tradition of German Baroque architecture – of which J.G. Specht's Abbey Church of Wiblingen (1772–83) stands as the clearest testimony. The last great abbey church, St Blasien (1772–83), and the last great episcopal Residenz, that of Coblenz (1777–86), were both designed in the severe idiom of French Neo-Classicism, by a Frenchman called Pierre Michel d'Ixnard (1723–95), though at Coblenz he was discharged in 1779 and replaced by a Frenchman from Paris itself, Peyre the Younger. In both cases the plans were submitted to a French Academy for approval – nothing could better illustrate the Germans' repudiation of their own architecture. In Germany, as in France, theory had won the day over practice, the trained architect over the craft builder; of what had been two parallel traditions – an aspiringly cosmopolitan palace architecture, and a fundamentally vernacular church architecture – the latter had been swallowed up by the former, and not until the last two decades of the nineteenth century did the magnitude of the achievements of Central European Baroque architecture begin to be perceived.

Austria

It is appropriate to begin this survey of Baroque architecture in Central Europe with Austria, not merely because the Austrian 'crown lands' – Upper and Lower Austria, Styria, and Carinthia – were the hereditary territories of the head of the Empire, but also because it was here that the most conscious attempts to wrest back architectural commissions from the hands of the peripatetic Italians were made. It was also in Austria that the *Reichsstil*[7] was forged. To translate this straight-forwardly as 'Empire style' would be misleading: it was more a tendency to plan on a scale and with symbolic elements expressive of Empire, that is to be found not merely in the buildings of the emperor and of his direct great subjects, but also in those parts of the Empire which were imperial rather than particularistic, like the episcopal states ruled by the Schönborns. For these rulers, it came naturally both to seek advice from a great Austrian architect like Hildebrandt, and to send their own architects, like Maximilian von Welsch, Neumann, and Küchel, to Vienna, just as others were sent (including Neumann himself on a previous occasion) to Paris, or to Italy. Finally, because Austria was the land of the emperor, it contained a capital city, Vienna, which alone amongst all the cities of Central Europe could compare with the other great European capitals – Paris, Rome, London or Naples – in the number and kind of architectural commissions that it afforded. Only Vienna supported a sufficiently rich and numerous aristocracy to require the building of enough town palaces and suburban villas to provide architects with an alternative lay practice to that of working for the ruling prince.

The states on the periphery of the Empire – Austria, Prussia and Saxony – having been won by conquest, were the most unitary. Their rulers were untrammelled by independent enclaves within them, whether secular, monastic, or episcopal. The Habsburgs were absolute sovereigns in their own right over the whole of Austria, Bohemia and Hungary (whose originally elective monarchies were made hereditary in 1621 and 1711 respectively). Once the Turkish menace had been lifted after the Relief of Vienna in 1683, and all of Hungary and much of the Balkans recovered from Turkish domination (by the Treaties of Carlowitz (1699) and Passarowitz (1718) in turn) Austria's eastern flank was secure. The sense of national identity induced by these successes was given further focus by rivalry with the other great continental power, France; although this arose less from any threat to Austrian interests than from Louis XIV's seizure of imperial and Habsburg territories in the west, and from dynastic rivalry between Habsburg and Bourbon over the throne of Spain. Austrian nationalism found expression in such propagandist works as Hörnigk's *Österreich über alles, wann es nur will* (1684) – 'Austria over all, when it but wills it' – and Wagner von Wagenfels' *Ehren-Ruff Teutschlands* (1691) – 'A call to the honour of Germany' – in which Austria and Germany were called upon to build up their own resources and throw off their servility to things foreign. Such exhortations were reflected in the growing demand for the employment of *'Teutsche'* rather than *'Welsche'* – Germans rather than Italians – as masons and architects. The more dynastic and imperial note on the other hand was struck in the ambitious scale and programmes of the buildings erected by the emperors and their immediate entourage, and in the plans to rebuild certain of the great abbeys.[8]

244 Salzburg Cathedral, interior

Austria, being contiguous to Italy, had been one of the first parts of Germany to be overrun by the peripatetic Italians, whose skill in the new bastioned method of fortification was in especial demand to guard against the Turks after the Battle of Mohacs (1526). Operating at first under the protection of the ruler, they succeeded in gaining admission to the Viennese masons' guild in 1627, whilst by 1660 they had established such a stranglehold over the guild at Graz that they were accused of a deliberate policy of excluding Germans.[9] Although these Italians were almost all from the periphery of Italy, they basked in the immense prestige of metropolitan Italian architecture. They came from around Lake Como and from the Italian-speaking parts of Graubünden, and the buildings that they put up were correspondly provincial and *retardataire* – e.g. the Cathedral at Salzburg (then an independent archiepiscopal state) *c.* 1614–28 by Santino Solari; the Servite Church, Vienna, by Carlo Canevale 1651–77; and the Leopoldine range of the Vienna Hofburg, by Filiberto Lucchese 1660–66. The exaggerated admiration for all Italian architecture is exemplified by the treatise on architecture that Prince Eusebius Liechtenstein wrote for his son around 1678.[10] In this he maintains that 'in its buildings *Welschlandt* (Italy) surpasses the whole world, so that its manner and no other should be followed, for it is fine, imposing, and majestic'. His naive views as to what constituted 'the Italian manner' can be seen in his admonition: 'never, never for all time put up any building without architectural adornment . . . and this consists in nothing other than the 5 Orders of columns, and in these alone'. For him, the ideal palace was one which would have '60 or more columns succeeding one another the same distance apart, and in 3 tiers' (an ideal that his son, advised by him, strove to achieve in Schloss Plumenau (Plumlov) in Moravia, 1680–85), and the ideal church a transeptless basilica without a dome, but with five superimposed Orders! When this treatise was first found it was thought to derive from the sixteenth century, and it clearly indicates that even a great and well-travelled magnate was not going to make any very sophisticated demands of the peripatetic Italians. The most influential works of the latter were in fact churches in which they deployed another of their special skills – stucco-work – to transform the internal appearance of an existing mediaeval building, as in the national pilgrimage-church of Maria-Zell (1644–83, by Domenico Sciassia and others) and the Benedictine abbey church of Kremsmünster (1680s, by G. B. Barberino and assistants).

The eventual relegation of the provincial Italians to a subordinate role in Austrian architecture took place in two ways: as the result of a greater awareness of contemporary or near-contemporary architecture in Rome, and through a nationalistic urge towards the employment of natives.

The desire to use native-born architects can be seen both as the result of pressures from below and as a reflection of conscious policy from above. In 1691 the Vienna guild forced Prince Johann Adam von Liechtenstein (the son of Prince Eusebius) to cancel the original contract with a Graubündener mason, Antonio Riva, to build his suburban palace, and to substitute another with a German. Again, in 1700, he had to appeal to the emperor for special permission to hire a *welsch* mason to execute the orangery, on the grounds that the plans, having been drawn up by a *welsch* architect, would be unintelligible to the local masons. On the other hand, when Hildebrandt petitioned the emperor Leopold I to succeed the retiring court builder Pietro Tencala in 1699, he began his application by saying, 'If this post is really once more to be filled with a worthy subject, and native vassals are to be given first consideration, may I then put myself forward, as a born child of this country, of German parents . . . .

At the same time, consciousness amongst clients of recent developments at Rome was increasing. Though only Prince Liechtenstein in Austria is known to have procured plans for a country seat from a leading Roman architect – from Carlo Fontana in 1696 – there was an eagerness to employ those with direct experience of the fountainhead. In two cases, that of J. B. Mathey (who was taken back from Rome to Prague by Archbishop Waldstein in 1675) and that of Domenico Egidio Rossi, painters were converted into architects. In 1690 Counts Harrach and Kaunitz succeeded in attracting the Lucchese Domenico Martinelli to Vienna from Rome, where he had been professor of perspective at the Academy. It was he who completed Count Kaunitz's town palace, after it had been bought by Prince Liechtenstein (1694–1700), and he who completed the latter's suburban palace (1700–11).[11] But the most

exciting event for aware patrons was the return in 1687 of Fischer von Erlach after almost sixteen years spent in Italy, chiefly in Rome. Within a year, Count Michael Althan, for whom Fischer was shortly to build the *Ahnensaal* at Schloss Frain (1688–92) in Moravia, was eagerly enquiring as to whether it was really true that Fischer was the man who had spent sixteen years with Bernini, whilst two other members of the Liechtenstein family were reassuring one another of the great pains that they were taking to nurse this 'great virtuoso' through an illness. In 1689 Fischer was identified with the patriot party through his appointment as tutor in civil and military architecture to the Crown Prince Joseph, alongside Wagner von Wagenfels as tutor in history and politics. The history that the latter composed for the private use of the crown prince had two leitmotivs: that the clergy should not be permitted to exceed their rightful sphere of influence, and that foreigners should not be preferred to native subjects. In 1690 Fischer thoroughly vindicated the latter maxim as far as architecture was concerned, by utterly outclassing the South Tyrolean Pietro Strudel in the two temporary triumphal arches that he designed to greet the Crown Prince Joseph on his return to Vienna after his election as king of the Romans. Wagner von Wagenfels celebrated Fischer's achievement the next year in his *Ehren-Ruff Teutschlands* (1691) in purely chauvinist terms – the profound and artistic German, 'who left it to his work, and not to his mouth, to speak' defeats the boastful foreigner – but Fischer's two triumphal arches are in fact a demonstration that, during his years in Italy, he had acquired a rich symbolic vocabulary greatly indebted to ancient Rome, and a mastery of complex architectural forms gained in modern Rome, beyond the scope of any rivals.

It is with Johann Bernhard Fischer von Erlach (1656–1723) that the history of a specifically Austrian Baroque architecture begins.[12] He was the son of a sculptor from Graz, and it was as a sculptor that he himself began, probably being sent to Rome by the local magnates, the Princes Eggenberg, like the painter Hans Adam Weissenkirchner, to improve his technique and broaden his horizons. Whilst in Rome, Fischer worked, if not directly for Bernini himself, for an assistant of his, Johann Paul Schor and his son, and mingled with a group of scholars that had gathered round Queen Christina of Sweden. The incorporation of sculpture and of sculptural features with an allusive significance was to be an important feature in Fischer's architecture, and he remained something of an intellectual. This is apparent both from his friendships, which, by contrast with those of Hildebrandt, were with scholars like Leibniz and Heraeus rather than with his clients, and from the publication towards the end of his life of the *Entwurff Einer Historischen Architektur*. Though only published in 1721, a manuscript copy is dated 1712, and Fischer began working on it around 1705.[13] The title is somewhat misleading because it is less a historical essay on architecture than a compilation of buildings from the past and from exotic countries, reconstructed with the aid of ancient coins and texts, or copied from travellers' sketches. The last two books contain a number of Fischer's own designs for buildings and vases, both realized and ideal. For Fischer, there was clearly no insuperable division between his own works and his reconstruction of works from the past. His particular sense

245 *Opposite* Salzburg, façade of the Cathedral built by Santino Solari, 1614–28 (the octagonal completions of the towers and the sculpture added later in the century)

246 *Above* Fischer von Erlach, engraving of an ideal design for
Schönbrunn, *c.* 1690

of history helped him to create an imperial idiom of architecture.

Fischer is not known to have executed any sculpture after his
models for the Trinity Monument in the Graben in Vienna
(1687–93), and here already, though not the designer, he
suggested that 'something unusual' should replace the proposed spiral column, because such columns were becoming
'almost two-a-penny in the villages'. The Italian theatre-
designer Burnacini thereupon designed a – not much more
sophisticated – cloud-wrapped obelisk instead, but it was
Fischer who had awed the Viennese into feeling provincial in
the face of his Roman experience. The transition to architecture
therefore occurred as naturally for him as for the painters
Mathey and Rossi; they were the *virtuosi* whose direct knowledge of Italy ensured that anything that they designed, from
palaces to catafalques, would be both up-to-date and ingenious
(the word *Ingenieur*, used to describe Fischer and other architects
at this period, merely betokened their ability to provide original
designs), whilst craft-trained masons guaranteed the solid
construction of their buildings. Unlike the painter-architects,
however, Fischer was alert to the possibilities of stone from his
training as a sculptor, enabling him to make such innovations
as the 'bulbous' arch – an arch that curves both upwards and
outwards, first executed in lath and plaster in the Triumphal
Arch of the Viennese Citizenry in 1690, and in stone in the
portal of the Court Stables at Salzburg (1693–94). Significantly,
it was this 'craft' feature in Fischer's work which had the

greatest vogue amongst the country architects building for
monasteries in Austria.

Fischer's work as an architect falls into three main spheres:
imperial projects, city and suburban palaces for the higher
aristocracy, and designs for churches and altars. One of the
immediate results of Fischer's appointment as tutor in architecture to the Crown Prince Joseph, who enjoyed the prospect
not merely of becoming emperor, but of reuniting the Habsburg
lines in Austria and Spain, was the project for a truly imperial
palace outside Vienna at Schönbrunn – a kind of counter-
Versailles. It was notorious that the imperial palace within the
city, the Hofburg, was as unbecoming to the dignity of the
emperors as was the palace of St James to the kings of England
– one French traveller in 1669 described it as being 'like the
ugliest houses of the *rue des Lombards* in Paris', without proper
courtyards or sets of apartments, and without any gardens at
all. Though the Emperor Leopold I had extended and embellished the range named after him (1660–66, and again after
a fire, 1668–81), using *émigré* Italians, his personal austerity
left him uninterested in any more far-reaching improvements. It
was, therefore, ostensibly for his heir that Fischer created his
first, ideal, design for Schönbrunn, misleadingly described in
the engraving that he subsequently made of it as an imperial
hunting-lodge. In fact it used every resource of site and symbolism to express the majesty of empire. The palace was to
stand at the top of the hill where von Hohenberg's Gloriette
now presides, with a prospect right over Vienna to the borders
of the Crown Prince's kingdom of Hungary. Massive arcaded
terraces and rock-hewn cascades descend to the entrance-gates,
flanked by Fischer's favourite imperial motif of two Trajanic

246

columns. The sculpture of the fountains and entrance bolsters the king/emperor's claims to be regarded as a second Hercules for prowess, and as a second Apollo for his triumph over the powers of darkness. The quadriga of the sun crowning the main block of the palace employs the same symbolism as at Versailles to equate king and sun, 'Schönbrunn' being interpreted in the completion medal to mean the 'fair spring' in the west at which the horses of the sun slake their thirst at the end of the day. The concave central court, enclosing an enormous basin, may have been inspired by Bernini's second design for the east façade of the Louvre, but Fischer treats the main block as if the palace were a secular Escorial, with the porticoed imperial apartments in place of a church at the centre. The setting on the other hand mixes elements of a lost monument of antiquity, the Temple of Fortune at Praeneste, with reminiscences of terraced garden settings such as had spread from Italy to France – e.g. St Germain-en-Laye.

How seriously Fischer envisaged the realization of this project it is hard to say; he later tried to interest Frederick I of Prussia in a reduced version (1704) – befitting a king as opposed to an emperor. But the emperor, unlike his mighty subjects, never had great sums available for architecture, and the expense of transporting materials to the hill-top site alone would have been enormous. When Schönbrunn was ultimately begun to a more modest design as – this time genuinely – a hunting-lodge for Crown Prince Joseph (1696ff), it was built at the bottom of

the site, where no one could see any point in it. The emperor insisted that the hunting-lodge be enlarged by two quadrangular blocks on either side for Joseph's retinue, making it into a full-blown summer-palace like his own Favorita, but upsetting its balance. Neither the stables and offices, nor the interiors, were however complete when Joseph died as emperor in 1711. The palace was then forsaken by Charles VI, and its present banal appearance, including the raising of the central block and the addition of a mezzanine storey all round, is due to Maria Theresa's architect, Nicolaus Pacassi (1744–49).

Fischer was unlucky in that, when his former royal pupil became emperor in 1705, Austria was engaged in the War of the Spanish Succession, thus precluding the grandiose reconstruction of the Hofburg envisaged by Fischer and his master. Under Joseph's brother and successor Charles VI (1711–40), Fischer was nevertheless entrusted with the construction of three imperial buildings incorporated in, or axially related to, the Hofburg – the Imperial Library, the Imperial Stables, and the Karlskirche.

The last-named was officially the fulfilment of a vow made by Charles VI to build a church to St Charles Borromeo, should Vienna be relieved from the great plague of 1713. In 1715 the emperor personally chose Fischer's design from a wealth of contenders. The fact that the names of the emperor and his votive saint were the same is exploited in the building's iconography. Fischer had designed the church from the first with the unique feature of two Trajanic columns between the outer towers of the façade and the portico. These make a secondary allusion to the two pillars, Jachin and Boaz, that stood in the porch of the Temple of Solomon, but they were

248

247 *Below* Vienna, plan of the Karlskirche by Johann Bernhard Fischer von Erlach

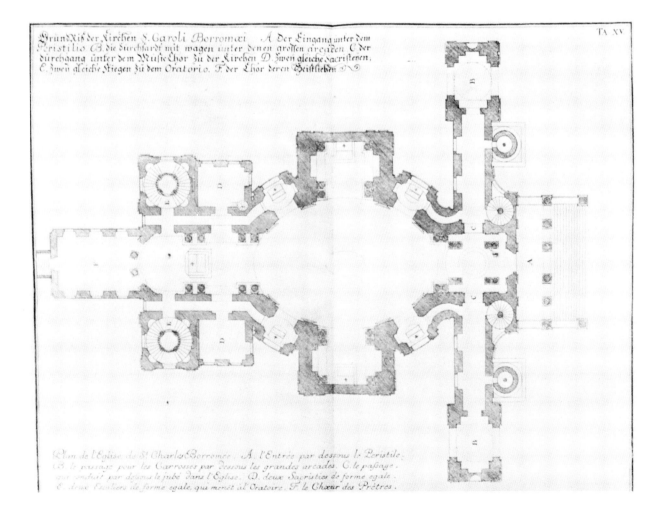

already a familiar feature of Fischer's imperial vocabulary. They had gained an added significance under Charles VI as emblematic representations of the Pillars of Hercules (reviving a device of Charles V's, expressive of his power reaching to the ends of the earth) – the classical name for the Straits of Gibraltar – betokening Charles's brief occupancy of, and claims to, the Spanish throne. The columns are still topped by crown-capped lanterns and imperial eagles, and Heraeus and Leibniz originally proposed that the reliefs should show scenes fom the lives of Charles VI's homonymous predecessors – Charlemagne and Charles the Good of Flanders. By 1721 the emperor had decided that the reliefs should show scenes from the life of Carlo Borromeo instead, but the two themes underlying the depictions on either column were to be Fortitude and Constancy, which happened to be both Charles VI's own election slogan as emperor, and the supposed meaning of Jachin and Boaz.

Visually, the columns do not so much mediate between the outer towers and the dome, as assert themselves as one pair of elements amongst several intended to be separately 'read' for what they symbolize or evoke. The plan gives a particularly good idea of the arbitrariness of the façade. This façade, with a pedimented centre set in front of a dome, and terminated by two towers with arched passageways beneath, recalls designs by Maderno and Bernini for St Peter's; but the pedimented centre has been promoted into a free-standing portico with an inscription, recalling the Pantheon (a precursor of the portico is to be found in J.C. Zuccalli's Church of St Erhard at Salzburg). The concave junctions and the balustraded attic linking the centre with the flanking towers evoke Borromini's S. Agnese, whilst the dumpy form of the towers themselves is more akin to Mansart's Church of the Minims – both churches with a domed centre similarly set back between outlying towers. The Karlskirche is thus a *summa* not merely of erudite iconography, but also of some of the major monuments of European architecture, imperial not only in its symbolism but also in its breadth of reference. Many of the present weaknesses of the design, especially in the interior, stem from the church's completion by Fischer's son Joseph Emanuel Fischer von Erlach (1693–1742).

The Imperial Stables (1721–25) were designed to form a prospect for the Hofburg, and to house the palace of the master of the imperial horse in the centre, in addition to six hundred horses (which it was previously the obligation of the citizens to stable). It is symptomatic of Fischer's grandiose imagination that for the layout he should have drawn on his reconstruction of the Golden House of Nero, even going so far as to take the cruciform temple from inside the hemicycle at the rear and place it outside, as a church for the grooms.

The Imperial Library was Fischer's last work, built posthumously between 1723–26 by his son, to whom the cooler French-influenced detailing of the exterior is doubtless due. When the idea of building a new library first arose, shortly after the Peace of Rastatt, in 1716, it was intended to erect a building for the proposed Academy of Sciences as well. Both were encouraged by Leibniz, who had been Librarian at Wolfenbüttel when Korb built the first free-standing library in modern Europe there. The incorporation of the Imperial Library into the Hofburg and its representative status, however, link it to the tradition of the great monastic libraries of Austria and South Germany (the Library at Melk is almost coeval with it). The Library occupies the two upper storeys of a building with

248 *Opposite* Karlskirche, exterior, built by Johann Bernhard and Joseph Emanuel Fischer von Erlach, 1716–33

249 *Above* Karlskirche, interior, completed in 1737, showing *The Glory of St Charles Borromeo* by F. M. Brokoff

stabling below. The domically vaulted transverse oval centre is flanked by two tunnel-vaulted arms divided by diaphragm arches supported on columnar screens. The arms originally merged directly with the central area, but signs of stress in the fabric forced Pacassi to insert arches, upsetting the effect and undermining the illusionism of Daniel Gran's central fresco (1763–69).

The columnar screens are clearly a reminiscence of the gallery in the Palazzo Colonna, and it is not necessary to see the columns as yet another allusion to the Pillars of Hercules. The sculptural decoration of the exterior and the fresco decoration of the interior are however richly programmatic. The sculptural programme is devoted to learning: a quadriga with Pallas Athene banishing envy and ignorance over the central pavilion, and the celestial and terrestial globes borne by personifications of the appropriate branches of learning over the arms. Daniel

Gran's frescoes within are to an immensely detailed programme drawn up by Konrad Adolf Albrecht von Albrechtsburg. Characteristically, that in the dome is a fulsome panegyric upon Charles VI, shown in a medallion supported by Hercules and Apollo, and his munificence in endowing the Library. This contrasts with the more modest celebrations of learning found in monastic libraries, two of which – at Altenburg and Admont – were nevertheless to emulate the Imperial Library in grandeur.

282
283

Fischer was invited to the sovereign territory of Salzburg by its prince-archbishop, Johann Ernst von Thun-Hohenstein (1687–1709), very soon after the latter's election. This man, from a German family originating in the South Tyrol, appears to have combined a passion for building with a marked anti-

pathy to Italians. On his accession he had promptly halted work on the church being built for the Italian-based Theatines, denied payment to the Italian stuccadors and architect, and only retained the latter (Johann Caspar Zuccalli) as court architect, until he could obtain the services of Fischer (1693).[14]

The first major work that Fischer executed for the archbishop, the Trinity Church (1694–1702), was in the nature of a calculated affront to their respective predecessors. The Theatine

250 *Below* Vienna, exterior of the Imperial Library designed by J. B. Fischer von Erlach, built by J. E. Fischer von Erlach, 1723–26

251 *Opposite* Imperial Library, interior, altered by Nicolaus Pacassi in 1763–69. Frescoes by Daniel Gran, completed in 1730

252 Salzburg, engraving of Trinity Church, by Fischer von Erlach,
1694–1702 *Vienna, Öst. Nationalbibliothek*

Church had been planned in association with a seminary. The
latter Archbishop Thun prohibited and instead asked Fischer
to design a church contained between a priests' hostel and a
school for sons of the nobility. Fischer took the oval plan
employed by Zuccalli in the Theatine Church and turned it
252   through 90°, to create a centrally planned church with longitudinal emphasis. The church has a concave façade between two
towers, in counterpoint to the dome over the oval, and convex
steps in front. Though the latter elements are derived from
37   Borromini's S. Agnese, which is likewise placed upon a square,
the Trinity Church is designed to dominate the end, rather than
to fit into the middle of its square – hence the assertive pro-
trusion of its towers. These formerly had squat terminations
with concave corners and a cornice bent upwards over oval
oculi – 'bizarre' detailing unlike the French sobriety of, above
all, the basement storey, but which was to remain a constant of
Fischer's ecclesiastical architecture. It was very probably
Fischer who proposed that the dome should be entirely frescoed
by Rottmayr in the Roman fashion, rather than heavily
stuccoed in the way envisaged by the 'provincial' Zuccalli for
his two Salzburg churches.

Fischer designed four other churches for the archbishop, but
three of them, the Hospital Church of John the Baptist
(*c*. 1695–1704) the pilgrimage church of Maria Kirchental
(1696ff) and the Ursuline Church (1699–1705), were of too
slight importance to evoke a sophisticated design, or to receive
detailed attention from Fischer at a time when he was
increasingly employed at Vienna.

The fourth church is altogether greater in stature, and was
indeed the only one of Fischer's Salzburg churches to be
included in his *Historische Architectur* – the Kollegienkirche
(1696–1707). Salzburg, which never admitted the exempt order
of the Jesuits, was the one territory in Southern Germany to
have a university not under their control, but run and sup-

ported by the Benedictines. Though founded in the first quarter
of the seventeenth century, this lacked even a permanent chapel
until Archbishop Thun supplied the endowment for the present
church in 1694. The archbishop clearly intended to have a
church as different as possible from the aisle-less, tunnel-
vaulted and galleried churches most characteristic of the Jesuits
in South Germany, yet as distinctive. In this Fischer did not
disappoint him, creating a memorable convex façade that was   254
thereafter adopted for most of the major Benedictine abbey
churches of South Germany. Fischer's use in the interior of the
plan of Lemercier's chapel of the Sorbonne ties in with the
archbishop's institution in 1697 of the same obligatory oath
upon the Immaculate Conception for all graduates that had
been required at the Paris University since 1497.

The plan of the church is not only that of the chapel of the   253
Sorbonne, but is also very similar to that of S. Carlo ai Catinari
in Rome, with which it also has the pierced-domed oval chapels
in the diagonals in common. The Kollegienkirche is however
unlike either of these models in the insistent verticality of both
the exterior and the interior. Counteracting this verticality is the
weaker longitudinal emphasis of the plan, which however
culminates in the remarkable light-flooded white stucco glory
of the Virgin Immaculate (the titular of the church) in the apse,
framed by two free-standing columns. These probably allude to
Jachin and Boaz, very appropriately for an institution devoted
to the pursuit of wisdom, and originally flanked a tempietto-
like tabernacle instead of an altar, so that God would have been
present only in the symbolic form of flooding light, making a
further *rapprochement* with the imageless sanctuary of Solomon's Temple. The archbishop decreed that after his death his
brain should be deposited in this church, just as his entrails
(symbolizing compassion) were to repose in the Hospital
Church, and his heart in the Church of the Trinity. He died in
1709, and with his death Fischer's architectural activity in
Salzburg came to an end; the next archbishop preferred Hildebrandt. Fischer's churches thus form a kind of interlude in his
career; with the exception of Karlskirche, they were all designed
within five years of one another, for the same patron and city.

Certain of their interior features, such as their relative plainness and sparing use of white stucco (the best by Diego Carlone and Paolo d'Allio) reflect the preferences of the archbishop acting upon the idiom of the region. It is above all in the remarkable diversity of their façades that the fecundity of Fischer's imagination can be seen, for example in trying out combinations and variations of certain features, some of which – like convexity and concavity – preoccupied him in his secular work as well.

The greater nobility of Austria was in essence a court-created aristocracy, which Leopold I had set out as deliberately to implant at Vienna, as Louis XIV had riveted that of France to Versailles. In Austria, however, there was no separation between court and capital, nor was there any accommodation in the royal palace for its courtiers. Instead, the second floor of every house in Vienna was compulsorily requisitioned for the use of court officers and officials. The construction of handsome

new palaces was encouraged by granting exemptions from requisition for a number of years, whilst other palaces were built to house certain ministers and their offices.[15] The court itself moved from palace to palace in Vienna and its environs at set seasons of the year, and the nobility emulated this by requiring not only a town palace but also a villa-like suburban palace, called a *Lustgarten* or *Lustgebäude,* to which to retreat, especially in summer.[16]

A number of such buildings, mostly one-storey pavilions, had been built on the outskirts of Vienna before the Siege of 1683, in the course of which they and the incipient suburbs had been destroyed.[17] The traumatic experience of the siege led to the stipulation thereafter that there was to be no building whatsoever on the 600-foot wide *glacis* in front of the city defences, nor building on vantage-points overlooking this, in order to deprive enemy artillery batteries of all cover. A complete caesura was thus established between the city of Vienna within the walls, which was one of the most crowded cities of Europe, and the untrammelled suburbs and 'gardens' (with their buildings ranging from pavilions to palaces) beyond the *glacis* (though mostly inside the outer lines drawn by Prince Eugene in 1704 against the marauding Hungarians). By the

253 *Below* Salzburg, plan of the Kollegienkirche (University Church) by Fischer von Erlach

254 *Below right* Kollegienkirche, façade. Built 1696-1707

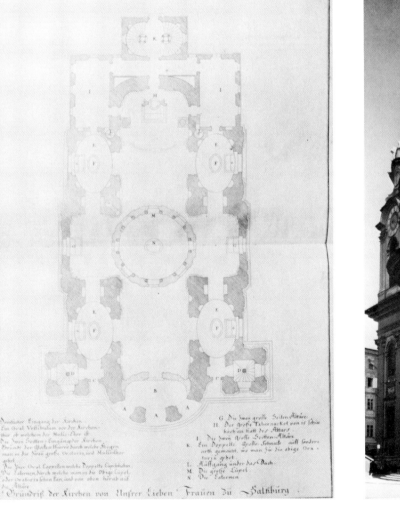

1690s it was sufficiently evident that the Turkish menace had been permanently removed for the intensive development of the suburbs to begin. The man coincided with the hour; though Fischer built town and suburban palaces alike, and though it is the former that have more successfully survived, his sketchbooks and engravings make it clear that it was in designing ever new variations upon the 'free' form of the garden palace and the garden pavilion that he took the greatest delight.

246   Fischer's earliest design for a palace in the environs of Vienna, the original design for Schönbrunn, was as we have seen, not for a *Lustgebäude* at all; nor would this be an apt description of the two first major suburban palaces by other architects: the new imperial Favorita by Burnacini (1687–90), and the Liechtenstein Garden Palace (the original design attributable to D. E. Rossi, 1691). The one was a dismal barrack of a building (later appropriately converted into the Academy for young nobles, the Theresianum), and the other, with its grandiose paired staircases and huge central saloon, placed representation above ease. Fischer's *Lustgebäude*, by contrast, seem designed for pleasure, open to the grounds about them – often to an extent that was not compatible with the harsh climate of the North, as opposed to the milder air of the Mediterranean, in which Fischer's imagination seems to have lingered. Several of them were therefore altered to keep out the cold, before being swept away altogether, with advancing urbanization.

255 Vienna, engraving of Strattmann (later Windischgrätz) Town Palace by Fischer von Erlach, 1692–93

Fischer's *Lustgebäude* commonly have flat, balustraded roofs, frequently raised into a belvedere over the centre, which is generally a bow-fronted or concave-cornered block housing an (often oval) saloon, with wings adjoining. There is sometimes an intricate curved set of ramps and stairs linking the house with the grounds, whilst the central portion, particularly in the ideal version of Fischer's designs, is formed out of open arcades on either side, so that breezes can waft through. What is probably the first of these garden palaces, the *Lustgebäude* in Neuwaldegg, built, like the first of his town palaces, for Count Strattmann in 1692, has most of these characteristics, though here it is only the lower part of the centre that is open to the air on both sides, forming a cross between the traditional *sala terrena* and a passageway, that to some extent prefigures Pope's Grotto under his house at Twickenham outside London. The atlantes supporting the balcony on one side of this and the shape of the staircase on the other clearly reveal the influence of Mathey's Schloss Troja – Fischer having just visited Prague, where he was sufficiently impressed by Mathey's Kreuzherrenkirche to ask permission to take drawings of it. But whereas on Schloss Troja this staircase is merely a highly sculptural adjunct to a fairly conventional building, Fischer's whole villa is conceived sculpturally, as an oval held between rectangular blocks with square projections, and is genuinely linked to the surrounding garden through the staircase and open arcades below. The projecting oval saloon in the centre is essentially a French idea (though at Schloss Frain Fischer had already created the *Ahnensaal* as a free-standing domed oval), taken from Le Vau's *châteaux* like Vaux-le-Vicomte and Le Raincy, and it was to be enormously influential in the Empire,

325

161, 424

especially in Bohemia; Fischer's innovation was to make this feature like a vestibule open to the world outside – an idea that ultimately proved unviable in the Austrian climate.

Fischer's subsequent *Lustgebäude* outside Vienna, both actual and ideal, vary the themes enumerated above. That of Count Althan (*c.* 1693) places the oval saloon (here closed) between four windmill-like arms, a formula that, whether by imitation or common preoccupation, was to be adopted by Boffrand in his second design for Malgrange (1712) and by Juvarra at Stupinigi (1729). The Villa Eckardt (built for Count Schlick, after 1690) employs an open oval vestibule on one side (cf. the Kollegienkirche), and a recessed front with concave corners on the other. These concave corners and the open arcading are retained in Fischer's design for a *Lustgebäude* just outside Salzburg for Archbishop Thun, Schloss Klesheim (1700ff), but the oval saloon has become a rectangle with rounded corners and the staircase has been placed inside, whilst in execution the arcades were glazed in. By the end of his career Fischer seems to have capitulated entirely to the exigencies of the climate – and, according to the inscription on the engraving, to those of his client – and in designing a *Lustgebäude* for the minister of the elector of Hanover (and future king of Great Britain), Baron von Huldenburg (1709–15), he made an enclosed cubic building with quadrant wings far nearer in spirit to the Palladian villas that were to be built in the latter country than to his own airy pavilions.

256 Salzburg, Lustschloss Klesheim, 1700ff. Fischer von Erlach's engraving, showing the intended open arcading

Fischer's town palaces had to overcome a different set of problems. In the crowded conditions of Vienna, in which, unusually for Europe at the time, the houses were of five or six storeys, and there was no room for gardens, the Italian *palazzo*, rather than the French *hôtel,* was the model generally adopted. The narrow streets placed a special premium on the scuptural enrichment of the façade, and of the portal in particular (which, however, required special permission if it was to project), whilst the multi-occupation of several of these palaces conferred especial significance on the semi-public staircase.[18]

The major town palace to be built immediately before Fischer began his career as an architect, the Dietrichstein (later Lobkowitz) Palace (1685–87 by G.P. Tencala), might almost be a textbook illustration of another of Prince Eusebius Liechtenstein's maxims: 'If a building is to be magnificent it must be long, and the longer the nobler. For a great row of evenly spaced windows one after another makes for the greatest effect and splendour'. Fischer's first town palace, for Count Strattmann (1692–93), strove by contrast for the maximum differentiation of its parts. There were projecting bays at either end, clothed with a giant Order of pilasters, the recessed centre had paired pilasters between the windows of the *piano nobile* and paired atlantid-herms (a habitual Viennese motif) between the attic windows, whilst the central portal had canted columns and a three-dimensional arch. Statues crowned the parapets over the projecting ends, and the whole building stood on a rusticated basement. There was also a striking staircase within. It was as if Fischer wanted to display his whole repertoire at a stroke.

In his next town palace, for Prince Eugene, which was

originally built with seven bays (c. 1695ff), but so planned that this could be expanded to twelve when an adjacent plot could be acquired (which it was in 1703), Fischer partially reverted to the infinitely extendable type of palace, with alternating windows and giant pilasters. Indeed in 1723/4 Hildebrandt, who had already superseded Fischer in the actual addition of the five bays and in the supervision of the decoration of the interior, added a further five. In this palace, however, Fischer's real claim to originality lay in his design of the staircase, which he was careful to proclaim as his own in an engraving produced after the construction of the palace had passed out of his hands.

Staircases were something that particularly exercised the minds of both architects and their clients at this period in the Empire; both because, as Guarini pointed out, they were the most difficult part of a building, for which Vitruvius had left no rules, so that a successful design afforded all the pleasure of a Baroque conceit, and because they played a crucial role in the reception of guests with the appropriate mixture of deferential etiquette and overawing context.[19] Before and during the period that Fischer was constructing the palace for Prince Eugene, Prince Johann Adam von Liechtenstein was acquiring two impressive sets of stairs in his town and garden palaces. In the garden palace Rossi had designed a majestic pair of dog-leg stairs setting out from each side of the vestibule and arriving on either side of the great saloon; for the town palace Martinelli had designed a rectangular welled staircase mounting two storeys, whose alteration at the whim of the prince during the architect's absence provoked him into fly-posting the palace with placards denying all responsibility for it. Both these Italian-designed stairs – though not the manners in which they were doubled – were of a kind already well-established in North Italy, and their construction and decoration were massive, majestic and grave. In Prince Eugene's town palace by contrast, Fischer created a staircase whose ascent is a progressive revelation of new spatial complexities. In essence it is of the type introduced to Vienna by Martinelli in the town palace of Count Harrach (c. 1690): starting with a single flight which bifurcates at the first landing into two arms that come together again in a balustraded landing over the beginning of the first flight. Fischer substituted remarkable serpentine volutes supporting vases for conventional balustrades in the first half of the staircase, and atlantes for columns supporting the upper landing, set the second pair of these slightly wider apart than the first, and placed doors up steps in the separately vaulted ends to the transept-like arms, so that at each turn the visitor is kept in uncertainty as to his ultimate goal, whilst the space about him expands as he ascends. The atlantes represent Atlas himself and Hercules, continuing the heroic imagery of the reliefs on the portals, as did the frescoes painted later in the palace, in allusion to Eugene's martial prowess; but their source is clearly the Titan-supported external staircase balcony at Schloss Troja in Prague, which Fischer took the bold leap of transposing indoors.

Fischer continued to design staircases, both conventional and unconventional, throughout his career, though none as remarkable as this. Two of the more unusual are those in the Bohemian Chancery and the Trautson Palace, both in Vienna. The former combines flights of stairs coming from the two fronts of the building in a central landing, from which the upper flights depart, with no more than balustrades and plinths making the divisions, under a unitary vault. The latter consists of one long flight, increasingly hemmed in by a pair of sphinxes

on plinths, four atlantes supporting a saucer dome over a transeptal landing, and the walls of the return flights, before emerging into the huge, light-filled void housing the upper part of the stairs. The Batthyany and Trautson Palaces both have three-aisled entrance passages, with the columns dividing the aisles being paired and grouped in fours respectively. All these stairs open off the side of the entrance-passage or courtyard; at Schloss Klesheim, as befitted a palace in the open, Fischer designed a staircase which took up the whole of the rear of the central block, and which had arcaded openings both to the central saloon and to the exterior. In effect, Fischer brought the paired stairs of the Liechtenstein Garden Palace together under one long, continuous ceiling, to meet at an upper landing acting as a vestibule to the saloon, now pushed to the front of the building. The meagre detailing of Archbishop Thun-Hohenstein's buildings was in this case accentuated by the prelate's death before its completion; what could be made of the idea is shown by Juvarra's staircase in the Palazzo Madama, where it is, however, rightly given pride of place at the front of the building.

Whilst Fischer's staircases seem to show him treating each as a separate exercise, following no one line of development, his later town palaces, in which some of them were housed, show greater convergence. These are the Bohemian Chancery (after-1708–14), the Trautson Palace (c. 1710–16: not strictly a town palace, though given the air of one), and the Schwarzenberg Palace (designed 1713) in Vienna, and the Clam-Gallas Palace (1713ff) in Prague. All of them have a pedimented centre, which in the case of the Trautson, Schwarzenberg and Clam-Gallas Palaces projects as a distinct block. There is a firm distinction between the channelled basement zone and that of the *piano nobile* and upper mezzanine (though in the Clam-Gallas, where the *piano nobile* is on the second floor, their relationship is inverted). The sense of the buildings as cubic entities, or as composed of interlocking cubes, is accentuated by the way in which their heavily framed windows are set into relatively plain walls, with a sense of interval between them. Although the tendency to link elements vertically is still apparent, and is particularly strong where portals are concerned, there is a much greater sense of repose, and of balance between horizontal and vertical, than in Fischer's earlier buildings. Sculpture and structure are more firmly distinguished. The Clam-Gallas Palace is the one in which these statements require most qualification, and it has several features not found in the other three: the absence of a central portal, and the placing instead of one at either end, the use of atlantes-support doorways, and the 'skeleton' treatment of the fenestration above these (derived from Schlüter's Stadtschloss at Berlin), and finally the separate projection of the ends in which these portals and window-structures are housed. Several of these features are concessions to local modes of building (the projections above the skyline and the two portals). Certain features of these late palaces have been described as 'Palladian' in the English sense. 'Classical' would be a better word, for it is doubtful that Fischer ever carried out his intention of visiting England in 1704 – where Palladianism was anyway not yet established. This Classical strain could as well have come from France as from England, but it is tempting to imagine that the alliance of England and

257 Vienna, staircase of Prince Eugene's Palace by Fischer von Erlach, 1695ff

258 Prague, engraving of Clam-Gallas Palace by Fischer von Erlach, 1713ff

Austria during the War of the Spanish Succession left its mark on the style of Fischer's old age. There are certainly signs of a reverse influence – in the work of Archer, and in Thomas Lediard's translation of the *Historische Entwurff*.

Jean Luca von Hildebrandt (1668–1745) is generally recognized as a foil to Fischer von Erlach, and treated as an architect of equal stature.[20] It is true that he was so regarded by most of his contemporaries. However, not only did his career as an architect begin almost a decade later than Fischer's early commissions (and continue for over two decades after Fischer's death), but it was also not until Fischer's active presence as a rival was removed (he was severely incapacitated by illness towards the end of his life) that Hildebrandt found his own idiom, and ceased to live off what were largely personal interpretations of Fischer's ideas. The two men were very different in character: Fischer was the scholar, said by one (nonetheless admiring) client to 'have a screw loose somewhere'; Hildebrandt was the genial, worldly, if temperamental figure, with whom his clients were happy to sit and plan as if he were an equal. We also know that there was a strong antagonism between the two. Fischer, who had been trained as a sculptor, was essentially an architect who thought in terms of shapes and solids, and used sculptural enrichment in a way that emphasized its plasticity. Hildebrandt, despite his training as a military engineer, was essentially a designer and a decorator, who was often consulted and asked for designs that would enhance the visual appearance of an already planned or existing building. Using the Frenchman Claude Le Fort du Plessy as a designer, Hildebrandt was responsible for introducing ribbon-work ornament to Austria, whence it was diffused into stucco decoration through much of Southern Germany. Hildebrandt was often asked to modernize some earlier building; Fischer never was. Hildebrandt was at his best as the frequently consulted family architect to a number of Austrian magnates – the Schönborns, the Harrachs, and Prince Eugene – creating and adapting above all their country and suburban houses, and inserting these into grounds (again, in collaboration with French gardeners) with trees, hedges, vases, statues, gates, and steps to create an enclosed world of which the house was but one element. His masterpiece, the Upper Belvedere, is not merely, like Blenheim, a building *sui generis* made for a hero, but the centrepiece of such a composition.

Hildebrandt was born in Genoa in 1668, the son of a German-born captain in the Genoese army. According to his own account, after studying civil and military architecture with Carlo Fontana and Ceruti respectively, Hildebrandt was attached to Prince Eugene's army in Piedmont as a fortifications engineer from 1695–96. The ending of the war in 1696 and, doubtless, the connections that he formed in the imperial army (though we do not hear of any contact with Eugene himself till 1702) determined Hildebrandt to try his fortune in Vienna, where the great wave of palace-building was by now under way. Almost immediately, he obtained a major commission – to build a garden palace for Prince Mansfeld-Fondi, for which the ground was bought and the first plans were drawn up in 1697.

The plans for this palace and its grounds were the most

259 *Opposite* Munich, interior of the Church of St John Nepomuk built by Egid Quirin Asam, begun 1733, with frescoes by Cosmas Damian Asam

ambitious of any of those in the suburbs of Vienna except the later Belvedere of Prince Eugene and the garden palace of Prince Johann Adam von Liechtenstein, upon which work was only to be recommenced in earnest in 1700. Prince Mansfeld-Fondi came under strong suspicion of having abused his position at court in order to obtain permission to place his palace so close to the *glacis*, on a site that could have provided cover for an enemy gun-emplacement. Hildebrandt's designs characteristically show not merely the palace itself and the *cour d'honneur* and stables, but also the terraced arrangement of the sharply tapering grounds behind, culminating in a pavilion and an open-air theatre, though we know that the actual gardens were designed by the Frenchman, Jean Trehet. For the palace, Hildebrandt took and simplified Fischer's favourite motif of saloon clamped between rectangular blocks. The saloon was not isolated in the centre of the building, but has a porch and a vestibule towards the forecourt, whilst the fenestration of the garden front was carried uniformly through the whole front including the projecting saloon. The palace also includes a chapel, which Hildebrandt designed most attractively with a cut-off and balustraded dome to the right of the vestibule. The most original feature was the roof of the saloon, to which Hildebrandt originally gave an ogee-shaped dome, but which was finally built with a flat roof, and a drum-like corona pierced by oculi transmitting light to a lantern illuminating the saloon from above. Inside, the saloon is not an oval, but a domed square extended by *exedrae* towards the garden and the vestibule.

When Prince Mansfeld-Fondi died without male heirs in 1715, only the right half of the palace was complete. It was bought in 1716 by Prince Schwarzenberg, who was unable to turn his attention to completing it until 1720, when his town palace was finished. He used the same architects for both – Johann Bernhard Fischer von Erlach and his son. Hildebrandt's lantern under the flat roof of the saloon having proved unviable, Fischer was forced to create a closed saucer dome (frescoed by Daniel Gran) in place of the lantern, and, in order to provide enough light, to open great round-headed windows on the garden front, thus interrupting Hildebrandt's undifferentiated fenestration and bringing the saloon nearer to his own preference for the expression of distinct volumes. Like so many garden palaces, the Schwarzenberg Palace (now a hotel) has suffered from the later substitution of more practical hipped roofs and a plain buttressing parapet for the flat roofs and statued openwork balustrade of the central part of the original design, and also of conventional triangular pediments for the curvilinear ones characteristic of Hildebrandt.

There was now an ecclesiastical interlude in Hildebrandt's career. Around the turn of the century three churches were planned, altered or built to a borrowed design by him; St Lawrence, Gabel (Německé Jablonné, Northern Bohemia), 1699ff; the Piarist Church of Maria-Treu, Vienna (planned ?1699, built 1716–54); and St Peter's, Vienna, 1700ff. All Hildebrandt's subsequent sacred buildings were either chapels or village churches, so that this trio of major churches would be of some interest in his *oeuvre*; yet in the case of only one of them – St Lawrence, Gabel – is his authorship certain, and even here he disclaimed all responsibility for the dome. Maria-Treu is a refined repetition in plan of St Lawrence; its designer is unknown, and its construction dragged on over the next half century. It is not impossible that Kilian Ignaz Dientzenhofer, who visited and drew the plan of the church in 1725 contributed

to the final design of the vaults. St Peter's was designed by an Italian engineer, Gabriele Montani, who left for Spain in 1703. If Hildebrandt, rather than the group of masons who credited themselves with the design, had anything to do with the church, this probably consisted in redesigning the façade with its two canted towers, in adaptation of the façade of St Lawrence, but without any relation to the lengthwise oval nave of the church behind. It is thus far from easy to determine the characteristics of Hildebrandt's ecclesiastical style; all the more so in that the first two churches display Guariniesque characteristics of the kind that one might have expected Hildebrandt to have introduced after his sojourn in Piedmont, but which do not occur subsequently in his work, whilst they do recur in the work of Bohemian architects who had an independent line of communication with Guarini's work through the designs that he had supplied for the Theatine Church of Maria-Ötting in Prague.

The one church Hildebrandt is known to have designed, St Lawrence, Gabel, was built at the expense of the imperial viceroy in Bohemia, Count Berka.

Hildebrandt supplied the design and made occasional visits to the site, but even at the laying of the foundation stone was represented by an itinerant mason, Pietro Bianco. Count Berka died in 1706, when the building had risen to the rim of the dome. Hildebrandt and Bianco were immediately dismissed, and when the execution of the building was subsequently entrusted to another Italian, Domenico Perini, Hildebrandt lamented in 1709 that 'the whole system of that fine work' had been changed, and that 'they did not want to finish it according to his model and designs, but wanted to spoil it'. The church was structurally complete by 1712, and furnished by 1717, but a fire in 1788 totally destroyed the furnishings and the roof.

In designing the church, Hildebrandt seems to have been guided by its dedication, modelling its plan to a considerable extent upon Guarini's Theatine Church of S. Lorenzo at Turin. But though both churches are octagons with convex sides protruding into the nave, Guarini's is inscribed in and enlivens a square shell, with each side almost equivalent in value, whereas Hildebrandt's, which is equally inscribed inside a square from which it protrudes only marginally at the sides,

261

83

260 *Opposite* Neu-Birnau, interior of the pilgrimage church by Peter Thumb, 1746–51. Stucco by J. A. Feichtmayr, frescoes by G. B. Göz

261 *Below* Německé Jablonné (Gabel), plan of the Church of St Lawrence

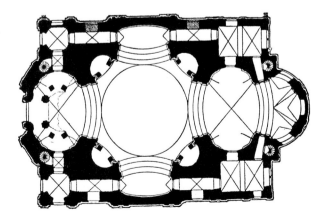

reverts towards the more traditional form of a cruciform nave, with niche-chapels in piers in the diagonals and tunnel-vaulted arms. It is this retreat from the more exciting possibilities of Guarini's plan (Hildebrandt also substitutes a straight balcony over the columns at the front of the diagonal chapels for Guarini's space-describing *serlianas*) that makes it doubtful that Hildebrandt ever projected any kind of dome as complex or interesting as Guarini's, despite his protestations over what finally was built. Even so, his church was not without importance for Bohemia; it initiated the use of three-dimensional arches at the junction of interpenetrating spaces, though in the hands of the Dientzenhofers these were to be transposed to the context of longitudinal churches. The façade, which must be all but entirely Hildebrandt's, is interesting for its subtly layered convex centre, cut back in the middle bay to house the simple portal and window above.

Shortly after the period at which St Lawrence was planned, Hildebrandt formed the most important connection of his career – that with Prince Eugene. In 1702 he provided the plans for the first of Prince Eugene's country houses, Schloss Ráckeve, situated on an island in the Danube below Budapest. In its original form this was a three-sided, single-storey summer palace round a court, with hollow chamfering to the two-storeyed central block housing the saloon. Hildebrandt presented the prince with a choice between a balustraded, flat-roofed termination with oculi underneath, as on the Mansfeld-Fondi (Schwarzenberg) Palace, or a dome-like mansard roof. Prince Eugene chose the latter, but Hildebrandt employed his alternative suggestion on the closely related *Lustgebäude* of Count Starhemberg (between 1700 and 1706). More clearly than Schloss Ráckeve, this building betrays the common ancestry of their hollow-chamfered central saloon, with an (originally) open vestibule in front, in Fischer's Villa Eckardt. Ráckeve and the Starhemberg garden palace, however, like the Mansfeld-Fondi, show how Hildebrandt flattens out Fischer's volumetric conception of his central saloons into mere projections above the roof-line and from the front of his evenly fenestrated façades. In the same year as he built Schloss Ráckeve, Hildebrandt displaced Fischer in the supervision of the extension and internal decoration of Prince Eugene's town palace.

In 1706 and 1707 Hildebrandt began remodelling buildings for members of two other families whose regular architect and architectural consultant he was to become: the garden palace acquired by Friedrich Carl von Schönborn, and Count Alois Harrach's family *Schloss* at Bruck on the Leitha. Friedrich Carl von Schönborn arrived in Vienna as vice-chancellor of the Empire in 1705, a post he had achieved through his uncle, Lothar Franz von Schönborn, archbishop-elector of Mainz and *ex-officio* chancellor of the Empire. Hildebrandt became Friedrich Carl's adviser in all matters of architecture, decoration and furnishing, the voice of all that was 'modern' in the Austrian capital, which for Friedrich Carl was fully the equal of the other pole of German palace architecture – Paris. Through Friedrich Carl, Hildebrandt's advice was obtained for his

uncle's and brother's, as later for his own, buildings in Franconia, thus helping to transmit something of the *Reichsstil* to this *kaisertreu* part of the Empire, which was further diffused through Neumann's employment by other members of the family, who held bishoprics ranging from Konstanz to Trier.[21]

Hildebrandt's involvement in the Schönborns' buildings in Franconia is more satisfactorily dealt with in that context; his work for Friedrich Carl in Austria can be treated briefly here.

Like every magnate, the vice-chancellor required a *Lustgebäude* in the suburbs, which Hildebrandt built round the core of an earlier building (1706–13). He gave this the appearance of a town palace towards the road, with a central section distinguished by a giant Order of pilasters, a balustraded mansard roof, and a triangular pediment-like eruption of the entablature over the combined portal and central window; the garden front was built around the three sides of a court, with a projecting hollow-chamfered pavilion in the centre. Hildebrandt's main imaginative effort went into designing the sculpture-filled grounds and the interiors, of which nothing remains but the staircase, which is the first to have his characteristic asymmetrical scroll-work balustrades – most probably inspired by Padre Pozzo's altar-rails in the Gesù, but licensed by Fischer's

262 *Opposite* Německé Jablonné, façade of the Church of St Lawrence designed and partially built by Jean Luca von Hildebrandt, 1699–1706 (completed 1712)

263 *Right* Salzburg, staircase of Schloss Mirabell rebuilt by Hildebrandt, 1721-27

257 very different scroll-work balustrades in Prince Eugene's town palace.

In 1710, the very year in which Lothar Franz acquired Pommersfelden, Friedrich Carl bought the domain of Göllersdorf. The next few years saw a lively interchange of suggestions, artists, and reports of progress between uncle and nephew, as each sought to convert his acquisition into a country estate. But whereas both of them originally intended merely to convert and adapt the existing fabric, Lothar Franz, despite his protestations that he was just building a family seat, ended by building 369 Pommersfelden from scratch with a representational staircase and *Kaisersaal*, whilst Friedrich Carl, who had deliberately left alone the seigneurial *Schloss* in order to transform a lesser building into his *Tusculanum* (the name of Cicero's villa-farm), progressively expanded his intentions, though never breaching the countrified silhouette of the original house. This was very

264 *Below* Vienna, façade of the Daun (later Kinsky) Palace by Hildebrandt, 1713-16

265 *Opposite* Daun-Kinsky Palace, staircase

similar to what Hildebrandt was to do to Prince Eugene's country property at Schlosshof (1729–32), and in both cases it 427 was to the quasi-architectural shaping of the grounds as an exterior continuation of the house that Hildebrandt's main attention was directed (1711–18). Since the whole village of Göllersdorf belonged to Friedrich Carl, he continued to ask Hildebrandt for a number of other designs for such works as a Loreto Chapel (consecrated 1715), a monument to the Virgin, and a delightful pierced-vaulted ciborium chapel to St John Nepomuk (1733), and the rebuilding of the parish church (1741–42). In 1729 Friedrich Carl was elected to the sees of Würzburg and Bamberg, where he continued to call upon Hildebrandt's advice on the completion of the Würzburg Residenz and the building of a summer palace at Werneck.

Hildebrandt's employment by the Harrach family was similarly extensive and varied, though less has survived. His most important task was to remodel the Mirabell palace for Johann Ernst von Thun's successor as archbishop of Salzburg, Franz Anton von Harrach (1709–27). Every archbishop of Salzburg tended to forsake the summer palace of his predecessor and to construct something new or reconstruct another, and Franz Anton was no exception. Within a year of his election, he stopped work on Klesheim and dispensed with the services of Fischer von Erlach, employing in his stead Hildebrandt, who had already remodelled three *Schlösser* for his elder brother Alois Thomas Raimund, to modernize Archbishop Wolf Dietrich's suburban villa called Mirabell, and to create new interiors in the Residenz. In the Mirabell Hildebrandt dexterously altered windows, doors, and staircases, and modernized the elevations to create a modern palace, whilst building up the old gate-house tower into a central feature that also alluded to those of the Harrach *Schlösser*. A fire in 1818 unfortunately undid most of this work, but the main staircase 263 survives to testify to Hildebrandt's skill in conversion: the old Renaissance configuration of a succession of flights mounting a central well, supported by slant-faced pillars, is lightened by the use of Hildebrandt's characteristic scroll-work balustrades all the way up, and by the omission of the pillars in the top half, so that the whole staircase opens out into a single area over the frothy balustrades. Hildebrandt's other significant work for a member of the family was the Chapel of the Teutonic Knights (now Seminary Chapel) at Linz (1717–21), for the Commander, Johann Joseph von Harrach, executed to his designs by the local Linz mason, J. M. Prunner. This is a small saucer-domed oval structure with a west tower, attached to the former Commandery, whose contrasted concave west front and convex 'arms' foreshadow certain churches by Kilian Ignaz Dientzenhofer.

The correspondence of the Schönborns and the Harrachs is punctuated by statements of alarm at the way in which Hildebrandt's plans 'tend fiendishly towards the grandiose', and by references to his impatience over the constraints of adhering to whatever had already been built or begun, when the result might seem to threaten his reputation if he was regarded as sole author. Yet, as we have seen, some of his most successful buildings were collaborative, or adaptations of some existing structure. Only one patron had the virtually unlimited resources to realize Hildebrandt's most extravagant designs – Prince Eugene. Hildebrandt's attempt to transform a great abbey – Göttweig – on a yet more grandiose imperial scale 266 faltered and failed (as did the attempt to create an Austrian Escorial at Klosterneuburg, to designs by Donato Felice d'Allio

266 Göttweig, Salomon Kleiner's engraving (1744) after Hildebrandt's ideal design for the reconstruction of the abbey, c. 1719. *Vienna, Öst. Nationalbibliothek*

and Joseph Emanuel Fischer von Erlach) because in Austria, as opposed to the Empire at large, the great abbeys simply did not have the resources or the freedom from state interference to realize such projects.

Hildebrandt's skill in making the most of an awkward site is best seen in the Daun (later Kinsky) Palace that he built in Vienna for the absent viceroy of Naples between 1713 and 1716. The façade of this palace combines the basic scheme of a palace generally accepted as having been designed by Fischer – the Batthyany/Schönborn (1699–1700) – with a portal combining the motif of a pair of atlantes standing on round shafts already employed on two other Viennese palaces, Fischerian vases, and an old-fashioned broken-headed segmental pediment framing a window, on which two female figures are perched, that is a straight adaptation of Carlo Fontana's portal of S. Marcello in Rome. The eclecticism of the Daun façade is continued in the interior. Here, following a columnar entrance-passage, Hildebrandt created a vaulted oval vestibule off which the staircase opens to the left. This sequence is reminiscent of that of certain Turinese palaces, which Hildebrandt would have encountered as a young man. The staircase itself is the most ingenious feature of the building. There were two problems: the long, hemmed-in site meant both that the main rooms had to be on

the second floor to obtain more light, and that the staircase itself could receive light only from the courtyard. Hildebrandt exploited these disadvantages by creating a crescendo of light and openness. Whereas the Liechtenstein Town Palace, whose main rooms were also on the second floor, had employed the conventional welled staircase, though drawing this out rectangularly, in the Daun Palace Hildebrandt suppressed the well, placing all the rising flights of the staircase against the closed wall along the outer side of the building, with corridor returns against the windowed courtyard side. But whilst the first flight is enclosed by the retaining walls and the saucer-and-groin vaults of the underside of the upper flight, the second flight is open above, yielding a view into yet a third zone, that of a continuous gallery on brackets below the frescoed ceiling, whilst putti on pedestals, with scroll-work balustrades between, replace the arcades of the lower part of the staircase. The idea is that of the Mirabell stairs, but applied to a rectangular staircase of a kind that arouses quite different expectations; and nothing prepares one for the surprise of a third, and apparently inaccessible, invisibly-lit zone between the upper corridor and the ceiling.

The chief merit of the executed portions of Hildebrandt's tremendous plans for the virtually total reconstruction of the Benedictine Abbey of Göttweig after the devastating fire of 1718 also resides in the staircase. Yet even this suffers from the lack of detailing in proportion to its grandeur, caused by his relinquishment of the responsibility for its execution. At Göttweig we encounter for the first time one of the vigorous abbots of great monasteries, who, though often of relatively modest birth, projected the reconstruction of their abbeys with the assurance of the great princes that they had become by office. In the case of the Imperial Free Abbeys *(Reichsabteien)*, whose abbots were princes of the Empire, and of one or two of the major Austrian subject abbeys with imperial connections, like Melk or Klosterneuburg, such grandiose projects can be explained in part as political affirmations. The unusual thing about Göttweig is that the abbot employed a metropolitan architect, though the abbey itself lacked any special tie with the imperial house; instead, this was a reflection of the personal career of the abbot, Gottfried Bessel (1714-49), with whose death all hope of realizing Hildebrandt's plans in full came to an end. Bessel was born in the territory of Mainz, where he entered the service of Lothar Franz von Schönborn, through which he came to the notice of the emperor. As a reward for serving him, he was appointed abbot of Göttweig, from which he had once, ironically, been expelled as a monk. The fire of 1718 gave him, Hildebrandt, and Friedrich Carl von Schönborn their chance to try something wholly new – the planning of an ideal abbey on a dramatic rocky plateau. Letters tell of the three men spending a whole day together, using Hildebrandt's talents as an architectural draughtsman, and of the resulting perfectly symmetrical plan that fulfilled their stated intention of creating something that 'would not have much of a monkish flavour to it' – in conscious contrast to Melk.

266   Hildebrandt's plan, cunningly incorporating one or two parts of the old monastery spared by the fire, envisaged massive bastioned fortifications surrounding the plateau, inside which the abbey was to be placed, with the domed church on the central axis at the rear of the huge first public court, and mansard-roofed pavilions emerging from the giant ranges to house the main representational features like the Library and *Kaisersaal*. The two chamfered corners at the front of the central court were each exclusively to house a ceremonial staircase; in the event, the left hand one of these was the only major representational feature of the abbey to be completed (1739) on the scale of the original project. The model for these stairs was clearly the autonomous staircase block at Pommersfelden, and, as there, the stairs mounted only to the first floor, inside a spacious chamber vaulted by a single frescoed ceiling immediately under the roof. But whereas at Pommersfelden the stairs form round an inner well and mount to a landing leading to the vestibule and *Festsaal* on an axis with the entrance, with Hildebrandt's three-storeyed arcades forming an outer layer disguising the barren walls, at Göttweig – where Hildebrandt was no longer in control – the stairs climb the sides of the chamber, returning in the centre to join a balustraded corridor that weakly departs to the sides.

If Göttweig exhibits a steady dilution of intention by want of resources, Prince Eugene's *Hoff-, Lust-, und Gartengebäude* (the name 'Belvedere' was only applied to the complex in the middle of the eighteenth century) illustrates the steady enhancement of an originally modest plan for a garden palace, facilitated by the accretion of wealth and honour to its owner, the victorious commander of the imperial forces against the French and the Turks.[22] In the Belvedere Hildebrandt succeeded in creating a unique building expressive of Prince Eugene's special status at Vienna: the cadet member of the ruling house of Savoy, who was at the same time the commander-in-chief of the imperial army and the absentee governor of the Spanish Netherlands. Eugene required a building which was not only a garden palace like its neighbours in the suburbs of Vienna, but also a building with representational pretensions; for he was entitled to his own 'court' *(Hof)* as a member of a ruling house, as well as being chosen to give audiences on behalf of the emperor – particularly to his humbled Turkish opponents. Eugene was moreover a bachelor, and one who seemed sublimely indifferent to his official heir (his niece Princess Victoria, who promptly set about selling his palaces and their contents after his death), so that there was no need to provide apartments for a possible family. He built purely for the pleasure that it gave him and the employment that it gave others, and in his carelessness about the eventual fate of his buildings, it would not even appear that he shared the ambition of Sarah, Duchess of Marlborough at Blenheim for her husband, to create a permanent monument to himself as a hero. This is not to say that any of these factors account for the Belvedere as Hildebrandt built it, but only that, in building it, Eugene and his architect had a uniquely free hand.

Eugene began acquiring ground for gardens adjacent to the Mansfeld-Fondi Palace in 1693, and by 1702 Hildebrandt was enquiring about the prince's intentions over what had clearly become a terraced, architectonic form of garden. By the time of the map prepared in connection with the defence of Vienna in 1704 the plan of the garden palace at the foot of the hill (the later Lower Belvedere) was established, whilst a true belvedere, or gazebo, was planned at the top of the hill on the emplacement of the later Upper Belvedere. The Lower Belvedere could not be built until the end of the War of the Spanish Succession, between 1714 and 1716. It is an unremarkable building from the outside, originally planned with a courtyard enclosed by wings with angled ends, and with a two-storey central pavilion housing the saloon only projecting above the roof-line from the broken-forward central section of the main one-storey range. The interior is lavishly decorated with stucco and stucco-marbling (carried up into the vault in the Marble Gallery) by Santino Bussi, and with frescoes glorifying the prince as Apollo by Martino Altomonte. The palace thus combines a representational role with the qualities of the more accessible *maison à l'italienne* derived from the Trianon and the Château du Val.

The Lower Belvedere was quite self-sufficient, but in 1720 the decision must have been taken to build another palace twice as grand on the site of the gazebo at the top of the hill (thus reversing the sequence of events at Schönbrunn), which was executed in an extraordinarily short space of time in 1721 and 1722. It is scarcely credible that the two palaces were built within seven years of one another by the same architect. In place of the monotonous rectangular blocks and stolid detailing of the Lower Belvedere, the Upper Belvedere appears as a fantastic concatenation of different-shaped roofs over an exuberantly ornamented base. Yet one contained the germ of the other. It was in the Lower Belvedere that Hildebrandt escaped from his half-hearted attempts to emulate Fischer's expression of the central saloon as a distinct volume, and recognized that his inclination was for a differentiated roof line above a horizontally united base. The central saloon of the Upper Belvedere emerges as one roof between two flanking

12

267 *Overleaf left* Vienna, Upper Belvedere, *sala terrena*

268 *Overleaf right* J. A. Feichtmayr. Putto in the pilgrimage-church of Neu-Birnau

269 *Opposite* Steinhausen, capital by D. Zimmermann, after 1728

270 *Above* Vienna, entrance front of the Upper Belvedere by Hildebrandt, 1721–22

270 roofs distinct from those of the rest of the range, just as in the Lower Belvedere, save that the differentiation is carried further and extended to the whole building. The paired pilasters of the central block of the Lower Belvedere are used throughout the Upper Belvedere. The Upper Belvedere, however, as if licensed by the difference of its scale and pretensions, employs the full repertory of Hildebrandt's idiosyncratic ornament: tapering pilasters, some of them labelled with a curious ornament derived from Mannerist pattern-books, some cross-banded, and others with grotesque face-capitals of almost Gothic ancestry; windows with indented jambs, ornate frames, and curvilinear pediments; and, on the lake front, the Borromini-esque pediment over the portico – a feature that Hildebrandt had already employed on the Göllersdorf and Halbthurn (Harrach) *Schlösser,* and that was to become almost a trade-mark denoting his intervention or influence.

The sloping ground on which the palace was sited meant that the garden side was lower than the lake side, which almost appears as a pretext for Hildebrandt's most ingenious staircase. This was so designed that the official visitor, approaching from the side of the *cour d'honneur* (the lake front), should be able to mount the gently ascending single flights of stairs leading to the 271

saloon. These stairs mount up either side of the rectangular chamber, whose vaulting springs from corbels supported by atlantid-herms, to meet in a platform before the door of the saloon. Between them, a third flight plunges downward under 267 the balcony of the platform, to the *sala terrena* acting as a prelude to the gardens on the other side. Against Hildebrandt's wishes, Prince Eugene at first had this covered with a ceiling, but when part of it collapsed, Hildebrandt was able to vault it as he had intended, supporting the arches dividing the sail vaults on massive atlantes, with military trophies above the entablature, in unmistakable allusion to Eugene's military prowess and conquests. The *piano nobile* is given over entirely to the private and state apartments of the prince, with the chapel and three particularly exquisite cabinets in the four octagonal corner-

towers that Hildebrandt appears to have incorporated as a deliberately archaic note, as if in make-believe that they were adopted from some older castle. The interior decoration, for which Hildebrandt used the Frenchman Claude Le Fort du Plessy as *dessinateur,* just as Eugene borrowed Dominique Girard from Max Emanuel of Bavaria for the gardens, is yet more sumptuous than that of the Lower Belvedere. The stucco is again by the immigrant Comasque Santino Bussi, but much of the painting is, significantly, by Italian-based

271 *Above* Upper Belvedere, staircase, stucco by Santino Bussi

272 *Opposite* Melk, interior of the abbey church by Jakob Prandtauer, built 1702–14

Italians – Giacomo del Pò and Francesco Solimena.

The Belvedere is Hildebrandt's supreme achievement and shows him at the height of his powers, finally in possession of an idiom wholly his own. It is therefore the more regrettable that, though he continued to work for his circle of magnates, and indeed for Prince Eugene himself at Schlosshof, he never again had *carte blanche* on a grand scale as he did here. His work at Schlosshof, though of a high order, as Bellotto's set of paintings of it testifies, was concentrated upon the perishable feature of the grounds, of which only sublime fragments remain. The grounds were also the *raison d'être* of the Harrach Garden Palace (1727–35), a sober building constructed round an earlier fabric. His loss of the commission to rebuild the Hofburg, and the failure to complete Göttweig, have deprived us of his two most ambitious later projects, even if it is not certain that their more public nature was suited to his talents. His most fruitful work henceforward was as the architectural adviser of Friedrich Carl von Schönborn, who, after his election as prince-bishop of both Würzburg and Bamberg in 1729, finally laid down his office of vice-chancellor and went to reside in Franconia in 1735. The effect of Hildebrandt's advice and interventions will be taken up in the section on palaces.

The introduction to Part IV has already mentioned the divide between what may be called the 'metropolitan' and the 'country-based' architects in Austria, a divide that concerns both the kind of commissions involved, and the nature and training of the men that executed them. Fischer and Hildebrandt, and certain other later architects who have not been considered, like the younger Fischer and Jean-Nicolas Jadot, operated in a European context. Their education and travels made them familiar with the most significant buildings outside Austria, to which their own make frequent reference. The country-based architects worked instead within a guild tradition, relying, particularly for certain forms of vault and arch, upon a repertoire of pragmatically evolved forms, some of which may have even have reflected the profound knowledge of vaulting and stereotomy accumulated in the mediaeval lodges. Unshackled by notions of correctness, novel elements in their work resulted not merely from the borrowing of features from

273 *Below* Melk, view of the abbey from the Danube

274 *Opposite* Melk church, detail showing dome frescoed by J. M. Rottmayr, 1719

the buildings of the metropolitan architects – as in Prandtauer's entrance block at Melk, or Prunner's adoption of Fischerian rounded central projections and Hildebrandtian pediments – but also from spontaneous invention – as in the towers of Zwettl and Dürnstein, or Prandtauer's terrace at Melk. In their inventiveness they were congenial to their clients, for whom architectural propriety took second place to ingenuity – a quality as prized by them in architecture as in a sermon, or in those favourite devices found adorning so many South German Baroque buildings – the emblem and the chronosticon. The metropolitan architects were employed by the emperor and the magnates – who also held the bishoprics – to build villas and palaces, and only exceptionally churches; the country-based architects were primarily employed by abbots and priors, who were rarely well-born, to build their monasteries and churches, and the occasional town house in provincial towns for the local aristocracy and their monastic employers.[23]

Whereas, as we have seen, the metropolitan architects virtually routed their Italian predecessors as adversaries (though some semi-assimilated Italians like Donato Felice d'Allio and Nicolaus Pacassi were subsequently still to find commissions), the first of the native-born country-based architects, Jakob Prandtauer (1660–1726),[24] simply succeeded to the monastic practice of the last dominant Comasque, Carlo Antonio Carlone (†1708). He succeeded Carlone at Kremsmünster, Garsten, and St Florian, after proving himself independently at Melk. 'Native' is not strictly accurate, for in contemporary terms Prandtauer, like his nephew Munggenast and a number of other craftsmen in Austria, was a 'foreigner' from the Tyrol, which, with Bavaria, helped to repopulate Lower Austria with people and skills at the end of the seventeenth century, after the ravages of the Turks and repeated plague. Prandtauer, who had been trained as a sculptor, settled in St Pölten in 1689, in the quarter belonging to the Austin Priory, and set about extending his competence to building.

He was first referred to as a *Baumeister* in 1695, yet in 1701 he was already being invited to rebuild the church of the major Lower Austrian abbey, at Melk. The man who invited him, Berthold Dietmayr (abbot 1700–39), the son of a monastic official, had himself only just been elected at the age of thirty, and was to be one of the most dynamic of all the Baroque prelates.[25] He invited designs for the church from a couple of Viennese masons and a stuccador (significantly, not from any metropolitan architect), and sent Prandtauer off to look at Carlo Antonio Carlone's church at St Florian with the prior. In view of this, and of the fact that Prandtauer is nowhere described as the *inventor* of the plan of the church at Melk, the overall design should probably be regarded as a product of the abbot's selection of particular features from churches and designs that had pleased him, welded into a whole by Prandtauer. These features might have included the decision to have a drummed dome, a twin-towered façade, and sail vaults (derived from St Florian – they were introduced to the Empire by the Comasques).[26] Prandtauer's personal contribution should then be sought in the detailing – in the busily layered and broken entablatures of the façade, the configuration of the dome, the bowed-out arch of the organ-gallery, and above all in the interplay of the concave, layered entablature of the nave with the broken-forward galleries beneath.

The distinctive profile of these broken-forward gallery arches was to be a characteristic feature of the country-based archi-

275 *Opposite* St Florian Abbey, upper flight of the staircase designed by Carlo Antonio Carlone and built (with alterations) by Prandtauer, 1706–14

276 *Above* St Florian, exterior of the staircase

tects' work. Whilst the inspiration for these goes back to Fischer von Erlach, it seems probable that Fischer himself was dependent for the realization of his ideas in stone upon the pragmatic knowledge of stereotomy built up in the marble quarries and stone-masons' guilds. These gallery arches are somewhat obscured at Melk – it is indeed easy not to notice that the middle pair have a subtly different profile – by the conversion of the gallery into a succession of *loges*. These are due to the theatrical designer Antonio Beduzzi, who also provided designs for the portal and the main altars. This intervention, and Rottmayr's illusionistic frescoes in vaults not really designed to receive them, again illustrate the role of the abbot in orchestrating the final ensemble.

Opposition amongst the monks forced the abbot to proceed cautiously with his plans for rebuilding the whole abbey; though an overall design for this was first spoken of in 1712, the cramped position and unspectacular design of the stairs, for which Prandtauer made a model in 1715, suggest that the reconstruction had to proceed piecemeal. To face the outside world, Prandtauer created an entrance front in 1723–24 whose palatial elevations are clearly indebted to Fischer's Trautson Palace. Between this and the river front of the abbey he enclosed the separate courts between enormously long ranges, barely relieved by breaks or adornment, that sophisticated contemporaries like the Schönborns condemned as 'monkish', which yet not only have a grandeur of their own, but also serve as a foil to his stroke of genius – the front of the abbey where it towers over the Danube.

Here there had previously been an enclosed atrium-like cloister before the church. Prandtauer converted this into a forecourt contained by a massive passage with rounded bastion-like projections over the cliff-face, bearing a terrace

Hall was completed or the Library begun, but since Abbot Berthold continued to construct them using only an executant mason, before finally appointing Prandtauer's nephew, Joseph Munggenast, as his successor, it cannot be doubted that they were to his design. Characteristic of Prandtauer is the almost total breaching of the wall between the pilasters by fenestration, with the abbreviated window entablatures of his later years.

The reputation that Prandtauer had begun to establish at Melk made him the natural successor as monastic architect to Carlo Antonio Carlone when the latter died in 1708, notably at the Austin Priory of St Florian.[27] Here, Carlone had rebuilt the church (still in its mediaeval position to the north of the monastery) as a twin-towered basilica with a calotte over the crossing and sail vaults over the nave. The lower part of the church, with its massive half-columns on high plinths and heavy balconies (cf. Salzburg Cathedral) was stuccoed by his brother Bartolomeo Carlone with the strongly sculptural white stucco characteristic of the churches decorated by this Comasque family of masons and stuccadors (e.g. Schlierbach, Garsten, and Passau Cathedral), but a change of prior resulted in inappropriate illusionistic frescoes in the vaults instead of stucco. Carlone's original design for the monastery envisaged housing the representational parts as spurs projecting from the enclosed courts, but in a second plan made some time before he died he had taken the momentous step of housing them in pavilions rearing out of the middle of these ranges, separately roofed in French *château* fashion. It now seems clear that it was also Carlone who had not only (before Pommersfelden) decided to house the ceremonial staircase in one such pavilion, but also to open this outwards in a series of arcades, ramping-arched below and round-arched above. As designed by Carlone, however, the stairs were sealed off by arcades (cf. Klesheim) from the corridors running the whole length of the prelatial and guest ranges behind them, to which they gave access. Prandtauer suppressed these arcades in the upper storey, unifying stairs and corridor under one vault, opened up the central bay above the entrance with a massive arch, made a recession in the balustraded platform behind it to attract the eye farther inwards, and designed remarkable open-work screens on the exterior and interior, so as to admit the maximum amount of light. As at Melk, his aim was to dissolve the barriers between within and without. At St Florian Prandtauer further designed the bombastic Marble Hall, whose decoration glorifying the emperor and Prince Eugene and their victories over the Turks is so little overtly religious that Bartolomeo Altomonte's fresco (1724) shows personifications of Austria and Hungary reverencing Jupiter trampling the Turk underfoot. This was appropriate to a part of the monastery which belonged to the secular sphere, being the climax of a set of apartments housing distinguished visitors, as both the monastic traditions of hospitality and the monastery's political role required. In Gotthart Hayberger's later Library (1744–51), which J. C. Jegg's undulating bookcases make into a masterpiece amongst Austrian monastic libraries, the balance was redressed. The prior declined Daniel Gran's idea of a fresco showing the Blessings of Austria under the Habsburgs, and opted for the blessings springing from the marriage of Virtue and Wisdom instead.

Prandtauer was succeeded by his nephew, Joseph Munggenast (1680–1741),[28] at Melk and Herzogenburg (rebuilt piecemeal from 1714ff), just as he had succeeded Carlone, but it appears that he had already begun to delegate lesser commissions to him before his death, notably Dürnstein. The story

277 St Florian, entrance portal, executed to an enriched version of Prandtauer's design by G. B. Bianco and Leonhard Sattler, 1712–13

connecting the Library and the Marble Hall. But the mock-fortification appearance of this passage (which can be compared with Hildebrandt's scenographically rather than earnestly meant bastions at Göttweig) is contradicted by the windows and the giant Serliana opening in the centre, by means of which Prandtauer attains his most characteristic effect – that of creating an optical link between within and without, making both a vantage-point for the inmate, and a device inviting the gaze of the spectator. Prandtauer concentrated the whole visual impact of the abbey upon this front, which would be the one seen by the traveller descending the major traffic artery of the Danube. For instead of placing the Library and the Marble Hall as two pavilions breaking through the middle of their ranges, as became the norm after C. A. Carlone's introduction of this device from palace to monastic architecture at Garsten and St Florian, he made them into spurs projecting slightly inwards from the long conventual ranges, framing the twin-towered façade and dome. Prandtauer died before the Marble

of the rebuilding of this Austin Priory shows it to be, in many ways, the most remarkable of all of the Baroque monasteries. Using the most slender resources, but exploiting his connections with the main Austin Priory of St Dorothy at Vienna and with his Benedictine neighbours at Melk, Prior Hieronymus Übelbacher (1710–40) managed to procure designs and work from some of the leading craftsmen of his day. His diary shows him thoughtfully noting what was being built elsewhere, for possible emulation, and narrowly specifying from what models and engravings his craftsmen should work.[29]

Prior Hieronymus began by rebuilding the monastery, probably to an overall design by Prandtauer, but employing Munggenast (who became an independent master-builder in 1717) or his foreman from at least 1719. The parts of the monastery were rebuilt where they stood, with no attempt to rationalize the mediaeval jumble. As a result, the most ornate feature, the portal leading to the church, does not stand in front of the church, but at one end of a narrow passage leading to a door in the north-west corner of it. The portal was begun in 1725, and it seems clear that it, like the church tower (1725–33), was the result of collaboration between Munggenast, who would have made the working drawings, and Matthias Steinl, who would have provided the original design. Steinl (*c.* 1644–1727) began his career as court carver in ivory, but as a corrodian of the Austin Priory of St Dorothy in Vienna, expanded into an *'Ingenieur'* employed by the order to design not only quasi-architectural features like high altars and pulpits, but also the rebuilt façade of St Dorothy's itself.[30] At this period the word *'Ingenieur'* could either mean an 'engineer' in the military sense, or simply an 'inventor' of designs. Steinl's designs reflect his training as a sculptor, and as such he needed the assistance of a mason to ensure their structural stability. Both the portal and the tower of Dürnstein are essentially conceived in sculptural and symbolic terms: the portal – which is shaped like an altar – illustrating the theme of redemption; and the tower, whose design is concentrated upon the two angled faces greeting those who come up or down the Danube, framing figures of the two protectors of those travelling by water – the Virgin and St John Nepomuk. The church itself (1721–23), whose construction, rather unusually for Austria at this period, is of the wall-pillar type, with sail vaults, has not been unanimously attributed to any architect. The old-fashioned wall-pillar plan and the undulating profile of the two convex galleries with a concave gallery between, all on three-dimensional arches, suggest Prandtauer, whilst the detailing of the choir suggests Munggenast. Steinl's name has also been put forward, but it is less easy to imagine his being responsible for a design in which structural subtleties like the bowed-out arches of the galleries, with pierced vaults behind (cf. the portal of the Court Stables at Salzburg) play such an important role. The church is exquisitely furnished, to detailed specifications laid down by Prior Hieronymus, whose proudest achievement was his acquisition of the stuccador of Prince Eugene's palaces, Santino Bussi, to create the vaults so unusually stuccoed with scenes in relief, instead of frescoes.

Munggenast and Steinl had collaborated on the design of a church tower once before, at the Cistercian Abbey of Zwettl (1722–8). Here, it seems to have been Munggenast who began by providing a conventional, planar design for the tower, to which Steinl then imparted life and plasticity, giving the façade an undulating profile, and creating great volutes and a bulbous base where the trunk of the tower itself began. Twin towers were the norm in Austria at this period, but a number of Cistercian abbeys employed a single west tower, possibly in a casuistical attempt to adhere to the letter of the Cistercian ban on stone towers by maintaining that these were an organic part of the façade. Such lack of regard for the statutes of the order may be contrasted at Zwettl with the remarkable decision taken at the same time to demolish the old Romanesque nave and raise it to the height of the Gothic hall-choir, using the same architectural forms: this at a period when the transformation into Baroque forms of earlier churches with fresco and stucco was the rage in South Germany.

Munggenast, like Prandtauer, was employed by a number of monasteries to regularize and modernize their conventual buildings. Only at the Benedictine Abbey of Altenburg, how-

278 Melk, interior of the Library designed by Prandtauer and completed by Joseph Munggenast, 1726–31

ever, did Munggenast have the chance to rebuild on a large scale, not only the church, but also representational rooms, including a great Library. He cunningly contrived to put the church inside the fabric of its mediaeval predecessor as a spacious oval nave preceded by a short entrance bay containing the organ gallery, and succeeded by a long monks' choir culminating in a saucer-domed sanctuary. The treatment of the oval nave was inspired by that of St Peter's, Vienna, from which Munggenast adopted the oval windows in the pendentives. These, however, are now flanked by pilasters, thus giving the effect of a quasi-drum in the absence of a real drum under the oval dome above. The object of this was to bring the fresco near, the fresco itself (by Paul Troger (1733–34)) being no longer some glory of miscellaneous saints in heaven, but a composite depiction of the 'Woman clothed with the Sun' described in the Book of Revelations. The desire to dispense with a drum at the base of domes, so as to make frescoes with their more complex iconography both more legible and more

immediate, spread from South Germany to Austria (hence also the suppression of the drum when the Piarist Church at Vienna was finally vaulted, to the benefit of Maulpertsch's frescoes). The high colouring of Troger's fresco, and more especially, the brilliant blue worn by the *Woman of the Apocalypse*, is taken up by F. J. Holzinger's lavish stucco and stucco-marbling – again a *rapprochement* with the Rococo churches of Bavaria and Swabia.

282   The Library (1740–42) is the most ambitious of all the Austrian monastic libraries, the equal of the church in scale and sumptuousness, and, in conception, taking its departure from the Imperial Library (and possibly from the Gallery at Clagny). The monastic buildings at Altenburg were not replanned symmetrically round the church, but built with enclosed courts

279 *Above* St Florian, Marble Hall by Prandtauer, built 1718–22, decorated 1723–24. Stucco-marbling by F. J. Holzinger, fresco by Bartolomeo Altomonte with *quadratura* by Ippolito Sconzani

280 *Opposite* Dürnstein Priory, tower designed by Matthias Steinl and built by Joseph Munggenast, 1725–33

and with projecting ranges linking the abbey more firmly with the landscape. One of these was built to contain the library over a massive substructure housing a crypt-like room decorated with grotesques whose purpose has never been properly elucidated. The Library consists of a domed centre with two arms – as in the Imperial Library – but with saucer domes over the ends of the arms as well. The amount of space

281 Dürnstein, interior of the church 1721–23, stucco by Santino Bussi

provided for books is minimal – there is not even a second tier of stacks reached by a gallery – instead, the upper zone and the vaults are given over to a series of frescoes by Troger glorifying the various branches of learning, and lavish stucco and stucco-marbling by J.M. Flor. The predominant colours are again, as in the church, blue and reddish-brown. More than any other library, save that of Admont, this one proclaims itself as an affirmation of the special role of the older, country-based orders – the cloistered pursuit of learning. The *Festsaal*, by contrast, here takes its place as merely one of a set of moderate-sized 'Marble Apartments' for distinguished guests.

There is one further country-based architect of this generation who merits attention – Johann Michael Prunner (1669–1739).[31] Born in Linz, after a period of *Wanderschaft* whose itinerary must have included Prague he settled in Linz as city mason in 1705. As the capital of Upper Austria, Linz afforded Prunner more commissions in the way of building town houses for the nobility and churches for the various religious orders than did St Pölten to Prandtauer or Mung-genast. One of these churches, that of the Commandery of the Teutonic Knights, Prunner built to designs supplied by Hilde-brandt (1718–25). Prunner also worked in Passau and Regens-burg. He did, however, work for a great abbey on one occasion, when he built the church at Stadl-Paura for Maximilian Pagl, the abbot of Lambach.[32] Pagl was, like Übelbacher of Dürn-   237

stein, a man who took a keen interest in the planning and
decoration of all his projects. Though the church at Stadl-Paura
was built in honour of the Trinity in fulfilment of a vow made
when the plague of 1713 (the same plague that gave rise to
the building of the Karlskirche) threatened Lambach, Pagl also
saw this as an opportunity to realize an ambition that he had
already nurtured to build a triangular church. He therefore
237 obtained from Prunner plans for a centrally-planned church
with three identical façades framed by three towers. In order to
perform their function, the towers had to be canted, so that the
resulting façades bear a distinct resemblance to that of St
Peter's, Vienna (which was erected by a Confraternity of the
Holy Trinity – making one wonder if Prunner did not have
access to some project of Hildebrandt's for a Trinitarian replanning of that church). Each portal was dedicated to a
member of the Trinity, round whom the symbolism of the altar
in the apse facing the portal was also designed. When it came to
the decoration of the dome of the church with frescoes by Carlo
Carlone in illusionistic settings by Francesco Messenta
(1719–23), a change of plan was made, possibly suggested by
the latter, as a result of which the retables of the altars were
merely painted on the walls of the apses, which were cut
through to reveal the altarpieces painted upon the back walls of
the towers behind – a device which may have been derived from
Bernini's Altieri Chapel in S. Francesco a Ripa, or from certain
Genoese altars with sculptural groups by Maragliano. Every
item of decoration in the church plays its part in the Trinitarian
symbolism of the whole.

With the deaths of Hildebrandt and Joseph Munggenast in
the first half of the 1740s, the era of creative architects in
Austria in both the capital and the countryside was virtually at
an end. Maria Theresa had first to fight for her throne and to
attempt to wrest back Silesia from Frederick the Great of
Prussia in the War of the Austrian Succession and the Seven
Years War. Thereafter she, like her son and successor, Joseph
II, concentrated more upon reforming and rationalizing the
laws and administration of Austria, in order to emulate Prussia,
than on building. The empress and Joseph II both lived simply,
and her piety was private, whilst he was a deist. The great
abbeys were prevented by a combination of a shortage of funds
and governmental interference from embarking on any further
grandiose projects – as the melancholy failure to complete the
Austrian Escorial – the Abbey-Residenz of Klosterneuburg –
reveals.[33] Only in the remote province of Styria were fresh
projects and ideas to be found.

There, the son of a masons' foreman in Vienna, Joseph
Hueber (?–1787), had succeeded by ability and marriage to the
practice of the last of the dynasties of local *welsche* masons
(another branch of the Carlones) in the capital, Graz.[34] From
there he built two pilgrimage-churches – St Veit am Vogau
(1748–51) and the Weizbergkirche (1656–58). These are unusual in that they combine a wall-pillar plan with a vaulting
arrangement that creates a centralizing effect in the middle of
the nave. Though comparisons have been drawn with
J. M. Fischer's churches in Bavaria and Swabia, it seems more
likely that the centralizing idea comes from Munggenast and his
son's churches at Altenburg and Herzogenburg, whilst the wall-
pillar plan was introduced to Styria by the Comasques. At the
Weizbergkirche, where the central bay is distinguished by a
saucer dome and columns on either side of the chamfered
pillars, the hybrid is particularly successful, combining the
receding stage-like effect – with the high altar as the focus – of

282 *Top* Altenburg Abbey, interior of the Library built by Munggenast,
with frescoes by Paul Troger and stucco by Johann Michael Flor,
1740–42

283 *Above* Admont Abbey, interior of the Library built by Joseph Hueber,
with frescoes by Bartolomeo Altomonte, 1774–76

the wall-pillar church, with the revelation of successive spaces. Examination of the Weizberg church encourages the opinion that it was Hueber who designed the last of the great Baroque libraries, at Admont (*c.* 1770). This is the only feature to survive from the Baroque abbey, which was partially rebuilt in the mid-century to an elephantine overall design by the Steyr architect Gotthard Hayberger (who also built the library at St Florian). Nothing either in Hayberger's plan or in his other work indicates that he was capable of the spatial imagination shown in the library at Admont, which consists of a saucer-domed central space defined by wall-pillars faced by half-columns, between arms each divided above into three sail vaults, but bound together below by continuous bookcases. The iconographic programme of the library, consisting of rather arid frescoes depicting personifications of all the branches of learning by Bartolomeo Altomonte (1774–76), remarkable sculpture from an earlier projected library by Thaddäus Stammel, including depictions of the 'Four Last Things' (cf. the portal at Dürnstein), and herm-pilasters representing all the most famous artists of antiquity and the modern world (including an invented son of Dürer's!), represents an apt summing-up of the programmatic ambitions of Austrian architecture and decoration.[35]

Bavaria and Swabia

Outside Austria, the range of activity open to an architect in the Empire was much more limited. In the absence of a focal capital or a wealthy aristocracy based on the land, the major commissions were those afforded either by one, or by a group, of the innumerable courts scattered through Germany, or, in the South, by the great monasteries. Balthasar Neumann was exceptional in being extensively employed on secular and ecclesiastical commissions alike. Johann Michael Fischer's tombstone, by contrast, proudly recalls that he worked for 22 monasteries and built 32 churches, but is vague about secular work, whilst François Cuvilliés, though consulted about the construction of palaces from Munich to Cassel, was never entrusted with a commission to build a church, even if, as the elector's architect, he was asked for advice on several.

To this dichotomy of employment corresponded a dichotomy of training; in general, the court architects were foreigners or foreign-trained, and they were of higher social status either through birth or through military rank, service as a military engineer being the one way to acquire a theoretical as well as practical knowledge of architecture, through the study of the art of fortification. The ecclesiastical architects customarily came from within the guild tradition, even if their training was not always that of a mason. Neumann again, as a craft-trained bell- and artillery-founder who was given the opportunity to study military architecture as an officer, and rose to be a colonel, bestraddles the two spheres. In other words, the division that was found in Austria between the metropolitan and the country-based architects is repeated in the rest of the Empire in a different form, in the division between court architects and craft architects. The latter had to be inscribed in the guild of a town, and unlike the city masons of Vienna, the Oedtls and the Jänggls, who generally worked as the executive masons of the metropolitan architects and were debarred from working in the country, found their most fruitful employment working for the great rural abbeys. Some, like the Asams, might not even belong to a masons' guild, but then the exempt status of the great abbeys released them from guild control. That the gulf between court and country architecture is not greater is largely due to the decoration applied to buildings; the Asams, Johann Baptist Zimmermann and a host of other stuccadors and frescoists, were able to work indifferently on court or ecclesiastical commissions, even if the most prestigious of these, such as the *Kaisersaal* and Staircase at Würzburg, or the major ceilings of the Neues Schloss at Stuttgart, were entrusted to foreigners.

Bavaria was a relatively compact state, smaller than Austria, but ruled by a dynasty, the Wittelsbachs, that nursed the ambition to head the Empire should the male line of the Habsburgs fail.[36] This, and not extravagance alone, accounts for much of the gilded and silvered splendour of the apartments in the palaces built by the Electors Max Emanuel (1679–1726) and Carl Albert (1726–45) – briefly but miserably the Emperor Charles VII. Max Emanuel's differences with Leopold I, after a heroic youth spent fighting the Turk on his behalf, led to his exile during the War of the Spanish Succession, from

284 Weingarten, pulpit by Fidel Sporer, 1762

1704–15, first in the Netherlands (of which he had earlier been governor for the Habsburgs), and later at St Cloud. Hence not only his acquisition as a page of the stunted Walloon, François Cuvilliés, whose architectural aptitudes only later became apparent, but also his enduring belief in the superiority of everything French, to the extent that he felt himself an exile amongst his own subjects, and employed Frenchmen or French-trained craftsmen whenever he could. Consideration of the palaces and pavilions built for Max Emanuel and Carl Albert will be deferred to a later chapter, but the intensity of the French influence prevailing at court in Bavaria must always be borne in mind, both as a foil to the very different climate in which ecclesiastical architecture was created, and as an important factor in the diffusion of French-influenced ornament into the latter sphere.

Bavaria was traditionally and zealously Catholic – the Wittelsbachs could indeed be said to have rescued Southern Germany and Austria for the Roman Church – and contained both important monasteries, whose foundation went back to

285 Weingarten, ideal project for the reconstruction of the abbey. After(?) Father Beda Stattmüller's design of 1723. *Benediktinerabtei Weingarten*

the missionary days of Christianity in Germany, and innumerable pilgrimages, mostly fostered by the orders. Ultimate control over the administration and expenditure of these monasteries was nonetheless exercised by a state body called the Spiritual Council. As a result, they were frequently held back from reconstructing their conventual buildings, whilst being more lavish in the adornment than in the structural ambition of their churches. As in Austria, spiritual control over the monasteries and over the parishes was exercised by bishops who were also the rulers of small ecclesiastical enclaves within or beyond the borders – in this case Freising, Eichstätt, and Augsburg. Monastic affiliations and ecclesiastical jurisdictions sometimes affected the locations in which craftsmen and artists worked.

Bavaria contained one Benedictine abbey, Wessobrunn, (founded by a member of the dynasty that had preceded the Wittelsbachs), that helped to foster one of the most remarkable examples of collective genius in the history of art: the so-called Wessobrunn School of stuccadors.[37] Craft activity in Bavaria was regulated by a network of guilds in the capital, Munich, and in most of the lesser towns. One such town to the south of Munich, Weilheim, fed the capital with sculptors and masons just at the time, around the turn of the sixteenth century, when Italians and Italian-trained Netherlanders were introducing the art of Renaissance stucco-work to the capital, in the Church of St Michael and the Residenz. Developing out of this association, the craftsmen from the hamlets nestling round Wessobrunn, which fell within the jurisdiction of Weilheim, began to specialise in stucco, as did the masons of another town called Miesbach. During the Thirty Years War the Wessobrunners were already working as far away as Innsbruck in the Tyrol. After the war, whereas the Miesbachers concentrated more upon masonry than stucco, the Wessobrunners succeeded in establishing a partnership with the Vorarlberg masons, working chiefly for the exempt abbeys of Swabia. In this partnership they employed a distinctive acanthus-based decorative repertoire, that was indebted to French engravings for its ornamental vocabulary, but to the Wessobrunners' own training as masons for its intelligent and lucid relation to what was built. This combination of ornamental modernity and sympathetic understanding of structure was to be a permanent characteristic of Wessobrunn stucco till the end of the eighteenth century.

In the 1720s it began to look as if the cohesion of the School was being threatened, both by the emergence of a new form of French-influenced ribbon-work ornament whose subordination to large illusionistic frescoes undermined the Wessobrunners' creative role, and by the action of several of them in settling elsewhere, and pursuing other skills: Dominikus Zimmermann, first in Füssen and then in Landsberg, learning the art of *scagliola* and then that of masonry; Johann Baptist Zimmermann, settling successively in Miesbach, Ottobeuren and Freising, before becoming court stuccador at Munich, whilst branching out into fresco-painting in addition; Joseph Schmuzer, following his ancestor Johann, and turning more to masonry; the Feichtmayr and Finsterwalder brothers, settling in Augsburg. However, this last move gave a decisive new impetus to the Wessobrunn School. Augsburg was the centre in South Germany not only of ornamental engravers – often pirating the latest French prints – but also of fresco-painting; as a result, the Wessobrunners based there had immediate access to the latest developments in ornament, and, by associating with the painters, evolved a kind of decoration that was complementary to their frescoes, which themselves began to turn their back on pure illusionism. A decisive final factor was that the brothers broadened their team to include another Wessobrunner, J.G. Übelhör, who had worked with J.B. Zimmermann on the court commissions at Munich, and brought with him a familiarity with the vital element of Rococo ornament – the ambiguous, shelly substance called *rocaille* – which was evolved in the decoration of the *Reiche Zimmer* and the Amalienburg. It was the Feichtmayrs and Übelhör who at Diessen in 1734–36 created for the first time on a monumental scale the *rocaille* cartouche ornament that was to prevail over the whole of South Germany, and influence developments as far afield as Prussia and the South Tyrol for the next generation.

Swabia, in contrast to Bavaria, was a land of fragmented sovereignties, chiefly of *Reichsstifte* and *Reichsstädte* – Imperial Free Monasteries and Imperial Free Towns. The latter were, with the single exception of Augsburg, whose significance has been alluded to above, no longer of any great importance; the monasteries (one or two of which were subsequently to be subsumed into Switzerland rather than into Germany) on the other hand felt an unparalleled need to give built expression to their sovereign status and to the religious triumph (as they saw it) of the Church and their orders.[38] This they did by rebuilding their monastic complexes symmetrically on a monumental scale and by rebuilding or redecorating their churches with fresco and stucco. Whereas mediaeval monasteries were as a rule built in a jumble to the south of the church, with the cloister as their only regular element, and the chief buildings of the common life, the chapter-house and the refectory, as their most distinguished features, Baroque monasteries had a very different order of priorities. For them the representational and hospitable parts of the monasteries – the main stairs, and the state apartments of the abbot and his guests, culminating in the *Festsaal* – were those on which the most attention was to be lavished, whilst a splendid library symbolized the monasteries' historic role as repositories of sacred learning. For Imperial Free abbeys, the *Festsaal* was more than just a saloon for great receptions – it was a *Kaisersaal,* a room that broadcast their status as sovereigns under the emperor. It was therefore appropriate that the direct models for their new symmetrical layouts should have been found in secular *Schlösser,* whilst their ideal inspiration came from the palace-cum-monastery complex of the Escorial, itself partly inspired by theoretical reconstructions of Solomon's Temple. Abbeys were still acquiring sovereign status as late as the second half of the eighteenth century; that this was no hollow presumption is shown by the fate of Weingarten, whose plans for the reconstruction of its abbey buildings – the most appealing of all ideal plans – were thwarted by the abbey's subjection to the emperor in his capacity as ruler of Austria. And whilst the scale and decoration of reconstructed monastic buildings asserted the abbeys' rights as rulers, the decoration of their churches embodied the special claims to venerability and sanctity of the orders that built them. In Swabia and Switzerland several of the great Benedictine abbeys also incorporated a reference to Fischer von Erlach's church of the Benedictine University at Salzburg through their bowed-out façades.

Certain of these Benedictine abbey churches – Einsiedeln, Zwiefalten and Weingarten – were, exceptionally, themselves pilgrimage churches. In general the old orders in South Germany, notably the Cistercians and Premonstratensians, though eagerly fostering this manifestation of popular piety, avoided the disruption of the claustral life that pilgrimages brought with them. Instead, the Cistercians at Neu-Birnau and Vierzehnheiligen, and the Premonstratensians at Steinhausen and the Wies, lavished all the resources of architecture and decoration upon building pilgrimage-churches set in the middle of the countryside, that nevertheless succeeded in attracting more than one hundred thousand communicants in a year. These pilgrimage-places were unlike those of the high middle ages, which were generally at sites linked with the life of Christ or with the resting-places of the earliest Apostles and Martyrs; instead, they sprang from the late-mediaeval and post-Tridentine susceptibility to miraculous visions and happenings, associated either with pre-Christian cult sites, or with crude images reflecting new intensities of devotion to the sufferings of Christ and the Virgin.[39] The custodianship of these places and images was one of the chief assets of the old country-based orders, as compared with the later urban orders of friars and

286 Obermarchtal, interior of the abbey church designed by Michael Thumb in 1684, built 1686–92. Stucco by Johann Schmuzer, 1689–94

congregations. The orders particularly associated with the Counter-Reformation either cultivated a more verbal appeal, and relative plainness in their churches – like the Capuchins and the Carmelites – or, in the case of the Jesuits, developed two specialized types of ecclesiastical building – galleried wall-pillar churches to house the largest possible number of auditors

285

254

– both their own students and the public – for their sermons; and rudimentary, but lavishly decorated, low rectangular rooms to house the communal devotions of the congregations that they fostered amongst their own students and the townsfolk.

The distinctive asset of Bavarian and Swabian Baroque architecture in the ecclesiastical field was a kind of structure that was, in its own way, as significant an invention for this region as that initiated by Alberti's S. Andrea and perfected in Vignola's Gesù was for Europe as a whole. This is the wall-pillar church: an aisleless, tunnel-vaulted building, with chapels placed between internal buttresses that are connected by small transverse tunnel vaults, springing at the same level as the main vault.[40] Such churches generally had an insignificant transept or none at all, a recessed apsidally-ended choir, and galleries running through the wall-pillars above the chapels. The want of a clearly-defined crossing, abetted by considerations of economy and spatial instinct, made domes rare. In many ways, the wall-pillar church was a synthesis of Late-Gothic and Renaissance structures – the wall-pillar system of chapels between internal buttresses that had been extensively developed in Southern Germany and Austria in the late middle ages, and the Renaissance revival of tunnel-vaulting, with galleries inserted to accommodate the Jesuit (and originally Protestant) accent on preaching. Appropriately then, it was a Jesuit church, St Michael's at Munich (1583–97, designed by Friedrich Sustris and Wendel Dietrich, executed by Wolfgang Miller) that initiated this type of church, and further Jesuit churches – at Dillingen (1610–17, by Hans Alberthal), and on the Schönenberg above Ellwangen (1682–86, designed by Michael Thumb and Heinrich Mayer SJ, executed by Christian Thumb) – that inaugurated the exploitation of it by the Graubündeners and Vorarlbergers respectively.[41]

The Graubündeners and the Vorarlbergers were to Bavaria and Swabia what the Comasques were to Austria.[42] The Graubündeners who, as we have seen, also extended their activity into Austria and Salzburg, were more concentrated in Bavaria, whilst the Vorarlbergers, though stemming from the westerly part of the Habsburg dominions, flourished in Swabia. Whereas the Graubündeners had begun moving into Bavaria and Swabia in the second decade of the seventeenth century, the Vorarlbergers emerge as a distinct group only with the founding of the *Auer Zunft* – the Au Guild and Confraternity – by Michael Beer in 1657. Although Beer almost immediately obtained a commission of more than provincial importance, (the first rebuilding after the Thirty Years War of a major abbey, at Kempten 1652ff), he was very shortly displaced there by a Graubündener, Giovanni Serro, so that the Vorarlbergers' heyday did not begin until the 1680s, with the Schönenberg Pilgrimage-Church, and the great abbey churches that followed. The Graubündeners, like the Comasques, but with less originality, combined the practice of masonry with stuccowork, whereas the Vorarlbergers came only late to the latter, and, as mentioned earlier, relied chiefly on the Wessobrunners for this essential complement to their architecture. Both the Graubündeners and the Vorarlbergers shared the virtues of mobility and adaptability that favoured them as itinerant masons against the hidebound guildsmen of the towns, but whereas the Graubündeners especially enjoyed the repute of being, in the words of the chronicler of Zwiefalten, 'a people superior to our own in speed and diligence', the key Vorarlbergers were conveniently ready to be the contractors for, as

well as the builders of, the buildings that they undertook.

Certain Graubündeners made contact with court and urban circles, and correspondingly enlarged the scope and range of their designs, but the Vorarlbergers remained almost exclusively in monastic employment, and their churches are almost all developments of the wall-pillar type. At one time it was even customary to refer to this design as the '*Vorarlberger Münsterschema*', though this categorization is now recognized as unduly confining. The series starts with the Schönenberg Pilgrimage-Church (1682–86), receives its classic formulation in the Premonstratensian Abbey Church of Obermarchtal (1686–92, designed by Michael Thumb – here replacing a Graubündener), and enjoys a last lease of life in the early churches of Peter Thumb (the Benedictine Abbey Church of Ebersmünster, 1719–27, and the Benedictine Abbey Church of St Peter in the Black Forest, 1724–27). All these churches have naves of wall-pillar construction, with a somewhat wider bay marking the centre of a barely projecting transept, usually followed by a choir with free-standing pillars, contrasting with the wall-pillars of the nave. Developments within this schema, and particularly within the *oeuvre* of the most fertile of the Vorarlbergers, Franz Beer (whose 'von Bleichten' denotes the title given to him by the emperor in 1722, albeit not for his architectural activity), include a growing approximation of the wall-pillars to free-standing pillars, and an increase in the autonomy given to each bay, through the employment of saucer-domes or sail-vaults – the latter doubtless borrowed from the Comasques. The employment of such vaults went hand in hand with the increasing importance given to frescoes at the expense of stucco, and with increasing illusionism within the frescoes themselves. Almost all these churches were stuccoed by members of the Schmuzer family from Wessobrunn; and whereas the earliest churches had only richly plastic, but sparing, acanthus stucco forming the focus of each vaulting-bay – Irsee (1699–1702) was the first to incorporate a cycle of paintings – the later churches, notably Weissenau (nave by Franz Beer, 1717–23) and Weingarten (1715–20), employ acanthused ribbon and diaper-work on the peripheries of their frescoed vaults.

Despite the increasing predilection for domical vaults, Weingarten was the only Vorarlberger church to be built with a full drummed dome over the crossing. It is in some sense the climax of the series, though neither the last to be built, nor exclusively attributable to the Vorarlberger architect who provided the basic plan, but left when he was not entrusted with the total conduct of its construction – Franz Beer. Drummed domes were contemplated at other Vorarlberger churches, at Disentis and Einsiedeln, but in both these cases, as later at Ottobeuren, the idea was dropped. Drummed domes ran counter to the South German taste for visual immediacy[43] so that whereas they are still to be found in churches that antedate the era of great unifying frescoes – for example, at Kempten, in the Theatine Church of Munich, and in Stift Haug at Würzburg – thereafter, if they were employed at all, it was generally not in the structurally logical place, over the crossing, but over the choir, where they had the iconological significance of a baldachin (e.g. at Seedorf, the Parish Church of St James at Innsbruck, and the Heiligkreuzkirche at Augsburg). This is in contrast to the more enduring taste for full domes in Austria, where Italian influences were always stronger. In various other places – at, for instance, Ottobeuren, Vierzehnheiligen, and Neresheim – the building of a full dome was considered, and in all three the final

286

287

decision went against it. Almost the last full dome to be built was Neumann's over the crossing at Münsterschwarzach (1733).

Weingarten[44] is a typical and early instance of the synthetic planning instigated and controlled by the client that was to be characteristic of most of the major architectural projects in South Germany. Even if he intervened in no other way, the client always had an important say in the final appearance of a building because he, rather than the architect, chose the artists – the frescoist, the stuccador, and the altar-builders – to complete the interiors. At Weingarten, however, Abbot Sebastian Hyller not only obtained alternative plans from several architects (Franz Beer, J.J. Herkomer and Joseph Schmuzer), but also employed Andreas Schreck, a Vorarlberger lay-brother from his own monastery, to 'improve' the plan chosen, and sought advice on further details – notably the dome, façade, high altar and galleries – from the Württemberg court architect, Donato Frisoni. One of the latter's most important contributions was to suggest the concave form of the galleries, which, with the clustered pilasters and entablature on the front end of the wall-pillars, and the broad, arched passageways through them above and below, went as far as was possible in creating free-standing supports. Light floods in from the sides of the church through two tiers of paired, broad-arched windows and Diocletian windows (perhaps suggested by Herkomer) above, and is reflected through the whole church by the plain white plaster detailing below, and Franz Schmuzer's delicate white ribbon-work stucco on a dove-grey ground in the vaults and on the galleries. In striking contrast is the saturated colouring of the frescoes, the first major cycle by Cosmas Damian Asam (1719–20), in some of which, whilst apparently resorting to Pozzoesque illusionism, he was already achieving, not a prolongation of the spectator's space, but an autonomous world above his head.

One other major Vorarlberger church, which also stands outside the customary schema, was frescoed by Cosmas Damian Asam, but this time in collaboration with his brother Egid Quirin as stuccador. This was the Benedictine Abbey Church of Einsiedeln, which, exceptionally amongst monastic churches, was also a pilgrimage-place, combining the two functions in an Upper and a Lower Minster of differing dates and construction. An earlier Vorarlberger builder, Hans Georg Kuen, had already rebuilt the choir of the monks' part of the church, the Upper Minster (which was in turn to be remodelled after the rest of the church in Rococo taste in 1746), when a Vorarlberger inmate of the monastery, Brother Caspar Moosbrugger, was instructed to make plans for the reconstruction first of the Upper Minster, and then of the Upper and Lower Minsters together. Nothing came of these plans and in 1702 it was decided to rebuild the whole abbey (begun in 1704). At this point occurred the decisive intervention by a Bolognese virtuoso, Count Marsigli, who submitted the plans to an unnamed Milanese 'pupil of Bernini's'. Whilst finding no fault with the monastic layout, which they interestingly confessed was quite

287 *Top right* Weingarten, interior of the abbey church. Stucco by Franz Schmuzer, 1718–21; frescoes by Cosmas Damian Asam, 1719–20

288 *Right* Weingarten, façade of the abbey church built by Franz Beer and Brother Andreas Schreck, 1715–20, with interventions by Donato Frisoni, 1717ff

unlike that of Italian monasteries, they made a suggestion crucial for the church: that both the area round the hermit Meinrad's Chapel housing the miraculous Black Virgin and the monks' choir should be singled out architecturally from the rest of the wall-pillar church (whose construction they clearly failed to understand), the former by creating a dome over it, and lateral exedrae to facilitate the circulation of the pilgrims, and the latter by another dome. Moosbrugger made a series of designs over the next fourteen years elaborating on these suggestions, and though he abandoned the idea of a dome over the Chapel in favour of an octagonal vault springing from the surrounding piers and meeting over an arch-linked pair of pillars above the Chapel, whilst the Chapter decided against his full drummed dome over the monks' choir in 1723, he retained and developed the idea of the church as a succession of domically-vaulted areas (built 1719–26). In the event, the spatial clarity of Moosbrugger's conception is overlaid, not merely by the Asam brothers' vigorously coloured and sculptural frescoes and stucco in the vaults (in which Cosmas Damian extended his illusionistic devices to include a circular stepped podium footing for his fresco of the *Last Supper,* and an all-round landscape setting for his fresco of the *Nativity* and the *Annunciation to the Shepherds*), but also by the unfortunate extension of this stucco and stucco-marbling to the unadorned lower parts at the end of the nineteenth century. Despite this, Marsigli's suggestions and Moosbrugger's church are interesting both as an early instance of the transmission of Milanese ideas (cf. Ricchino) of combining centrally-planned spaces to South Germany, and as a probable spur to Moosbrugger's experimentation, in drawings that were to influence Dominikus Zimmermann, with an ambulatoried oval as the focus of a pilgrimage-church.

Church architecture in Bavaria at this period presented a far less unified picture than in Swabia. The Italian wife of the Elector Ferdinand Maria of Bavaria, Henriette Adelaide of Savoy, unfortunately failed to get Guarini to pass through Munich on the way to Paris in 1662 to design the great new Theatine Church that she and her husband built in gratitude for the birth of a long-awaited son. Instead, the Bolognese architect Agostino Barelli (1627–79) designed a conventional domed basilica based on S. Andrea della Valle that remained virtually without influence in Bavaria. The two major Benedictine Abbey Churches, Benediktbeuern (1681–86) and Tegernsee (1684–88), the former by an unknown architect (probably the Wessobrunner Caspar Feichtmayr), and the latter by the second-rank Graubündener Antonio Riva, are less notable for their architecture than for their frescoes by the Asams' father – the first by a native artist since the Thirty Years War.

By the end of the century, however, two Graubündener architects were operating in Bavaria, extending the range of architectural designs more fruitfully than Barelli. These were Enrico Zuccalli (*c.* 1642–1724) and Giovanni Antonio Viscardi (1645–1713).[45] The two were lifelong enemies, so that, despite their approximately equal ages, Viscardi only flourished when Zuccalli, as the elector's favourite architect, was eclipsed during Max Emanuel's exile and the Austrian occupation. Zuccalli's work for Max Emanuel will be dealt with later; his ecclesiastical activity appears less important than that of Viscardi, either because his designs remained unrealized (Altötting), or because they merely clad an existing Gothic church in Baroque forms (Ettal), or because they were merely for chapels. In the latter, however, he shows a predilection for oval plans (also employed

289

289 *Top* Einsiedeln, plan of abbey church

290 *Above* Rohr, interior of the Priory Church of the Assumption built 1717–22, with retable of the Assumption, by Egid Quirin Asam, 1722–23

291 *Opposite* Ingolstadt, interior of the Prayer-Hall of the Marian Congregation built 1732-36, fresco and stucco by the Asam brothers, 1734

292 Aldersbach, vault of the abbey church, with fresco by Cosmas Damian Asam, 1720, and stucco by E. Q. Asam

by his cousin Johann Caspar Zuccalli, for the Theatine Church at Salzburg), often inscribed within a rectangular shell, that should probably be recognized, along with Moosbrugger's studies, as an influence upon Dominikus Zimmermann.

Viscardi's ecclesiastical buildings exhibit greater diversity, partly occasioned by the widely differing nature of the commissions involved. At Freystadt (1700–10), he rebuilt the pilgrimage-church for Count Tilly on a Greek-cross plan with an extended choir and a vestibule, covered by an old-fashioned ribbed and stuccoed dome with a plinth instead of a drum, and with awkwardly stilted arches over the galleried chapels in the diagonals. At Fürstenfeld he had a hand in planning (1699/1700), but did not live to see built (1716–28) the Cistercian abbey church as a massive wall-pillar structure. Fin-

ally, in Munich itself he built the plain, rectangular congregational prayer-hall, the Bürgersaal (1709–11), and the votive church of the Holy Trinity (1711–14). Here he again employed a Greek-cross plan with an extended choir, but with much greater suavity than at Freystadt. There are solid chamfered piers with pendentives above in the diagonals and the dome is wholly frescoed by C. D. Asam (1714/15). The dome has no drum, so that Viscardi was able to tuck it away behind the canted-sided façade, which expresses, whilst concealing, its octagonal casing, an ingenious adaptation of Ricchino's S. Giuseppe at Milan.

Viscardi's Munich Trinity Church and Zuccalli's church at

Ettal are unusual in the Bavarian context for the attention lavished on their façades – the serpentine façade of Ettal is, exceptionally, of stone and not plaster – and for their use of full columns. The bases and entablatures of those on the Trinity Church are angled in keeping with the canted centre, which is crowned by a jagged, broken double pediment with outward-turning ends. The multiple layering of the entablature and pediment is not uncommon in the Empire at this period (cf. Kremsmünster and Melk, and Ottavio Broggio's churches in Bohemia), and, in this exaggerated form, seems to derive from North Italy (cf. Carlo Emmanuele Lanfranchi's S. Giuseppe at Carignano).

As in Austria, the dominance of the Italians in Bavaria was first challenged by virtuosi with direct experience of Rome and Italy – Cosmas Damian (1686–1739) and Egid Quirin (1692–1750) Asam.[46] But whereas Fischer von Erlach was instantly taken up by the Viennese court and aristocracy, the Asam brothers only built churches, though Cosmas Damian also worked as a fresco-painter in palaces as well – at Schleissheim, Bruchsal, Mannheim and Ettlingen. In Bavaria the court side of the Graubündeners' activity was taken over by those with a quite different training gained in Paris, Effner and Cuvilliés. The Asams were sons of the painter Hans Georg Asam, and they appear to have been sent to Rome on his death in 1711 by his client the abbot of Tegernsee, to improve their respective talents as painter and sculptor. But whereas Cosmas Damian is known to have studied under Ghezzi and to have won a prize at the Academy of St Luke in 1713, and began accepting fresco commissions immediately after his return in 1714, Egid Quirin came back to serve a regular apprenticeship under the sculptor Andreas Faistenberger.

The two brothers' tender for the construction of Fürstenfeldbruck between 1714 and 1716 shows that they were eager to collaborate as architects from the first, though they were not actually able to work together till 1720, when they built a sumptuous chapel at Weihenstephan and decorated the church at Aldersbach. Their close collaboration as decorators enjoins caution over placing too much weight upon the documented responsibility of one brother, rather than the the other, for the design of what they built. It must also be remembered that they enjoyed a very brief vogue as architects. Almost everything that they designed from scratch was begun by 1720; thereafter came only Egid Quirin's own church, and the church of the Ursuline convent at Straubing, for which Cosmas Damian forwent his fee in exchange for his daughter's entry into the convent. Everything else was a work of decoration or interior transformation, for which the brothers were sought after from Bohemia to Switzerland. There is a curious discrepancy between the interiors that they created in the churches of other architects or periods and those of their own two major works, Weltenburg and the Asamkirche in Munich. The former grew out of, and contributed to, the vernacular tradition; the latter were evocations of Roman richness and theatricality that had no successors in Bavaria.

The most significant novelty introduced to Bavaria by the Asams was that of frescoes with a curvilinear frame uniting the major part of the nave vault of longitudinal churches.[47] These used foreshortening and *di sotto in sù* to suggest, not an extension of constructed space, but narrative episodes enacted upon a stage above the congregation's head.[48]

The first provision for a vault-uniting fresco was made over the nave of the Augustinian Priory Church of the Assumption (1717–22) at Rohr, though ultimately a painted Marian monogramme was executed inside the gilded and mildly curved frame instead, doubtless because nothing was to distract attention from the Assumption group in the apse. Though Egid Quirin is described as having built the church, his hand is apparent only in the architectural detailing. In construction this transeptal basilica with a shallow domical vault over the crossing would appear to be a belated realization by the Wessobrunner mason-stuccador, Joseph Bader, of a plan made for the church by Antonio Riva in connection with his reconstruction of the monastery. Save in the vaults and side-chapels, the church is entirely conventional; its remarkable feature is Egid Quirin's retable-like construction behind the canons' stalls, framing a stucco *tableau vivant* of the Assumption. Though Bernini is usually quoted as the inspiration for this, what it really represents is a permanent embodiment of the temporary, illusionistic, *theatra sacra* raised to a new art by Padre Pozzo – a celebration of the feast-day of the Virgin throughout the

293 Freising, interior of the Cathedral, transformed with fresco and stucco by the Asam brothers, 1723–24

year – an appropriate manifestation of the new spirit of joyous triumph that underlay the extraordinary wave of church building and refurbishing in South Germany at this period.

At the Cistercian Abbey Church of Aldersbach, Cosmas Damian did execute a fresco spanning three bays of the nave, representing St Bernard's vision of the Nativity (1720). Surprisingly for a fresco of this size, however, he employs a bastard form of illusionistic projection that is convincing only from the west end of the church, and one which is, moreover, like a stage-set, empirically rather than scientifically constructed. He uses *quadratura* solely for the balustrade, because it is in a projection of this that St Bernard sits, and it is he and the stucco putti supporting a scroll inscribed in Latin with the words 'For God so loved the world that he gave his only begotten Son' that mediate between the vision of the Nativity and the spectator; Cosmas Damian thus succeeds in using degrees of illusion to structure the content of his fresco. Here and at Rohr Egid Quirin's plum-coloured stucco, which makes use of the *Régence* ribbon-work originally brought into the decoration of the Wittelsbach palaces by Joseph Effner, introduces a new note of colour and reintroduces plasticity into the vaults, notably in the four massive cartouches (at Aldersbach containing stucco figures of the Evangelists), deployed in a quite new way to express the forces usually implied in transverse arch-bands. Egid Quirin's stucco transcends the work of other stuccadors to second his brother's achievement with sculptural elements (like the Evangelists) beyond ornament and putti, and also continues below the entablature. In some churches, most notably in the Premonstratensian Abbey Church of Osterhofen (built by J. M. Fischer 1726–28; decorated and furnished 1730–35), he was able not merely to design and sculpt the high altar and side altars (the stucco-marbling and stucco sculpture of altars was also the *forte* of the Wessobrunners), but also to organize the side chapels in such a way that the altars are put against the outer walls Italian-fashion as at Rohr. As a result the whole church – with Cosmas Damian's main fresco again embracing three bays of the nave (but this time being taken farther down the vault, and making the innovation of setting four scenes from the life of St Norbert before 'mansion'-like structures in the middle of the continuous architectural setting round each of the four sides), the rich greens and golds of Egid Quirin's stucco, stucco-marbling, and painted diaper-work, and his altars – appears to be wholly the work of the Asams, who decorated it, rather than of Fischer, who built it.

On no other church by a contemporary architect did the Asams so completely set their stamp, because their intervention was more narrowly confined to the vaults and altars. Only in the interior transformation of mediaeval churches, notably Freising Cathedral (1723–24) and the Benedictine Abbey of St Emmeram at Regensburg (1732–33), were they free to conjure the ancient fabric away under their plaster and fresco.[49] In Freising the vault of the long Romanesque nave was almost exclusively given over to Cosmas Damian, who made a rare excursion into pure *quadratura*, painting it with simulated coffering, transverse arches, and frames either containing feigned *quadri riportati*, or surrounding fictive openings containing a painted dome over the non-existent crossing, and a 'Glory of St Corbinian' over the central bays of the nave – in which Cosmas Damian was adopting, not merely the illusionistic tricks of Pozzo in S. Ignazio and Baciccio in the Gesù, but feigning the setting of the latter in paint as well. Cosmas Damian also painted a series of scenes from the life of St

Corbinian along the walls of the nave (evoking the tapestry decoration originally intended for the Cathedral's jubilee), whilst Egid Quirin stuccoed the aisles and galleries, and created pilasters in the nave with a stucco-marble revetment like *Régence boiseries* (foreshadowing Osterhofen). In St Emmeram, the ornament of the vault is stuccoed and not painted, and Cosmas Damian perversely turns the illusionistic tables by framing his frescoes on the vault and walls in heavy gilded frames more appropriate to canvases, whilst indulging in no more illusionism than a little compromise foreshortening.

Little in any of these churches prepares us for the Asams' masterpieces, two churches indubitably built and decorated by them (the Prayer-Hall of the Marian Congregation at Ingolstadt of 1734 is too rudimentary to be called architecture, even if it were certain that it was built by either of the brothers): the Benedictine Abbey Church of Weltenburg (built and frescoed by Cosmas Damian 1716–21, but with decoration continuing long after), and Egid Quirin's own Church of St John Nepomuk in Munich (the Asamkirche: 1733–46). Whereas the churches that they merely decorated are light-filled, predominantly white and pastel, and sparing in their use of marbling and gilding, particularly in the lower zones (though Osterhofen is more sumptuously sombre), these two churches are essentially dark, as a foil to the dramatic foci of light, mostly from concealed sources, and aglow with rich marbling and gilding overlaying the walls, supports, and entablatures. In both, moreover, the visitor has the sense of being enveloped by static architecture with defined boundaries, that only gives way to the indefinite in the zone of the vaults, in complete contrast to the feeling of open, circulating space conveyed by the generality of South German churches in the Baroque era.

Weltenburg is not merely exceptional within the *oeuvre* of the Asams, it is exceptional for its function – that of an abbey church. Instead of the massive longitudinal structures with monks' choirs beyond the crossing almost as long as the nave, Weltenburg adopts a lengthwise oval plan more typical of urban chapels, tucking the monks away behind the organ-screen at the west end as if they were nuns. Under this is an oval vestibule (decorated in 1734–36), decked out with confessionals to produce and symbolize the purity of heart necessary to enter the House of the Lord, whilst at the east end there is a short choir with two *loges*, and a high altar retable with an arched opening in the centre, framing a *tableau vivant* of St George rescuing the princess from the dragon, silhouetted against a light-filled and frescoed apse behind. There are arched recesses for altars in the diagonals, and two large gilt-framed frescoes with rockwork bases (cf. the façade of the Asam Church) above the confessionals in the middle of the sides, one showing the arrival of the Benedictines in America with Columbus, and the other framing the pulpit with a statue of St Benedict on the tester. Two lunettes above these provide the only direct lighting, cutting into the cut-out oval dome, of which the lower part is shaped like a cove upon a plinth, and decorated with gilded

294 *Opposite* Ottobeuren, font-reredos designed by J. J. Zeiller and executed by J. M. Feichtmayr and Joseph Christian, before 1766

295 *Overleaf left* Ottobeuren, detail of a side altar by J. M. Feichtmayr and Joseph Christian, by 1766

296 *Overleaf right* Weltenburg, dome of the abbey church built and frescoed by Cosmas Damian Asam, 1716–21 (see also plan in plate 428)

reliefs of the arch-angels and scenes from the life of St Benedict. Putti supporting a gilded crown perch on the rim of this (over which leans a plaster figure of Cosmas Damian), holding it in readiness for the coronation of the Virgin taking place inside a domed rotunda in Cosmas Damian's fresco, which is lit from concealed windows set back at the hidden foot of the fresco behind the cove, creating an effect of miraculous suspension.

It is at first hard to see why the abbot of Weltenburg, Maurus Bächl (1713–43), accepted such an exceptional design from a young and untried painter, whom he had met as prior of Ensdorf, where Cosmas Damain had painted his first and unremarkable frescoes in 1714. At one level it was simply that he was the *protégé* of a sister Benedictine house in Bavaria, and fresh from study in what was still, for Bavarians, the artistic capital of the world (in 1720 the Spiritual Council was to insist that church painters were to adhere to the style of the *'grossen Maîtres der Italiäner'* and not adopt the vulgar realism of the Dutch and German masters). This in itself would not have been sufficient pretext to depart from the norm for monastic churches, but Weltenburg, though small and remote (apart from its situation on the Danube) had special ties with the ruling house of Bavaria. Not only, like so many communities, did it get financial assistance from the electors to rebuild, but it also seems to have played some part in Carl Albert's revival in 1727 of the knightly order of St George, the titular of the church. It is true that this revival and the apse fresco celebrating it post-date the building of the church by some years, but the prominence given to the chivalric accoutrements of St George in both altar and nave fresco suggest that the plan had long been maturing. The imagery of the church is a synthesis of these elements relating to St George with others relating to the Benedictine order and to the Virgin Immaculate (who reverses the relationship of the princess and the dragon), and in the same way the church itself combines the sumptuous privacy of a chapel, with the requirements of an abbey church that has to serve both monks and people.[50]

One of the countries in which Cosmas Damian, at least, found frequent employment was Bohemia, and it was doubtless thus that the bachelor Egid Quirin was caught up in the devotion to a newly fashionable Bohemian martyr, St John Nepomuk, canonized in 1729.[51] Relics of this saint were granted only to those who promised to build a chapel or church to house them, and in the year of the canonization Egid Quirin began to acquire houses in Munich with a view to building a church, flanked by a house for himself and another for priests. From 1733, when the foundation-stone of the church was laid, to 1746, when it was consecrated, all of Egid Quirin's resources (with subventions from the elector) and much of his energies (with help from Cosmas Damian for the frescoes) were devoted to the church. After completing his brother's frescoes in the Ursuline Convent Church at Straubing after Cosmas Damian's death (†1739; the façade is a simplified version of that of the Asam Church), Egid Quirin allowed nothing but the occasional creation of altars to distract him from his own church. When he did take up a decorative commission again it was, surprisingly, to fresco the Jesuit Church at Mannheim, whilst working on which he died (1750).

297 *Opposite* Weltenburg, high altar retable by Egid Quirin Asam, 1721

298 *Above right* Munich, Church of St John Nepomuk by Egid Quirin Asam, 1733–46

The 'artist's (or architect's) house' is a well-defined genre in architecture; an 'artist's church' is unique. Like any prince – or, more precisely, like the prince-bishop of Würzburg, whose Court Chapel is exactly contemporary with his – what Egid Quirin did was to create altars on two levels: one for worshippers   259
coming in from the street, and the other on a level with his own apartments, visible from his bedroom, and accessible via a continuous gallery. Above this, as at Weltenburg, he created a projecting cove, behind which the concealed lighting and the foot of his brother's fresco in the vault are situated. Again as at Weltenburg, the focus of the church is (or was, before nineteenth-century alterations) a sculpture of the titular saint of the church silhouetted against the east window behind the upper altar. Egid Quirin's stroke of inspiration was, by contrast with   305
the Würzburg Court Church, to develop this upper altar as the main altar of the church, standing its Salomonic columns upon the gallery, and bringing their entablatures into connection with the mouldings of the cove, so that the Throne of Grace (Trinity Group) which they frame is in its turn silhouetted against the light from the concealed window above and behind the cove. Entering the long, narrow church, with light filtering in from above as if (as the rocks framing the portal of the façade   298

299 Günzburg, nave vault of the parish church built by Dominikus Zimmermann, 1736–41, stucco by Pontian Steinhauser and fresco by Anton Enderle, 1741

suggest) he was in some underwater cavern, the eye of the visitor is drawn irresistibly toward the altar and upwards, with St John Nepomuk (who was martyred by drowning in the Moldau) rising up to the sculptural group of the Trinity, and to his life and apotheosis in Cosmas Damian's fresco in the vault. Enveloping the visitor are walls rich with marbling, gilding, frescoes and sculpture, and given movement by a series of blind niches below, and by the broken, curvilinear profiles of the gallery, entablature and cove above. The confessionals in the small oval vestibule, and the sculpture and inscriptions above the confessionals in the church, incite the sinner to repentance, to enjoy the eternal life promised by the eucharistic symbols and the angel-herms round the lower altar; and, as if in token of the humility needed to accompany repentance, an angel-herm in the vestibule holds a votive picture of the two brothers praying in their church, painted with deliberate crudity appropriate to the genre.

The kind of churches that the Asams produced when working as architects had, as has been said, no successors in Bavaria; their innovations as decorators, and more particularly Cosmas Damian's innovations as a frescoist, found a greater response. Pupils like Matthäus Günther and Christian Thomas Scheffler diffused Cosmas Damian's stage-like settings, which were also taken up by the Catholic director of the Augsburg Academy, Johann George Bergmüller, and the innumerable fresco-painters that came under his influence. Such large-scale frescoes in turn forced a reappraisal of the role of stucco, which was facilitated by the presence in Augsburg of Wessobrunner stuccadors like the Feichtmayrs and the Finsterwalders, as previously described.

Cosmas Damian's landscape settings were, with Amigoni's at Schleissheim and Ottobeuren, an important influence upon Johann Baptist Zimmermann (1680–1758). J. B. Zimmermann was, both as court stuccador at Munich and as an important frescoist and stuccador in Bavarian and Swabian churches and monasteries, the crucial link between the French-influenced ornamental innovations of Cuvilliés in palace interiors, and the new *rocaille*- and cartouche-based stucco decoration of churches.[52] Because he came from an earlier generation than the Feichtmayrs, and as one who in his last years came to practise primarily as a painter, he was late in adopting wholeheartedly the new vocabulary, but two of his assistants, Johann Georg Übelhör and J. G. Funk, transmitted elements of it to other troupes of stuccadors, whilst his own brother not only took up *rocaille*, but ended by using it in such a way as to dissolve the boundaries between stucco and architecture.

Dominikus Zimmermann (1685–1766) was, as a Wessobrunner, by training a stuccador.[53] He began his career as a specialist in scagliola antipendia to altars, and he was also a competent fresco-painter, but after settling in the Upper Bavarian town of Landsberg (of which he was to become mayor) in 1716, he became in increasing demand as an architect. His two most successful works, both pilgrimage-churches, Steinhausen and the Wies, were built in association with his brother as decorator, which naturally evokes a parallel with the Asams; but whereas Egid Quirin Asam was a sculptor without a mason's training, who therefore seems to have been dependent upon others to assist in realizing his architectural and decorative conceptions (and he signed himself *Pildhauer*, sculptor, in the fresco over the nave of the Church of the Holy Ghost at Munich), Dominikus Zimmermann, as a Wessobrunner, enjoyed a craft familiarity with both masonry and stucco (and signed himself ARCHIT. E. STUCKADOR under the organ gallery at Steinhausen). Moreover, whereas Egid Quirin and his brother drew their architectural inspiration from Rome, Dominikus Zimmermann is not known to have ventured beyond South Germany and Lake Constance in his journeyman years, and drew upon local and Vorarlberger traditions and experiments in his work. Other Wessobrunners also graduated from stucco to architecture, notably Johann and Joseph Schmuzer, but in none did the one skill remain so firmly rooted in the other as in the case of Dominikus Zimmermann.

Dominikus Zimmermann's earliest churches were chiefly for nuns–for the Ursulines at Landsberg (1720–25) and for the Dominicans at Mödingen (1716–19) and Siessen (1725–29). These were all aisle-less churches with a recessed chancel, a two-tiered nuns' choir at the rear, and wall-pilasters calibrating the nave. At Siessen, however, Dominikus Zimmermann not only introduced a succession of domical vaults (doubtless learnt from Franz Beer, whose Church of the Dominican Nuns at Wörishofen he had stuccoed), but also – as in the parish church at Buxheim of 1726–27 – Diocletian windows with idiosyncratic lobes, that were to remain his trademark (the idea of using Diocletian windows derives from J.J.Herkomer of Füssen, in the hands of whose pupil J.G.Fischer – and his pupil F.X.Kleinhans – they were also given lobes).

Siessen was the first sign that Dominikus Zimmermann was escaping from his conventional beginnings, albeit only in detailing. It served however as his introduction to the nearby Premonstratensians – henceforward his particular patrons as an order – of Schussenried, who in 1727 procured from him a 'neat little design' for the total reconstruction of their parish-cum-pilgrimage church at Steinhausen. This contact with the Premonstratensians of Schussenried was crucial to Zimmermann's development, because – possibly in connection with never-realized plans to reconstruct their own conventual church – they had acquired a bundle of plans by Caspar Moosbrugger, in which, taking Serlio as his starting-point, he had considered the idea of an oval choir with an ambulatory. This combination of an oval plan with the construction of a Late-Gothic hall-choir (that is, with free-standing pillars, and ambulatory vaults springing from the same level as those over the

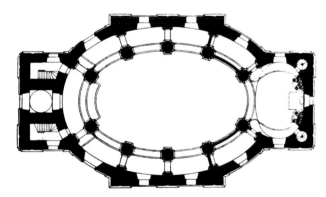

choir) was realized by Dominikus Zimmermann in the naves of Steinhausen and the Wies.

300   Steinhausen is the simpler of the two, with a narrow vestibule and staircases to the tower at the west end, and a small transverse oval choir at the east end. Ten pillars faced with

269   clustered pilasters, with freely-invented capitals and dosserets above, divide the nave from the ambulatory, which continues into the choir as a gallery beginning behind two subsidiary altars placed between the last pair of pillars on either side of the nave, and doubtless once crossed in front of the first double altar in the apse. Such double altars, with the mensa and tabernacle below, and the miracle-working image and altarpiece above, were, with the necessary ambulatories and galleries to provide access to or circulation round them without trespassing into the sanctuary, a frequent solution for pilgrimage-churches. Dominikus placed ten stucco apostles over the pillars, and over these and the arches created in stucco a continuous undulating zone out of volutes, mascarons, garland-bearing putti, plinths, and vase-supporting balustrades, that

301, 302   both serves as a base to Johann Baptist's 'irrational' landscape setting of his fresco glorifying the Virgin, and participates in it. The stucco repertoire is Johann Baptist's (though several of its

300 *Below left* Steinhausen, plan of the parish-cum-pilgrimage church built by Dominikus Zimmermann, 1728–33

301 *Below* Steinhausen, nave vault, with fresco by Johann Baptist Zimmermann, 1730–31

components ultimately derive from Egid Quirin Asam, as does the freedom and colouristic vigour with which the architectural detailing is handled), but the way in which the stucco ceases to be mere infill, and instead becomes a kind of hybrid between the architecture and the fresco, doing away with the idea of a distinct frame, betokens a collaboration between the two brothers even closer than that between the Asams. The church firmly established Dominikus Zimmermann's credit with the Premonstratensians, despite the fact that it had cost over four times the sum specified by the chapter of Schussenried; for this Abbot Ströbele was held responsible, and was exiled to another monastery in Lorraine after the consecration of the church in 1733.

Dominikus Zimmermann's next work was the parish church of Günzburg, rebuilt after its destruction by fire in 1735 on a surprisingly ambitious scale, for reasons of both national prestige and *campanilismo*: it was an Austrian exclave in Swabia, so that the emperor made a substantial donation, and the townsfolk sent collectors of alms for the church as far afield as the South Tyrol. A Poor Clare convent also used the church, and it appears to have been the original intention of the magistrature for the nuns to bear much of the cost of the rebuilding by designing the church for the dual use of convent

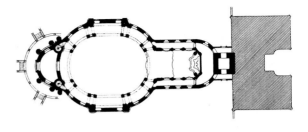

and parish. For this reason it has an oval nave, whose three-quarter detached columns appear to be the relic of some plan for a galleried ambulatory, and an unusually long, galleried choir culminating in a double altar: all elements of a pilgrimage-church, save that here the idea was to provide a separate altar and means of circulation for the nuns. In the event, the latter baulked at the expense, and contented themselves with a conventional screened-off double gallery, with its own altar, at the west end of the church, adjoining the convent. Nonetheless, the long choir, enclosed below but with paired free-standing pillars forming a gallery above, was retained; in its combination with an oval nave this contained the germ of the Wies. Because of the outbreak of the War of the Austrian Succession (1740–48), it was impossible to collect adequate funds to decorate the church in a way worthy of its architecture; Dominikus Zimmermann did not return after 1741, and the stucco and frescoes were left to indifferent assistants and local artists.

299

The last years of Dominikus Zimmermann's active life were spent on his masterpiece, the *summa* of all that he had ever built, the pilgrimage-church of the Wies (1746–54). The origin of the pilgrimage was a crude image of the Scourged Christ at the Column, devotion to whom in this form goes back to the installation of the supposed column at which he was scourged in S. Prassede at Rome in 1223, and which was given fresh impetus in Bavaria in the eighteenth century by the visions of the Blessed Crescentia of Kaufbeuren. The image was made for Good Friday processions by the Premonstratensian monks of Steingaden in 1730, cast out as 'too affecting' a few years later, and finally begged-for and taken in by a pious woman, who built a little field chapel for it in 1739. Tears seen to be shed by the image then provoked one of the most rapidly growing yet enduring pilgrimages in Bavaria. The field chapel at once became too small, and in 1745 it was decided to build a new church. Steingaden not being a sovereign abbey, it was necessary to procure permission for this both from the bishop of Augsburg and the elector of Bavaria. The latter was assured that, should the pilgrimage die down again with the rapidity with which it had sprung up, Dominikus Zimmermann's plan provided for the viability of the choir as a church on its own. No such thing happened, but despite the pilgrimage's continuing popularity the revenues from pilgrims were never enough to recover the considerable costs of building and decorating the church, and the abbey was encumbered with the debt until it was secularized in 1803. Dominikus became so closely identified with the church and pilgrimage that the Wies almost deserves to be called the Zimmermannkirche, on the analogy of the Asamkirche. Not only did he and his brother build and decorate the church, but his son married the pious harbourer of the image, and he himself, having been refused as a corrodian at

302 *Opposite* Steinhausen, detail of nave vault fresco by Johann Baptist Zimmermann

303 *Above right* Pilgrimage-church of the Wies, plan. Built by Dominikus Zimmermann, 1746–54

304 *Overleaf left* Wies church, pulpit and choir

305 *Overleaf right* Würzburg, Residenz, interior of the Court Church by Neumann with stuccoes by Bossi and frescoes by Byss, 1732–44

Schussenried, built a little house for himself beside the church, where he died in 1766.

In essence, the Wies is a fusion of the nave of Steinhausen with the choir of Günzburg, refined in certain particulars, and embellished with full *rocaille* decoration. Where the rather elongated oval nave of Steinhausen has single pillars evenly spaced, the Wies (going back for fresh inspiration to Moosbrugger's paper experiments) has a broader nave with paired columns and wider intervals on the main axes. Whereas the choir of Günzburg is walled-in below and has paired, plain white pillars marking off the gallery above, the choir of the Wies has arched openings below, and single blue-marbled columns above (alluding to the Virgin, as the red-marbled columns of the high altar refer to Christ and to the column at which he was scourged). Johann Baptist's fresco over the choir shows angels holding out the column, the Cross, and the other instruments of the Passion to intercede with God for humanity; over the nave, in a remarkable revival of Byzantine imagery, he depicts the *Etimasia* – the moment before the Last Judgement and the ending of time, with the gates of eternity not yet opened, and the judgement seat awaiting Christ, who is enthroned on a rainbow amongst the elect, showing his wounds (again an allusion to the column) in token of the mercy that will temper his judgement. As at Steinhausen, the architecture again dissolves into stucco in the vault, but here *rocaille* takes the place of all but a few figurative elements, cartouches play an important role (though still employed in a more planar fashion than in churches stuccoed by the Augsburg Wessobrunners), and holes pierced through the plaster between the vaults of the aisles and galleries, and over the *rocaille* volutes taking the place of arches linking the columns in the choir, wholly banish any sense of weight and thrust from the architecture. This is partly because Dominikus Zimmermann's lath-and-plaster vaults have anyway reduced load to a minimum, thus also allowing him to open up the walls with his idiosyncratically outlined windows to the maximum extent. In these penetrations of the vaults, yielding views of frescoed scenes behind, there are curious and unexplained parallels with Vittone's and others' churches in Piedmont. As a result of the amount of light flooding into it and the number of openings permitting angled views into whatever is beyond, the church is acutely sensitive to the quality and intensity of light of the different times of day and seasons of the year. Even on the gloomiest days the sheer whiteness of the walls and supports, and the gilding and brightly keyed colouring of the furnishings and frescoes make the church radiant. Yet there is always a bass-note established by the blood-red marbling of the columns of the altars, and taken up in the main frescoes, bringing the eye and the mind back to the Scourged Christ at the column framed in the middle of the double pilgrimage altar, the origin of the whole church.

The churches that Dominikus Zimmermann built were few,

303

304

308

and Steinhausen and the Wies were too singular, even as pilgrimage-churches, to have any successors. Nonetheless Zimmermann's churches grew out of, and recognizably belonged to, the vernacular tradition of South German Baroque architecture, and in the case of one of them, Günzburg, contributed strongly to this tradition in Swabia. The rather anomalous vaulting of the nave, with its cove-like zone decorated with cartouches and fragmentary transverse arch-bands, the shallow arched recesses for the side altars, and the idiosyncratic outlines of the windows, became the elements out of which Hans Adam (1716–59) and Joseph Dossenberger (1721–85) created a charming series of churches – most notably the Fugger votive church of St Thecla at Welden (1756–58) and the churches at Scheppach. Another architect who contributed to the vernacular vocabulary of church building in Swabia was J.J.Herkomer's pupil, Johann Georg Fischer (1673–1747).[54] Over the wall-pillar nave of the Schloss Church at Wolfegg (1733–38) and over the aisle-less nave of the church of the Poor Clare nuns at Dillingen (1736–40) he created great trough-shaped vaults, in these churches wholly filled by frescoes, that became a popular device in Swabia. One of the most appealing characteristics of South German architecture is the high quality of the lesser churches dotted about the countryside. In Swabia especially the plethora of small sovereign authorities and jurisdictions enabled several local architectural practices to develop alongside one another, each employing a limited number of architectural motifs, but with an attention to detail and an inventiveness within their repertoire that make the results endlessly delightful.

In Bavaria it was a Wessobrunner stuccador, Joseph Schmuzer (1683–1752), who was most successful in creating a local practice as the architect of parish churches, extending his competence from stucco to masonry like his father Johann before him.[55] Some of his earliest churches were round Augsburg, but it was in South Bavaria that he won most of his mature commissions, establishing an informal partnership with the Augsburg-based frescoist from a village nearby to Wessobrunn, Matthäus Günther. Schmuzer's development was towards the creation of a succession of centralized and variously vaulted spaces, as in the parish churches of Mittenwald 1737–40) and, most successfully of all, Oberammergau (1736–41). In these last two churches Schmuzer can also be seen tentatively adopting the accentual system of *rocaille* cartouche stucco evolved at Diessen, and indeed the new developments in stucco seem to have given a fresh impetus to the end of his career. Oberammergau belonged to the Austin Priory of Rottenbuch, by whose Prior Schmuzer was also employed as a mason and stuccador utterly to transform the interior of the mediaeval Priory Church with rampant pink *rocaille* stucco and Matthäus Günther's frescoes (1737–45). It was whilst stuccoing the interior of another monastery church, part mediaeval and part Zuccalli, that of the Benedictine Abbey of Ettal (1745–52), that he died.

Two Vorarlbergers, Peter Thumb (1691–1766)[56] and Johann Michael Beer von Bleichten (1700–67), continued to uphold the building traditions of their people beyond the middle of the century. The latter probably made a decisive intervention in the

299

309

306 *Opposite* Vierzehnheiligen, pilgrimage-church by Neumann, begun 1742, pilgrimage altar by Küchel, 1762

307 Neu-Birnau, exterior of the pilgrimage-church built by Peter Thumb, 1746–51

involved planning of the Benedictine Abbey Church of St Gallen (1749). Peter Thumb's earlier churches (already mentioned page 222) were backward examples of the wall-pillar type for their time, but later in his career he built a series of churches with aisle-less naves and recessed choirs. That upon which his fame rests, the pilgrimage-church of Neu-Birnau (1746–51), owes much, but by no means everything to its exquisite decoration by the frescoist G.B.Göz and the stuccador Joseph Anton Feichtmayr, within a range of green, yellow and ochre colours probably laid down by the former. Yet the undulating gallery with its vaulted underside running round the whole church, and the centralized nave vault enlivened by triangular penetrations all round, link this with Thumb's other masterpiece, the Library of the Benedictine Abbey of St Peter in the Black Forest (1739–53), and show that he had a fine sense of the modulation of simple spaces.

The one church architect in Bavaria and Swabia, apart from the Asams and Dominikus Zimmermann, to achieve more than provincial stature was Johann Michael Fischer (1692–1766).[57]

307

268

Unlike these, he was the son of a mason and trained in the craft tradition, going as far afield as Moravia during his journeyman years – an experience which his earliest churches reflect. Although he then came to Munich as the foreman of the city mason Johann Mayr, acquired citizenship in 1723, and married Mayr's daughter in 1725, the posts of city and court mason at Munich were preempted by Mayr's stepsons from Miesbach, Johann (1692–1763) and Ignaz Anton (1698–1764) Gunezrhainer. The only significant commission that he obtained at Munich was, therefore, early on in his career, to build the Hieronymite Church of St Anna am Lehel. His chief employment, as his tomb proudly declares, was as a monastic architect – working both for the great sovereign abbeys of Swabia and for the more modest religious houses under the jurisdiction of the elector of Bavaria (involving a difference of scale which must always be borne in mind). He also built parish churches, but never, surprisingly, a 'pure' pilgrimage-church (as the churches of Our Lady of the Rubble at Ingolstadt and Our Lady of the Snows at Aufhausen were built as much with the Austin Friars and Oratorians that served them as with their pilgrimages in mind). Not only was he called in with unusual frequency to build and partially redesign churches begun by other hands or incorporating older fabric, but he also suffered from interference with his designs during execution and after his death. Like all builder-architects, he had to renounce the responsibility for his churches after completing the vaults, leaving them to the hands of the frescoists and stuccadors, but in his case the problems of adaptability that this posed must have been all the greater in that his career spanned a period of extraordinary mutability in ornamental vocabulary, from the heyday of ribbon-work to not only the birth, but also the final phase of *rocaille*, so that he was called upon to provide the architectural matrix for decorators as different as the Asams and the Feichtmayrs. In some ways his most considerable achievement was, from Diessen to Rott am Inn, to evolve an architecture to whose chasteness and lucidity *rocaille* cartouche stucco was the perfect foil. There is no sense in asking whether and how Fischer was a Rococo architect, because the architectural criteria that are used to decide this question bear no necessary relation to the characteristics of the ornament from which the idea of a Rococo 'style' comes; what one can say is that Fischer created churches – and this can be judged by comparing them with those Rococo churches that are merely recladdings of earlier fabrics, or re-employments of traditional building types like the wall-pillar church – that are perfect vehicles for Rococo decoration: not only for *rocaille* stucco, but for Rococo frescoes and furnishings as well. Rott am Inn is the supreme example of that much abused word, the *Gesamtkunstwerk* – the total work of art – produced not by a fortuitous concatenation of structure, decoration and furnishing from different decades, but by architect, artists, and craftsmen all working together in conscious sympathy with and adaptation to one another's contributions. The Asams and the Zimmermanns created *Gesamtkunstwerke* as brothers working in unison designing virtually the totality of their churches; Rott am Inn is a *Gesamtkunstwerk* produced by wholly independent artists working in the assurance of a common idiom at its moment of perfection.

For the reasons mentioned above – the diversity of commissions, the changes in decorative idiom, and the number of occasions on which Fischer was faced with completing someone else's work – it is misleading to divide up his work too neatly

308 *Opposite* Wies church, nave. Stucco by Dominikus Zimmermann and fresco by Johann Baptist Zimmerman

309 *Above* Rottenbuch, interior of the priory church, transformed and stuccoed by Joseph Schmuzer, with frescoes by Matthäus Günther, 1737–45

into periods or categories, or to speak too glibly of the constants in his work. Nonetheless, his buildings do group themselves to a certain extent, and within his work there is a tendency towards the creation of churches out of communicating yet ever more clearly defined spaces. His first two significant churches, Osterhofen (1726–28) and St Anna am Lehel (1727–29), are both somewhat ill-defined spatially, and in both the dominant element is the Asams' decoration. There followed a church – Diessen (1732–34) – in which the *rocaille* cartouche method of stucco decoration was first deployed by the Feichtmayr troupe. Then came a group of three churches, Berg am Laim (designed 1735, executed and decorated 1735–44), Aufhausen (designed 1735, executed and decorated 1746–51), and Ingolstadt (1736–40), in which Fischer played variations upon a dominant centrally planned nave, covered by a domical vault,

310, 311

312

313

314

from the first with an almost wholly frescoed vault, ruling out any possibility of continuing his three-dimensional arches into the vault. So whereas in Bohemia the subsequent taste for frescoes obliterated and made nonsense of several of the Dientzenhofers' subtle vaults, Fischer, being confronted with this taste at the outset, let his architecture take a different course.

For the small community of Hieronymite Friars in Munich, Fischer created in St Anna a church composed of a transverse vestibule, succeeded by an ovoid nave created out of two   311 intersecting circles, and terminated by a three-quarters-round choir. Unusually, even when employing this fashionably ovoid nave, Fischer persisted in the use of wall-pillars, with curved recesses housing the altars between. The composite geometry of the plan of the nave still has something of the Bohemian Guarinian tradition in it, but the elevations run counter to this, and the creation of ancillary spaces in the flanks of the church is foreign to the Bohemian treatment of walls as a negative, skin-like feature behind the main element – the baldachin-like system of supports. The vault overhead, sustained by arches of varying shape and radius, is equally empirical, and merely serves as the matrix for Cosmas Damian Asam's fresco in its restlessly curvilinear frame.

At Osterhofen Fischer had been constrained by the retention of the stumps of the Romanesque towers and the Gothic choir;   310

310 *Left* Osterhofen, interior of the abbey church built by Johann Michael Fischer, 1726–28; stucco, frescoes, and altars by the Asam brothers, 1730–35

311 *Below* Munich, interior of the parish church of St Anna am Lehel built by J. M. Fischer, 1727–29; stucco, frescoes, and altars by the Asam brothers, 1729–39 (photograph taken before partial destruction by bombing in 1944)

312 *Opposite* Diessen, interior of the priory church built by J. M. Fischer, 1732–34; stucco by the Feichtmayr troupe; frescoes by J. G. Bergmüller (nave fresco 1736); consecrated in 1739

315, 316
317–19

320, 321

310

with saucer-domed spaces attached. After this, he was called upon to execute the two most grandiose works of his career, the Imperial Free Abbey Churches of Zwiefalten (1741–47) and Ottobeuren (1748–54), together with the Cistercian Abbey Church of Fürstenzell (1740–48) – in all of which he was under the constraint of beginnings made by other hands. Lastly came two churches, Rott am Inn (1759–60) and Altomünster (1736–66), that took the centrally planned designs of his middle years, using them as the core of more elongated designs appropriate to conventual churches.

St Anna am Lehel and Osterhofen have already been partially discussed in the context of the Asams. Of the two churches, it was upon the Premonstratensian Abbey Church of Osterhofen that they set their mark more pronouncedly – with such lavishness that the abbey's continued indebtedness led to its suppression fifty years later. As far as Fischer is concerned, its chief interest lies in the residual Bohemian/Moravian elements: the convex balconies supported on three-dimensional arches, the three-dimensional arches eating into the tunnel vault of the nave from the ovoid spaces above the chapels, and the concave entablatures of the wall-pillars and corners of the nave. These entablatures make it appear that Fischer reckoned

the saucer-dome over the choir, and as cartouche-clamps fastened on to the crown of arches, windows, and other nodal points. Other *rocaille* ornament is sparingly employed at focal points round the edges and in the centre of blank spaces, on the same principle as in *boiseries*. The result of all this, despite the common use of a wall-pillar nave united by a single fresco overhead (doubtless at the behest of the prior after seeing the Asam fresco at Osterhofen, for this was the first of the kind that J.G. Bergmüller painted), is very different from that at Osterhofen. There the decoration is richly coloured, extending evenly over every surface, both of the walls and the vault, and the chapels are decorated in their own right; the total impression is one in which architecture and decoration are fused. At Diessen the effect is the opposite: fresco, stucco, furnishings and architecture all stand out from one another; there are no longer chapels, but richly gilded altars placed in an old-fashioned way against the western faces of the wall-pillars – like the wings of a theatre – leading to a focus in the high altar. Yet the common employment of gilding and *rocaille* link together furnishings, framed frescoes, and stucco against the white of the architecture, whose plainness is deliberately retained in the lower zone, in contrast to the teeming vault – which is where the 310

313 *Above* Berg am Laim (Munich), interior of the confraternity church built by J. M. Fischer, 1735–44; stucco and frescoes by J. B. Zimmermann, 1743–44

at the Austin Priory Church of Diessen he was called in by an energetic prior, Herkulan Karg (1728–55), to raise an entirely new church over foundations laid by a local builder a decade before. Most significant for this church was that the prior made two journeys, one with Fischer the year before the church was begun in 1731 to inspect Fischer's own churches in Lower Bavaria (i.e. notably Osterhofen), and the other in 1733, when the carcase of the church must have been approaching completion, as far as the South Tyrol, to gather ideas for its decoration. The result of this second trip was that he rejected any idea that he might have had of employing the Asams, and instead decided upon a combination – that he must have come upon both at the Cistercian Abbey Church of Stams near Innsbruck and at the chapel of the Teutonic Knights at Sterzing in the South Tyrol – of Augsburg frescoists and stuccadors. At these two churches the latter, in the person of the Augsburg-based Wessobrunner Franz Xaver Feichtmayr, had taken the first steps towards evolving a form of decoration based primarily upon the cartouche, used both as a frame and a clamp, for accent and emphasis. At Diessen, Franz Xaver and his brother 312 Johann Michael Feichtmayr (who had themselves already made tentative use of asymmetry) came together with another Wessobrunner, Johann Georg Übelhör, who had been working under Johann Baptist Zimmermann on the *Reiche Zimmer* of the Munich Residenz, where the first use of the *rocaille* is to be found. There French influences and the native repertoire of ornament converged, and the same is true is Diessen, where *rocaille* cartouche stucco was being employed from 1734 onwards – the very years in which the suites of engraved *rocaille* 194, 195 ornament by Meissonnier, Lajoue and Mondon were being published (and, soon after, pirated by the Augsburg engravers). The novelty of Diessen was the employment of this on a monumental scale, as framing cartouches in the pendentives of

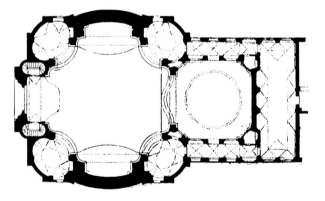

314 *Above* Ingolstadt, plan of the Austin (later Franciscan) friary church built by J. M. Fischer, 1736–40 (destroyed in the War)

focus of Rococo churches was henceforward to be. It was also at Diessen that Fischer introduced what was to be the habitual scheme of his façades: a giant Order (usually of pilasters) below, on a high base, supporting a straight entablature on either side of a bottom-broken pediment above the portal; above this a freely designed gable with a central niche.

The paths of Fischer and the Feichtmayr-Übelhör troupe diverged for the decade after Diessen, and whereas the latter went on to diffuse the new mode of *rocaille* cartouche decoration as far afield as Upper Austria (Wilhering, 1740–51) and Franconia (Münsterschwarzach, 1737–49, and Amorbach, 1744–51), Fischer found himself working in Bavaria with stuccadors under the guidance or influence of J. B. Zimmermann. Though largely responsible for introducing *rocaille* into stucco, he had become more used to working as a stuccador on court commissions and was thus slow to perceive the significance of the use of monumental cartouches in church decoration. Because of his ambitions as a frescoist, however, he did adopt something of the more sparing, concentrated deployment of stucco ornament.

J. B. Zimmermann was the frescoist and stuccador in two of Fischer's three centrally planned churches of the mid 1730s to the early 1740s – the Confraternity Church of the Order of St Michael at Berg am Laim, outside Munich, and the Pilgrimage-cum-Austin Friary Church of Our Lady of the Rubble (an image of the Virgin supposedly rescued from profanation by the Jews) at Ingolstadt. At Berg am Laim a plan of Fischer's published in 1735, which envisaged joining an octagonal nave onto a horseshoe-shaped chapel, was reluctantly chosen for execution in 1737 by the nephew and successor of the founder of the order, both as grand master and as archbishop of Cologne, Clemens August von Wittelsbach. Local interests however pushed forward the Munich city mason, Philip Köglsberger, as executant, who made his own alterations to and enlargements of the plan, including preparations for a much more expensive solid stone vault. This led to his discharge in 1739, and to the reinstatement of Fischer, who had to take over both his predecessor's foundations and the twenty-six-foot high trunk of his façade. In its final form the church emerged as a succession of spaces tapering – after the transverse oval vestibule – towards the choir, in which it is not unlike Rainaldi's S. Maria in Campitelli at Rome, save that the vaults assert the spatial separation of the parts more strongly. Curved walls in the diagonals, a saucer-dome raised over stilted arches above the arms, and curious circular-ceiled vaulting penetrations above the windows in the diagonals, erode any indication of the nave's octagonal plan, and in the choir there is a similar discrepancy between plan and elevation, and absence of clear spatial definition. The focus of the church lies in the succession of J. B. Zimmermann's landscape-set frescoes recounting the discovery and miracles of the Grotto of St Michael at Monte S. Angelo (1743–44), whose dominant colour is picked up by the apple-green marbling of the columns and entablature.

At the Pilgrimage-cum-Oratorian Church of Our Lady of the Snows at Aufhausen (both frescoist and stuccador unknown) Fischer again assembled the church out of a succession of centrally-planned spaces – vestibule, nave and choir – but with a more conventional elevation in the nave, where there are saucer-domed chapels, with saucer-domed galleries above, in the diagonals. This is a reversion to Viscardi's treatment of Freystadt, albeit with more refinement in the details – including a low domical vault above an undulating cornice in the nave, containing a single fresco (only in the choir are pendentive cartouches employed), and brightly illuminated side-chapels. The Pilgrimage-cum-Austin Friary Church at Ingolstadt (frescoed and stuccoed by J. B. Zimmermann 1739/40, destroyed 1944), whilst dispensing with a vestibule, refined yet further upon this plan. Here the diagonal chapels were not merely oval in their vaults but oval in plan, whilst filled with light both below and in the galleries above. Ingolstadt must have been the most perfect of the three centrally planned churches of Fischer's middle years, in which the fluid treatment of space resulting from the juxtaposition of independently lit and vaulted spaces was realized in the side-chapels as well, and its loss is the more regrettable; not until two decades later was Fischer again given a free hand to experiment further in the same vein, at Rott am Inn.

One substantial and two major commissions intervened, in all of which Fischer advised on and modified already begun buildings. At the Cistercian Abbey Church of Fürstenzell

313

314

315 Zwiefalten, interior of the abbey church built by J. M. Fischer, 1741–47

Fischer was asked in 1740 to replace a sculptor, J. M. Götz, who had attempted to pose as an architect without the requisite technical knowledge. After making fresh designs, Fischer directed the building from a distance, whilst his site manager, though tearing down the earlier masonry, does not seem to have altered the foundations – hence the somewhat rudimentary construction of the church, with tunnel-vaults to both the nave and chancel, whose appearance has been further diminished by the destruction of the original monks' choir behind J. B. Straub's high altar, and the moving of the latter to the rear wall. The chief interest of the church lies in its decoration, in which the abbot played a leading role. He had already obtained the services of a good local stuccador, but one who had never worked on this scale, Johann Baptist Modler (1697–1774), and wanted an Austrian frescoist – Troger or Altomonte. Fischer, however (and it is an interesting indication that he had yet to perceive the significance of the decoration of Diessen) wanted J. B. Zimmermann, on the grounds that he could give directions to Modler as well. The troubles of the War of the Austrian

originally intended seven and to build a new ashlar façade, but also to construct proper stone vaults, rather than the lath-and-plaster ones usual in South Germany. It was the construction of these vaults, which was beyond the competence of the local masons (called Schneider) who had begun to rebuild the church in 1739, that led to Fischer's employment. Though he advised demolishing everything but the towers hugging the west end of the narrowed choir, it would seem that he was either constrained by the retention of portions of the mediaeval foundations, or by the local prestige of the Vorarlberger tradition, and of the *reichsfrei* Weingarten in particular, into adopting – as at Diessen and Fürstenzell – a wall-pillar plan for the nave. Moreover, instead of the varied succession of centrally planned spaces found in his churches of the previous decade, Fischer alternates tunnel-vaults over the nave and choir with saucer-domes over the crossing and sanctuary. It is likely that tradition and prestige also required his incorporation of a somewhat inorganic transept, though by this period – in contrast to Weingarten – it was thought preferable to have a clearly frescoed saucer-dome rather than a full dome with a drum over the crossing.

315

The really successful elements of the church derive from the combined decorative talents of Fischer himself (mitigating the severity of the wall-pillar schema with convex galleries and stucco-marble columns), the fresco-painter F. J. Spiegler (1691–1757), the sculptor J. J. Christian (1706–77) and the stuccador J. M. Feichtmayr. Though nothing is said of Spiegler being accorded the overall control enjoyed by Zeiller at Otto-beuren, this was probably the case; it is suggested by the striking colouristic harmony of the church – notably between his frescoes and the rich golden capitals and reddish-brown shafts of the paired columns placed on the front face of the wall-pillars, and between these and the stucco-marble altars – and by the complex design of the pulpit and counter-pulpit (together forming an interlocking tableau of the *Vision of Ezekiel* and the

316 *Left* Zwiefalten, vault of the nave; stucco by J. M. Feichtmayr and fresco by F. J. Spiegler, 1751

317 *Below* Ottobeuren, plan of the abbey church built by J. M. Fischer, 1748–54

318 *Opposite* Ottobeuren, interior; stucco by J. M. Feichtmayr and frescoes by J. J. and F. A. Zeiller, 1754–64

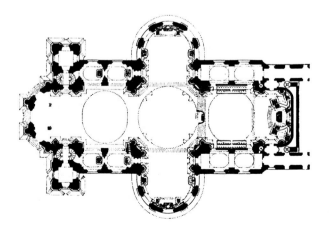

Succession intervened, and when work on the church began again in 1744, the abbot had his way to the extent that he obtained Troger's pupil J. J. Zeiller to fresco the church, whilst Fischer procured a former assistant of J. B. Zimmermann, J. G. Funk, to assist Modler with the stucco, notably with the cartouches – of whose importance Fischer was now fully aware – which Modler ruined twice. The difference in treatment between the choir (stuccoed by Modler in 1741) and the nave (chiefly stuccoed by Funk 1747–48) reveals the significant integrating effect of *rocaille* cartouches between architecture and fresco, even though, having been executed by one who was not a member of the Feichtmayr troupe, they are still somewhat planar, and lacking in balance within their asymmetry.

One year after he was called in to redress the situation at Fürstenzell, Fischer was summoned to advise on, and in the event to redesign, the church of the Benedictine Abbey of Zwiefalten. This church, the first of the two monumental buildings of Fischer's career, was built in affirmation of the status that the abbey aspired to, and which it obtained in 1750 – that of *Reichsfreiheit*. Only this can explain the decision not merely to extend the choir by thirty feet instead of the

319 Ottobeuren, choir stalls and organ; joinery by Martin Hörmann and sculpture by Joseph Christian, 1755–64

ities by rebuilding the church, which was designed from the first to jut out in continuation of the central spine of the abbey. The pronounced transept, and the convex façade between two towers, clearly alluding to the Benedictine University Church at   253 Salzburg, are also features of the church as built that go back to the earliest designs for the reconstruction of church and monastery by an inmate, Father Christoph Vogt (*c.* 1711). Between this date and the laying of the foundation-stone of the church in 1737 Abbot Ness, in the characteristically autocratic way of German clients in the Baroque era, procured a series of plans from almost every architect working in Swabia, including Dominikus Zimmermann, Joseph Schmuzer, and the Comasque stuccador of the abbey, Andrea Maini, before taking aside his local mason, Simpert Kramer, indicating the features that he wanted selected from each design, and telling him to combine them in a workable plan. It is not a little surprising that, after receiving such interesting projects as Zimmermann's for either a pure rotunda or a longitudinal building with an ambulatoried oval crossing, and Maini's unexpected adaptations of S. Carlino and S. Ivo (but then he and Borromini shared a common Comasque homeland), the final plan should have been so archaic. Not only on account of the apsidally ended transepts and choir, which are reminiscent of Salzburg   245 Cathedral (itself retrospective), but also on account of the low aisles, whose lean-to roofs on the exterior look quite mediaeval. A full dome over the crossing was considered after the church was begun, but rejected in favour of a calotte. Ness's successor as abbot had doubts about the design, and called in for consultation the eclipsed Munich court architect Joseph Effner, who straightened every wall that he could, created a saucer-dome over the now straight-ended sanctuary, and placed four massive columns against the façade. Kramer's inadequacy must however have become patent, and in 1748 Fischer was finally invited to produce revised designs, replacing him the next year   317 when the church had already begun to rise out of the ground. Fischer's most successful intervention was in the crossing, where he enlarged and curved the piers, and flanked them with attached columns, in such a way that they advance the crossing into the arms (abetted by steps mounting into the transepts and chancel) so that it dominates the church. He vaulted the crossing with a calotte and created a domed double bay on either side of it, respectively continued by an apsidal ending to the west and a vaulted sanctuary to the east. In the nave the twin   318 arched openings in the double bay house chapels, with altars set away from their eastern walls to allow passage between them; in the choir they are closed behind J.J. Christian's *mouvementé* choir-stalls-cum-organ-case below, but open to the vaults of the   319 sacristy and vestry respectively above.

Fischer can thus only be accounted as an 'improver' of the plan and elevations at Ottobeuren, albeit a successful one, whilst his responsibility for its decoration is demonstrably less. Surviving drawings show that his elevations were handed to competing stuccadors to sketch out their projected ornament upon, while we know that the chief fresco-painter, J.J. Zeiller, was entrusted with the design of both the pulpit and font-   294 reredos, and of the paving of the crossing and choir. The Zeiller cousins as frescoists apart, the decorative team was the same as at Zwiefalten, with J.J. Christian as sculptor and J.M. Feicht-mayr as stuccador. The stucco is more selectively employed here than there; it is at its most striking in the massive cartouches on the pendentives, though arguably, as one of the competing stuccadors realized, the scale is too great for them. Christian

316   *Way of Redemption*). Spiegler's own main fresco over the nave is a remarkable vertical composition showing an involved chain of salvation extending from the Trinity via the Virgin, and diffused through her images in the main Marian pilgrimage-places served by the Benedictines. This fresco, like those at Osterhofen and Diessen, extends over all four bays of the nave, but its frame is entirely dissolved into C- and S-shaped sections, with eruptions of *rocaille* stucco at the junctions and over into the fresco, which, correspondingly, has a discontinuous setting, sharply receding and advancing in curved strips of wall and steps: nowhere is the close symbiosis of developments in stucco with those in fresco better exemplified.

The church at Zwiefalten led to his commission to take over the church at Ottobeuren,[58] another great Swabian Benedictine abbey, which had achieved *Reichsfreiheit* in 1711, but whose dynamic abbot, Rupert Ness (the son of a blacksmith from Wangen), preferred to rebuild the abbey buildings on a palatial scale before wounding the more conservative monks' sensibil-

295 and Feichtmayr were again responsible for the sculpture and stucco-marbling respectively of the altars and columns, vitally contributing to the overall effect; and here the pulpit and facing font-reredos celebrate, the one the Transfiguration, and the other the Baptism of Christ.

In 1753, on Neumann's death, Fischer applied to take over the construction of the church at Neresheim. His application – it is fascinating to speculate upon the way in which he might have modified Neumann's plans – was rejected, and he reverted from the monumental churches of Swabian *reichsfreie* abbeys to the more modest scale of churches in Bavaria. Yet it was with one of these that he achieved the most perfectly realized church of his career – that of the Benedictine Abbey of Rott am Inn. It was originally intended merely to transform the interior of this church with plaster and fresco as was done so often at this period, but the old fabric was voted unsafe, and in 1759 Fischer was entrusted with the task of rebuilding the church altogether, incorporating nothing but the two east towers from the old. Left thus with an almost free hand, Fischer

321 reverted to his centralized plan with extensions, as in the mid-1730s: Rott is rather like a cross between the naves of Aufhausen and Ingolstadt, fitted between two domically-vaulted bays the width of the axial openings to east and west, with a concealed sacristy behind the high altar one end, and a horizontally divided bay, containing the tomb of the founders below and an organ gallery above, the other end. The effect,

320 however, is much chaster, because at Rott all curvature has been eliminated from piers, entablatures, and balconies; the frescoes rise behind unbroken circular, or all but circular, cornices, and the stucco is pared back to a minimal system of accentual grey cartouches with pink putti, standing out against the white and yellow fields of the architecture. This exquisitely composed stucco is the work of F.X. Feichtmayr and his assistant Jakob Rauch, whilst the frescoes (drawing heavily on a *bozzetto* left by the prematurely deceased J.E. Holzer for the glory of the Benedictine order in the central calotte) are by the accomplished Augsburg-trained Bavarian Matthäus Günther. A namesake, but no relative, Ignaz Günther, designed and carved the elegantly mannered painted wooden (instead of the usual marmoreal white stucco) figures of the altars, with the aid of his pupil Joseph Götsch. The remarkable stylistic unity of the church is partly to be accounted for by the fact that it was vaulted within the extraordinarily short space of a year, stuccoed and frescoed in another four, and furnished by 1767. It is also interesting that in this particular case Fischer acted as the overall contractor as well as the architect. All this was achieved through cheap loans, and led to not unjustified criticism of the abbot for his precipitancy, for the abbey was unable to proceed to the reconstruction of its conventual buildings, and was still heavily encumbered with debt when secularized in 1803.

The last church that Fischer designed and supervised, and the last major Rococo church in Bavaria, was that for the Brigittine community at Altomünster (1763–66). Here again he opted for a centrally planned nave with extensions, but his design had to accommodate itself to a series of local peculiarities. On the one hand it had to retain the two-tiered Gothic choir at one end, and a Romanesque tower housing steps mounting up to the level of the church at the other; on the other hand it had to provide for the quadripartite constitution of the Brigittine community – nuns, monks, lay-brothers and parish congregation – and for the separate, and sometimes concealed, circulation of all these to their respective portions of the church. The

320 *Top* Rott am Inn, interior; stucco by F. X. Feichtmayr and Jakob Rauch, frescoes by Matthäus Günther, 1760–63

321 *Above* Rott am Inn, plan of the abbey church built by J. M. Fischer, 1759–60

322 Rott am Inn, apostle-light sconces, incorporating symbols of Saints
Simon and Bartholomew

upper part of the east end housed the monks' choir, with its own
altars, screened off by the parish altar below, and three altars
for the contemplation of the nuns above. The nuns' choir was
placed over the lay brothers' choir, looking into, but screened
off from, the choir with the altars on one side, and the nave on
the other. The congregation sat in the saucer-domed octagonal
nave, which is surrounded by passages below, by screened-off
galleries for monks on five sides half way up the pillars, and by a
screened-off gallery all the way round above the entablature for
the nuns. Thus, though the interior plan is similar to that of
Rott, the outer envelope of passages and galleries creates more
solid elevations, through which the light filters at one remove,
and which express the octagon more clearly than ever before.
The (typically late Rococo) apple-green stucco by Rauch is as
sparingly applied as at Rott, but the Tyrolean Joseph Magges's
fresco over the nave has the more sombre colouring and
synthetic composition that betoken the first chill draughts of
Neo-Classicism. In another major church in Swabia for which
Fischer supplied designs – those for the *reichsfrei* Benedictine
Abbey of Wiblingen (*c.* 1757) – which were only executed in
starkly modified form by J. G. Specht after his death (1772–83),
Neo-Classical influences gained the upper hand; it is significant
that when it came to the decoration of the vaults Specht was
discharged (1778), and the frescoist Januarius Zick given
overall control. For in South German churches it was in
painting that the first intimations of Neo-Classicism's de-
thronement of the Baroque came from Rome: preceding the
French architects and French engravings that introduced the
new modes of architecture and ornament from France.

Bohemia and Franconia

Though Bohemia and Franconia were two very different political entities – Bohemia being one of the dynastic kingdoms of the
Habsburgs, and Franconia less an entity than, like Swabia, a
congeries of diverse sovereignties – the architecture of the one
was intimately connected with that of the other. This connection had two main causes. One was that both looked to
Austria for inspiration – Bohemia because it was ruled by a
Catholic aristocracy largely implanted by the Habsburgs after
the Battle of the White Mountain, and Franconia because its
dominant rulers saw in a strong imperial authority the best
hope for the lesser constituents of the Empire (such as themselves) and therefore oriented themselves by Vienna. The other
was that members of a fertile architectural family, the Dientzenhofers, emigrated from Bavaria to dominant architectural
positions in both areas. It should be said that, for the purposes
of architectural history, Bohemia can be held to have embraced
the margravate of Moravia, and also the dukedom of Silesia
until its annexation by Prussia, whilst the tone of Franconia
was set by the two prince-bishoprics of Bamberg and Würzburg, rather than by the secular marches of Ansbach and
Bayreuth (which will be considered in the chapter upon palace
architecture).

The reason for the commanding architectural authority of
the two prince-bishoprics was that, for the crucial earlier half of
the eighteenth century, one or both sees were held by members
of the remarkable Schönborn family.[59] This family, originating
in the petty nobility of the Rhineland, took its first step to
greater stature with the energetic prince-bishop of Würzburg
and archbishop-elector of Mainz (1642/47–1673), Johann Philipp
von Schönborn. Johann Philipp, the 'German Solomon', was
too preoccupied with reconstructing and preserving peace in
the Empire after the Thirty Years War to be a great builder, but
one of his nephews, Lothar Franz von Schönborn, had no
sooner been elected to the see of Bamberg in 1693 than he began
to make plans for reconstructing the palace there, despite an
election oath to the contrary, and continued to build in his two
sees of Bamberg and Mainz (to which he was elected in 1695) till
the end of his life in 1729. He had a whole brood of nephews,
who were no less avid to build than to accumulate the political
and ecclesiastical dignities that provided the excuse and the
funds for their buildings: Friedrich Carl, vice-chancellor of the
Empire (1705–34) and prince-bishop of Bamberg and Würzburg (1729–46); Johann Philipp Franz, prince-bishop of Würzburg (1719–24); Damian Hugo, cardinal (from 1715) and
prince-bishop of Speyer (1719–43) and Konstanz (1740–43);
and Franz Georg, archbishop-elector of Trier (1729–56),
prince-bishop of Worms and prince-provost of Ellwangen
(1732–56). Of all these, the two who were the most obsessed by
the demon of building (which they referred to resignedly as their
'*Bauwurmb*'), and took the most informed and detailed interest in every aspect of construction and decoration,
were Lothar Franz and Friedrich Carl. The two kept up a
vigorous correspondence, swapping suggestions and craftsmen
with one another, and tapping a whole set of architects for
advice, not only on their own projects, but also on those of
Johann Philipp Franz. It was largely through these
two – Lothar Franz was, *ex officio* as archbishop of Mainz, the
chancellor of the Empire, whence the appointment of his
nephew to the executive post of vice-chancellor at Vienna – that

a Viennese/Franconian architectural axis was created, with the most fructifying effects for Franconia. It was also Lothar Franz who, by employing two of the Dientzenhofer brothers as his court architects, ensured the continued division of this gifted family between Franconia and Bohemia.

Having been one of the earliest parts of Central Europe to attract the Comasques (to build the Belvedere at Prague, 1534–41), Bohemia[60] was also to remain longest under the domination of Italian architects – or architects of Italian descent - never wholly dispensing with them throughout the Baroque period. It seems possible, indeed, that nascent nationalist feelings put difficulties in the way of indigenous architects, whether Czech- or German-speaking; and it is certainly noteworthy that, whilst the most distinguished family of German architects working in Bohemia, the Dientzenhofers, originated in Bavaria, the foremost Bohemian-born, German-speaking architect, Balthasar Neumann, made his career in Germany.

The two Comasque architects who dominated the scene in the middle years of the seventeenth century were Carlo Lurago (c. 1618–84) and Francesco Caratti (died in 1677). Both worked in a ponderous, emphatic idiom belonging more to the sixteenth than the seventeenth century, and achieved their chief exterior effects through the repetition of the same elements over enormously long façades. Both their masterpieces make striking use of a very plastic giant Order. Caratti's was the Czernin Palace (1669ff),[61] built at the opposite end of the hill on which Prague Castle stands, in a kind of defiant over-trumping of the latter, for a man who was himself a dilettante architect, but who was also a rare survivor of the old Bohemian aristocracy resentful of

the new, Count Humprecht Johann von Czernin. Lurago's masterpiece was built not in Bohemia, but just over the border – the Cathedral of the sovereign bishopric of Passau (1668ff.). In plan, the Cathedral (which Bishop Thun wished to be based on that of Salzburg) is a conventional cruciform basilica with a full dome over the crossing (as was still the vogue at this period; Caratti had introduced one of the earliest to Bohemia in 1648 over the crossing of the late sixteenth-century church of St Salvator in Prague). The church's greatest importance lay in its introduction of a succession of sail vaults over the nave – the first time that this form of construction had been used in the Empire and an important contribution to the trend towards the dissolution of churches into a number of centralized units. But Lurago, who was himself a stuccador, was

323 *Left* Prague, exterior of the Church of the Crusader Knights built by Jean-Baptiste Mathey, 1679–88

324 *Above* Prague, façade of the Czernin Palace built by Francesco Caratti, 1669ff

also responsible for the overall design of the enormously influential decoration of this church (executed 1677ff by his fellow Comasques, the frescoist Carpoforo Tencalla, and the Carlone stuccador troupe), which for the first time in a church of this kind combined expansive frescoes with richly plastic cartouche stucco.

Two non-Italians broke the Comasque hegemony in the last quarter of the seventeenth century, Jean-Baptiste Mathey (c. 1630–95)[62] and Abraham Leuthner (c. 1639–1701). Both had been (or, in the case of Leuthner, claimed to have been) in Rome, and both invigorated the architectural situation in Bohemia with new ideas, the one by example and the other by precept. Mathey was a Burgundian by birth and, characteristically for this stage of Central European Baroque architecture, not an architect but a painter by training, who had been associated with Claude in Rome. There he became painter-in-ordinary to a scion of the family raised to greatness in the person of Wallenstein, Johann Friedrich Count Waldstein. When this man was elected archbishop of Prague in 1675, he took Mathey back with him, and at once entrusted him with the reconstruction of his archiepiscopal palace, and kept him busy with commissions over the next twenty years. Mathey's two most notable works both served as sources of inspiration for Fischer von Erlach, who was reported to 'nurse a special

325 Prague, Schloss Troja, garden front showing the staircase built by
Mathey 1679–96

affection for the said Mathey from acknowledged experience in architecture'. One was the Church (1679–88) of the Crusader
323 Knights with the Red Star, a chivalric order based in Prague (to which the Karlskirche was later to be entrusted), of which Waldstein had been Grand Master since 1668. This church broke with Comasque traditions in the lucidity of its planning and in the elegance and low relief of its detailing. The latter is French in inspiration (notably the overall rustication of the exterior), but the plan combines the then fashionable oval (though this had already been employed a century before for the 'Wälsche Kapelle' of the Italian colony) and a full dome above, with cruciform arms (alluding to the Crusaders) extended by a saucer-domed choir to the east. The other work was Schloss Troja (1679–96), a *villa suburbana* for Count Sternberg. This not only broke away from the massive block-like or quadrangular Italian *Schlösser* through Mathey's introduction of the French pavilion system and projecting wings, but also has
325 attached to it on the garden side a remarkable oval staircase incorporating a *gigantomachia* sculpted by the Heermanns. Mathey, as a 'foreigner' untrained in architecture, was still dependent on the Italians for the execution of his projects, which in all cases but the Church of the Crusader Knights seems to have led to an intrusion of coarser and inappropriate detailing. And though breaking the dominance of the Comasques, his work lay outside the mainstream of development in Bohemia, so that his real importance resides in his part in the formation of Fischer von Erlach, during the latter's fruitful visit to Prague in 1691.

Abraham Leuthner, by contrast, arose out of the milieu of the Comasque masons, enriching the practical knowledge that he gained from them with theoretical speculation of his own, and passing the fruits of both on to the earliest generation of Dientzenhofers. He first appears working as a mason on the
324 Czernin Palace, and his one important building was the Cistercian Abbey Church of Waldsassen (1681–1704) in the re-

catholicized Upper Palatinate. In this church certain features of Passau Cathedral – the domically treated sail vaults over the nave, and the same combination of richly plastic white stucco by the Carlone troupe and large frescoes (by the Prague artist Jakob Steinfels) – are married to reversions to a more indigenous type of church – the calotte, rather than a full dome over the crossing of the non-projecting transept, and the aisleless nave with galleried side-chapels all but sealed off from one another, but with wide arched openings to the nave underneath the gallery and the entablature. A striking innovation that Leuthner made in this church, and that subsequently enjoyed enduring popularity, was the piercing through of the vaults of these side-chapels to the galleries above. More important than what Leuthner built, however, was his theoretical treatise, the *Grundtliche Darstellung der funff Seullen* (1677), written, as he claimed in the foreword, from a 'true German heart', and going beyond a mere treatment of the five Orders to illustrate a number of interesting plans, including both that of a wall-pillar church and those of a number of centrally planned churches, some of symbolic form. The latter, curiously, were translated into imaginary designs for garden pavilions by Fischer von Erlach, who conversely turned Leuthner's simplified redaction of Archduke Ferdinand's star-shaped Schloss outside Prague (1555–58) into the design for a church. Leuthner's whole treatise was drawn on for another compilation by the Bayreuth court architect, C.P. Dieussart, which was in turn re-edited by J.L. Dientzenhofer in 1695. Surviving collections of ideal designs from the Dientzenhofer circle reveal how strongly they were influenced by the symbolic plans of Leuthner in particular.

Waldsassen came to serve almost as a private academy of the Dientzenhofers; at least three of the six architect brothers from this remarkable Bavarian family served in a subordinate capacity under Leuthner or his successor on this building.[63] Christoph Dientzenhofer also acted as executant mason for Abraham Leuthner on Schloss Schlackenwerth (1685ff – the Schloss from which came Sibylla Augusta of Sachsen-Lauenburg, the later margravine of Baden-Baden) – and their two families came, in addition, to be closely connected by marriage. It may have been guild exclusiveness in their native Bavaria that drove the Dientzenhofers to seek work farther afield, at first in Prague and then in the Upper Palatinate and Franconia as well. The eldest brother, Georg (1643–89) is first heard of in Prague in 1681, and then as Leuthner's foreman on Waldsassen in 1682. He went on to build the symbolically trefoil-planned pilgrimage-church of the Holy Trinity at Kappel (1685–89) for the abbey, and the sail-vaulted, wall-pillar Jesuit Church of St Martin in Bamberg (1686–89), before being 326 removed by an early death. Georg paved the way for the careers of two other brothers in the Upper Palatinate and Franconia: Wolfgang (1648–1706) and Johann Leonhard (1660–1707). Wolfgang took up residence in Amberg, whence he built a number of abbey churches in the Upper Palatinate on fairly rudimentary wall-pillar plans, possibly basing himself on designs by his brother for the earliest of them. Johann Leonhard worked under Georg at Waldsassen till he was appointed architect to the Cistercian Abbey of Ebrach in 1686. Through taking over the execution of his brother's church of St Martin, he also put himself into position to become architect to the see of Bamberg in 1690, thus cementing his base in Franconia. With the election of Lothar Franz von Schönborn as bishop of Bamberg in 1693 he was assured of a busy career, though nothing that he built had the distinction of the works created by his youngest brother, Johann (1663–1726), who succeeded him as architect to the see on his death in 1707. Lothar Franz's own doubts about Leonhard's capacities are attested by his refusal to appoint him as architect to his other see of Mainz in 1698. He was nonetheless summoned fairly far afield to build his major project, the Cistercian Abbey Church of Schöntal (realized after his death 1708–27), which was designed, like one or two other major churches of the period (e.g. Grosscomburg and the Jesuit church at Heidelberg), on fundamentally late-mediaeval lines as a hall-church, but in Renaissance garb, with panelled pilasters applied to the four sides of the pillars, and sail vaults.

Although all the Dientzenhofer brothers appear to have begun their careers in Prague, only Christoph (1655–1722) settled there, to become a Bohemian architect by adoption. The history of Bohemian architecture is fraught with uncertainty over the authorship of certain key buildings, and the earlier *oeuvre* of Christoph Dientzenhofer and Santini Aichel in particular suffers from some crucial uncertainties. It nonetheless seems feasible to argue back from Christoph Dientzenhofer's attested later works and from a common strain running through both his work and that of his son, Kilian Ignaz, so as to assemble as his earlier work a group of churches having one very important feature in common – indebtedness to Guarini.

Guarini impinged upon the Bohemian scene both directly and indirectly. In 1679 he submitted plans for a Theatine church in Prague to be dedicated to the Blessed Virgin of Ötting. The church was not built till some years later, and then to different plans, and with a façade by Santini Aichel. Guarini's designs had no immediate resonance, but in 1699 Hildebrandt designed his earliest church, for Count Berka at Gabel in northern Bohemia, a church clearly indebted in plan to its namesake of S. Lorenzo in Turin. Hildebrandt's adaptation of one of Guarini's central plans was not directly imitated; instead it seems to have provoked a keen interest in Guarini's plans for longitudinal churches – which had in the meantime been published (1686) – notably those for the Theatine church in Prague, S. Maria della Divina Provvidenza in Lisbon, and the chapel of the Lazarist Mission (now the Archiepiscopal Palace) at Turin (1673–75 and 1695–97) – though this was not in fact one of those published amongst the plates later used for the *Architettura Civile*. What ensued was less an imitation of Guarini – the principle behind the intersecting vaults is very different – than the use of Guarini to license unconventional forms of vaulting that owed much in technique to indigenous traditions of masonry. Guarini's respect for Gothic architecture is well known, and it is no coincidence that the one country to take inspiration from Guarini's experiments in vaulting, Bohemia, should also have been the country to engender Santini Aichel's fanciful reconstructions of Late-Gothic vault-rib patterns.

The first of the Guarinesque churches attributed to Christoph Dientzenhofer (partly on analogies in detailing with his earliest known work, the symbolically heart-shaped Magdalen Chapel at Skalka, 1692–93) is the church of the former Sternberg Schloss at Smiřice (1699–1713). This combines elements from a surprisingly heterogeneous variety of sources: an interior plan which is virtually that of St Lawrence, Gabel, but which, lacking the corridored envelope of the latter, displays undulating walls to the exterior – to which the first step had been taken at Skalka – and a star-shaped rib-vault so faithful to its Gothic model that this can be dated to the early years of the sixteenth century, though at Smiřice the severies are filled with

programmatically organized frescoes in stucco frames. The vault, though startling, is explicable; for this church is dedicated to the Adoration of the Kings, who were led to Bethlehem by just such a star (and the Prophets and Sibyls in the frescoes foretold the birth of Christ as the star had). The star also alludes to the name of the family (lit. 'Starmountain'). The idea of exposing the interior plan as undulating walls to the exterior doubtless derives from S. Maria della Divina Provvidenza. Christoph Dientzenhofer's innovation, which was to remain a distinguishing feature both of his own work and of the early work of his son, was the way in which the system of supports sustaining the vault and the walling between are sharply distinguished from, and bear no necessary relation to, one another – the so-called 'baldachin-system'.

The next church of the group, the Church of St Joseph attached to the Pauline Friary at Obořiště (1702–12), is the first to have what are apparently Guarinesque vaults. In fact, though the plan of the church is clearly indebted to that of the Archiepiscopal chapel at Turin, from which it derives the idea

326 Bamberg, façade of the Jesuit church of St Martin built by Georg Dientzenhofer, 1686–89

dome over the centre, absurd though it looks, echoes the essential 'illogicality' of Christoph Dientzenhofer's vaults in relation to his bi-axial ground-plan.

At this point comes a church whose attribution to Christoph Dientzenhofer is reasonably secure, the Jesuit Church of St Nicholas, Malá Strana (the 'Lesser Side' of Prague). The building history of this church proceeded in fits and starts. Though the foundation stone was laid in 1673, it was not until 1703 that the church was begun, to new plans by Christoph Dientzenhofer. Shortage of funds caused building to be broken off after the church was roofed in 1705; and the nave was only vaulted and the façade built in 1709–11. The east end was closed by a provisional, illusionistically painted wooden screen until the domed choir and single tower were built by Kilian Ignaz Dientzenhofer in 1737–59.

Perhaps because it was for a Jesuit House of Profession, Christoph Dientzenhofer adopted a form of construction unusual for Bohemia – that of a galleried wall-pillar church. However, not only did he support the front of the galleries on three-dimensional arches, he also set the pillars to face diagonally into the nave, with the intention (as proven by early copies of his plans) of setting over them a syncopated series of three-dimensionally curved transverse arches meeting tangentially over the centre of the bays (i.e. the 'voids') beneath, and leaving vacant lens-shaped areas of vault between them, corresponding to the pillars (the 'solids'). These plans show that the genesis of these apparently Guarinesque ribs, which were to be adopted with such enthusiasm in Franconia by Christoph's brother Johann, and from him by Neumann, was entirely non-functional: they were to be decoratively applied to a continuous

329

327 *Above* Smiřice, exterior of the Schloss church of the Adoration of the Magi built by Christoph Dientzenhofer, 1699–1713

328 *Right* Smiřice, interior of the church

of a nave composed of two rounded bays with a subsidiary bay between, and intersecting vaults, these vaults are quite differently constructed. Where Guarini designed domes with a skeletal framework of tapering ribs, Christoph Dientzenhofer created three slightly *bombé* vaults, with groins at their junctions with one another, eaten away by deep triangular penetrations arising from the arches of the clerestory windows and those of the east and west ends. This is exactly the same kind of empirical vault-construction, more Gothic survival than Guarinesque, that can be seen in the two symbolically planned churches, both connected with the Dientzenhofer circle, at Westerndorf (1668) and at Kappel. At Obořiště, however, another device characteristic of Christoph Dientzenhofer emerged: the 'syncopation' of the vaults in relation to the plan. Where the eye expects – and Guarini had created – domes or domical vaults corresponding to the concave-walled bays at either end of the nave, only two broad V-shaped ribs touching at the tips are left by the penetrations; where the eye would have expected a double transverse rib over the 'closed' central section formed by the clustered wall-pilasters, is a smooth section of domical vault expanding out into the adjacent bays. In 1733 the vault was crudely frescoed in such a way – as so often in these churches – as to mask the architect's original intentions; nonetheless, the illusionistic

330

tunnel-vault. It·is possible that these plans represent *ex post facto* rationalizations of the executed vault, which is of empirical wavy construction, with concealed ribs on the outside, and that the idea of exploiting them visually only came later, for at the Benedictine Abbey Church of St Margaret, Břevnov (begun in 1708, taken over and completed by Christoph Dientzenhofer 1709–15), they are also to be found over the westernmost bay of the choir (1714–15) but not over the earlier nave. Over the nave of Břevnov, and over that of the Church of the Poor Clares at Eger (Cheb, 1707–11), commonly attributed to Christoph, is to be found his more usual system of intersecting sections of vault – syncopated at Břevnov, and bi-axially organized at Eger (though a sectional plan exists of Eger, showing three-dimensional ribs). It was his brother Johann who, at Banz (1710–19), took the further step of amalgamating the syncopated system of intersecting vaults with these three-dimensional ribs. Unfortunately, at St Nicholas, as at Obořiště, Christoph's vaults were again found too disturbing for the eye, and were obliterated under a vast illusionistic fresco by J.L. Kracker in 1760–61. This subsequent overpainting obscures the extent to which the canted pillars and ribs would have formed an autonomous system – the so-called 'baldachin-system' – within the otherwise conventional plan of the church. This emerges much more clearly at Břevnov, in which Dientzenhofer used the same canted pillars, placed against the walls (which themselves bow slightly outwards) very much in the manner of the shafted buttresses of the earliest Gothic wall-pillar churches. In the façade of St Nicholas, and in the side elevations – treated as façades – of Břevnov and Eger, his love of curvature and of the interplay of advancing and receding sections is given full rein, as

329 *Bottom left* Prague, nave of the Jesuit church of St Nicholas on the Lesser Side, built by Christoph Dientzenhofer, 1703–11

330 *Below* Obořiště, nave vault of the friary church built by Christoph Dientzenhofer, 1702–12

331 *Bottom right* Břevnov (Prague), interior of the abbey church built by Christoph Dientzenhofer, 1709–15

332 *Opposite* Prague, exterior of St John Nepomuk 'on the Rock' built by K. I. Dientzenhofer, 1730–39

333 *Above* Prague, façade of the Villa Amerika built by Kilian Ignaz Dientzenhofer, 1717–20

at Smiřice, but without the same compulsion from the plan.

Such are the main features of the most important of the churches known to be by, or attributed to, Christoph Dientzenhofer – a man whom the Latin chronicler of a monastery described in 1699 as 'with a fine understanding of his art, working far and wide, though quite incapable of either reading or writing' (not strictly true, as he could certainly sign his name). Though extraordinarily diverse, these churches display an inner consistency as well as, in the literal sense, a family resemblance to the works by other Dientzenhofers. Whereas, however, his brother Johann immediately exploited his three-dimensionally curved ribs and galleries at Banz, his son Kilian Ignaz (1689–1751) at first struck out on his own, and only in the 1730s began to exploit certain of his father's ideas.[64] Unlike his father, he received a formal education before being sent as a journeyman to Vienna in 1707. He did not return from there till 1717, making a further study trip in 1725, and it is evident that his experience of the metropolis inclined him at first to more conventional solutions, and to the central plan in particular. It seems clear that the somewhat staid vaults of the Loreto Church in Prague, for which his father signed the contract in March 1722, dying in June of the same year, are due to Kilian Ignaz, whereas the picturesque screen front to the whole site, begun in May 1721, is almost entirely Christoph's.

Kilian Ignaz's *oeuvre* was vast, and included everything from town palaces and churches to monasteries and little chapels in the countryside. Certain idiosyncrasies of detailing recur in his work, several of them Hildebrandtian – label-like capitals to pilasters, often linked together, heavy curvilinear pediments isolated in the wall, windows cut out of the wall like patterns in pastry, piers crowned by broken segmental pediments in the interiors of his churches – but his catholicity of approach in planning his churches is almost too great for a consistent preference to be sought or a clear line of development found. Almost all his designs are, however, variations upon a central plan; and when the circumstances of the commission required a longitudinal church, the nave was generally bi-axial.

Kilian Ignaz's first work on returning to Prague from Vienna was the exquisite little summer pavilion for Count Michna, the so-called Villa Amerika (1717–20) which combines Hildebrandtian decorative motifs with local features like the dormer window set in an attic balustrade. This was followed by two orthodox centrally planned churches, St John Nepomuk on the Hradschin above Prague (1720–28) and the pilgrimage-church of the Virgin's Nativity at Nicov (Nitzau, 1720–27). St John Nepomuk is like a straitened version of the Piarist Church at Vienna (whose ultimate vaulting with a drumless, pendentive-less dome like St John Nepomuk may even derive from suggestions made by Kilian Ignaz when he studied it in its unfinished state in 1725). At Nicov, though equally innocent of any debt to his father, Kilian Ignaz nonetheless seems to have timidly resorted to inspiration from Guarini's own churches for the tapering ribs of the conched arms, and for the drumless dome with oval windows between the tapering ribs, disguised as

333

an octagon on the exterior. More important, however, is the way in which Kilian Ignaz runs a well-lit gallery behind the piers of the dome. For whereas Christoph, with his 'baldachin-system', created an autonomous skeleton of wall-pillars and vaults within the neutral outer envelope of the walls of his churches, Kilian Ignaz was to arrive at a more organic solution in which whole piers were isolated from the walls as the structurally significant elements sustaining the vaults. The vaults themselves, in consequence, were usually treated as unified (generally frescoed) wholes, sustained by wall-arches round the perimeter, but not articulated by ribs. Neither church yet exemplifies this fully, though in both the system is adumbrated by the way in which the entablature of the piers is carried into the cross arms, only to stop short at the outer wall, creating a clear distinction between the vault-sustaining and the infilling parts of the church.

In Kilian Ignaz's longitudinal churches this treatment results in buildings whose exterior, in which the walls play the major part, is governed by a love of alternating convexities and concavities, whilst their interior is defined by the system of supports, with the walls as a negative element behind and between. The first major church in which this is exemplified is the Benedictine Abbey Church of Wahlstatt (Legnickie Pole, 1725–31) built as a triumphant reassertion of Catholicism in Protestant Silesia by the abbot of Braunau (Broumov). Externally this is an ovoid church, extended by a rounded choir at one end, and faced by a twin-towered façade with a convex centre the other. Inside, however, the nave is characteristically divided by Kilian Ignaz into two equal parts, so that the central cross axis is closed by a wall-pillar on either side. These wall-pillars, and those at the extremities of the nave, are treated like the clustered columns of Gothic churches, with pilaster fragments supporting the wall-arches, and attached columns taking the peripheral arches of the vault (which is unified by a fresco by C.D. Asam). In the choir a heavy layered entablature is supported by attached columns placed in front of the walls, and supports arches framing the windows above, creating the effect of walls and windows being stretched behind the essential scaffolding of the fabric, as in the nave. A very similar treatment to that of the choir was applied by Kilian Ignaz to the nave of one of his most attractive churches, the picturesquely sited St John Nepomuk 'na Skalce' ('on the Rock' 1730–39) in the New Town at Prague. This has a twin-towered façade similar to that of Wahlstatt, save that here the towers are canted, as in St Peter's, Vienna. Behind this, the nave is shaped as a concave-sided octagon, with a transverse oval bay at either end, and a three-quarter circle choir to the east. Though the intersections of these areas produced three-dimensional arches in the vaults, these, as in Guarini's centrally planned churches, are the logical consequence of the intersections, and not wilfully introduced like those of Kilian Ignaz's father. The complete frescoing of the vaults again highlights the outer perimeter of arches sustaining them. It was not until the Jesuit church at Opařany (Woporschan, 1732–35) that Kilian Ignaz used a pair of tangential three-dimensional ribs; and it is characteristic that he neither applied them ornamentally like his father at Břevnov,

334

332

334 *Above right* Prague, interior of St John Nepomuk 'on the Rock'

335 *Right* Carlsbad, choir of St Mary Magdalen built by K. I. Dientzenhofer, 1733–36

nor in syncopation to the structure below, like his uncle at Banz. The plan of the nave of Opařany is again bi-axial – and indeed derived from Eger – and the tangential ribs are the result of the projection into the vault of the two transverse ovals out of which the nave is notionally constructed. In contrast to Banz, they meet over the piers, and not over the voids between, as in the modified copy of Christoph's sectional plan of Eger. Below, the attached columns from which they rise are linked by Kilian Ignaz's characteristic broken segmental pediments; whilst the articulation of the whole church into vault-sustaining supports and integument-like walls is again lucidly carried through.

At this point Kilian Ignaz produced one of his most successful churches, in the series of plans for which the vitality of his imagination is also best exemplified – the Church of St Mary Magdalen (1733–36) standing on the slope above the hot springs of Carlsbad (Karlovy Vary). In his first two plans he intended to exploit the conspicuous site, as with St John 'na Skalce', by setting the twin towers diagonally – with a recessed centre in the first version, and as part of a continuously curved façade in the second. Behind this in the first version he planned an octagonal nave with a star-shaped rib vault eaten into by three-dimensional arches emanating from the oval spaces in the axes and the niches on the diagonals, and in the second version a symmetrical succession of transverse oval vestibule, lengthwise oval nave, transverse oval choir, and octagonal eastern towers, resulting in a remarkable double-waisted plan. The final plan was more sober: a rib-domed lengthwise oval nave, with concave-sided spaces on the axes, prolonged by a transverse
335 oval choir at the east, and with rib-headed exedrae on the diagonals. The ribbed dome and diagonals are reminiscent of Nicov, and Kilian Ignaz exploited the ideas of that church yet further by taking an undulating gallery right round the church to the high altar, to describe a light-filled path behind the structural skeleton of the church – the segmental-headed 'piers' framing the diagonal openings. In this church Kilian Ignaz's lucid distinction between the tectonic and the enveloping parts of his buildings is most fully and happily realized; he thereby comes close, not through the imitation of his father, but by pursuing his own development, both to Guarini and to the never wholly submerged Gothic tradition in Bohemia – of which his projected star-shaped rib vault over this church was but another instance.

At the same time as St Mary Magdalen was being put up, Kilian Ignaz was designing the much more bizarre centrally planned church of St Nicholas (1732–37) in the Old City of Prague for the abbot of the Benedictine Emmaus monastery. Some of the strangeness of this church is due to the site, and to the subsequent clearances around it. St Nicholas was the rebuilding of a church that had been for two centuries in the hands of the heretical Utraquists – thus requiring its architecture to be something of an affirmation – on a site so hemmed in that it could only be developed upwards. Kilian Ignaz created the main façade out of the long south flank, setting a strongly
336 detached tower at either end to flank the set-back dome, to make a picturesquely composed group from afar, repeating this triadic arrangement in the centrepiece framing the portal

336 *Above right* Prague, side façade of St Nicholas in the Old City built by K. I. Dientzenhofer, 1732–37

337 *Right* Prague, interior of St Nicholas in the Old City

337 dominating the street. In the interior of the nave the church is divided into supporting and enveloping elements, as at Nicov, with a wrought-iron balconied gallery running round behind the supports; but the contribution of light is missing, despite the pierced domes of the diagonal chapels (cf. the Kollegienkirche at Salzburg). Instead, to obtain light, the vertical emphasis is taken to extremes: the segmentally-pedimented attached columns flanking the diagonals are carried up as caryatids in the intermediate zone, then as recessed attached columns flanking pilasters in the drum, to culminate as tapering ribs in the lanterned cloister-vault. The interior is also unusual amongst Kilian Ignaz's churches for the amount of stucco ornament (by Bernard Spinetti) complementing C. D. Asam's frescoes.

Kilian Ignaz was never able to realize the major con-

ventual church for which he produced such stimulating designs for the Ursulines of Kutná Hora – with the church forming the diagonal of an irregular hexagon (cf. Caspar Moosbrugger's second plan for St Gallen) – but at the end of his career he was appropriately chosen to add the domed choir and single east tower to his father's church of St Nicholas, Malá Strana (1745–53), for the Jesuits. The choice was appropriate in familial rather than stylistic terms, for the massive sobriety of the interior of Kilian Ignaz's domed triconch contrasts strongly with the undulating fluidity of his father's nave. By setting the drummed dome upon curved pendentives, Kilian Ignaz even lost the opportunity to create three-dimensional arches at the intersection of the circular centre and the conches. Moreover, the paired columns placed in front of the piers and in the drum are now purely rhetorical devices, not distinct structural features. But Kilian Ignaz is thoroughly vindicated by the unforgettable contribution that his dome and tower make to the silhouette of Prague. Even though it is clear that a single tower at the south-east corner of the Jesuits' site was a feature of the earliest designs for rebuilding their House, and that the tower was executed by Kilian Ignaz's son-in-law Anselmo Lurago, it required genius to balance dome and tower through contrast rather than conformity – setting concavity off against convexity, tapering against roundedness, and richness against bulk. It is perhaps appropriate that this last major achievement of the Bohemian Baroque should evoke, without imitating (though there may well be an allusion in the seraph-herms of the penultimate southern nave window), the similar collocation of dome and single tower in Borromini's completion of S. Andrea delle Fratte.

In following through the particular strand of Bohemian Baroque architecture represented by the Dientzenhofers, strict chronology has been disregarded. Bohemia, like Austria itself, despite the reassertion of native, or at least German talent in the building world, continued to harbour a number of *welsche* architects, though many of these were by now second or even third generation immigrants. Ottavio Broggio (1668–1742), for instance, from Leitmeritz (Litoměřice) dominated architectural activity in that region, building churches – e.g. the Cistercian Abbey Church of Ossegg (Osek, 1712–18) – and *Schlösser* – e.g. Ploschkowitz (Ploskovice, 1720–25), for the estranged wife of Gian Gastone de' Medici – characterized by richly profiled mouldings and a Dientzenhofer-like interplay of convexity and concavity. Italians were particularly in demand to build town palaces and country *Schlösser,* and in carrying out these commissions were instrumental in giving secular architecture in Bohemia a far more Austrian stamp than church architecture. Both D. E. Rossi and Domenico Martinelli came from Vienna, the former in 1692 to supervise the completion of the interiors of the Czernin Palace in Prague, and the latter on various occasions between 1692 and 1705 to make designs for Schloss Aussee (Moravia) and Schloss Landskron (Bohemia) for Prince Liechtenstein, for Schloss Austerlitz (Moravia) for Count Kaunitz, and for the Sternberg Palace in Prague. A notable feature of both the Sternberg Palace (c. 1700ff) and Schloss Austerlitz (post 1698ff.) is that they make use of a

338 *Above left* Schloss Karlskrone, exterior built by J. B. Santini Aichel, 1721–22

339 *Left* Sedlec, nave and aisles of the abbey church built by Santini Aichel, 1702–06

projecting oval saloon in the centre. A yet clearer instance of inspiration from Fischer von Erlach is Schloss Liblitz (Liblice) built from 1699 onwards by G. B. Alliprandi (1665–1720), who had come from Vienna to Prague in 1695 to take over the supervision of the Czernin Palace from D. E. Rossi, in direct imitation of a design of Fischer's later engraved for the *Entwurff*. The projecting oval saloon maintained its popularity in Bohemia till the 1740s and beyond, being found for instance in Schloss Ploschkowitz, on both fronts of J. Augustoni's Schloss Trpist, and in three *Schlösser* inspired by Fischer's Althan Garden Palace – the Czech F. M. Kańka's (1674–1766) Weltrus (*c*. 1715ff.), Santini Aichel's three-winged Karlskrone (1721–22), and the anonymous Karlshof (post 1730).

426
338

Schloss Karlskrone was the last work of Johann Blasius Santini Aichel (1677–1723), the most remarkable of all the indigenous Italians.[65] Though to his contemporaries he was most renowned as a secular architect – in 1722 he was said to be serving over forty noble clients in Bohemia and Moravia – it is not for Karlskrone or the Kolowrat/Thun-Hohenstein (1710–20) and Morzin/Czernin (1713–14) palaces in Prague that he is now remembered, so much as for his single-handed invention of a new genre of church architecture, since christened 'Baroque Gothic'.

Santini Aichel was the grandson of an Italian immigrant mason, and the son of a stonemason who frequently worked for Mathey. Whether inspired by the latter's example, or because he was a cripple, Santini Aichel left it to his younger brother to pursue his father's craft, and himself trained as a painter. Yet in 1702, with no other known work to his credit, he was already considered competent to replace the Bohemian German archi-

tect P. I. Bayer (1650–1733) in the rebuilding of the Cistercian Abbey Church of Sedlec – a choice as bold as that of C. D. Asam for the rebuilding of Weltenburg. Sedlec had been burnt down by the Hussites in 1421, and its reconstruction therefore took on the character of a reassertion of the pristine faith, from which Utraquism, the Bohemian Brethren and Lutheranism had been so many aberrations. Gothic was chosen both as a conscious reversion to the past, and because in Bohemia there were still echoes of Ferdinand I's insistence, in the midst of a precocious adoption of the Italian Renaissance for secular works, that Gothic forms – and particularly vaults – were alone 'churchy'. The reversion to Gothic was also the architectural equivalent of the religious politics involved in the resurrection or creation of the cults of Bohemian national saints, culminating in the virtual re-invention of St John Nepomuk. And just as in Southern Germany the old orders rebuilt their abbeys and churches, and filled them with frescoes and sculpture glorifying their history, in Bohemia the same orders – the Benedictines, the Cistercians, and the Premonstratensians – employed Santini Aichel to build in his historicizing 'Gothic' style.

339

There were other instances of the imitation of genuine Gothic vaults, as we have seen in Smiřice and Kilian Ignaz Dientzenhofer's first design for Carlsbad, but Santini Aichel, exploiting the possibilities of stucco and taking his cue from the non-

328

340 *Left* Kladruby, interior of the abbey church

341 *Above* Kladruby, exterior of the abbey church built by Santini Aichel, 1712–26

tectonic nature of Late-Gothic rib vaults in Bohemia, went beyond this to an imaginative recreation of such Late-Gothic vaults in terms of a different geometry. The exteriors of Sedlec and Kladruby could pass muster as the genuine article at least as well as Hawksmoor's quadrangle at All Souls, Oxford, but their vaults are unmistakably personal. At the Benedictine Abbey Church of Kladruby, indeed, razed both by the Hussites and in the Thirty Years War, and rebuilt by Santini Aichel (1712–26), the abbot showed how far even the clients were from aiming at archaeological accuracy by writing of the Bohemian-crowned crossing-dome that it was *'more Gottico nondum viso'* – in a hitherto unheard-of Gothic manner – particularly rich in pinnacles. At Kladruby, Santini Aichel not only created pistachio-green rib vaults of a patterned complexity worthy to vie with Kutná Hora, but also designed altars that terminate in a riotous thicket of crocketed nodding pinnacles; but this exuberant adoption of Gothic was not taken so far as to preclude very Baroque frescoes by Cosmas Damian Asam on the high walls of the nave and in the crossing-lantern.

Santini Aichel's Gothic ventures, which included the rebuilding of the Premonstratensian Abbey Church of Želiv (Seelau, 1713–20) as a galleried hall-church on the lines of Kutná Hora, and the addition of three-dimensionally curved galleries to the Gothic Cistercian Abbey Church of Žd'ár (Saar, *c.* 1710), did not preclude churches in a more orthodox Baroque vein, in which his ingenuity was manifested in the invention of striking plans. Two of these, Kiritein (Křtiny, *c.* 1710) and Maria-Teinitz (Mariánské Týnice, 1711ff.), were Greek cross-shaped pilgrimage-churches, which Santini Aichel found new ways of integrating into the containing cloister that was a traditional feature of Bohemian pilgrimage-sites. At Maria-Teinitz (now a ruin) the fourth side of a quadrangle with kidney-shaped chapels in the corners was clamped on to one arm of the church thus creating an imaginary prolongation of the cloister through the church past the image, like the walk of a Carthusian monastery. At Kiritein the same occurs, yet with the additional complexity that, whilst the cloister, set with a tower-shaped chapel, clasps and enters the two sides of the south arm of the church, the east and west arms are mantled by two-storey ambulatories also opening into the church. In both Kiritein and Maria-Teinitz the interiors are distinguished by detailing in very shallow relief and the rounding inwards of piers and pilasters, emphasizing continuity with the drum-less domes and vaults above. This undistracted expression of interior space is given full rein in the Benedictine Abbey Church of Raigern (Rajhrad, 1722ff., completed posthumously), which is composed, behind a somewhat eclectically detailed concave façade, as a succession of drum-less oval-domed spaces – a lengthwise oval, followed by an octagon, which protrudes externally from recessed walls, and finally a cross-wise rectangle with rounded piers. It is a remarkable spatial sequence, different in character from those later to be found in the works of Kilian Ignaz Dientzenhofer or J. M. Fischer, both in the smooth continuity between walls and vaults, and in the flowing transitions, the sense of flux and reflux, between the voluminous wholes thus created. Typically, the three spaces have a symbolic justi-

342 *Above right* Křtiny, vaults of the pilgrimage-church built by Santini Aichel, *c.* 1710

343 *Right* Zelená Hora (Žd'ár), exterior of the pilgrimage-church built by Santini Aichel, 1720–22

fication, revealed by an inscription on the arch over the altar: *Faciamus hic tria tabernacula* – St Peter's impetuous reaction to the Transfiguration.

The most remarkable of all Santini Aichel's churches is governed by symbolism in its very essence; it also represents a striking synthesis between his two modes of building – the 'Gothic' and the Baroque. Like any Bohemian architect, his *oeuvre* contains a number of centrally, and often symbolically planned votive chapels, of which the most successful is the domed triangular chapel of St Anne (celebrating the trinity of St Anne, the Virgin and Christ). One of Santini Aichel's most constant clients was the abbot of Žd'ár, for whom he not only rebuilt the abbey and modified the church, but also put up a variety of symbolically shaped buildings, including out-buildings in the form of the abbot's initials, a court in the shape of a lyre, and a chapel to the Virgin at Obyčtov like a tortoise in plan (betokening constancy). In 1719 the tongue of John of Nepomuk, supposedly martyred for his refusal to utter the secrets of the confessional, was miraculously rediscovered in an undecayed state. Thereupon, the abbot, whose monastery had been transplanted to Žd'ár from Nepomuk exactly five centuries before, decided to build a votive chapel on an adjacent hill, itself rechristened Zelená Hora (Green Hill) after the hill at Nepomuk, in the shape of a five-pointed star – an allusion not only to the five stars that had hovered round the martyr's head when he was thrown into the Moldau, but also a reference to the abbey's quincentenary. Santini Aichel, however, entered so far into the spirit of the abbot's conception that every feature of the building is imbued with symbolic significance, whilst trans-cending symbolic pedantry (as exemplified in, say, Sir Thomas Tresham's triangular lodge at Rushton) as consummately as in S. Ivo della Sapienza. The plan of the chapel, with its five tangential oval chapels alternating with five tongue-shaped altar-niches, is a cross between Fischer von Erlach's crypt-chapel at Schloss Frain and his designs for garden pavilions. The word tongue-shaped is used advisedly, because this shape recurs not only in the elevation of the niches, but also in the doors, windows and narrow openings to the chapels, whilst the saint's tongue is represented in stucco as the centre-piece of the dome. Santini's adoption of – appropriately named – lancet windows thus has a dual significance, alluding both to the 'Sword of the Lord, the Sword of Gideon', as the saint's tongue was lauded for its steadfast refusal to utter the secrets of the confessional, and to the mediaeval past of Žd'ár. Triangular windows lighting the ambulatory and gallery have a similarly dual significance. Throughout the church, five-, six-, and eight-pointed stars celebrate St John Nepomuk, the Virgin, and the Cistercian order. Inside, the straight balustrades of the tribune emphasize the decagonal plan of the body of the church, whilst the alternately projecting and receding concave sections of the upper gallery, scored with Gothic ribbing underneath, bring out the five-pointed star again. And whilst at the lower level the five altar-niches are closed, and light floods in from the lancet openings to the chapels, above the situation is reversed. Out-side, the precinct round the church is contained by a ten-pointed cloister housing five chapels, both in calculated anti-strophe to the church, and in further allusion to the decagonal Gothic fountain embodying Žd'ár's Latin name – *Fons Mariae*. Such a wealth of symbolism results in a church whose idiosyn-cracy verges upon the bizarre; but the way in which this is translated on the exterior – which has a more angular, Gothic appearance – and in the interior – where there is a more Bar-

oque play with convexity and concavity and with light – into interpenetrating forms and plans is both intellectually and aesthetically exciting.

One of the sources of inspiration for Santini Aichel's sym-bolically planned churches was Kappel and the series of sym-bolic plans that this inspired the Dientzenhofers to create. The only one of the five brothers (a sixth barely seems to have functioned as an architect) not to have been considered so far is the one who acted as the vital link between the progressive architecture of Bohemia and that of Franconia, Johann (1663–1726), the youngest, who appears to have begun his career by turning his back on unconventional architecture. He first worked as executant mason for his brother Leonhard, and thus came to the notice of Lothar Franz von Schönborn, who in 1699 sent him to Rome 'to profit from the sight and observation of the most notable palaces and buildings of those parts'. Johann was the only one of the brothers to have this direct experience of Italy, and the clear implication was that he was being groomed to build palaces for his patron. For the moment, however, his brother held the post of court architect, there were no funds for other projects, and so on his return in 1700 Johann took up the post of court architect to the prince-abbot of Fulda.

Fulda was one of the oldest Benedictine monasteries in Germany, and housed the bones of the German Apostle, St Boniface. It was therefore natural that the church should be rebuilt as the abbey approached its millennium (1704–11), and that Johann Dientzenhofer, whose task was complicated by the original insistence (common at the time) on retaining the two west towers as emblems of the past, should – fresh from Rome – have done so on a conventional Latin-cross plan using a dome and the maximum Roman *gravitas*. The weakest feature is, ironically, the vaulting – a plain tunnel vault divided into alternating sections by transverse arches, and with deep pene-trations from the clerestory windows.

In the meantime Leonhard Dientzenhofer had died (1707), and Johann succeeded his brother in his various posts at Bamberg, and also at the Benedictine Abbey of Banz.[66] As court architect at Bamberg his chief employment was, from 1711 onwards, to build Schloss Weissenstein at Pommersfelden for Lothar Franz, which will be considered in the section on palace architecture; but at the same time he began to build the church at Banz (1710–19). It was in this church that Johann introduced syncopated vaults with three-dimensional ribs, a combination of two ideas that his brother Christoph had as yet only made upon paper. The church consists of a broad two-bay nave and a long, narrow choir. The nave is thus bi-axially divided, with canted and curved ends creating an overall effect of centralization, as at Obořiště and Eger. However, Johann has here brought the concave central pier of these two churches out from the wall, making it a wall-pillar, pierced by a gallery supported on three-dimensionally curved arches either side, like a fragment of the nave of St Nicholas, Malá Strana.

It was likewise the unexecuted plan of St Nicholas that inspired the syncopated vaults, with three-dimensional arches meeting over the voids, and lens-shaped sections of vault over the supports. But whereas St Nicholas was a longitudinal church with its syncopated divisions superimposed on a tunnel-vault, Banz is bi-axial, and has three tangential sail vaults – bounded by twisted three-dimensional ribs, with the central one not only more distended than those at either end, but also marked out as the centre of the whole vault by an illusionistically set fresco of Pentecost. In marked contrast to

344

343

345

346

the decoration of Christoph Dientzenhofer's churches, Melchior Steidl's frescoes and J.J. Vogel's Bérainesque stucco are not afterthoughts, but integral to the conception of the interior. And though in some respects Banz appears like an eclectic combination of Christoph's ideas, the result is so organically coherent – not least the three-dimensional ribs, which here twist with the curvature of the vaults that they bound – that one is driven to wonder whether in his last churches Christoph was not borrowing from his brother, rather than the other way about. Further evidence of Johann's inventiveness is provided by the high altar, which overcomes the Tridentine ban on *jubés* cutting off the congregation from the monks' choir and high altar by an illusionistic trick. The monks' choir is here placed behind the congregational high altar in the old-fashioned way – but both share the same altarpiece, which is placed on the rear wall of the choir, and only appears to be framed by the altar surround!

It is regrettable that the see and principality of Bamberg did not afford Johann Dientzenhofer the same wealth of commissions as his brother and nephew. His craft status precluded him from a pivotal role in secular commissions, whilst Franconia – much of which had gone Protestant – lacked the plentiful religious houses of Swabia and Bavaria. Towards the end of his life, however, he came into contact with Balthasar Neumann, who appears to have inspired him to use his empirical skill in constructing vaults in a new way. How exceptional these skills were we know from a letter of 1724 of Lothar Franz von Schönborn to his nephew Friedrich Carl, regretting that Dientzenhofer's gout and consumption made it impossible to send him to construct a vaulted *sala terrena* in Schloss Göllersdorf like that in Pommersfelden (which has tangential three-dimensional ribs), and saying that he knew no one else competent to do so (the fact that Friedrich Carl made the request shows that it was beyond Hildebrandt's competence – which is not without signficance for the arguments about his role in the planning of the Court Church and Schönborn Chapel at Würzburg).

In 1720 Lothar Franz lent Johann Dientzenhofer to another nephew, Johann Philipp Franz, to supervise the building of his new Residenz at Würzburg. This task he performed for the next three years, under Balthasar Neumann, who as yet lacked practical experience of architecture. We know that this assistance also extended to making designs at Neumann's request. In 1721 Johann Philipp Franz decided to rebuild a chapel built on to the north transept of the cathedral as a mausoleum for himself and his family.[67] With his usual impetuosity he demolished the old chapel straight away, and set about procuring plans for the new from as many designers as possible. Most of the designs share a generic similarity, because Johann Philipp Franz's way of inviting designs was to send out a redaction of his own ideas for modification and criticism. This now lost design, which, with certain alterations, remained the basis for the executed chapel, laid down a domed central area housing the altar and outside entrance in opposite niches on one axis, and two kidney-shaped recesses housing a pair of monuments on the other axis. The junction of the vaults of the kidney-shaped recesses with the central rotunda produced pronounced three-dimensionally curved arches. This is the inevitable consequence of any arched opening to a cylindrical space, albeit one requiring considerable skill in construction. It is no accident that some of the most successful instances of its accomplishment were in France, where Gothic skill in stereotomy was applied to classical designs – by Delorme in the chapels at Anet and Villers-Cotterets, and by François Mansart in the Visitandine Church in Paris. In one version of the design three-dimensional arch-ribs tangential to these arches departed from pilasters set against the rear curve of the recesses. The author of this seminal lost design is not known. Neumann, in the inscription placed traditionally in the knop of the dome, only described himself as 'director' of the work. All the evidence, however, points to Johann Dientzenhofer, here applying his peculiar skills to the problem of a chapel centred – in accordance with his patron's express wish – on a *'Cuppola all'italiana'*.

The attribution is made almost certain by the evidence of the

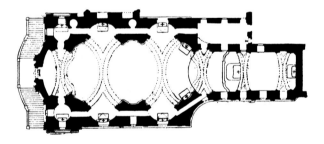

competing designs made for Fulda's priory of Holzkirchen by Neumann and Johann Dientzenhofer between 1724 – the date of election of the new prior, Bonifatius von Hutten, the brother of J.P.F. von Schönborn's successor as prince-bishop of Würzburg the same year – and 1726, the year of Dientzenhofer's death. Whereas Neumann's surviving design for the church – which was the one chosen for execution, probably on the grounds of economy – is simply for a domed octagon, Johann Dientzenhofer's two alternative designs both envisaged a domed central area thrusting outwards with a three-dimensionally curved arch into two arms, to be met tangentially by a similar arch-rib – just as in the Schönborn mausoleum chapel. In one design the central rotunda predominates, and the concave-ended arms (cf. Banz) are clearly distinct; in the other   345

344 *Below* Zelená Hora, gallery of the pilgrimage-church

345 *Right* Banz, plan of the abbey church built by Johann Dientzenhofer, 1710–19

the result is more like a quatrefoil. In both designs Dientzen-hofer placed the church at the pointed angle of the court-yard – foreshadowing Schlaun's similar design for the Brothers Hospitaller at Münster. It is regrettable that these designs never came to fruition, and all that was executed (1728–30) was Neumann's plain octagon. Yet once he had recovered from the first flush of architectural rectitude ensuing on his return from Paris in 1723 (like Dientzenhofer's after his return from Italy), and having acquired the techniques of vault-construction from Johann Dientzenhofer, Neumann continued to experiment with and develop ideas of intersecting vaults and three-dimensional arches.

Balthasar Neumann's career (1687–1753) is in many ways the most remarkable of any architect in Germany at this period,[68] for he worked his way up from humble craft origins as the son of a cloth-maker in Eger (Cheb, a free city in Bohemia) to become the favourite architect of both the Schönborn prince-bishops of Würzburg, and the architectural consultant to every prince in South Germany bar Bavaria. Not only this, he designed the two most ambitious churches of the time – Vierzehnheiligen and Neresheim – giving evidence in the de-signs of a sophisticated mathematical intelligence unsurpassed by any architect in Europe. All this he originally achieved by pursuing the one *carrière ouverte aux talents* available to the ambitious in the eighteenth century – the army – in which, as an engineer, there was every opportunity to turn the mathematical and planning skills acquired in fortification to civil architecture. It is, significantly, a bastioned trace that Neumann holds in his hand, whilst pointing to the Würzburg Residenz, in Kleinert's portrait of 1727.

Neumann arrived in Würzburg in 1711 as a journeyman cannon- and bell-founder who had already shown signs of broadening his skills to cover waterworks as well. His pro-fession brought him into contact with a man who perceived his rare intellectual abilities, Engineer Müller, through whose encouragement (and a remarkably enlightened series of loans from the city fathers of Eger) he was enabled to renounce his craft calling and study the theoretical basis of civil and military architecture for four years, achieving a commission as an artilleryman ensign in the Episcopal Bodyguard at the end of it in 1714. For the next five years Neumann's career was largely military. He was promoted captain, and took part in campaigns in the Balkans and North Italy. But he also accompanied the episcopal architect, the Vorarlberger carpenter Joseph Greis-ing, on his tours of inspection, thus acquiring some practical knowledge of architecture. As a result, when Johann Philipp Franz von Schönborn was elected bishop of Würzburg in 1719, and Greising was too closely identified with the corrupt admin-istration of his predecessor to be retained, Neumann was the man that Schönborn chose to act as his architectural aman-uensis, so that he could hold his own against his brother and uncle with their *Baudirigierungsgötter*. Neumann, in his turn, at first had Johann Dientzenhofer at his elbow, to help him with the practical side of building, of which he as yet had little, if any, experience. Though responsible for putting forward Johann Philipp Franz's ideas in the collaborative planning of the Würzburg Residenz (as will be seen in the chapter on palace architecture), Neumann's talents were soon recognized by Lothar Franz and Friedrich Carl, who regretted only that he lacked the sophistication that a year or two in Rome and Paris would bring. In the event, once the overall plan for the palace had been settled and building begun, Johann Philipp Franz did

send Neumann to Paris for three months in 1723, both to get the plans for the Residenz 'corrected' by de Cotte and Boffrand (who himself came to Würzburg the next year), and to collect ideas about or acquire what was up-to-date in decoration and furnishings. Not long after he returned, however, in 1724, Johann Philipp Franz died of a stroke, and his austere suc-cessor, von Hutten, halted work on the palace. Neumann's reputation was already such that he found plentiful work farther afield, both in the ecclesiastical sphere, as architect of the church at Münsterschwarzach from 1727 onwards, and as adviser to princes, at Mergentheim and Bruchsal. In 1729 von Hutten and Lothar Franz von Schönborn died, and Friedrich Carl von Schönborn succeeded to their sees of Würzburg and Bamberg. For the next fifteen years Neumann was his archi-

346 Banz, detail of the nave

tectural genius, in everything from the completion of the Würzburg Residenz to the design of parish churches with constructed vaults, whilst at the same time travelling all over South Germany to advise other princes on their palaces – and on the knotty problem of staircases in particular. With the death of Friedrich Carl in 1746, Neumann was dismissed by his half-mad successor, von Ingelheim. This left him free to reach the apogee of his career elsewhere, with the construction of the Abbey Church of Neresheim, and the submission of a design for rebuilding the Hofburg in Vienna – not executed, because of the War, but for which he was rewarded with a golden snuff-box by Maria Theresa. When von Greiffenklau succeeded to the see of

Würzburg in 1749 Neumann was reinstated as director of building, whilst continuing his ubiquitous career as architectural consultant to the end of his life in 1753 – having lived just long enough to see his bold ceiling over the staircase at Würzburg frescoed by Giambattista Tiepolo, and himself included in the fresco – in the uniform of a colonel.

Neumann's first independent church design was, as we have seen, for the very staid priory church of Holzkirchen, built shortly after his return from Paris. This conventionality persisted in his first major church, that of the Benedictine Abbey of Münsterschwarzach (1727–43). This Neumann designed as a cruciform basilica with a full lanterned dome over the crossing, and with tunnel vaults over the nave and choir divided into bays by broad arch-bands springing from the paired columns below. The church was demolished in 1837 after the suppression of the abbey, but its appearance is recorded in an engraving. Its loss is greatly to be regretted, as Neumann's solemn architecture was relieved by some of the earliest Rococo stucco by the Feichtmayr troupe, and above all by J.E. Holzer's frescoes – the masterpieces of this short-lived artist.

Properly to come into his own as an ecclesiastical architect, however, Neumann required the stimulus of an informed patron: in his case Friedrich Carl von Schönborn. Through Friedrich Carl's direct authority as both bishop and ruler, Neumann was to make designs not only for court chapels and parish churches, but also for pilgrimage-churches as varied as Gössweinstein, the Käppele and Vierzehnheiligen.

Gössweinstein (1730–36) was a Trinitarian pilgrimage, yet Neumann turned his back on symbolic solutions like those once projected by Johann Dientzenhofer, and created a gallery-less, wall-pillar church with a transept. The façade of the church is a flat, twin-towered screen, and the choir and the arms of the transept are apsidal within but polygonal on the exterior. The only unusual note is the shallow saucer dome pincered over the crossing. The basic ordinariness of the design – though it may be partially explicable, as later at Vierzehnheiligen, by Friedrich Carl's desire to play down the 'exotic' aspect of pilgrimages – also points to an ambivalence in Neumann himself. He frequently seems to have settled for relatively conventional solutions, sometimes enlivened by experiment with one particular feature, and only to have been stimulated to produce his most exciting designs as the result of competitive planning – as in the case of the court church at Würzburg – having to cope with the unexpected – as at Vierzehnheiligen – or as the result of creative friction with his clients – as at Neresheim.

305   It was in the court church of the Würzburg Residenz (built 1732–34, decorated and furnished 1735–44) that Neumann had the courage to revert to the Dientzenhofer tradition of intersecting vaults. After several migrations of position and mutations in form from the time of the original plan of the Residenz, it was at Neumann's insistence that the church found its ultimate site in the south-west corner, where it could rise to the full height of the building, without – as Friedrich Carl would have liked – having his apartments above. In the masterplan that resulted from the conference in Vienna in September 1730, in which Hildebrandt played the leading role, the chapel was planned with two domed bays and an apse behind the high altar. In Hildebrandt's revised designs of April 1731, this was reduced to one dome flanked by tunnel-vaulting. Neumann criticized the technical aspects of Hildebrandt's vaults, and, though promising to adhere to Hildebrandt's plans, was in-

spired to produce his own first design, which was for a longitudinal oval vault intersected by tunnel-vaulting on either side – thus giving rise to single three-dimensional arch ribs at the points of intersection. Elaborating further on this idea, in 1732 he came up with the final design of a longitudinal oval vault intersecting with a transverse oval vault over the chancel and over the vestibule on either side of it, further cut into by fragments of vault over the windows between these, bounded by three-dimensional arches representing the projection of the ovals as conceived in plan. The slanting of the system of supports below helps to make legible the succession of ovals, which are, however, inter-penetrated by a secondary pair of ovals adumbrated underneath the tangential three-dimensional arches. The complexity of all this is by any reckoning considerable, and its legibility is impaired by the sharp horizontal division into two zones, occasioned by Hildebrandt's insertion of a gallery, so treated that it runs above a heavy entablature supported on free-standing marble columns, whilst above it tapering pilasters support the vaults. Such a division into an upper and a lower level is a customary feature of court chapels, in order to allow the participation of spectators below in the devotions of the prince in a *loge* to the rear. In Friedrich Carl's case, however, the rear gallery served for musicians, whilst that at the other end gave access from his apartments to his own invention (but inspired by pilgrimage-churches) of a secondary altar above the high altar for his private devotions. It was also Hildebrandt who supplied the basic designs for the decoration and furnishings, laying down the refulgent harmonies of dark marble and gilded stucco that proclaim this so strongly as a court church. The stucco is the earliest surviving work in the Residenz by the gifted Comasque Antonio Bossi, who, with the ageing Swiss fresco-painter Johann Rudolf Byss, designed most of the detail of the decoration.

Having taken the plunge with the court church at Würzburg, Neumann experimented with a variety of different vaults over the next few years, further developing both the idea of inter-penetrating vaults and that of a system of supports describing a shape unrelated to that of the outer walls. The chapel of Friedrich Carl's new summer seat at Werneck (planned 1734ff., finished 1744–45) was designed with an oval vault supported by downward tapering pillars with round niches between, contained within a trapezoid.

Friedrich Carl was especially keen on keeping parish churches in good repair, establishing a fund for the purpose, employing Neumann as surveyor, and insisting where possible on constructed vaults, and on the claims of structure to take precedence over those of decoration. Most of the churches that had to be rebuilt are devoid of artistic significance, but in two (both built 1742–45), the bishop's interest resulted in a special effort by Neumann. The parish church at Gaibach was in the village of one of the Schönborn's family seats. Neumann designed the church with a trefoil east end in such a way that the domical vault over the crossing expanded out with a three-dimensionally curved rib into the vaults of the arms, where it encountered a similar rib tangentially – the very idea of Johann Dientzenhofer's for Holzkirchen on which Neumann's design had then turned its back. The parish church at Etwashausen was the result of the Protestant refusal to contribute to the repair of the 'simultaneous church' that they shared with the Catholics there, and of Friedrich Carl's decision to build a fresh church for the Catholics alone, dipping into his own pocket to make sure that the church could hold its own. Characteristically, as at Gaibach, he expressly stated that he saw no reason to contribute to any interior embellishment. Etwashausen is Latin-cross-shaped, and here it is the vaults of the arms that take great bites out of the domical vault of the crossing. The distinctive feature of the latter is that it is supported on paired columns standing out from the angled corners, to which they are attached by short sections of tunnel vault – a solution which, making the main vault a kind of inner membrane, can be paralleled in the Garden Saloon of the Würzburg Residenz (1744), and looks forward to the crossing-vault at Neresheim.

The most celebrated of the churches that Friedrich Carl got Neumann to design was one on which the *locus standi* of both was open to question, Vierzehnheiligen.[69] This involved the rebuilding of a church built over the spot where in 1445 a shepherd had had a vision of the Christ child surrounded by fourteen other children, later interpreted as the Fourteen Saints in Time of Need. The church belonged to the Cistercian abbey of Langheim, over which Friedrich Carl was ruler as bishop of Bamberg, with whom the abbey had to share the proceeds of the pilgrimage. This effectively gave Friedrich Carl a blocking position over the proposals of a new abbot, Stephan Mösinger (1734–51), to rebuild the church. He used this to reject designs for the church made by the Protestant architect to the prince of Saxe-Weimar-Eisenach, G.H.Krohne, in 1739, and another made by the Bamberg architect J.J.M.Küchel in the winter of 1741–42 – both of which were decorative but relatively cheap – and to impose instead the most orthodox of a number of designs made by Neumann in 1742, on a Latin-cross plan and providing for constructed vaults. The lack of intrinsic architectural interest in Neumann's chosen design makes it likely that Friedrich Carl's grounds for rejecting those of Krohne and Küchel were liturgical and constructional, not aesthetic. On the one hand, neither met his passionate insistence on fireproof stone vaults, and on the other, whilst Krohne tucked the *Gnadenaltar* (placed over the miraculous spot) away in a trefoil choir and made inadequate provision for the circulation of pilgrims, Küchel made all too much – placing the *Gnadenaltar* in the middle of a central rotunda with entrances in the four cardinal axes, to the exclusion of any normal high altar at the east end. Neumann's plan placed the *Gnadenaltar* in the centre of the crossing – a solution like that employed in the late mediaeval pilgrimage-church at Dettelbach nearby.

Friedrich Carl could not impose his own architect upon Abbot Mösinger, and when the foundation stone was laid for the church to be built to Neumann's plan in April 1743, Krohne was the executant builder. When, however, Neumann and Küchel visited the site on a tour of inspection in December, they found that Krohne was blithely departing from Neumann's plans and carrying out some new design of his own that truncated the choir, thus placing the *Gnadenaltar* at the end of the nave before the crossing, rather like the congregational altar of some pre-Tridentine monastic church, with unbuttressed walls that were clearly not intended to take a stone vault. To appease Friedrich Carl, Abbot Mösinger hastily dismissed Krohne, whilst Neumann set to work to produce a second set of designs that would incorporate what had already been built,

347 *Top right* Vierzehnheiligen, plan of the pilgrimage-church, built by Balthasar Neumann, 1743ff.

348 *Right* Vierzehnheiligen, exterior of the pilgrimage-church

taking account of the fact that the site of the *Gnadenaltar* would now have to be in the nave. Neumann's second set of designs was ready when it was possible to start building again, in March 1744. In these he employed the device that he had used in the court church at Würzburg and that he had toyed with in his first designs of Vierzehnheiligen, deploying a succession of oval vaults – here one larger longitudinal oval vault between two smaller ones – like an inner membrane on a system of supports quite unrelated to the walls of the church. In a true stroke of genius he also borrowed the old Dientzenhofer idea of syncopation, placing the largest oval vault so that it spanned not the crossing, but the *Gnadenaltar* in the eastern section of the nave. As a result the three-dimensional arches marking the junctions of the oval vaults fall over the crossing – where one would normally expect a dome – and over the pseudo-crossing created to balance this in the western section of the nave. At the same time as sustaining the vaults, Neumann's supports house aisles and galleries between themselves and the outer walls, thus permitting the circulation of pilgrims round the sides of the *Gnadenaltar;* the effect of all this, with light streaming in from the broad windows in the walls behind, is diaphanous, whilst any alteration in position on the part of the visitor throws the spaces described by the supports into a new relation both with one another and with the outer walls, creating disorienting yet stimulating new vistas.

347

Friedrich Carl died in 1746, thus severing Neumann's connection with the church. His place was taken by Küchel, as architect to the see of Bamberg, who faithfully carried out Neumann's plans as far as the architecture was concerned, whilst himself designing the free-standing *Gnadenaltar* – one of the high points of Rococo construction – along the lines proposed in his original plan of 1742. Building proceeded slowly, and it was only in 1762/63 that the church was vaulted. Through Küchel, and perhaps because of the Bavarian origin of the reigning bishop, Adam Friedrich von Seinsheim, the Feichtmayr-Übelhör troupe was employed to stucco the church – its last major commission – round frescoes by the itinerant Italian Giuseppe Appiani. The decoration was only completed, and the church consecrated, in 1772. There was thus a full generation between the planning and the completion of the church, and no necessary relation between the decoration and the architecture as planned by Neumann (whose draughtsmanship was anyway always too poor for him to design ornamental detail himself); yet the two complement one another perfectly. Nor would anyone anticipate the interior from the somewhat pedantic stone exterior of the church, whose twin-towered façade looks out over the valley of the Main to – appropriately – Banz on the other side.

306

Shortly after the death of Friedrich Carl, one of Neumann's consultative journeys in 1747 took him into Württemberg, where he met the abbot of Neresheim, who invited him to take over the rebuilding of the church,[70] for which preparatory work had been in progress for the previous two years. Neumann was originally asked to produce a church modelled on the one he had built for the Benedictine Abbey of Münsterschwarzach, and it seems likely that a design along these lines had already been prepared by one of the monks who later became abbot, Benedict Maria Angehrn. Neumann however insisted that this should not be 'just a church like another', and between 1747 and 1750 produced a series of designs of varying degrees of ambitiousness that progressively departed from the conventional conception of a cruciform basilica. The abbots of

348

Neresheim had a special reason for falling in with the idea of a distinctive church themselves, which was that they were aiming at *Reichsfreiheit*, which they finally achieved, emancipating themselves from the suzerainty of the princes of Öttingen, in 1763.

In his earliest designs Neumann envisaged an aisled church whose most singular feature was to be the set of three interlocking domes over the crossing and transepts. The first step to the final design was taken when Neumann decided to support the oval dome over the crossing on paired columns placed in front of the piers – developing the baldachin effect that he had employed at Etwashausen. The aisles of the nave and choir were then reduced to narrow passages, and a pair of transverse oval domes over the former and of round domes over the latter added to those already planned for the crossing and transepts. Finally, the domes over the choir were also converted into transverse ovals. Neumann had thus arrived at both the 'inner membrane' effect and the succession of oval domes employed in the Würzburg court church and Vierzehnheiligen, but the domes are now side- rather than end-on to one another, save in the crossing, thus preserving their integrity, in keeping with the proto-Classical urge towards spatial clarity that has also been noticed in J. M. Fischer's late churches. This distinctness is underlined by the design and setting of Martin Knoller's frescoes (1770–75), which are painted in feigned saucer domes within the ovoid vaults. At Neresheim, as at Vierzehnheiligen, the decoration considerably postdates the design of the church, which was only vaulted in 1769–70. But in the case of Neresheim, this led to the church being given the kind of superficial Classical garb referred to by Germans as the *Zopfstil*, after the way of dressing men's hair in a queue popular at the time. The abbot was a great friend of Duke Carl Eugen of Württemberg, who favoured the first stirrings of German Neo-Classicism, whilst Knoller was one of the first artists working in South Germany to have been influenced by Mengs in Rome. In a

349

350

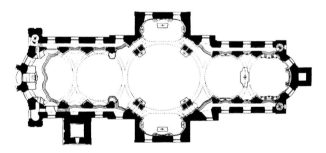

349 Neresheim, plan of the abbey church built by Neumann, 1750ff.

treatise that he left he even states that he changed his manner for 'meinen lieben Neresheim', and though his frescoes continue to use illusionistic Baroque settings, their composition and execution betray the new desire for clarity. The ornamental parts of the vault were all painted under Knoller's supervision rather than stuccoed – itself an innovation in a church of this size – whilst the stuccoing of the lower parts was carried out – after an unfortunate experience with an inadequate Italian recommended by Knoller – by Thomas Schaidhauf from the Stuttgart Academy. Yet though this decoration is not what Neumann envisaged (he died in 1753), its cool and uncluttered

350 Neresheim, interior of the abbey church

appearance is not inimical to the increased lucidity of his designs, but rather, by taking its place alongside churches with full Rococo decoration, and others with none at all, expands our way of looking at his architecture. The real betrayal of Neumann's intentions occurred in the construction of the vaults. Neumann had intended these to be of stone. His son's twice-repeated offer to build them was turned down on the grounds of his youth – though he was to become a brilliant engineer, who pioneered new methods of solid vault-construction. Instead, in 1759 the abbey decided to execute them in lath-and-plaster, which meant both flattening them and renouncing Neumann's intended lantern over the crossing. Ironically, the vaults have given trouble ever since, and the church has only just emerged from a nine-year campaign of restoration, largely occasioned by the vulnerability of the vaults to sonic booms.

With the death of Neumann the great tradition of Bohemian and Franconian Baroque architecture came to an end. The great church commissions were past – Langheim, which had built Vierzehnheiligen, never rebuilt its own abbey church, despite the plans that Neumann made for this, whilst Ebrach, in a belated effort at modernization, contented itself with a bizarre *Zopfstil* revetment of the interior of its Gothic abbey church in stucco. Franz Ignaz Neumann had as great a technical understanding of architecture as his father – if not greater – but was never given the chance to employ it in original works. Instead, he gave invaluable assistance in preserving and completing the fabric of Mainz and Speyer Cathedrals, displaying a sensitivity to Gothic that contrasts sharply with the stucco-encrustation of Ebrach, and points to the dawn of another age.

Palace architecture in the Empire

Frederick the Great of Prussia (writing in French as was his wont), says of German princes in the *Anti-Machiavel:* 'There is not one of them, down to the youngest son of a youngest son from an appanaged line, who does not preen himself upon some resemblance to Louis XIV; he builds his Versailles; he has his mistresses; he maintains his standing armies.' Liselotte, the Palatine wife of the duc d'Orleans, had already observed and re-gretted the bedazzling effect of Paris and Versailles upon young German royalty and nobility on their Grand Tour at the end of the previous century. War with France, as Freschot observed, had not prevented infatuation with 'French *galanterie* and French fashions... the antics of French dancing-masters and all the little knick-knacks of French hairdressers' from afflicting even the Austrian capital. Montesquieu, indeed, perceived the irony of the fact that it was only after the War of the Spanish Succession, in which Louis XIV had had most of the princes of the Empire ranged against him, that the contagion really took hold: 'Versailles has ruined all the princes of Germany, who are now susceptible to the slightest subsidy. Who could have foretold that the late king would have established the power of France by building Versailles and Marly?'

It is an over-simplification to maintain that the thorough-going reconstruction of German palaces in the late-seventeenth and early-eighteenth centuries was purely the result of such emulation.[71] Other factors played their part: the Thirty Years War had already caused a hiatus in the normal process of building and rebuilding, whilst in the Rhineland the French themselves had been responsible for considerable destruction – as the palace at Heidelberg still testifies – that needed to be made good. There were also several princes who had yet to descend from their mediaeval eyries into submissive towns, like the prince-bishops of Würzburg and Eichstätt, and others who wished to move away from insubordinate towns, or from the proximity of Free Cities not under their control, like the elector palatine (who moved to Mannheim), the prince-bishop of Cologne (who made his main palace at Brühl), and the prince-bishop of Speyer (who created a new town and palace at Bruchsal). But the form that the reconstructions and new constructions took nonetheless clearly points to France as the spur.

German princes frequently referred to Marly or the Trianon – less often to Versailles itself – as their model, or baptised their pavilions with French names – Mon Plaisir, Solitude, Mon Bijou, Sans Souci – indicative of the source of inspiration for such sophisticated retreats. Inside their palaces planning was governed by the French concept of the apartment, replacing the outmoded – but itself once French – idea of the *enfilade*. The decoration and furnishing of these interiors was to a significant extent designed and executed by French or French-trained designers and craftsmen, and much was actually pro-cured from France. Not only did the taste for intimate rooms come from France, but also the original inspiration for ex-quisite cabinets, decorated with mirrors or lacquerwork. Gar-dens were always laid out in the French manner, often by French gardeners; and frequently presiding over everything were French architects, particularly in the little Protestant principalities, because they had given refuge to the Huguenots after the Revocation of the Edict of Nantes (1685), and in the Rhineland principalities, because of their proximity to France.

Sometimes, as in the prince-bishoprics of Cologne and Würzburg, there were Parisian architects – de Cotte, Boffrand, or Oppenord – sending plans or advice (and in Boffrand's case, actually visiting his clients in 1724). More usually, however, there were their deputies – men like Guillaume Hauberat or Michel Leveilly in Cologne – or simply Frenchmen eager to make more challenging, also more precarious, careers outside France – Nicolas de Pigage in the Palatinate, de la Guépière the Younger in Württemberg, and Peyre the Younger in Trier. Nearly all of them added 'de' to their names, in accordance with the unspoken law that every Frenchman abroad was an aristocrat, whilst some invented new names for themselves altogether: d'Ixnard to conceal his humble craft origin – his real name was probably Michel – and Louis-Rémy de la Fosse (Nicolas Lerouge) for some reason unknown. La Frise du Parquet, the architect to Speyer, almost sounds as if he was making fun of the whole convention! Their employers generally had first-hand experience of French architecture from the 'Kavalierstour' – the German equivalent of the Englishman's Grand Tour. In addition, they enjoyed the advice of a new breed of dilettante architect-offical – the 'Kavalierarchitekten' – whose training and orientation was similarly French. The von Zochas at Ansbach were gentlemen-architects of this kind, and there was a particularly strong concentration of them at the courts of the Schönborns – the Barons von Erthal and von Rotenhan, and the von Ritter zu Groenesteyn brothers.[72] As has been explained in a previous section (see pp.172 and 175), their professional architects, when they were not of foreign origin, were also of higher social standing than the mason-architects employed on ecclesiastical commissions, almost invariably having officer status as military engineers (a profession that was itself set upon a new footing by the French).

This strong French inclination of German palace architecture means that there is often little that is specifically Baroque about it, particularly in the north, where the academic and classicizing strain in French architecture was reinforced by the resort to Dutch, and even English, models.[73] The Rococo decoration of interiors was of course, as the example of Palladian houses in England bears out, independent of the orientation of the architecture. Yet there were three factors influencing German palace architecture in a more Baroque direction. The first of these – the sheer continued preference for grandeur over intimate comfort – sustained the other two: the enduring influence of Italy and Italian architects, and the inclination towards Vienna of (particularly the episcopal) German courts. Sometimes French and Austrian/Italian influences met head-on – as in the remarkable Opera House at Bayreuth (1746–48), whose façade is an academic French exercise by Joseph Saint-Pierre, whilst the auditorium, by Giuseppe and Carlo Galli-Bibiena, is strongly indebted to designs for a new Viennese Opera House by Francesco Galli-Bibiena of 1704.

The instructions given to Tessin the Younger over the design of a château at Roissy-en-France for the président de Mesmes just before 1700 already reveal a northern architect being instructed in the growing French aversion to vast public rooms. At one point, for instance, he is told: 'There is absolutely no call for a Salon – it occupies half the house, and no one ever goes there'. By the time that L. C. Sturm published his Vollständige Anweisung Grosser Herren Palläste . . . nach dem heutigen Gusto schön und prächtig anzugeben in 1718, it was his opinion – with his gaze fixed upon France – that 'Not so many Grand Saloons

are made now as previously, nor are they required to be so vastly big as before'. The contrary had, however, been demonstrated at – for instance – Ludwigsburg and Pommersfelden just before he wrote, and was to persist in both the palaces of the Austrian capital – e.g. the Upper Belvedere – and those of the princes of the Empire.

In the section dealing with France (see above pp.106–142) Christopher Tadgell has explained that it was less that France witnessed a move away from great state apartments than that there was for a time a lack of royal commissions to engender them. In France, as Liselotte had to explain to her German half-sisters, there was only one 'Hof', or Court – that of the king – requiring the full hierarchy of state and private apartments. In Germany, not only were there innumerable dynasties, fragmented into more than one line, each with its own court, but there might also be, within these, a dowager or a brother with a court – and thus a palace or palaces – of his or her own. The ceremonial of German courts, all of which took their cue from Vienna – where indeed the expression 'etiquette' seems to have been invented – was more formal than that of France, and encouraged a greater number of rooms for the nice observance of distinctions in treatment of courtiers and guests.[74] In addition, much more was made of the Festsaal (often called the Kaisersaal, when its decoration paid homage to the prince's ultimate overlord), for great occasions, and much greater attention was paid to the staircase, which had a crucial role to play in the reception of a guest – both in impressing him from the moment of his arrival, and in defining his position relative to his host, according to where the latter awaited or came to meet him. German punctiliousness over etiquette was at its most acute in Ratisbon (Regensburg), where the business of the perpetual imperial diet could be held up for months at a time over unresolvable issues of precedence. The English dramatist, Sir George Etherege, who was envoy there between 1685 and 1689, was an alternately amused and exasperated observer of this, claiming that:

The Plague of Ceremony infects
Ev'n in Love the softer Sex:
Who an essential will neglect
Rather than lose the least respect.
With regular approach we storm
And never visit but in form:
That is, sending to know before
At what a Clock they'll play the Whore.

Whilst Lady Mary Wortley Montagu observed, when she passed through on her way to join her husband in his embassy at Constantinople in 1716, and having failed to enter into any disputes over precedence: 'I begun to think my selfe ill-natur'd to offer to take from 'em, in a Town where there is so few diversions, so entertaining an Amusement. I know that my peaceable disposition allready gives me a very ill figure, and that 'tis publickly whisper'd as a piece of impertinent pride in me that I have hitherto been saucily civil to every body, as if I thought no body good enough to quarrel with'. This fine sense of social distinction and precedence is reflected in Sturm's discussion of apartments: he not only distinguishes between the

351

351 *Opposite* Bayreuth, Opera House auditorium by Giuseppe and Carlo Galli-Bibiena, 1746–48

number of rooms and anterooms appropriate to the palaces of respectively a great lord, a ruling prince, and a king (remarking in an aside that the contemporary enlargement of princely households required the addition of yet another antechamber), and calls for at least eight sets of apartments in the palace of a ruling prince, but he also says the apartments for guests 'must be laid out with hierarchically diminishing space and comfort, so that one is never at a loss to lodge the persons of Princes commodiously, yet with due regard to their station'.

A most distinctive feature of German palaces was the 'core' arrangement of the key areas – vestibule, *sala terrena* or garden room, ceremonial staircase, and great saloon – in the centre of the palace, above and alongside one another. This 'core' arrangement was first adumbrated at the Brunswick-Wolfenbüttel *Lustschloss* of Salzdahlum (by J. B. Lauterbach and Hermann Korb, 1688–94), and received one of its most successful formulations at Pommersfelden.[75] Boffrand professed himself lost in admiration when he visited this *Schloss* in 1724, particularly on account of the stairs and the great saloon, freely confessing that there was nothing comparable to these in France. Another un-French feature that he did not specifically remark on at Pommersfelden, but which formed part of the above mentioned core, was the *sala terrena*. As the rock- and shell-work, or illusionistically painted 'ruin' decoration of these betrays, they were derived from the grotto. Their singularity was that – in a tradition going back to Sustris's Grotto Loggia in the Munich Residenz (1581–6) and Solari's grotto under the Salzburg archbishops' suburban retreat at Hellbrunn (1613–15) – they were not isolated features in the grounds, like the Grotto of Thetis at Versailles (which, significantly, was already dismantled in Louis XIV's lifetime), but integral with the palace, forming a hinge between without and within, 'Nature' and 'Architecture'.

Over and above the taste both for summer palaces and for small informal buildings and pavilions in the parks of, or yet farther away from, the main palaces, fostered by Louis XIV's Marly and Trianon, German princes favoured two especial types of retreat – the hermitage and the hunting lodge. Hermitages were a religious sub-species of the grotto, also decorated with 'natural' materials, and sometimes simulating a ruin, in which princes could either play at or live out in earnest for a brief period the austere life of the hermit. The *Jagdschloss* or hunting lodge – which might be a pheasant shooting box, as in the case of the Amalienburg; a place for heronry, like Falkenlust; or a centre for stag-hunting, like Clemenswerth – embodied the escape from the constricting etiquette of the palace household in a form particularly congenial to the Nimrod-like princes of the Empire (Montesquieu went so far as to claim that at one time certain of them used to measure their might by the number, not of their subjects, but of their stags!). Such buildings, precisely because they were for informal use and small, allowed the architect the greatest licence; whilst the expression of their purpose in the decoration of their interiors allowed the German aptitude for combining fantasy and nature in ornament free play; they are among the most successful and appealing products of the German Baroque. Of other features – 'ruins', 'Chinese' or 'Indian' pavilions, open-air theatres, bath-houses, and the like – many of which were common to Europe as a whole in this period, it is only necessary to single out one: the frequently hemicyclic orangery that so often closed one prospect of a *Schloss,* because in a famous case – the Zwinger at Dresden – this evolved into a unique building in its own right.

The intimate relation between the architecture and the life of a court was itself an inducement to princes to take a more active part in the planning of their buildings than other kinds of client in theirs, and was manifested in such ways as the Schönborns' insistence upon the creation of lower mezzanine floors to house their domestics, in keeping with Italian and Viennese practice, but contrary to French ideas of seemliness. When it came to the ceremonial staircase, for which again the models were more often sought in Italy than France, and in which – as Sturm contemptuously observed – inventiveness was more highly prized than was 'correctness' elsewhere in the palace, the client might essentially design his own, as Lothar Franz von Schönborn did at Pommersfelden. But the involvement of clients sometimes extended to more than the design, or insistence upon the incorporation, of particular features. Several took pleasure in designing their own buildings. In the case of Frederick the Great of Prussia, this is notorious, for the whole career of the aristocratic ex-officer architect, Georg Wenzeslaus von Knobelsdorff (1699–1753), depended upon his collaboration with the king, from their first association in the design of the Temple of Apollo at Neu-Ruppin (1733), to its culmination and breakdown in the construction of Sanssouci (1745–47), when the king insisted upon the omission of a basement against the advice of his architect. A training in drawing and in the classical vocabulary of architecture formed a customary part of the education of princes at this period, but this did not necessarily result in a competence in architectural draughtsmanship. Frederick the Great contented himself with rough sketches and indications, which he expected his architect to work up into a realizable building; Augustus the Strong of Saxony and Poland (1694–1733) on the other hand, produced detailed architectural drawings of his projects, which were then 'corrected' by one of his team of architects. Klengel had been his tutor, as Fischer von Erlach had been Joseph of Austria's and Chambers was to be George III's. Augustus the Strong also made a number of ideal designs, in which he showed a strong predilection for the central plan. Max Emanuel of Bavaria claimed during his exile that the only things capable of diverting him from his mel-

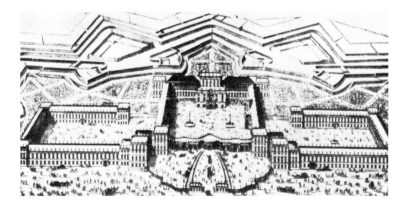

352 *Opposite* Nymphenburg (Munich), the Amalienburg, alcove in Yellow Room designed by Cuvilliés, decoration by J. B. Zimmermann and Joachim Dietrich, 1734–39

353 *Right* Mannheim, engraving of the Residenz, probably designed by Louis-Rémy de la Fosse, begun 1720

ancholy were 'des maisons de campagne, des jardins...des ajustements, meubles, et pareille chose', and that 'I couldn't exist without making designs. I form an idea of the sites, and thereupon I draw and make plans...being quite content to have scribbled away without regard to execution...the mere thought of a future building gives me pleasure when I look at my drawings'.

All princes took a keen interest in interior decoration and furnishings, since in these, as in their clothes, ballets, and firework-displays, they were intent upon being abreast of the latest French fashions. No prince attempted to design interiors himself – but in two famous cases women did so. These were the Dowager Margravine Sibylla Augusta of Baden-Baden (1675–1733) and Frederick the Great's sister the Margravine

354 Schloss Favorite, Rastatt, interior designed by the Dowager Margravine Sibylla Augusta of Baden-Baden, 1711–29

354
355

Wilhelmine of Bayreuth (1709–58), whose feminine skills and independence of character led them to design interiors, in the Favorite near Rastatt (1711–29), and the Neues Schloss at Bayreuth (1754–58), that are a genre apart within the German Baroque and Rococo. The remarkably various and fragmented picture that German palace architecture presents is not a little due to the role played by the dilettante passion for architecture of such a plethora of sovereigns.

The domination of Italians was most marked in the south of the Empire at the beginning of our period; in the Protestant courts of the north and in Westphalia, Netherlanders and Scandinavians like Philipp de Chieze and Peter Pictorius were more in evidence, establishing a sober classicism that was taken up by their German pupils and successors – men such as Johann Arnold Nering (1659–95) in Prussia and the theorist L. C. Sturm (1669–1719) in Brunswick and Schwerin. Only in Saxony in the north did Wolf Caspar von Klengel (1630–91) introduce a more Baroque note, as the result of his first-hand experience of Italy in the years 1651–55. The consequence of the

hegemony of the Italians in the south was – since innovations in layout and planning no longer stemmed from Italy, but from France – that the earliest palaces were decidedly old-fashioned. Barelli's villa-type *Lusthaus* at Nymphenburg (1664ff) for the Elector Ferdinand Maria of Bavaria's wife Henriette Adelaide of Savoy was originally a plain, five-storeyed cube with monotonous fenestration. Antonio Petrini's (1624–1701) country *Schloss* for the prince-bishop of Bamberg, the Marquardsburg or Seehof (1687–95) is a quadrangular building with corner-towers modelled on Georg Ridinger's *Schloss* at Aschaffenburg, put up at the beginning of the century. A quadrangular layout was also originally intended by Zuccalli both for the Elector Max Emanuel of Bavaria's country *Schloss* at Schleissheim near Munich (planned 1693 onwards, foundations laid 1701), and for his brother the Elector Joseph Clemens of Cologne's Residence at Bonn (1st campaign 1695–1702). The War of the Spanish Succession and the consequent exile of the two electors in France, however, put a stop to both these projects, and when they were resumed, it was to plans considerably modified by the French architects – most notably Robert de Cotte – whom the brothers had consorted with during their exile, and with French or French-trained architects directing their construction and decoration. Before continuing with the account of these palaces however, it is necessary to speak of what was being built in the meantime in other states of the Empire that did not suffer from *interregna* caused by the war.

These years when the emperor, already indebted for the Relief of Vienna (1683) and the final annihilation of the Turkish threat to his satellite princes, was now in league with most of them against France, were also the years in which the prestige of the architecture of the imperial capital and its outposts began to spread, spurring on the electors of Brandenburg and Saxony to create appropriate settings for their new-found royalty, as kings of Prussia and Poland respectively, and inspiring other princes to found new residences whose idiom and aspirations were imperial, even when the model for their layout was Versailles. Two whose plans were so ambitious that neither approached realization, were the Residence planned by the Venetian Count Matteo Alberti for Jan Willem, the elector Palatine, to replace the devastated castle at Heidelberg (1697), and Louis-Rémy de la Fosse's plans for a new Residence for the Landgraf of Hesse-Darmstadt (1715ff). Both of them aspired to house the emperor and all eight electors (though the latter made provision for the landgraf's hopes of becoming the ninth), and in the new Palatine Residence the symbolically octagonal staircase alone was to be 225 feet high and 125 feet wide, and adorned by 158 statues. Ultimately, a new Palatine Residence of at any rate colossal length – almost 1500 feet – was built by Jan Willem's successor Carl Philipp onto the new town of Mannheim (1720ff), owing to a dispute with the citizens of Heidelberg. It is thought that the plans for this too were supplied by de la Fosse, though their execution between 1720 and 1731 lay in the successive hands of the Mainz architect Johann Kaspar Herwarthel, the Speyer architect Johann Clemens Froimont, and the de Cotte *protégé* formerly at Cologne, Guillaume Hauberat, with subsequent additions of an Opera-House (1741–42) by Alessandro Galli-Bibiena, and interiors – including the famous Library, destroyed with the rest of the (now rebuilt) Residence in the last war – by Nicolas de Pigage (1752ff). In all three of these residences, projected and realized, the monumental treatment evokes Fischer von Erlach's designs for

353

Schönbrunn, whilst the detailing of the exteriors – despite the almost exclusive involvement of Frenchmen at Mannheim – is indebted to Italy rather than France. In one respect, however, they all took after Versailles, and that was in the creation of a *cour d'honneur* in front of the palace. This was also the case with the first of all the wholly new residences to be built in South Germany, Rastatt, even though here the architect, D.E. Rossi, was an Italian who had been working in Vienna. It was begun as a *Jagdschloss* in 1697, and redesigned as a residence, with a planned town associated, in 1700.[76] In other respects, however, Rastatt clearly betrays the Italian provenance of its architect and the orientation towards Vienna of the man for whom it was built – 'Türkenlouis', the margrave of Baden-Baden. When announcing his new designs to the margrave, and making special mention of the 'core' arrangement of the *sala terrena*, twin stairs, vestibule and saloon, Rossi assured him that they were 'of such a *Simitri* and *Magnificentza*... that no better could be found of these dimensions... I am prepared to stake my life on it that, if realized, the whole world will approve, and say that it is one of the finest buildings not just in Germany, but in Italy even'. It is significant that, whilst the thoughts of the Catholic margrave of Baden-Baden and his architect were on Italy and Vienna, those of his Protestant kinsman, the margrave of Baden-Durlach, who was soon employing Rossi's more tractable foreman, Giovanni Mazza, without reference to Rossi, were on Tessin the Younger's New Palace at Stockholm (1697ff), which we also know to have been taken as a model by the Protestant ruler of Prussia for his new *Schloss* in Berlin. Since Tessin's main source of inspiration was Bernini's plans for the Louvre, the ultimate orientation towards the Baroque models of Italy was the same, but it is illuminating that the choice of exemplar was dictated by political and religious affiliation.

Rastatt in turn served as a model for another *Jagdlusthaus* converted into a residence, with a planned town attached – Ludwigsburg (1707ff), built by Duke Eberhard Ludwig of Württemberg for himself and his notorious mistress, Wilhelmine von Grävenitz, turning his back on his lawful wife

356

and ancestral palace in Stuttgart.[77] The hunting lodge at Ludwigsburg was designed by the Stuttgart theologian and mathematician P. J. Jenisch, but for its conversion into a full-scale palace in 1707 the duke turned to a military engineer of unknown training, Johann Friedrich Nette (1672–1714). The sources of Nette's architecture, and the fact that in 1709 he went to Prague to recruit craftsmen – chiefly Italians – to make up for the deficiencies in local talent, are sufficiently indicative of links with the Habsburg crownlands. Moreover, whilst taking the idea of a *cour d'honneur* over from Rastatt, he exploited the ground falling away on the opposite side to create a quite Italian terraced garden, in keeping with the Italian detailing of his *corps-de-logis*. On his death in 1714, the duke appointed one of those whom he had recruited in Prague, the Comasque stuccador Donato Giuseppe Frisoni (1683–1735) to succeed him as architect, over the protests of his officials, who only wanted to recognize this mere craftsman as an *Ingenieur*, or designer. Frisoni continued to add to the complex of buildings – most interestingly in the trefoil-shaped court church – and it was he who, when all these additions still left the court short of living accommodation, had the ingenious idea of closing the *cour d'honneur* with a second *corps-de-logis,* placing it over an awkward fall in the land (1725–33). The lavish decoration of the interiors with stucco and illusionistic frescoes was entirely executed by Comasques in the modes usual in Austria and Bohemia. Frisoni also designed a more intimate retreat called the Favorita (1715–19) on the hill opposite the original *corps-de-logis,* with a virtuoso external staircase in the same spirit as that on the similarly-named building of the Bohemian-born dowager margravine of Baden-Baden and those in Bohemia itself. Ludwigsburg was the last major palace to be built and decorated by Italians in this Austro-Bohemian manner; Frisoni's executant builder was his nephew, Paolo Retti, and it is symptomatic of the change in taste that, when the interior completion of the residence at Ansbach was entrusted to his kinsman Leopoldo Retti between 1734 and 1745 (it had been rebuilt in successive stages by Gabrieli de' Gabrieli, a Graubündener from Vienna, from 1705–15; by the two von Zocha brothers, from 1716–30; and by Retti himself from 1731

onwards), he sought craftsmen who could work in the new French-based Rococo manner from Bonn and Munich.

In the two major northern courts of Brandenburg-Prussia and Saxony-Poland there was meanwhile a brief Baroque interlude, before French-oriented academic taste–replacing the earlier adherence to Dutch classicism–was imposed by a group of French *émigrés* and their adherents, two of whom–Jean de Bodt (1670–1745) and Zacharias Longuelune (1669–1748) – pursued their careers in both kingdoms.

In Berlin this interlude was represented by the career of Andreas Schlüter (*c.* 1660–1714).[78] Schlüter was a sculptor of unknown origin, who arrived in Berlin from Warsaw in 1694. His career as an architect started on the Arsenal, a building probably designed by the French academic architect François Blondel, and begun by Nering in the year of his death (1695). In 1696 Schlüter was commissioned to carve over a hundred keystones for this building, exploiting the opportunity and the martial connotations of the project to include a whole series of dying warriors, instead of the grimacing masks and old men more usual in such a location. This led to his employment as architect of the fabric as well, which allowed him to increase the sculptural component. In 1699 he forfeited the architectural direction of the building to Jean de Bodt, on account of the first of several collapses that dogged – and ultimately ruined – his career as an architect; Berlin was built upon reclaimed marshland, and this and the lack of skilled and experienced craftsmen in the mushroom city were doubtless responsible for his misfortunes, since his Bernini-like role as not only sculptor and architect, but also artistic overseer, must have overtaxed his powers of supervision. Nonetheless, Schlüter continued to supervise the reconstruction of the Stadtschloss, with which he had been entrusted in 1698, preparatory to the Elector Frederick III's elevation to be king as Frederick I. A number of factors–piety towards the old *Schloss* of the Great Elector, the influence of Tessin's new palace at Stockholm (1697ff) and, beyond that, of Bernini's designs for the Louvre–led to the retention of a quadrangular layout, but in the elevations, and above all in the interiors, Schlüter revealed a remarkable gift for the sculptural conception of both structure and decoration. The politically motivated destruction of this war-damaged *Schloss* in 1950 was one of the most regrettable losses in the aftermath of the war. Faulty construction led to cracks in this fabric, too, finally becoming Schlüter's undoing when it came to the erection of a water-tower at the north-west corner of the palace, called the Münzturm from its proximity to the Mint (1702–06). This was a remarkably imaginative structure, like an openwork belfry over a rockwork fountain base, but overloading of the old foundations threatened imminent collapse, which Schlüter forestalled by taking the tower down. In disgrace with the court, Schlüter nonetheless went on to build a house with an undulating, strikingly astylar façade for Ernst von Kamecke (1711–12). The succession of the thrifty Frederick William I in 1713 led, however, to the drying-up of all significant architectural patronage, and in the next year Schlüter left to try his fortune at the court of Peter the Great of Russia, only to die shortly after his arrival. Schlüter's rivals, de Bodt–who concentrated increasingly on his military career – and the Swede Eosander von Göthe – whose most notable work was the extension of Nering's palace of Charlottenburg (1701–12), and the addition to this of a dome (a Baroque feature out of keeping with the sobriety of the architecture beneath, probably insisted upon by Frederick I) – meanwhile held the field. It is a pointer to

the future that, before undertaking the work at Charlottenburg, Eosander was sent on a study tour to Paris; the results show that he was impressed by the extended Versailles. Under Frederick William I, however, Eosander, de Bodt, and de Bodt's former assistant, Longuelune, all left Prussian employ, ultimately for that of Saxony, where, in the later 1720s, they began to carry through an academic reaction against the Baroque of the preceding years.

The Baroque strain in Saxon architecture had a long genesis, and is by general consent traceable back to the palace in the Grosser Garten at Dresden (1679–83), raised by Klengel's successor Johann Georg Starcke (*c.* 1640–95) on the basis of a sketch by the crown prince. This H-shaped building included motifs from sixteenth-century French architecture in a strongly sculptural treatment of the exterior, with a pair of outdoor staircases filling the hollows of the H. The Elector Augustus the Strong, who unexpectedly succeeded his elder brother Johann Georg IV in 1694, and was elected king of Poland in 1697, had not been brought up to rule. Instead, he had travelled widely and had become a votary, not just of the more carnal pleasures (he ate prodigiously, and the margravine of Bayreuth calculated that he sired 354 illegitimate children), but of the more refined, if profligate, ones of operas, pageants, ceremonial camps, and architecture.[79] Of the latter he himself wrote to Count Wackerbarth, his superintendent of buildings (1695–1728) in 1711, making quite clear his attitude to the role of his architects: '... so We, from Our special love of the art of building, wherein We are particularly wont to amuse Ourselves, have before now Ourselves invented various designs, put them down on paper, and ordered Our architects in Our own Person to put them into complete execution...and have reserved the final say once and for all to Ourselves as Master'. The architects with whom he chiefly chose to work as his instruments in this way were, first of all, Marcus Conrad Dietze, a sculptor and draughtsman, whose lively designs for the rebuilding of the *Schloss* at Dresden were never realized because of war, and his death in a fire in 1704, and Matthäus Daniel Pöppelmann.[80]

Pöppelmann arrived in Dresden from Herford in about 1680, and proceeded to acquire his architectural knowledge in the electoral office of works – the first German architect to have what can be called a professional training. Appointed *Baukondukteur* – draughtsman and surveyor – in 1691, his creative opportunity did not come until he succeeded Dietze at the

357 Berlin, Royal Palace, rebuilt 1698ff. by Andreas Schlüter (destroyed 1950)

358 Dresden, the Zwinger by Matthäus Daniel Pöppelmann, 1709ff. in a painting by Bellotto. *Dresden, Staatliche Kunstsammlungen*

age of forty-two in 1704. The Elbe wing of the *Schloss* at Dresden had burnt down in 1701, whereupon Dietze had been sent to Italy for two years to gather ideas for a total reconstruction of the whole *Schloss*, on the plans for which he had been working since his return in 1703 (Augustus had also written to Berlin to ask for Schlüter's plans for the *Schloss* there, to provide ideas). Sufficient funds never became available to realize the intended palace, for which Pöppelmann also made a whole series of designs between 1704 and 1718; instead, what was at first intended as a mere appendage to the reconstructed *Schloss*, the Zwinger-Garten, took shape as a building in its own right.[81]

358   The Zwinger takes its name from the dry moat between two ramparts in which wild animals were very often kept. It was in such a sheltered location that in 1709 Augustus the Strong decided to place his orangery, and made a rough sketch of his intentions, which soon became more ambitious. The next year Pöppelmann was sent to Vienna and Rome 'to examine the current manner of constructing both palaces and gardens, but in particular to consult with the outstanding architects and artists over the designs entrusted to him of the present palace'. Augustus the Strong, who recovered Poland in 1710 through the defeat of Charles XII of Sweden at Pultawa the year before, and who was to be made vicar of the Empire in 1711, had the strongest political reasons for pressing ahead with his ambitious plans for splendid representational palaces in both Dresden and Warsaw; nevertheless, neither of these was ever built as intended, and the history of the Zwinger seems to show that he somehow realized that he had found a project that was not only – even if it exceeded his purse – within the limits of his credit, but also peculiarly apt as a built memorial to his reign. As Augustus wrote to his son in 1719, 'Princes win immortality through great buildings as well as great victories'. His own martial career had been inglorious, and the Zwinger is instead a permanent embodiment of his creations in the other field in which he yearned to excel – the truly Baroque one of festivals, pageants, processions and tournaments. It is like a petrifaction of the pavilions and grandstands put up for the spectacles created to celebrate the upturn in Augustus's fortunes and the visit of the king of Denmark in 1709. For the Zwinger steadily evolved: from being a simple orangery framing a garden, it became an orangery enclosing an arena for spectacles, to which

its galleries and pavilions could serve as the stands; in 1718 it was accepted that the rebuilding of the *Schloss* would have to be postponed indefinitely, the Zwinger was recognized as a building in its own right, it was decided to repeat symmetrically on the south-east what had already been built on the north-west, and the work was pressed on frantically in order to be ready for the crowning festivities of Augustus the Strong's career – those celebrating the marriage of the crown prince to the emperor's daughter in 1719; finally, in 1728 began the installation of the king's library and all his collections bar those of his works of art.

Yet all this had been foreseen by Pöppelmann almost from the first. One of the things that he acquired when he was in Rome was Carlo Fontana's engraved reconstruction of the Campus Martius, and in the prefatory inscription to his publication of a set of engravings of the Zwinger in 1729, he implied that this had been his inspiration all along: 'Just as indeed the Ancient Romans, amongst their other astonishing structures, also used to build such huge public buildings for show and amusement that these took up a vast area, and incorporated yet other buildings, such as race-courses, fencing-quintain- hunting- and animal-baiting rings, stages, covered- and open-air walks, colonnades, forecourts, public dance- and assembly-halls, baths, dining-rooms, cabinets of curiosities, libraries, temporary stands, triumphal arches, tiered seats for operas and plays, waterworks, gardens and the like – but above all a long round-ended *Schau-Burg* or arena, for victory-carnival- and state-parties ... so the fabric of this royal so-called Zwinger-garden is so cunningly laid out that it embraces all the above-mentioned things.'

The buildings that Pöppelmann created for the Zwinger show that he had been impressed above all by Viennese architecture – at the time of his visit Hildebrandt was creating the gardens and orangery of the Schönborn garden palace – by its fusion of sculpture and ornament with architecture, by its delight in stairs, and in convexity and concavity. Other features show that he had absorbed the lessons of French *maisons de plaisance* like the Trianon (he had visited France in 1715), and had been impressed by designs as various as the gardens of Frascati and that for an orangery in Paul Decker's *Fürstlicher* 359 *Baumeister* (which had come out in 1711, a copy being immediately acquired by Augustus the Strong). Most memorable is the contrast between the low, regular, and flat-roofed galleries and the fanciful, highly sculptural gates and pavilions projecting from these. Here a crucial contribution is made by the carving of the Salzburg-born sculptor Balthasar Permoser. This is rich with symbolism that plays on the three themes of Nature, the Gods, and the State. Crowning the masterpiece of the whole ensemble, the *Wallpavillon* (1716–18), which is honeycombed with stairs within and without, is Hercules supporting the globe, at one and the same time an allusion to the political responsibilities of Augustus the Strong, and to his escape from these into pleasure-grounds encompassed by an orangery–like Hercules in the Garden of the Hesperides.

None of Pöppelmann's other executed buildings have the exciting qualities of the Zwinger; before the liberating experience of his journey to Vienna and Italy he was too staid, and during and after its construction – on such projects as the Elbe-side Schloss Pillnitz (1720–24, noteworthy for its 'Chinese' roofs), and the conversion of the Holländisches Palais into a 'Japanese Palace' of porcelain (1728ff) – he was inhibited by collaboration with other architects like Longuelune and de Bodt. After the death of Augustus the Strong and the succession of Augustus III in 1733 the latter held sway with the 'correct', chaste, and academic manner. The new *Baureglement* of the reign was simply parroting a previous memorial of de Bodt's when it stated: 'In future, we want efforts to be made to see that there is something *noble* in all details and features of a building, and that there is nothing excessive, and even less, contrived and unsuitable, about the decoration and ornament... that the architecture is not oppressed or obscured by the ornament applied... We believe that in this way two-thirds to three-quarters of the carving and sculpture that up till now has been applied here, there, and everywhere, can be dispensed with'. Designs for the completion of the north side of Pöppelmann's Zwinger (ultimately filled by Semper's Picture Gallery) show how little sympathy remained for his approach. The surviving elements of the Baroque tradition in Saxony (which, it should be remembered, was the country of Winckelmann) were only to be found in church architecture, notably in the Protestant Frauenkirche (1726–43) by the carpenter-architect Georg Bähr (1666–1738), and in the rival Catholic Hofkirche (1738ff) by Gaetano Chiaveri (1689–1770).

Gardens and garden palaces had been the first feature of German architecture to fall under French influence. Henri Perronet laid out French gardens in connection with the Brunswick-Lüneburg residences of Celle (1673ff) and Herrenhausen (1674ff), the latter being amplified into the finest formal gardens in Germany by Le Nôtre's pupil Martin Charbonnier at the urging of the Electress Sophia (1689ff). Zuccalli was sent on a study tour to France when the *Lustheim* at Schleissheim was begun (1684), and Hermann Korb was sent specifically to examine Marly during the construction of Salzdahlum in the 1690s. Marly was also the inspiration of the pavilions added to the grounds of the palace in the Grosser Garten at Dresden by the garden-designer Johann Friedrich Karcher (1650–1726), whilst Maximilian von Welsch (1668–1745) was to convert yet another Favorite, Lothar Franz von Schönborn's suburban retreat outside Mainz (1717ff), into a complete copy of the French *maison de plaisance* and its satellite pavilions. But it was in 1715 – the year in which, as we have seen, Pöppelmann was sent to France to gain ideas for the Zwinger – that the floodgates of French influence were released in Germany. The Treaty of Rastatt the year before had established peace between France and the Empire, one of whose provisions was the return from their exile in France of the Wittelsbach brothers, the electors of Bavaria and Cologne.

Both electors had had, as noted above, uncompleted palaces in hand when driven into exile, and both had consulted French architects about them. Joseph Clemens, the elector of Cologne, had established more exclusive relations with Robert de Cotte, whilst Max Emanuel, the elector of Bavaria, had not only had consultations with Alexis Delamair and de Cotte, but had also employed Germain Boffrand to build him an octagonal hunting pavilion called Bouchefort (1705) at the focus of radiating rides cut through the forest of Soignies in the Netherlands, and to complete the redecoration of his house at Saint-Cloud (1713). The decoration of this house had been begun by a Bavarian *protégé* of his, Joseph Effner (1687–1745),[82] the son of the head gardener at Dachau, whom he had sent to Paris in 1706, at first to study garden design, but subsequently architecture. The difference between Max Emanuel and his brother, was that, whereas the latter continued to depend heavily on French advice, French architects, and French goods and craftsmen after his return from exile, the former – who had a more considerable state from which to draw them – attempted to train his own subjects in the new modes and techniques by sending them to the fountainhead.

An extensive correspondence survives, at first between Joseph Clemens himself and de Cotte,[83] and then between the latter and the successive architects that he sent the elector, exposing the elector's dependence upon de Cotte for plans, advice and help. The correspondence reveals that it was the 'grand et magnifique' of the regal monuments of the previous reign that obsessed him, rather than the intimate planning of the Régence, though he made contradictory demands upon de Cotte to shape his designs to a purse more limited than that of the French king (whose subsidies were, however, the source of such funds as the successive electors of Cologne could spare for building).

Joseph Clemens, having originally intended the incorporation of Zuccalli's half-completed residence at Bonn into a much grander design by de Cotte, was soon forced to limit the latter's help to making some additions and modifications to counter

359 Paul Decker, engraving of a design for a royal palace from the *Fürstlicher Baumeister*, 1711

the monotony of Zuccalli's façades and the lack of grandeur or variety in his planning. He did however succeed in building a suburban palace on the axis of the residence to de Cotte's plans–Schloss Clemensruhe at Poppelsdorf (1715ff)–whose plan resembles that of the central palace at Marly, save that the circular centre is an open, arcaded court rather than an enclosed saloon, whilst its polychrome exterior and play of bulbous roofs attractively betray its German location.[84]

In Bavaria, Joseph Effner immediately took over the effective responsibility for the whole of the elector's *Lustbauwesen* on his return in 1715, though Zuccalli remained nominally chief architect until his death in 1724.[85] Effner's chief task, as the elector tactfully attempted to explain to Zuccalli, was the fitting up of the interiors of Schleissheim and Nymphenburg with 'certi ornamenti alla francese del novo gusto'–in other words in the by then well-established French mode of so-called *Régence* decoration, which chiefly meant painted grotesque ceilings in the manner of Audran, and ribbon-and-diaperwork *boiseries* and stucco coves. But Effner–who seems to have remained untouched by a winter study trip to Italy in 1717–also designed one of the best sets of pavilions of any German palace in the grounds of Nymphenburg: the Pagodenburg (1717–19), a miniature reminiscence of Bouchefort, with little Chinese to it but the name; the Badenburg (1719–21), a bath-house with an appropriately 'Roman' vestibule; and the Magdalenenklause (1725–28), a hermitage built in the form of a ruined cell, with mingled Classical and Gothick detailing that would be surprising even in England at this date. At Schleissheim, whilst Effner designed apartments with *Régence boiseries* and stucco coving that were passably French, but for the slight over-exuberance of the carving and the blue-and-silver Wittelsbach colour scheme, the old-fashioned vastness of Zuccalli's core features, and Max Emanuel's similarly old-fashioned predilection for narrative and allegorical frescoes and sculptural stucco, led to the summoning of the French sculptor-stuccador Charles Dubut from Saxony, and the Venetian painter Jacopo Amigoni and the Wessobrunner stuccador Johann Baptist Zimmermann from

working on the abbey buildings of Ottobeuren (1720). The latter, though working to Effner's–and subsequently to Cuvilliés'–overall designs, brought with him a taste for the exuberant modelling of the forms of Nature, that played a crucial role in the indigenous evolution of Bavarian Rococo decoration.

Effner's sway lasted little over ten years, for in 1724 François Cuvilliés (1695–1768) returned from spending four years in Paris.[86] Though officially employed as Effner's draughtsman, his imaginativeness as a decorator, allied to his first-hand acquaintance with current Parisian fashions, soon won him commissions in his own right, particularly with the death of Max Emanuel and the succession of Carl Albert in 1726. It was however Max Emanuel who had first taken Cuvilliés, who was born near Bouchefort at Soignies, into his household in 1708. Cuvilliés is already recorded as a cadet and a draughtsman in 1716; the often quoted notion that he was a dwarf probably arose from an exaggeration of the fact that his slight stature prevented him pursuing his military career further. In Paris it is likely that he studied with, rather than under, Jacques-François Blondel. After his return, he was given his first major opportunity not by Carl Albert the new elector of Bavaria, but by his brother Clemens August, the new elector of Cologne, in 1728. In that year the latter had just finished realizing a project of his uncle and predecessor Joseph Clemens–the reconstruction of the old moated castle of Brühl as a modern palace (1725–28), in a region noted for falconry.[87] Clemens August had not followed

360 *Above left* Nymphenburg (Munich), the 'Saletl' in the Pagodenburg

361 *Above right* Nymphenburg, exterior of the Pagodenburg built by Joseph Effner, 1717–19

362 *Overleaf left* Nymphenburg, interior in the Magdalenenklause built by Effner, 1717–19

363 *Overleaf right* Pommersfelden, Mirror Cabinet, stucco by Daniel Schenk, wood-work by Ferdinand Plitzner, 1713–18

the plans procured by his uncle from de Cotte and Hauberat, but had instead obtained fresh ones from the architect of his chief friend and minister, Count Ferdinand von Plettenberg–Johann Conrad Schlaun (1695–1773). Schlaun, like Plettenberg, however, came from another of Clemens August's sees–Münster–a strongly Dutch-influenced region of brick buildings, and had little familiarity with French interior decoration.[88] Cuvilliés was therefore called in to supply this, beginning with the so-called Yellow Apartment in the north wing (1728–30), and continuing with the remodelling of the whole *Schloss* and the design of dependent buildings such as the informal *maison de plaisance* for falconry, the Falkenlust (1729–37).[89]

In the design of the *boiseries* and stucco ceilings of the Yellow Apartment[90] Cuvilliés showed that he had a mastery of the latest manner of French interior decoration–of the kind then, or just subsequently, practised in the *hôtels* de Lassay, de Matignon, and de Roquelaure, and publicized by the plates in Mariette's *Architecture Françoise* (1728ff.)–that was fully the equal of anything done in France itself. With the *boiseries*, the ends of the outer mouldings of the panelling were curved, and dissolved into ornament. With the ceilings, ornament broke the confines of the cove and rose into cartouche- or canopy-like points of emphasis in the axes, with a rosette in the centre. Most of this ornament was gilded on a white ground, but some of the ceilings were white on white. But the new element that Cuvilliés brought to this decoration, particularly in the Audience Chamber, where the cove was entirely broken up into a series of curvilinear fragments, was the depiction of Nature–here falconers, herons and their nests–as an element in its own right, not formalized or distorted into ornament.

The Italian stuccadors of the Yellow Apartment at Brühl and of Falkenlust (where another former subordinate of de Cotte, Michael Leveilly, acted as Cuvilliés' draughtsman) influenced Cuvilliés' designs back to the previous de Cotte manner with which they were familiar. When he came to work independently in Bavaria, Cuvilliés found instead that his designs received a further impetus towards naturalism and the incorporation of that metaphor for Nature–*rocaille*–from his executant stuccador, J. B. Zimmermann.[91] Cuvilliés' chance came in 1726 with the accession as elector of Bavaria of Carl Albert, who wished to create a whole new set of richly decorated state apartments, of an imperial grandeur that anticipated his bid to become emperor on the extinction of the male line of the Habsburgs. Working as Effner's draughtsman, and with J. B. Zimmermann as stuccador, Cuvilliés at first began to transform Effner's decorative schemes from within, and then from 1728, when he was given parity with Effner, openly. This can be seen in the surviving lower room of the Munich Residence–the Ancestors' Gallery–where Cuvilliés' looser, more naturalistic ceiling-decoration is superimposed upon Effner's stiffer, yet over-luxuriant, panelling and cove. A savage fire in December 1729 destroyed much of what had been done, but a fresh start was immediately made the next year upon what came to be known as the *Reiche Zimmer*–the 'rich rooms'.[92] Here Cuvilliés was completely in control, designing for and directing teams led by J. B. Zimmermann as stuccador, and Adam Pichler, Wenzel Mirofsky, and Joachim Dietrich as woodcarvers. These apartments (which have been remarkably restored since their partial destruction in the last war) are not overpowering, despite their profusion of gilding, because of the way in which, above all in the ceilings, they include a wealth of relief sculpture

235

364 *Opposite* Würzburg, garden front of the Residenz by Neumann and Hildebrandt

365 *Above* Nymphenburg, exterior of the Amalienburg built by François Cuvilliés, 1734–39

whose *raison d'être* is symbolical, but whose execution is of a charmingly sophisticated naïveté – the countryside, animals, and rustic gods come to court, the ornamental equivalent of Lancret and Desportes. Mere ornament plays a subordinate role, but in the succession of rooms, from the Mirror Cabinet (1731) to the Green Gallery (1733) the increasingly important part played by–now asymmetrical–cartouches and *rocaille* can be observed. Comparison with the suites of engraved ornament that Cuvilliés himself published (1738ff) suggests that much of the *al fresco* informality and naturalistic detail was due to the initiative of J.B. Zimmermann.

Both these elements are very much to the fore in Cuvilliés' next work, the Amalienburg (1734–39), a pheasant shooting box added to the ranks of the pavilions in the park of Nymphenburg, and surpassing them all.[93] Whereas the Falkenlust, despite the immense charm of its interior decoration, centred on the theme of falconry, was basically an adaptation of the French suburban villa that reflected Cuvilliés' Parisian apprenticeship, the Amalienburg is a true one-storey pavilion, combining French interior planning with exterior architecture indebted to Viennese *Lusthäuser*. The climax of the building, held between a concave front on one side and a pedimented projection with convex steps on the other, is the central circular Mirror Saloon. Framed by rooms decorated in silver on lemon yellow either side, this is resplendent with the silver and azure of the Wittelsbach arms. The mirrors create angled vistas and redouble the glinting richness. The undulating play of their rounded heads is communicated to the cornice, which in turn becomes the 'ground' upon which a whole realm of nature rests – trees, fountains, birds, animals, nymphs and putti. The supreme achievement of Bavarian court Rococo, it stands alone, even in Germany, whilst the contemporary French

365

352, 366

366 Nymphenburg, the Mirror Saloon of the Amalienburg, stuccoed by Johann Baptist Zimmermann

paragon that is so often held up alongside it – the Salon de la Princesse in the Hôtel de Soubise – is sober by comparison. Unlike the Salon de la Princesse, the Mirror Saloon of the Amalienburg employs a minimum of conventional ornament and incorporates no paintings; instead, everything is taken from the real world, whilst the stucco in the vault usurps the role of a fresco in feigning a world above our heads.

Cuvilliés designed another set of apartments in the Munich Residence to celebrate Carl Albert's election as the Emperor Charles VII (1740–43), but after the emperor's luckless death in 1745 the rooms were dismantled, and part of the woodwork employed to furnish a much more modest set of apartments – the Kurfürstenzimmer – whose name and simplicity proclaimed the rule of realism under Max Joseph III. Cuvilliés himself fell into disfavour, but was asked for designs by the landgraf of Hesse-Cassel. In 1750 his services were again required, to design the Residence Theatre, but in 1754, having been already passed over in favour of Johann Gunezrhainer for the succession to Effner as chief court architect, he was even

367

refused a rise in salary on the preposterous grounds that: 'apart from his mannered Opera House, we know nothing of Cuvilliés' supposed services'. He accordingly took his son to Paris for a year (staying with the painter Chardin!), where they absorbed the tempered Rococo taught by his old *confrère*, Jacques-François Blondel, as may be seen from the town houses designed by Cuvilliés after his return. Cuvilliés' heyday was however already over with the death of the spendthrift Carl Albert, and his career uncharacteristically closed with the termination of the façade of the Theatine Church (1767) for the court, whilst for the next century his memory was only kept opprobriously alive by his engravings.

The brilliance of Cuvilliés' interiors at Brühl and Munich established a new paragon for the building-mad princes of South Germany. Leopoldo Retti, engaged in fitting up the interior of the Ansbach Residence between 1734–45, sent a plea for a stuccador from Johann Zimmermann's troupe in 1734, because the craftsmen in Munich 'are so good of their kind, that one will not find a better in Paris or in the whole of the rest of Germany', and in 1738 sent craftsmen to make careful drawings of the *Reiche Zimmer* and the Amalienburg. The interiors of the Ansbach Residence are indeed a tempered version of the

Reiche Zimmer. The Bamberg architect, J.J. Küchel saw and admired the Amalienburg and the *Reiche Zimmer* on his study tour of 1737, and it is probable that the drawings made by his draughtsman influenced Antonio Bossi's stucco in a Rococo direction at Würzburg. We have already seen in an earlier chapter how J.G. Übelhör carried *rocaille* over into church decoration in stucco, and Wessobrunner stuccadors were summoned to work on palaces as far afield as Potsdam and Bruchsal.

In terms of architecture, as opposed to decoration, it was however another figure whose prestige caused him to be summoned for advice on almost every palace in South Germany in the second quarter of the century – Balthasar Neumann, whose career has already been described above,[94] (cf. p.267). The basis of his fame was his work for the Schönborn family, and in order to put this in context it is necessary to go back to the first of the family to be stricken by the *Bauwurmb* – Lothar Franz von Schönborn, prince-archbishop elector of Mainz and prince-bishop of Bamberg. He had marked his election to the see of Bamberg in 1693 by promptly laying plans for the reconstruction of the residence–the Neue Hofhaltung–which were carried out on rather old-fashioned lines by Johann Leonhard Dientzenhofer (1695–1705). In Mainz, Lothar Franz could not justify rebuilding the residence, but instead built a suburban retreat, the Favorite (1704ff)–whose conversion into a 'little Marly' has already been alluded to.

It was in 1711, the same year as his nephew Friedrich Carl began to rebuild Göllersdorf, that Lothar Franz began to build a new country *Schloss* at Pommersfelden, with money acquired from his support of the election of the Emperor Charles VI at Frankfurt.[95] When in 1710 he inherited the old castle, half of which was held in fee from Bamberg, and half from Bayreuth, it was his intention simply to make it habitable. Its ruinous state, however, led him first to plan a new three-winged *Schloss* on the site of the old quadrangular one, and then, when the problems of repartitioning this between Bamberg and Bayreuth, whilst keeping the chapel on the Bamberg (Catholic) side, became insuperable, to transfer it to a new site. All this time Friedrich Carl, who regarded his uncle's architects as second-rate provincials, was urging him to send plans of the site so that his own architect, Hildebrandt, could produce a design. Lothar Franz at first refused, on the grounds of economy, and when he relented, forestalled Hildebrandt with 'a design according to my own fancy and comfort ... I am making provision for future women and children [when he bequeathed the property], and so I am not making a court with lots of antechambers and galleries, but a really fine, large, and comfortable country house, which will also look well and make a bit of a show.' These plans were made by Johann Dientzenhofer, whom he appointed to succeed his brother Johann Leonhard in 1711, on the basis of his own suggestions; so when Lothar Franz in 1712 finally had his plans taken to be given a more metropolitan polish by 'you Sir *virtuosi, curiosi, et sumptuosi* at Vienna', he had already begun his own wing, which could not be changed, and was insistent that 'my staircase, which is of my own invention and my masterpiece, must remain'. Nonetheless the

next year, when Dientzenhofer was sent to Vienna to be shown all that was new by Hildebrandt, and to mull over the plans further with him, the latter came up with modifications to the staircase that turned it from a bizarre into a beautiful idea. 369

The singularity of Lothar Franz's stairs was that he wanted them to be housed in a pavilion of their own, projecting from the *Schloss* like the centre bar of an E, and that they were not, in the usual way, to hug the walls, but to stand free like outdoor stairs, with passages between them and the walls. Because of the 'core' arrangement of the main rooms – *sala terrena*, leading to the garden on the ground floor, and a small cut-off, domed oval vestibule leading to the two-storey saloon on the first floor–it 370 was only necessary for the main stairs to rise through one storey to the vestibule, which gave directly on to the saloon

367 *Above right* Munich, Residence Theatre built by Cuvilliés, 1751–53, reconstructed after being seriously damaged by bombing in 1944

368 *Right* Pommersfelden, exterior of the Schloss built by Johann Dientzenhofer and others, 1711ff.

straight ahead, and was continued on either side as a passage giving access to the two wings. Although Lothar Franz prided himself upon his 'invention', the form of the stairs themselves derives from a twin staircase designed by Palladio for the Casa Civena in Vicenza, and employed by Fischer von Erlach for his 'Staircase for the Empress' at Schönbrunn (demolished under Maria Theresa). His innovation, that of detaching the stairs from the walls and letting them stand free as if they were an outdoor staircase (and indeed the visitor was intended to dismount from his carriage in the dry in the staircase-hall), was precisely what Hildebrandt did away with. Rightly maintaining that the hall would be too echoingly vast (a lesson not remembered at Göttweig!), Hildebrandt drew on a feature of some very similar stairs designed by Claude Perrault for the

369 *Left* Pommersfelden, the ceremonial staircase designed by Lothar Franz von Schönborn and Hildebrandt

370 *Below* Pommersfelden, the *sala terrena* vaulted by Johann Dientzenhofer, with *rocaille* by George Hennicke, 1719–23

371 *Opposite* Pommersfelden, the Mirror Cabinet, ceiling stucco by Daniel Schenk, *c.* 1715

Louvre, creating a gallery right round the first floor, with a similar gallery above, supported by single fluted columns at the corners and paired fluted columns on the sides (themselves exceptional in German Baroque architecture, and inspired by Perrault's east front of the Louvre), with 'Imperial' capitals derived from a version of the French Order. The narrower well made possible a pavilion vault, supported on the herms of the upper arcade, later illusionistically frescoed by Marchini and Byss (1717). Hildebrandt could do little to alter Dientzenhofer's somewhat dry – though attractively roofed – exteriors, but inside he supplied designs for Daniel Schenk's stucco, which introduced Viennese ribbon-work to this part of Germany. Dientzenhofer's special achievement was the vaulting of the *sala terrena* with interpenetrating vaults and three-dimensional

368

370

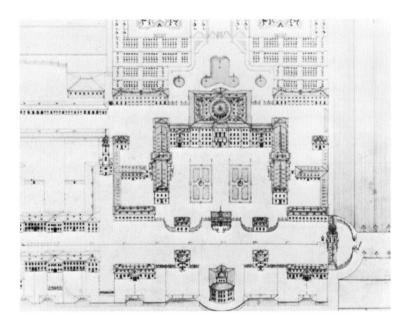

372 *Top* Bruchsal designed by Maximilian von Welsch and others, begun 1721

373 *Above* Bruchsal, contemporary bird's-eye view

ribs; the superlative 'grotto-work' decoration was executed by Georg Hennicke (1722–23). Finally, Lothar Franz's Mainz architect, Maximilian von Welsch, was called upon to give a French touch to the whole, by laying out the gardens, and by designing the semi-circular stables as a feigned orangery in front of the house.

No sooner had Lothar Franz completed Pommersfelden than two of his other nephews, Damian Hugo and Johann Philipp Franz, were elected to the prince-bishoprics of Speyer and Würzburg respectively (1719), and immediately set about thinking of the relocation and reconstruction of their residences. The architectural collaboration that had grown up between Lothar Franz and Friedrich Carl (who felt aggrieved that he had been passed over for his brother by the canons of Würzburg) now developed into a sustained barrage of criticism and advice directed at this supposedly jejune pair – both of whom had perfectly clear ideas of their own.

Damian Hugo was given good grounds for building an entirely new residence at Bruchsal (1721–32, 1738ff)[96] by the obstacles raised by his see – the free city of Speyer – to his residing there and rebuilding the old bishops' palace razed by the French in 1689. In 1720 he chose a virgin, level and unconfined site at Bruchsal, on a slight elevation, with splendid views over the valley of the Rhine, and building materials in abundance. The plans he procured, not from the expatriate French architect to Speyer, Froimont, but from his uncle Lothar Franz's Mainz architect, Maximilian von Welsch. Welsch's plans are lost, so we do not exactly know what he designed with Damian Hugo whilst they both took the waters at Schlangenbad, but the unusual arrangement of the palace as a series of detached or semi-detached blocks round a court was probably insisted upon by Damian Hugo, who subsequently justified this as a measure to prevent fire spreading, in a land where war always threatened. The flanking buildings, which were begun first, were certainly designed by von Welsch. It is a sign of Damian Hugo's confidence in his own abilities that he employed architects only in a consultant, but never a supervisory capacity, preferring instead to direct operations himself through a succession of masons, whilst he was for ever falling out with those who worked for him. When it came to the main *corps-de-logis* in 1725, Damian Hugo turned to another Mainz architect, the gentleman-amateur Anselm Franz von Ritter zu Groenesteyn, who helped to incorporate what must have been an idea of Damian Hugo's – a circular staircase-well, with two flights diverging from the vestibule to climb the outside walls and meet on the opposite side. This unusual feature was to occupy the centre of the building, with a saloon on the *piano nobile* on either side, which thus had to be connected by a bridge over the centre of the well. The next year however, Damian Hugo, belatedly realizing that he had not allowed for sufficient rooms to lodge his household – and there was no town for them to take quarters in – high-handedly got his builder to insert a mezzanine between the ground floor and the *piano nobile*. Not only did this offend against von Ritter's French notions of propriety – and he was not to be won over by Damian Hugo's bluster that: 'of course one sees this in the most distinguished modern palaces in Rome and Italy, of which I still have a fresh picture in my mind' – but it also meant that the staircases had an extra half-storey to climb, so that they no longer fitted. Once his suggested device of prolonging the stairs into the vestibule had been rejected, von Ritter washed his hands of the problem, leaving Damian Hugo to bemoan the 'hole' in the centre of his

373

372

palace for the next four years. In 1728 he had the good fortune to procure the services of Balthasar Neumann from the then bishop of Würzburg, Christoph Franz von Hutten, who had no desire to order any but essential work to be done on the Würzburg Residence. Neumann began by designing the completion of the rest of the *corps-de-logis* (which was given

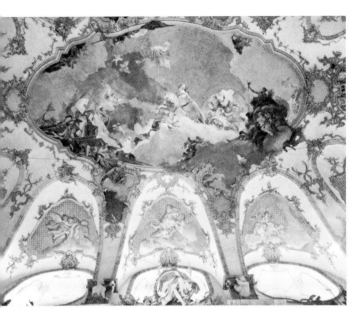

374 *Below left* Würzburg, the *Kaisersaal*, with stucco by Antonio Bossi and frescoes by G. B. Tiepolo, 1751–52

375 *Below right* Bruchsal, upper landing of staircase by Neumann, begun 1731. Stuccoes by J. M. Feichtmayr, frescoes by Johann Zick, 1752. Photograph taken before the bombing of the Schloss in 1944. The staircase and most of the stucco-work has now been brilliantly restored

376 *Right* Würzburg, exterior of the Residenz built by Balthasar Neumann and others, 1720ff

illusionistic exterior detailing *à la Marly* by Marchini), and early in 1731 set to work with Damian Hugo, who stood by to '*mit componirn*', to redesign the core.[97] Not only did he fit the stairs in, he also substituted a solid circular platform for von Ritter's bridge. The entering visitor was (and is again, thanks to the brilliant restoration of the flattened *Schloss* after the war) thus faced with three openings leading through darkness to light: the central one leads through a dimly lit grotto simulating a ruin to the garden room on the other side, whilst the two arms of the staircase begin as darkish passages climbing the sides of the central cylinder, slowly emerging into the pure, light-filled 375 domed rotunda between the two saloons. The experience is made into a true climax by the superlative *rocaille* stucco by J.M. Feichtmayr and the illusionistic fresco by Johannes Zick (1752), who were recommended to Damian Hugo's extravagant successor, Franz Christoph von Hutten, by Neumann.

Damian Hugo's palace, though begun a year after Johann Philipp Franz's, was structurally complete within his own reign, and only decorated under his successor, whereas the construction (1720–44) and decoration of the Würzburg Residence extended over the reigns of six bishops, spanning the whole period from *Régence* to the German equivalent of Louis XVI, the *Zopfstil*.[98] Its beginnings were modest enough, and lay in the desire of Johann Philipp Franz – ironically approved by his chapter on the grounds of economy! – to transfer his residence from the Marienberg, a modernized mediaeval castle on a hill on the other bank of the Main, into the town near the cathedral.

Though his uncle and brother instantly began to seethe with plans and to lay him under regular siege with their architects, Johann Philipp Franz at first kept his head and announced his intention of cutting his coat 'according to the slender measure of my lands and purse', which meant enlarging a '*Schlösslein*' already in the town, and rejecting the '*castelli in aria*' proposed

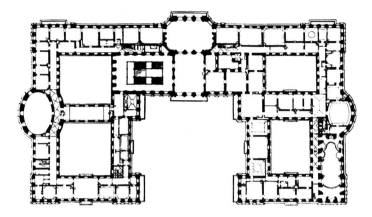

by Hildebrandt (who passed through in 1719). Despite the urging of Friedrich Carl to build something 'princely and worthy...*pro dignitate tanti episcopatus et principis*', the bishop clearly resented the assumption that his brother and uncle knew so much better, and preferred to correspond with another brother, Rudolf Franz Erwein, about his *own* plans. The discovery of the ruinous state of the fabric of the *'Schlösslein'* first gave the *'castelli in aria'* a chance, and gave Lothar Franz his cue to obtain the point that the new palace should be aligned on the point of the bastion (cf. the Zwinger). Meanwhile Hildebrandt went to work on one set of plans, and a group of Mainz gentlemen-architects – Philipp Christoph von Erthal, the master of horse von Rotenhan, and von Welsch – under Lothar Franz on another. Against this formidable battery Johann Philipp Franz could only field the 'Engineer' Balthasar Neumann, who, though winning the admiration of the other Schönborns for his abilities, was crucially disadvantaged in their eyes by never having been to Italy or France. At this stage he was anyway only acting as architectural amanuensis to Johann Philipp Franz who was criticized for understanding neither architecture nor architectural plans and, despite putting himself in his uncle's hands as a mere novice, for deciding everything *ex cathedra*, forcing Neumann to put a whole series of wretched ideas down on paper, threatening to ruin the whole project, both the Mainz collective's designs for the interior and Hildebrandt's designs for the interior.

At this point, in January 1720, an unlikely *deus ex machina* appeared – Jakob Gallus, the confidential minister of the previous bishop. His defalcations were found to have been so enormous, that 'in these pinched times... from so wicked a servant may be made a good paymaster': he was forced to buy himself off charges with the enormous sum (for the period) of 600,000 florins. Johann Philipp Franz instantly wrote off to ten architects inside and outside Germany for plans, whilst Lothar Franz sent the word to Hildebrandt – '*Nur wacker bauconcepten her*' – 'plan boldly away', and Hildebrandt took him at his word by even drawing Prince Eugene and General Althan into his planning sessions. However, when the foundation-stone of the new and now enlarged palace was finally laid on 22nd May 1720, the honours went not to Hildebrandt but to the Mainz team of von Erthal and von Welsch, who had enjoyed the advantage of coming to Würzburg to mull their plans over with Johann Philipp Franz. Even so, there were some points on which Johann Philipp Franz was adamant; significantly these concerned, not the architectural *ordonnance* and detailing, which he was perfectly happy to leave to the Mainz team, but

matters of lodging and access: he was insistent upon a triple entrance, so that a carriage could deposit him dry at the foot of the stairs and turn out again (though it would also have the symbolic value of a triumphal arch, like that on the Berlin Stadtschloss), and upon a mezzanine between the ground and first floors as well as one above. This idea emanated from Hildebrandt, and caused much head-shaking among the Mainz team, who finally persuaded the bishop at least to drop it from the *cour d'honneur*, in order to create variety. Though the Mainz team professed themselves exasperated by six weeks of chopping and changing their plans to accommodate Johann Philipp Franz' 'caprices', and at times regretted any association with such a 'wrecked and crippled abortion of a building', the final result in most essentials repeats their original design, albeit on a yet more spacious scale. The palace is a hybrid between the three-winged *château* round a *cour d'honneur* and the multiple courtyard type found in the ambitious designs for Rhineland residences. There are two courtyards in either wing, with oval projections – originally designed to hold the chapel and the *sala terrena* – in the centre of their outer façades. The latter was placed where it was because the entrance in the centre of the *corps-de-logis* was to be driven right through to the garden front, with a three-armed staircase placed on either side of the vestibule. The elevations of the wings, which were essentially designed by Hildebrandt, remained canonical for all but the *cour d'honneur*. 376

It is a token of the Mainz team's responsibility for the design that von Welsch was paid an annual salary to come and inspect the building at intervals, though Neumann, assisted by Johannes Dientzenhofer for the technical aspects, was put in day-to-day control. Once work on the north block (which was where the bishop intended to live whilst the massive task of completing the rest of the palace was accomplished) was well advanced, Johann Philipp Franz belatedly took up Lothar Franz's suggestion of broadening Neumann's experience, sending him to Paris for three months to gain ideas for furnishings and interior decoration, and to consult with the leading French architects, de Cotte and Boffrand, over the plans for the Residence.[99]

Faced with these plans de Cotte could only comment that there was 'much in the Italian manner and something German about them', whilst most of his suggested improvements were made in a take-it-or-leave-it fashion that took no account of the bishop's requirements – as Neumann shrewdly remarked, 'his own designs give him the most pleasure'. One suggestion that he made was, however, of great importance, because Neumann later adopted and adapted it for his own, despite his patron's proprietary interest in the forsaken design – that of suppressing one staircase and so enlarging the other that it had a platform all round the top and took light from the end as well as from the side. Boffrand was more accommodating in his planning, but as implacably French in his exterior elevations, as the designs that he published in his *Oeuvres d'Architecture* reveal. On Neumann's return a joint planning session was held to incorporate some of the Parisian suggestions, and in July 1724 Boffrand himself came on a visit, tactfully praising Pommersfelden and the Residence in terms of there being nothing in France to

377 *Top left* Würzburg Residenz, plan of the first floor by Neumann with the help of Maximilian von Welsch, Hildebrandt and other architects

378 *Opposite* Würzburg, the ceremonial staircase, built by Neumann, 1737–42, frescoed by G. B. Tiepolo, 1752–53

compare with them! A month later Johann Philipp Franz was dead, and during the rein of his successor, Christoph Franz von Hutten (1724–29), no more was done than to complete the north court, bar the oval projection. With the election of Friedrich Carl von Schönborn (1720–46) the realization of the whole grandiose project was assured, with the important difference that Vienna, rather than the French-inclined Rhineland, now set the tone, and that Neumann finally came into his own as an architect, favoured by his fidelity to the Schönborns and their projects during the interregnum. Though elected to the sees of both Würzburg and Bamberg in 1729, Friedrich Carl did not leave Vienna till forced to vacate the vice-chancellorship in 1734. He naturally dismissed von Welsch, for he already had Hildebrandt as his architect and friend. For 1730 Neumann cautiously proposed building the south block on the same lines as the north, but the cogency of his suggestions was already revealed by Friedrich Carl's reluctant assent to his idea for the

305 placing of the court church (see p.268). In the crucial planning session held in Vienna in September 1730 Hildebrandt was given the task of redesigning the *cour d'honneur* fenestration, the garden front, and the main *corps-de-logis*, but Neumann's adoption of the vast single staircase and his relocation of the *sala terrena* and redesigning of this and the vestibule found favour. In succeeding years Neumann's mastery of vaulting techniques enabled him to prevail over Hildebrandt in two important matters – the shaping of the interior of the court church, and the vaulting of the staircase. As originally envisaged by de Cotte, and as perpetuated in Boffrand's engravings and Neumann's earliest designs, the upper gallery was to be surrounded by a colonnade, upon which the vault over the well of the staircase would be supported. However, abetted by the lightness and mastery of German roof-timbering (remarked on by Boffrand), Neumann was able to construct a single vault

378 over the whole staircase area (1742–43), thus providing the matrix for G.B. Tiepolo's masterpiece (1752–53). His son tells an amusing tale of Hildebrandt offering to hang himself from the vault should it hold, and Neumann countering this by offering to fire cannon underneath it – and indeed in the last war the vault (and hence Tiepolo's fresco) survived, when so much else went up in flames. Though Hildebrandt still supplied designs for certain special features like the furnishing and decoration of the court church, with Friedrich Carl's removal to Franconia Hildebrandt lost control of the interiors of the Residence as well. Ornamental draughtsmanship was not Neumann's forte, and control over this passed instead to the team of J. R. Byss the painter, J. W. von der Auwera the sculptor, and the superlative Comasque stuccador Antonio Bossi, whose two surviving masterpieces are the purely stuccoed *Weisser Saal*

374 (1744–45) and the *Kaisersaal*, in which he supplied the gilded stucco and stucco-marble setting for Tiepolo's trial frescoes (1749–53). Hildebrandt did not even receive such honour as was due to him in Würzburg, and in 1743 we find him writing sadly to Friedrich Carl to complain of this and of the engravings being made that credited not him but Neumann with the Residence, so that he could truly say, '*et hos versulos feci, tulit*

alter honores. It grieves me very much, that another should parade himself in my clothes....' This was indeed an injustice, but as we have seen no single person could claim credit for the Würzburg Residence; it is the most remarkable example of collective planning in Baroque Germany.

Borrowed clothes or no, the Würzburg Residence set the seal on Neumann's reputation as a planner of palaces in general, and of staircases in particular. Friedrich Carl himself employed him to design and build his country *Schloss* at Werneck (1733–45), whose chapel has already been mentioned (cf see above, p.268); for yet another member of the Schönborn family, Franz Georg, archbishop-elector of Trier, he built a *Sommerschloss* called Schönbornslust near Coblenz (1748–52, destroyed in 1793), and through the Trier architect Johannes Seitz his influence was perpetuated in the region. After Friedrich Carl's death Neumann was particularly at liberty to travel ceaselessly, and the palaces upon which he gave or sent advice included Stuttgart (1747–49), Carlsruhe (1750–51), and even 425 the Hofburg at Vienna (1746–49).[100] His most distinguished intervention was, however, over the staircase of Schloss Brühl (1744–48).[101] Neumann was employed by Clemens August in a consultative capacity on the staircase at Brühl from 1740 onwards, despite the retention of Cuvilliés. It was indeed Cuvilliés' alterations to Schlaun's plans – his abolition of the real and mimic mediaeval round towers in 1735–36, and his transfer of the show side from the *cour d'honneur* on the east to the garden side on the south – that necessitated the relocation of the staircase. Neumann moved the staircase to the north, creating an extra saloon in its place, so that the visitor successively mounted the stairs and passed through the *salle des gardes* before entering the last and most sumptuous of all the sets of apartments created at Brühl (*c.* 1750–64). The entrance to the staircase, as a censorious English travel-writer noted in 1794, 'is peculiar for the palace of a prince; and by no means favourable to the idea of his dignity. It is by means of a gateway, which runs through the centre of the building, after the manner of some large inns...'; a single central flight of stairs mounts to the right, ascending towards a remarkable tomb-like monu-

379 *Opposite* Brühl, the ceremonial staircase, added by Balthasar Neumann, 1743–48, frescoes by Carlo Carlone, 1750, stucco by Giuseppe Artari, C. P. Morsegno and G. A. Brilli, 1748–63

380 *Above right* Brühl, *Salle des gardes*, fresco by Carlo Carlone, 1752, stucco by C. P. Morsegno, 1754

ment to Clemens August, framed by paired columns on consoles; the two return flights are on bridges supported by trios of caryatids at the foot, and paired stucco-lustro columns over the entrance-passage; two passages held in by the same exquisite wrought iron-work as the stairs run back towards the apartments in the north wing, whilst the landing acts as a prelude to the main apartments in the south wing; above, the beginning of a flat ceiling supported by paired herm-brackets is cut open to reveal a circular gallery and a dome-like fresco (a device reminiscent of the Daun-Kinsky staircase in Vienna) celebrating the glory of Clemens August beyond. Only the structural design of the lower part of the staircase is Neumann's, and it is masterly; the shaping of the upper zone and the decoration of the whole were designed and executed by the team of draughtsmen and craftsmen who combined to make Brühl surpass any other palace in sheer splendour: Michel Leveilly the architect; Johann Adolf Biarelle (now back from Ansbach) the draughtsman; the stuccadors Giuseppe Artari, Carlo Pietro Morsegno, and Giuseppe Antonio Brilli; and the frescoist Carlo Carlone.

It is a curious fact that Johann Conrad Schlaun (1695–1773),[102] who conducted the reconstruction of Brühl until he was set aside for the more 'modern' Cuvilliés in 1728, should have been responsible for designing and building what may be considered the last Rococo palace in the Empire – the Münster Residence (1767–84) – at a time when Salins de Montfort and d'Ixnard were introducing the severe massivity of Neo-Classicism from France. Despite his displacement from Brühl, Clemens August had never given up employing him in his Westphalian territories, and working in the idiom of this region – subtly layered brickwork, with freestone dressings and slate roofs – Schlaun produced a series of buildings noteworthy for their spectacular adaptation to their sites, and for their achievement of considerable effects with the most modest means. Conspicuous amongst them is Clemens August's *Jagdschloss* at Clemenswerth (1737–44), an original adaptation of Boffrand's *maison de chasse* at Bouchefort for Clemens August's uncle Max Emanuel, with additional inspiration from the Falkenlust. Here a cruciform hunting lodge with a circular central saloon below stands in the middle of eight rides cut through the forest, with eight pavilions (one of which is a chapel) placed between the rides. In the interior an ingenious miniature two-armed staircase leads to the rooms on the first floor, whilst the rooms are decorated with lacy stucco very similar to that in the Falkenlust, and also designed by Michel Leveilly. Though it is not a palace project, mention must be made of Schlaun's Church and Hospital of St Clement (1744–54) for the Brothers Hospitaller in Münster, because of its ingenious exploitation of an acute-angled corner site, which serves as a foil to Schlaun's subsequent exploitation of an oblique-angled corner site for the Erbdrostenhof (1753–57) in the same city. The design has surprising affinities with Johann Dientzenhofer's unexecuted design for the priory at Holzkirchen (see above, pp.266–67). The hospital buildings occupy the four sides of an irregular quadrilateral, whilst the domed tri-apsidal church is placed at the junction of the two longest sides, with one apse forming a bowed-out entrance with concave extensions on either side. For the Erbdrostenhof, built for a member of the local aristocracy, Schlaun made the front angle of the site into a triangular forecourt, which was closed by the receding curve of the palace, interrupted by the pedimented projection of the concave-fronted *corps-de-logis*. For the front façade of the central pavilion of the otherwise conventional

381 Münster, Erbdrostenhof, exterior designed by J. C. Schlaun, 1753–57

three-winged Münster Residence, Schlaun employed a convex pedimented projection, with concave flanking pieces, rather as in the façade of St Clement. Though by no means palatial, Schlaun's own country house, Haus Rüschhaus (1745–48), should also be mentioned for its idiosyncratic creation of a gentleman's country seat, complete with forecourt flanked by offices and formal gardens, out of buildings modelled on vernacular farm architecture.

With Schlaun, the indigenous tradition of Central European Baroque architecture comes to an end; there are provincial survivals in places like Hungary, but in Germany itself a fresh wave of immigrant Frenchmen imbued with the ideals of Neo-Classicism banished the old freedoms. The last great residence to be built in Germany, before the Revolution swept all the petty and ecclesiastical sovereignties away, was designed by one of these – the palace of the archbishop-elector of Trier at Coblenz, by Michel d'Ixnard (1777–86).[103] Yet as if to demonstrate that even this tutelage was not tight enough, d'Ixnard's plans were themselves strongly criticized by the Académie d'Architecture in Paris, so that the elector meekly asked d'Angiviller, the *Directeur des Bâtiments* of the French king, to send him a replacement for d'Ixnard; the younger Peyre being chosen. It was like the situation at the beginning of the century, save that this time the German lack of confidence was no longer caused merely by the prestige of a new style. It derived from the fact that the sovereignties of the Empire were too fragmented and old-fashioned to offer architects the manifold opportunities in public and private building to afford them a regular career such as was now possible in England and France, and could never combine to found a school of architecture producing such a high level of architectural competence as that produced by the Académie d'Architecture, Blondel's Academy (till its amalgamation with the former), and the directorate of the Ponts et Chaussées. Three-quarters of a century of vigorous building had failed to produce a new generation of professional architects in the Empire, or any consciousness of a contemporary national style, and for the next hundred years Germans, adopting French disparagement of Baroque architecture as their own, remained unaware of the originality of their own achievement.

Russia

The foundation of St Petersburg as the new capital of Russia in 1703 was a symbol of Peter the Great's determination to open up Russia and to establish commercial, diplomatic, and artistic links with the countries of Western Europe. He was also intent on making the city worthy of comparison with the capitals of Western European countries that he had visited on his journey of 1697–98: Amsterdam, London, Dresden, and Vienna (Paris he avoided because he was on bad terms politically with the government of Louis XIV).

The emperor realized immediately that the Russian architects available to him were not adequate to the task of planning and building a great modern city. The architecture of Moscow had hardly changed for several centuries; the great mediaeval building tradition had declined and had not been renewed, and stylistically the only innovation had been the importation of a few crudely applied Italian decorative details. Further Peter wanted to build his city of brick and stone and the Muscovite architects were trained primarily in wood construction.

The emperor invited a number of architects, mainly German, Swiss, and French, to Russia to help in the construction of his capital. The most distinguished of them, Andreas Schlüter (see above, p.278), died a few months after his arrival in 1714 and left no mark on Russian architecture. Much more important was Domenico Trezzini (1670–1734), an Italian-Swiss architect from the Ticino, who was working for Frederick V of Denmark when he was recruited for the emperor in 1703 by the Russian ambassador in Copenhagen.

Trezzini provided the designs for the smaller houses to be built in St Petersburg, many of which had at this time to be constructed of wood and have disappeared, but his main commission was for the fortress of St Peter and St Paul, begun in 1703 as a protection against possible invasion by the Swedes. There is hardly anything specifically Russian about Trezzini's work. The Petrovsk Gate to the fortress is based on French mid seventeenth-century models, which the architect could have known through engravings. The cathedral is more interesting. It is built on the simplest of three-aisled plans but has a very tall dome over the crossing, which was to become a feature of many eighteenth-century Russian churches. Its west façade leads to a tower, a pattern borrowed from south or west Germany, but transformed here by the addition of the tall gilded spire (altered after being struck by lightning in 1756), which echoes the similar spire on the Admiralty on the south bank of the Neva, built for Peter the Great by a Russian architect, Ivan Korobov, but completely submerged – except for the tower and spire – in the early nineteenth-century Neo-Classical additions of Zakharov. The two other Italian architects who worked for Peter in Russia, Niccolò Michetti – a pupil of Carlo Fontana – and his assistant, Gaetano Chiaveri, put up few buildings, most of which have been altered or destroyed, but Chiaveri's library in the emperor's Kunstkammer is conveniently and soberly designed, in a style which reflects the emperor's practical approach to architectural problems.

More important than these Italian architects in the development of St Petersburg was the Frenchman Jean-Baptiste-Alexandre Le Blond, who came to Russia in 1716 and died there in 1719. He supplied the original plan for the lay-out of St Petersburg on a grid-system with a network of canals. Unfortunately his plan, though admirable theoretically, failed to take into account certain important factors of practical convenience, particularly in the matter of communications, and had to be modified. Le Blond also built the palace of Peterhof, some ten miles to the west of St Petersburg (altered and extended later by Rastrelli for the Empress Elizabeth), and laid out its gardens, which run down to the Gulf of Finland. Le Blond was accompanied by Nicolas Pineau (see above, p.139), who executed at Peterhof some of the most original and delicate of early Rococo decoration. After the death of Peter the Great in 1725 he returned to Paris.

The official building campaign at St Petersburg was personally directed by the emperor but his favourite, Prince Menschikov, built two vast palaces for himself to the designs of the German architect Gottfried Schädel, one on the north bank of the Neva, opposite the Admiralty, and the other at Oranienbaum, not far from Peterhof. Both palaces were drastically remodelled in the early nineteenth century, but from engravings showing their original state it is clear that they were among the boldest Baroque inventions of the period, with wings curving forward and ending in domed pavilions, and terraces and steps leading down to the river.

During the remainder of the eighteenth century Russian history was dominated by a series of powerful Empresses – Anna Ioannovna (1730–40), Elizabeth (1741–62), and Catherine (1762–96) – under whose guidance St Petersburg developed into one of the great European capitals.

Of the three empresses Anna Ioannovna was the least active, and the Winter Palace which she built was engulfed in the vast building put up by Elizabeth, who was an enthusiastic builder, with a love for rich and exuberant decoration. Under her patronage there flourished a style which can be regarded as a real Russian variant of the Baroque. The creator of the style was Bartolomeo Rastrelli (c. 1700–71), the son of an Italian sculptor, also called Bartolomeo, who had settled in Paris, where the younger Bartolomeo was born. In 1716, on the invitation of Peter the Great, the family moved to St Petersburg, where the father made a successful career as a sculptor and the son soon established himself as an architect. He is known to have travelled abroad – certainly in 1725, and probably in 1719–21 – to get training as an architect, but it is not recorded which countries he visited. The style of his mature works suggests that he went to Dresden and possibly to Berlin and Vienna. It is not known whether he went to Italy, and the evidence supplied by the style of his buildings is inconclusive: the Roman details could easily have been learnt from pattern-books, but some of his buildings are so close in feeling to Piedmontese works that a visit to Turin seems possible.

Rastrelli's early works are highly eclectic. The palace which he began for Biron, the Empress Anna's favourite, at Ruhenthal (Rundal) in 1736 is basically French in design, with slightly projecting pavilions and triple-arched openings in the middle section, but the altar in the chapel is like that of an Austrian monastic church and the niches flanking it recall the Zwinger at Dresden. On the other hand his design for the Summer Palace in St Petersburg suggests that he had been looking at the Palladian designs in *Vitruvius Britannicus*.

By the end of the 1740s, however, he had evolved a personal style, which he displayed in a series of vast buildings for the Empress Elizabeth: the Smolny Convent (begun 1748), the rebuilding and extension of Peterhof (1746–58), the Palace of Tsarskoe Selo (1749–56), and the Winter Palace in St Petersburg (1754–68). These buildings show a new – sometimes a

358

reckless – indulgence in the architectural forms of the Late
383   Baroque – curved and broken pediments, massive columns,
repeated atlantes – to which an added vitality is given by the
colours with which the buildings are generally decorated (the
Palace at Tsarskoe Selo is painted blue and white). The details
would have shocked any architect from western Europe; the
windows boldly varied from Roman models and heavily decorated with sculpture would have distressed a Frenchman;
and the proportion of the arches and the supporting Orders
would have surprised even a provincial Italian architect; but
Rastrelli designed with a gusto that makes the modern visitor to
Tsarskoe Selo forget his prejudices and enjoy the spectacle,
particularly in the interior, which contains some exceptionally
rich Rococo decoration.

What is more serious than Rastrelli's reckless treatment of
conventional forms is the fact that he could not really conceive
buildings on the grand scale demanded of him. Tsarskoe Selo,
for instance, is composed of a series of sections almost wholly
unrelated to each other (one, incidentally, which is composed
383   of giant columns carried by atlantes, looks more like a piece of
stage-architecture than a real building). He is much more at
ease when working on a small scale. Even the Stroganov Palace
is more coherent than the Imperial Palaces, and Rastrelli is
particularly successful in the small pavilions at Tsarskoe
384   Selo – the grotto beside the lake and Mon Bijou (destroyed but
known from engravings).

The same applies to his few works of ecclesiastical architecture. The Smolny Convent in St Petersburg is an ambitious
design and would have been even more striking if the tall spire
shown in the surviving wooden model had been carried out, but
his most successful translation of the traditional Russian
church with four elements round a central dome is the little
382   Cathedral of St Andrew at Kiev, in which the subsidiary domes
are replaced by elegant towers in the idiom of Juvarra. This is in
fact the one of Rastrelli's buildings which supports the theory
that he may have visited Turin, because not only are the towers
Juvarresque but the wavy entablature round the bottom of the
dome is reminiscent of the unusual arrangement on the exterior

382 *Below* Kiev, Cathedral of St Andrew by Bartolomeo Rastrelli

383 *Top* Tsarskoe Selo (now Pushkin), façade of the Imperial Palace by
Bartolomeo Rastrelli, 1749–56

384 *Above* Tsarskoe Selo, grotto by Bartolomeo Rastrelli

of the Cappella della SS. Sindone. No Italian architect, however, would have tolerated the little curved pediments over the
coupled columns on the corners of the building!

Rastrelli had a few Russian followers, of whom the most
talented were S. I. Chevakinski, who built the naval church of St
Nicholas in St Petersburg, and Feodor Argussov, who built an
attractive variant of Rastrelli's Tsarskoe Selo grotto in the park
at Kuskovo near Moscow.

The Baroque, however, went out of favour under Catherine
the Great, who preferred the more Classical manner of the
Italians Rinaldi and Giuseppe Quarenghi, the Frenchman
Vallin de la Motte, and the Scottish architect Charles Cam-
eron, who created some of the most beautiful early Neo-
Classical buildings in Russia, notably the wing which he added
for the empress to the Palace of Tsarskoe Selo. This phase was
the preliminary to the great Neo-Classical movement in Russia,
dominated by native architects such as Adrian Sacharov and
Alexander Voronichin, who built the Admiralty and the other
monumental buildings which make Leningrad today one of the
most splendid of all Neo-Classical cities.

Part V

The Iberian Peninsula and the New World

The evolution of Baroque architecture in the Iberian peninsula differs in many ways from its development in other parts of Europe. Owing to their geographical isolation Spain and Portugal were not open to the gradual penetration of Italian ideas which characterized the formation of the Baroque in Austria and South Germany; instead we find two different, almost opposed traditions running side by side: a strong local tradition, having its roots in the sixteenth-century architecture of the country, and an imported style, introduced by foreign architects, usually from Italy but sometimes from France or Germany, which never took root or fused with local traditions. The last stage of the story takes place in Latin America to which Iberian architectural styles were transplanted by the Conquistadores, producing works which, however brilliant and fascinating they may be, burst through any acceptable definition of the Baroque.

385 Murcia, façade of the Cathedral by Jaime Bort Miliá, 1736–49

Spain and Spanish America

In the first half of the sixteenth century Spain produced a style of architecture, called Plateresque, which is one of the most successful examples of the fusion of Italian decoration with Late Gothic planning and structure. The style derives its name from *plateria* or silver-work on account of its elaborate and delicate low-relief decoration; but this name does not take into account its real qualities of design, which are considerable and distinctive. Works such as the Hospital of Santa Cruz in Toledo, the Casas Consistoriales at Seville, or the sacristies in the cathedrals of Seville and Sigüenza show a real feeling for spatial design rare in architecture of this date outside Italy, and in certain features, particularly the planning and construction of staircases, the Spaniards were far ahead even of their Italian contemporaries. This period also produced one highly sophisticated building, Pedro Machuca's Palace of Charles V in Granada (begun in 1527), which shows a familiarity with the architecture of the High Renaissance in Italy in the use of the Orders and in the handling of masses, and is unusual in being built round a circular court, an idea adapted from Raphael's designs for the Villa Madama, Rome, though the architect may also have had in mind a mediaeval Spanish model, the royal castle of Bellver near Palma de Mallorca.

Classical tendencies and knowledge of contemporary Italian architecture remained characteristics of Spanish royal taste throughout the sixteenth century. Even before he became king on his father's abdication in 1556, Philip II was concerned with the building of the Alcazar at Toledo, begun in 1538, on the design of Alonso de Covarrubias (1488–1570), but essentially the work of Juan Bautista de Toledo (d. 1567), who had been trained in Naples. The latter designed the spacious court with two superimposed arcades and the magnificent staircase, the earliest surviving example of the type known as the imperial staircase.

In 1562 Juan Bautista de Toledo took the first steps in the designing and building of the greatest Spanish monument of the sixteenth century, the royal palace and monastery of El Escorial, about forty miles north-west of Madrid. The grid-plan of the Escorial is due to Juan Bautista, who actually built the Cloister of the Evangelists in a style derived from Antonio da Sangallo the Younger's court of the Palazzo Farnese, but the character of severe grandeur which marks the whole building is due to his assistant and successor, Juan de Herrera (c. 1530–97). This characteristic appears most clearly in the entrance façade,

386 Granada, façade of the Cathedral by Alonso Cano, 1664

the choir was circular and planned in conscious imitation of the church of the Holy Sepulchre in Jerusalem, which had been taken as the model of some earlier Italian churches, for instance the SS. Annunziata in Florence. Siloe planned the façade with two tiers of arched recesses, the middle one on each floor being higher than the outer two, making a design like two Roman triumphal arches superimposed on each other. The cathedral was, however, unfinished at Siloe's death in 1563, and the façade was added in 1664 by the sculptor-painter Alonso Cano (1601–67). Cano made one radical change in Siloe's original design by eliminating the lower tier of arches, creating three enormously tall recesses broken by a strongly marked cornice which follows the planes of the wall and piers. In making this change Cano destroyed the likeness of the design to a Roman triumphal arch and brings it much closer to a type of mediaeval façade with three tall, recessed arches running the full height of the building of which the most famous example of this type is Lincoln Cathedral. Given the direct allusion to a mediaeval design in the choir of the cathedral, it is not impossible that the architect should have intended a reference to a mediaeval model in the façade. The façade of Granada Cathedral has the sharp severity of Herrera's school, but Cano has introduced certain decorative details which had not apparently been used in Spain before this date and which are important in relation to later developments. The curious feature about them is the fact that they are derived from sixteenth-century northern models. The circular windows in the upper storeys of the two side-niches are based on the very simplest kind of 'strap-work', the type of decoration invented in France by the architects of the School of Fontainebleau in the 1530s and 1540s, and the features, almost like keystones, over the windows below them come from the same tradition, but probably from the modified form which it received at the hands of Flemish artists. Both the French and the Flemish designs were widely disseminated over Europe by decorative engravings produced in great quantities in both countries.

386

A different type of influence from the sixteenth-century north is visible in two of the most impressive Spanish church façades of the early eighteenth century: that of the chapel attached to the college of San Telmo in Seville, built in 1724–34, probably by Leonardo da Figueroa, and that of the cathedral of Murcia by Jaime Bort Miliá (1736–49). In San Telmo the design, consisting of three storeys flanked by coupled columns with single columns set back outside them, derives from a tradition established in France by Philibert de Lorme at Anet in the 1550s and continued by Salomon de Brosse in the church of Saint-Gervais and by François Mansart at the Château of Maisons in the first half of the seventeenth century. Nothing, however, could be less French than the detail of the façade. The Doric columns on the ground floor are carved in high relief with clustering figures and oval medallions, of which the upper ones contain flaming hearts and are capped with royal crowns. The Ionic and Corinthian columns of the upper storeys are fluted, but in a manner contrary to all Classical principles. In fact the zig-zag pattern on the Ionic columns is taken directly from an engraving in Wendel Dietterlin's treatise on architecture, first published in Nuremberg in 1593, and that on the Corinthian, though not exactly traceable in Dietterlin, is entirely in char-

387

with its huge single granite half-columns, and the impressive interior of the church, articulated with sharp-edged Doric pilasters, also in granite.

Philip III was not much interested in the arts, and his successor, Philip IV, though a great patron of painters, built little, and that little is without interest. Generally speaking the severe style of Herrera continued to dominate Spanish architecture till well into the seventeenth century, though in some areas, particularly in Andalusia, it was qualified by the addition of fairly rich, carved decoration, as in the Sagrario at Seville (1615). This richness of surface treatment was to increase during the century – an extreme example is the stucco work on the dome of Santa Maria la Blanca in Seville, which dates from 1659 – and was to become a dominant feature in the architecture of the early eighteenth century.[1]

One of the most curious buildings of the mid-seventeenth century is the façade of Granada Cathedral. The cathedral itself was mainly built by Diego de Siloe from 1528 onwards, on a plan which was basically mediaeval, with one unusual feature:

387 *Opposite* Seville, façade of the chapel in the College of S. Telmo by Leonardo da Figueroa, 1724–34

acter with his style. The richness of surface decoration, so conspicuous on this and many other early eighteenth-century Spanish buildings, has been described as a revival of the Plateresque manner and has been associated with the nationalist spirit in Spain at the time, but it is important to notice that the actual decorative themes have little in common with early sixteenth-century Spanish architecture and are derived from North European sources. In the façade of the cathedral of Murcia the Baroque features are more marked, for instance the deep curve of the central niche and the broken pediment over the main door, which in form is not unlike the type regularly used by Hildebrandt – for instance on the entrance front of the Upper Belvedere in Vienna – with a double curve interrupted by a right-angled break; but there are other features, such as the rectangular elements dropped into the arch of the door, which, like the flutings of the columns of San Telmo, are close in character to North European Late Mannerism.

The most celebrated Spanish façade of this period is that of the cathedral of Santiago de Compostela, the great pilgrimage centre built round the relics of St James, the patron saint of Spain. In the first half of the seventeenth century his position was challenged by the partisans of other saints, such as St Joseph and St Theresa, but his claim was maintained and the authorities of the cathedral determined to celebrate the fact by restoring the building, which had been much neglected, and completing it by adding a façade. The first addition was a tower – designed by Peña de Toro in 1667 (the one on the left was actually built later) – and in 1738 the façade itself was begun from the designs of Fernando de Casas y Nova. The silhouette of the towers suggests a Gothic cathedral, and they were no doubt consciously conceived to continue the character of the mediaeval building, but their 'spires' are composed of superimposed tiers of volutes which remind one of Longhena's Salute. The theme of volutes is carried on in the façade itself to create a broken silhouette which in many ways recalls a Flemish town house rather than a southern church. The façade is rich in relief, created both by sculpture and by free-standing columns, and the dramatic effect of the whole is heightened by the steps which lead up to it from the plaza.

Church planning in Spain remained conventional for most of the Baroque period, but some of the new forms invented in Rome penetrated the country at a fairly early date and were applied competently, though rarely inventively. For instance, the oval ground plan was used as early as 1617 in the church of the Bernardines at Alcalá de Henares, probably by Sebastian de la Plaza, and again by Diego Martínez Ponce de Urrana for the Desamparados of Valencia. Pedro de la Torre, a Fleming trained in Rome as a sculptor, was more ingenious: for the Ochavo in Toledo Cathedral (1632) he used an octagonal plan,

388 *Opposite* Santiago de Compostela, façade of the Cathedral

389 *Above right* Madrid, door of the Hospicio de San Fernando, 1722

390 *Right* Toledo, the Transparente in the Cathedral by Narciso Tomé, 1721

391 *Overleaf left* Seville, detail of the high altar in S. Luis by Leonardo da Figueroa

392 *Overleaf right* Valencia façade of the Cathedral by Conrad Rudolph, begun 1703

and at San Isidro in Madrid (1643), a sequence of square spaces, of which the largest is covered by an octagonal dome. Generally speaking, however, Spanish architects clung to the traditional rectangular or Latin-cross plans, though in the case of the latter they often used the modified form invented by Vignola for the Gesù, with shallow transepts and domed crossing. About the turn of the seventeenth century more advanced Roman ideas were introduced. In 1680 Carlo Fontana supplied plans for the church of St Ignatius at his birth place, Loyola, and, though they were modified in execution by local architects, the bold lines of the porch, curving under the heavy dome, opened the eyes of Spanish architects to the new style. In the Jesuit church of San Luis at Seville (1731) the architect, who was probably 391 Leonardo de Figueroa, copied the plan of S. Agnese in Piazza Navona almost slavishly, though the decoration is entirely in the local style of Andalusia. The same plan was used about the same time by Pedro de Ribera in the Virgen del Puerto in Madrid, though the exterior has a typical Castilian severity. One of the few really original designs of the early eighteenth 392 century is the façade of the cathedral of Valencia, begun in 1703 by Conrad Rudolph, an architect of German origin trained as a 6 sculptor in Rome. The plan of the façade is a bold version of the double-S of S. Carlino, the articulation of which is emphasized by superimposed free-standing columns. The composition centres on a cartouche with the 'M' of the Virgin carried by angels like those supporting Bernini's altar at Castel Gandolfo. The whole is a clever solution to the problem of making an impressive façade on a narrow site, limited on the left by the mediaeval belfry. The principles of design used by Rudolph in this church were applied by a local architect, Vicente Acero y Arebo, in the façades of the cathedrals of Guadix (1714) and Cadiz (1722). The plan of the latter, for which Acero was also responsible, follows Diego de Siloe's cathedral at Granada in that the choir is a complete rotunda in imitation of the church of the Holy Sepulchre.

The greatest and most original creations of Spanish Baroque are to be found in a series of altars and doors, dating from the first half of the eighteenth century, in which architecture, decoration, and sculpture are fused in a uniquely fantastic manner. The favourite ingredients in these productions are the Salomonic columns, revived by Bernini and popularized by Andrea Pozzo, and the *estipite,* a pilaster broken up into different zones by secondary capitals, geometrical panels, and cartouches often with low-relief sculpture. The *estipite,* which is not found in the architecture of Spain or Italy at earlier periods, is in fact an invention of northern Mannerism, specially of Dietterlin, who has already been referred to as a source for the fluting on the façade of San Telmo, Seville.

The Salomonic column was already established in Spain before the end of the seventeenth century, a particularly rich example being the high altar of the Caridad in Seville, designed by Bernardo Simón de Pineda in 1670. A simple form of 389 the *estipite* is to be seen flanking the door of the Hospicio de San Fernando, Madrid, dating from 1722. Here the *estipite* has a second 'capital', composed of scrolls and cherubs' heads, below which is a block of stone held in the *estipite* itself by a clamp. The lower part of the shaft is bound to the wall by bands of rustication decorated with projecting diamond-shaped panels. The jambs of the doors are ornamented with plume-like motifs, and the 'pediment' over it is dissolved into ogee forms, scrolls, trefoils, and figure-sculpture. The silhouette of the door is enveloped in stone drapery hanging from the entablature. The *estipites* of the upper storey are extremely attenuated, with bands of fruit twisted round their shafts. The whole design ends at the top with a curiously broken pediment of which the three parts are joined together by a band ornamented with diamond projections, like the rustications round the door. In Castile the most celebrated example of this new style is the Transparente in 390 Toledo Cathedral, designed by Narciso Tomé in 1721. It stands with its back to the high altar of the Gothic cathedral and occupies the full height of a bay of the ambulatory. In structure it consists of a single concave bay, flanked on each side by two superimposed columns, the entablatures of which curve steeply downwards to create an effect of greater depth for the niche – a device recalling some of Borromini's tombs in the Lateran. On the actual *mensa* of the altar stand marble putti who carry a sort of tabernacle with statues of the Virgin and Child enclosed in a niche, the top of which is more than a semi-circle – possibly an echo of Moorish arches – and seems to close in on them like pincers. Immediately above is a glory of angels round the mystic 408 rose of the Virgin, more riotous than anything that Bernini ever invented. Above this again is the 'upper room', in which Christ and the Apostles are eating the Last Supper, and at the very top stands St Longinus, holding the spear which pierced Christ's side. The Transparente has neither Salomonic columns nor *estipites* but its columns are equally strange in their own way. They are fluted, but the fluting is covered with an imitation of either torn parchment or skin, probably the latter, because the effect recalls the partially skin-covered skeletons which Late Gothic and Mannerist sculptors loved to add to their tombs. The sinister character which the device has in the tomb-sculpture is cancelled out in the Transparente by the cherubs' heads which peep out through the interstices of the 'skin'.

This fantastic style, of which the Transparente was the extreme example, was employed in Castile by other architects, such as José Benito de Churriguera (1665–1725), whose high altar in San Esteban at Salamanca makes free use of richly clustered Salomonic columns, carved with vines and putti, but it was in Andalusia that the style reached its fullest expression through Francisco Hurtado Izquierdo (1669–1725) and his followers, for instance in the chapel of San José in Seville.[2] 395

Hurtado was born in Andalusia, where he spent the greater part of his working life, and his works have the exuberance typical of Southern Spain. His earliest works, two mausoleums, one for the counts of Buenavista in the church of the Victoria at Malaga (1694), the other for the cardinal-archbishop in Cordova Cathedral (1703), reveal his talents as a decorator in stucco, but his altars in the Sagrario (chapel of the Sacrament) 393 of the Cartuja (Carthusian monastery) of Granada (1713) and for the same Order at El Paular, near Segovia (1718), are much more ambitious. In these Hurtado makes free use of Salomonic columns in coloured marbles and of rich, somewhat heavy, gilt acanthus stucco decoration, but he breaks up the architectural forms – as, for instance, in the door separating the two chapels at El Paular – with greater boldness than his predecessors. At

393 *Opposite* Granada, detail of the altar in the Sagrario of the Cartuja by Francisco Hurtado Izquierdo, 1713

394 *Overleaf left* Granada, detail in the Sacristy of the Cartuja, 1730–47

395 *Overleaf right* Seville, interior of San José by Hurtado Izquierdo

Granada he treats the entablature over his columns in a series of
layers, patterned almost like strap-work, a device which is
reminiscent of northern Mannerism, and the strange cartouches, almost like human ears, at the top of the altar derive
from the same source. At El Paular the effect depends largely on
the careful disposition of light and shade, the outer chapel
forming a dark foreground to the brilliantly lit inner sanctum,
with its fantastically formed and richly carved baldacchino,
carried by twisted columns and with Mannerist layering in the
panel immediately over the arch. In these two altars Hurtado
does not use the *estipite*, but in that of St James in the cathedral
(1707) and that of the Convent of Zafra at Granada (after 1720)
it is the principal ingredient, though it is treated with restraint,
the pilasters being relatively simple in form and all being set in a
single plane, but in other altars by followers of Hurtado – such
as those in the churches of San Matías and Santo Domingo at
Granada – they were used with much greater freedom. One of
the richest and most fanciful examples of the Andalusian style is
the high altar of the chapel of San José at Seville, where – as at El
Paular – carefully disposed light heightens the dramatic effect of
the broken and gilded forms.

The most celebrated – and the most violently abused
– example of this style is the sacristy of the Cartuja at Granada, begun in 1730 and decorated between 1742 and 1747,
except for the altar, which was finished in 1770. The decoration
shows signs of influence from Hurtado but is fundamentally
different in character. The *estipites* are more fantastic than any
produced earlier, even in Andalusia, The second 'capital' is
composed of the inverted segmental pediment fragments,
invented by Buontalenti for the covering of a door but never
used in a capital, and below these is even what might be
considered a third 'capital', composed of Ionic volutes. The
shafts are completely broken up by bands of curved or zig-zag
strap-work, sometimes repeated in layers in the manner of
Hurtado. This repeated layering is carried to a hitherto
unknown pitch in the panels between the upper and the lower
windows, in a pattern which suggests the carving over a wooden
door rather than any model in stone or stucco, except where it
twists in almost liquid form round the piers behind the *estipites*.
An origin in wood-carving is also suggested by the mouldings
round the arches over the windows and across the vault of the
nave, but in this case the model would be a carved frame rather
than a door panel.

The author of the decoration of the sacristy is not known.
The only architect of distinction recorded as working in Granada in the 1740s is José de Bada, and if the Sagrario at Lucena is
correctly attributed to him – which is far from certain – he may
indeed be responsible for the sacristy, but most of his works are
in a much more restrained style. The style of the sacristy is
found in the Sagrario at Priego, but that dates from 1784 and its
architect, Francisco Xavier Pedraxas, was not born till 1736.
The Sagrario, which is as fantastic in its decorative forms as the
sacristy of the Cartuja, is yet another example of the late
survival in remote districts of a style quite out of date elsewhere.

But what style? Baroque? But all the decorative motifs derive
from Late Mannerism, and even their disposition in layers on
the walls can be paralleled there. Rococo? Hardly, because not
a single Rococo motif appears, and the work lacks the lightness
and elegance associated with the term Rococo. Churrigueresque? But it is not like the works of any of the Churriguera
family. In some ways the sacristy can most accurately be
described as 'neo-Mannerist'; but it would be a pity to invent a

396 *Opposite* Granada, Sacristy of the Cartuja, decorated 1742–47

397 *Above* El Paular, Sancta Sanctorum in the Cartuja by Francisco
Hurtado Izquierdo, 1718

stylistic term for a single building. In fact the sacristy is *sui
generis*.

Generally speaking, however, the art of Andalusia, as it is
represented by Hurtado and his contemporaries, is one of the
supreme manifestations of popular Baroque, not 'popular' in
the sense of made by the people for the people, but made by the
Church for the people – a Marxist would say as a distraction
from the ills of this world, but 'consolation' might be a fairer
word. Whichever explanation one prefers, it is certain that this
art, with its richness of materials, agitated forms, dramatic light
effects, and ecstatic figure-sculpture, appealed widely to the
people of Spain. At first sight its emotional tone seems to have
something in common with the painting and sculpture of the
late-sixteenth century in Spain, but in fact it is fundamentally
different. The intense religious feeling expressed in the painting
of El Greco was based on a highly sophisticated and intellectual
mode of thought, combining neo-Platonism with traditional

398 *Above* Madrid, exterior of the Royal Palace by Giovanni Battista
Sacchetti, begun 1738

399 *Opposite* Madrid, state-room in the Royal Palace by Matteo
Gasparini, after 1760

theology, and intended to appeal to a limited public cognizant
of such matters. To appreciate the art of Hurtado all that is
needed is familiarity with the legends of the saints and a belief
in their miraculous power. For the full effect of these churches
to be appreciated they must be seen when a great service is
taking place in them, with the candles lit, the organ accompany-
ing the harsh Spanish singing, and a procession carrying the
figure of a saint gaudily accoutred and clouded with incense.
But of all moments the best is Holy Week, when the white stalks
of the new corn are laid out on the floor in front of the altars.
This may not be great intellectual art, but it performs its
intended functions perfectly.

   While this outburst of religious art was taking place in
Andalusia – and to a lesser extent in other parts of Spain – a
totally different style of architecture was flourishing at the court
of Madrid. The lack of royal building projects already noted as
characteristic of the reigns of Philip III and Philip IV was even
more marked under Charles II, partly because of the severe
economic decline under which Spain suffered after the wars
with France, which ended with the Peace of the Pyrenees in
1659. This decline continued through the War of the Spanish
Succession provoked by the conflicting claims to the throne of
Spain by France and the Empire on the death of Charles in
1700, but when Philip V, the grandson of Louis XIV, was finally
established on the throne by the Treaty of Utrecht in 1713, a
recovery began to take place, and soon the king embarked on a
vast campaign of building which included the Royal Palace in
Madrid and the country palaces at Aranjuez and La Granja.
The building histories of these palaces are long and complicated
and illustrate the varying fortunes of the Spanish monarchy and
the successive intervention of different foreign influences. Philip
was a Frenchman, brought up at the court of Versailles, and his

two queens were Italian – Savoy and Farnese respectively – so it
is not surprising that the king should have preferred French and
Italian architects to native Spanish designers, whose style
he would no doubt have found provincial, even distasteful.

   The two country palaces were each built round a nucleus of
sixteenth-century buildings – in one case an unfinished palace
by Herrera begun for Philip II, in the other the cloister of a
monastery – and the plans for the extensions were frequently
changed. At Aranjuez the work was begun by two French
military engineers, at La Granja by a local architect; at Aranjuez the building was taken over by a Spanish architect,
Santiago Bonavia, after a fire in 1748, whereas at La Granja
two Italian painters, pupils of Carlo Maratta, added the north
and south courts, and the main façade was built, from 1736
onwards, by Giovanni Battista Sacchetti, a pupil of Juvarra, on
his master's design. In the case of both palaces the most
remarkable feature is the garden, laid out by French designers
but extensively modified in the later eighteenth century.

   The decoration of the interiors of the two palaces also dates
largely from after the death of Philip V, and the most enchanting room of all, the Porcelain Cabinet at Aranjuez, was commissioned by Charles III when he moved from the throne of the
Two Sicilies to that of Spain in 1759, no doubt to recall the
similar room which he had commissioned for his country palace
at Portici, near Naples. One would like to think that this was the
room in which the great *castrato* singer, Farinelli, sang to the
kings of Spain, but, alas, it was the two unhappy predecessors
of Charles – Philip V and Ferdinand VI – whose melancholy
Farinelli soothed. In fact on the accession of Charles he fell
from favour and left Spain for Italy.

   The Royal Palace in Madrid was a much more ambitious
project. As originally designed by Juvarra it was a vast affair,
planned round four courts, with a front of seventy-nine bays on
the garden side, but it soon became apparent that this scheme
was unrealistic, and in 1738 Sacchetti produced a new design
round a single court. The plan was based on that of the Louvre,
with pavilions at the four corners, double flights of rooms in the
wings, a vast, columned vestibule, and two giant staircases. The
elevation was directly taken from Bernini's third project, but   173
with the proportions altered, so that the rusticated ground
storey, which contains a main floor and two mezzanines, is
almost as high as the upper part enclosed in a giant Order of
pilasters, which cover the *piano nobile,* a mezzanine and another
full storey, making six storeys in all, to which must be added an
attic between the entablature and the crowning balustrade,
which was to have carried statues. The result is a ponderous
building, awkward in its proportions, and fussy and repetitive   398
in its fenestration. In its dimensions – particularly in its
height – it must have reminded Charles III of Caserta, when he   126
arrived from Naples in 1759, but it lacks the dignity of its rival.
The interior contains some fine rooms, including one of the rare   399
examples of full Rococo to be found in Spain.

   If the royal palaces built for Philip V and his successor were
lacking in distinction, a certain number of houses were built for
private individuals which share some of the inventiveness of
contemporary ecclesiastical architecture. The most notable is
the palace in Valencia remodelled in 1740–44 for the Marqués
de Dos Aguas by Hipólito Rovira y Brocandel. The façade was
originally painted, and the window-surrounds were replaced in
stucco in the 1860s – perhaps with some additional frills – but
the door survives in its original state and is a striking example of   400
the adaptation of the contemporary type of Spanish sculpture

400 Valencia, door of the Palace of the Marqués de Dos Aguas by Hipólito Rovira y Brocandel, 1744

to a flat surface (it is not irrelevant that Brocandel was primarily a painter). The rocks, clouds, trees, scrolls, and other decorative motifs flow, almost like soft clay, over the surface of the wall and even the figures – the two Michelangelesque river-gods of the Dos Aguas below, and the fish-tailed water-nymphs above – avoid disturbing the integrity of the plane. The whole effect fore-shadows the Art Nouveau which was to be so popular in Spain a century and a half later.

About the middle of the eighteenth century the general European tendency towards a more Classical spirit was felt in Madrid. This may have been partly due to the accession of Charles III, who in Naples had shown his preference for the new taste by calling Vanvitelli and Fuga to work for him, but it was probably also due to general influence from France and Rome. The most remarkable architect of this phase was Ventura Rodríguez (1717–85), a pupil of Santiago Bonavia. In his earlier works, such as the Church of San Miguel in Madrid (1749), he followed the style of his master, based on the study of Carlo

Fontana, but his later buildings, of which the most impressive is the façade of the cathedral of Pamplona, built in 1783, represent a revival of the severity of Herrera seen through Neo-Classical eyes; but it is typical of the barriers which separate the different provinces in Spain that Rodriguez' cold and impressive portico is exactly contemporary with the exuberant stucco with which Pedraxas was decorating the Sagrario of the parish church at Priego.

Spanish America

The first churches to be erected by the Spaniards in the New World were mainly built by the great missionary orders, first the Dominicans, Franciscans, and Augustinians, and later the Jesuits.[3] A few of these churches were in a more or less pure Gothic style, but most of them are in a mixed style, like contemporary churches in Spain. Many of them, such as those at Acolmán, Actopan, and Tepotzotlán (all in Mexico), have a fortified appearance outside and were sometimes used for defence against the Indians. The interiors are tall and spacious, usually with Gothic vaulting but Plateresque decorative detail, particularly in doors and windows. Gothic cloisters are a regular feature, and their walls are often painted with scenes in black and white, copied from the wood-cut illustrations in the books of hours which the Friars brought with them. The mixture of mediaeval and Plateresque elements characteristic of these churches is to be found in a few houses, of which the most complete is the Palace of Cortés at Cuernavaca (Mexico).

Sometimes Moorish influence is visible, transplanted from Spain. For instance, the Capilla Real at Cholula (Mexico) is built on a square plan, with seven aisles, like a mosque, and a number of wooden *mudejar* ceilings survive in Mexico and even as far south as Quito (Columbia), Lima (Peru), and Suere (Bolivia).

Towards the end of the sixteenth century the Spaniards began to build a series of cathedrals on a much bigger scale than the churches of the missionary orders. The cathedral of Mexico City was begun in 1585 and became the model for others further south, such as Puebla in Mexico and Lima and Cuzco in Peru. The architect mainly responsible for the cathedral of Mexico City was Claudio de Arciniega, a Spaniard by birth, who took as his model the cathedral of Jaén in Andalusia. These cathedrals are hall-churches, with three aisles of almost equal height, separated by Classical columns of awkwardly elongated proportions.

The style employed in Spanish America in the sixteenth century survived till very late, and in Mexico there are no new developments to notice till the early eighteenth century. In Peru – perhaps owing to the enormous wealth derived from the gold and silver mines – architects were more adventurous, and an original form of church façade was invented, of which examples are to be found at Lima (San Francisco) and Cuzco (the cathedral and the Jesuit church, or Compañía), all dating from about the middle of the century. The design consists of a series of steeply stilted arches, of which the one over the door is usually interrupted by a niche or window. The curves of this lower register are repeated above in a cornice which curves over three round-headed windows, and yet again in the sky-line which, in the cathedral at Cuzco, consists of a curved pediment flanked by two lower half-pediments, but in the Compañía takes on a cusped form, covered by a heavy, almost Borrominesque, entablature.

This type of structure is also found in gilded, wooden altars in

Peruvian churches, and it is possible that the design may originally have been invented for wood and only later transferred to stone. An analogy could be found with certain types of sixteenth- and early seventeenth-century façades of Spanish churches, which seem to be derived from the many-tiered high altars of slightly earlier date. This type of façade has some resemblance to that of the cathedral of Santiago de Compostela and, more closely, to the Gatehouse of Santa Clara in the same town, but these both date from the mid-eighteenth century, and it seems that in this case the form was invented in the colonies and imported thence into Spain. It is often suggested that the Late Baroque of Andalusia and the sacristy of the Cartuja at Granada were influenced from Mexico, but this is certainly untrue, and the 'Cuzco façade' seems to be a very rare – perhaps unique – example of influence flowing back to the mother country.

The façades of the Cuzco churches include pairs of rather squat towers, a pattern familiar in Spain since the sixteenth century, but the towers now take on a new and interesting form, ending in domed octagonal turrets, surrounded by four smaller turrets or domes. It is almost as if the architect had transferred the traditional arrangement of a central dome with four sub-sidiary domes from the crossing of a church to the tops of the towers.

From the point of view of planning or spatial invention, there are hardly any churches in the Spanish Colonies which deserve to be called Baroque (the Capilla del Pocito at Guadalupe, near Mexico City, is one of the few examples which qualify), and the most remarkable churches of the eighteenth century carry on the tradition of Andalusian architecture with its use of the *estipite*, probably transplanted to Mexico by Lorenzo Rodríguez, a pupil of Hurtado, who built the façade of the Sagrario attached to the Cathedral of Mexico City and several other churches of importance, including the Santísima Trinidad in Mexico City and probably that of Tepotzotlán. In these churches and in others in much the same style at Taxco and Ocotlan façades and altars are composed exclusively of *estipites*, arranged in layers and of a bewildering variety of shapes, some purely decorative, others broadening out in the middle, so that they can hold niches with statues. Only the doors and the framing-piers of the façades show any architectural features at all, and inside the churches the *estipites* cover the walls, leaving only the pilasters and arches visible. The effect is heightened by the use of gold-leaf, which covers all the ornament of the interiors,

388

401
429

producing sparkling reflections from sun or candlelight. These churches have even less claim than the sacristy of the Cartuja of Granada to be called Baroque. Every decorative element is taken from the Late Mannerist vocabulary – in the cases quoted above from Dietterlin, in others, such as the Capilla del Rosario in the church of Santo Domingo at Puebla, from French engravings – and the manner in which the *estipites* are clustered can also be paralleled with engravings of Dietterlin. In view of these points the term 'neo-Mannerist' suggested for the Cartuja sacristy seems even more appropriate here.

The decoration of these Mexican churches was carried out by Indian craftsmen, who were heirs to a great tradition of decorative stone-sculpture from their Maya or Aztec ancestors, but the suggestion that they introduced elements of their

Portugal and Brazil

The history of Portuguese Baroque architecture can never be fully written because, when the earthquake of 1755 destroyed the whole centre of Lisbon, it annihilated all the evidence about the architecture of what was certainly the most important centre of building activities in the country, so we can now only piece together a picture of Portuguese architecture in the seventeenth and early eighteenth centuries from the buildings remaining in less important centres, such as Evora, Tomar and Oporto.[1]

For part of the period under consideration – the years 1580–1640 – Portugal was under Spanish domination, but her

403 *Above* Peru, Cuzco, façade of the Jesuit Church (The Compañia)

404 *Above* Oporto, choir of the church of São Bento

ancient pagan symbolism in the decoration of Christian churches seems to be without foundation. At most one can say that the love of rich, overall decoration was typical of both Maya and Aztec architecture, and that the ecclesiastical authorities realized that the glittering gold interiors would impress on the Indians the power of the Church and therefore encouraged the style, but in all fundamental respects it derives from Spanish models and was designed by architects who usually had been born and trained in the mother country. It is only in remote districts and usually at a later date that the design of the decoration is so clumsy as to suggest that it is due to an Indian artist.

architecture always remained distinct from that of her neighbour, and in the two periods of her great wealth – the Age of Discovery in the reign of Manuel I (1495–1521) and the Age of Brazilian Gold under João V (1707–50) – Portugal produced architecture of real distinction and originality, though, owing presumably to the position of the country, it never made any contribution to the mainstream of European Baroque.

In the basic elements of its make-up the Manueline style is the Portuguese equivalent of the Spanish Plateresque, but it has marked characteristics of its own and in its greatest achievements – the unfinished chapels at Batalha, or the church of the Hieronymites at Belém – it reaches a grandeur in conception

405 Bom Jesus, near Braga, steps to the pilgrimage-church. Begun 1727, the church dates from the 1780s

and a controlled fantasy of decoration which has no parallel elsewhere in Europe. In particular the door of the chapel at Batalha has a use of interlacing curves which was to reappear in much Portuguese Baroque, notably in the architecture of Oporto and the Minho district in the north of the country.

About the middle of the sixteenth century this ornate style gave way to a more strictly Italianate manner, and in the cloister at Tomar (begun 1557) the most talented architect of the period, Diogo de Torralva (1500–66), produced a monumental design fully in the spirit of the Italian High Renaissance. Diogo de Torralva was Spanish by birth, and the cloister has something of the severity of Herrera's architecture, but it is enlivened by the use of deep Serlian arches on the upper storey, which create dramatic contrasts of light and shade.

This severity continued for more than a century and can be seen in the façade of two typical churches of the period: São Vicente de Fora in Lisbon (begun 1582), which miraculously survived the earthquake of 1755, and the Jesuit São Lourenço (the 'Grilos') at Oporto (1614–22). São Vicente, which is by the Italian architect Filippo Terzi, is the more regular of the two, but the Portuguese architect of the Grilos, Baltasar Álvares, has introduced curious features, such as secondary pediments overlapping both the towers and the central frontispiece, which give a broken, Mannerist character to the whole design.

During the seventeenth century the austerity of the earlier period was relaxed. The practice of decorating churches with *azulejos* or coloured tiles, which had begun in the later sixteenth century, became more widely employed, and from being mere repeating patterns the *azulejos* became – like the tapestries of the period – whole compositions, often reproducing paintings or engravings. At the same time the use of carved wood decoration, usually gilded, became common, and this form of decoration was much more extensively used in the first half of the eighteenth century, when the discovery of Brazilian gold had made the metal readily available for decoration in the form of gold-leaf. Walls and vaults of the churches could be entirely covered with intricate gilt wood-carving in high relief. In the north of Portugal the decoration often incorporated mediaeval

406 *Above* Lamego, façade of the pilgrimage-church of Nossa Senhora dos Remédios, 1750–60

407 *Opposite* Coimbra, the library of the University, probably designed by Gaspar Ferreira and decorated by Claudio de Laprada, 1716–28

features. For instance, the high altars of the Dominican church at Aveiro and at São Bento at Oporto are framed in what is almost a Romanesque arch with rows of half-cylindrical mouldings – enveloped, admittedly, in very un-Romanesque foliage. In the church of São Francisco at Oporto the effect is more bizarre – and perhaps less successful – because the decoration is applied to a late Gothic building, the slender arches of

404

which do not provide the solid surface needed by the rich and heavy ornament. Portuguese architects of the late seventeenth and eighteenth centuries invented one unusual type of plan for their churches, based on an oval or, more usually, an elongated octagon, with corridors flanking the choir and leading to the sacristy, usually covered by galleries. Externally churches became more impressive, partly through the increased richness of their decoration, and partly because of the dramatic situations in which they were placed. Both these features are well illustrated in two great places of pilgrimage in the north of Portugal: Bom Jesus near Braga, begun in 1727, and Nossa Senhora dos Remédios at Lamego, built between 1750 and 1760 (the towers were only finished in the nineteenth century, but certainly according to the original design). Both churches stand at the top of steep flights of steps, flanked by chapels containing representations of the Stations of the Cross, and ornamented with urns and obelisks which, at Bom Jesus, are continued by box-trees cut into conical shapes. At the top is a sort of *piazza*, from which the pilgrim ascends to the church by further steps – at Lamego a repeated double-flight of straight steps, at Bom Jesus a pair of curved flights. The church of Bom Jesus was not begun till the 1780s and already has something of the coldness of Neo-Classicism, but at Lamego the façade has the liveliness typical of Northern Portuguese Baroque. The sky-line is a variant of Borromini's Oratory pediment, ending in an extra curve on each side, and the façade itself, although articulated with rather heavy Doric pilasters, is enlivened by windows with curved frames, lifted pediments and tassels hanging from their sills. Both these churches are broad in their proportions, but some of the churches of the north are marked by their tallness. In the case of the Clerigos in Oporto, built by a Tuscan, Nicola Nasoni, who lived and worked in Oporto from 1725 to 1773, the tower rises to a height of 250 feet, has a projecting balcony in the top-stage, almost like the tower of the mediaeval Palazzo Comunale in Nasoni's native Siena, and is possibly unique in having the two corners adjoining the church cut off straight by a plane at an angle of 45° to the sides, whereas the other two are rounded and broken by clustered pilasters.

The Baroque buildings of Northern Portugal depend to a great extent for their effect on the hard dark-brown granite in which the architectural features are executed. Occasionally, as in the church of Santos Passos at Oporto, the effect is heightened by the use of *azulejos* on the façade, but usually the stone stands out in dramatic contrast to the whitewashed walls. At Bom Jesus and Lamego the forms are simple, but in other cases, for instance in the chapel of Santa Maria Madalena near Braga, which dates from 1783, the carvings round the door burst into the wildest Rococo forms.

The most remarkable expression of this style is, however, to be found in a series of town-houses built in Braga and Guimarães in the decades after 1750, when the district enjoyed a great revival of prosperity owing to the appointment as archbishops of Braga – who were also primates of Portugal – of two illegitimate members of the royal family. In these houses the forms invented by Borromini are developed with a degree of fantasy that they never attained elsewhere, except perhaps in South Germany. The town-hall at Braga is relatively simple, except in the middle bay, where the niche is covered by a flower-

like hood and the pediment curves up steeply in an almost Late Gothic ogee-curve, but in the Raio house at Braga and in the Lobo-Machado house at Guimarães all the windows have hoods of extreme complexity. In the former they are of two types: in one, Borromini's favourite form, which he invented for the Palazzo Barberini and used to the end of his life, as at S. Carlino, is given an extra curve at the end – almost as on the façade of Lamego – and then the straight ends are slanted downwards; in the other the middle-section of the hood is almost rectilinear, but it ends in S-curves, and under the central section are three heavy voussoirs. In the middle bay the jambs of the doors, which are composed of scrolls at top and bottom, are canted, and the pattern is repeated for the window above with even livelier scrolls, two of which support statues. The Lobo-Machado house is more restrained. The outer windows are fairly close to Borromini in design, but the pediments of the inner ones are broken in a manner unknown to him or to his Italian followers. The whole design is framed by pilasters which are unfluted but have fantastic asymmetrical capitals and support a splendid, richly moulded cornice – it cannot really be seen as a full entablature – which moves to a climax in a Borrominesque 'pediment' in the central bay. The cornice must originally have formed the sky-line, and its effect is weakened by the addition of an attic which bears no clear relation to the façade below.

The wealth which King João V derived from his royal fifth share of the gold discovered in Brazil enabled him – like his contemporary Philip V of Spain – to build on a greater scale. He evidently felt – perhaps rightly – that there were no Portuguese architects capable of conceiving buildings of the grandeur that he envisaged, and he turned to other countries for suitable candidates. His first choice, Juvarra, was in every way logical, since in his capacity as architect to the duke of Savoy, king of Sicily and later of Sardinia, he was engaged on enterprises of similar magnitude, but in fact the plans which he provided for a new palace in Lisbon were never carried out, and when in 1717 the king had to choose an architect for his most ambitious project, the convent-palace at Mafra, north of Lisbon, he selected a German, Johann Friedrich Ludwig (1670–1752), known in Portugal as Ludovice, who had been trained – mainly in Rome – as a goldsmith. The result was a vast building – larger than the Escorial – which, rather surprisingly, is of chilling architectural purity. The general plan is reminiscent of certain German monasteries, such as Weingarten in Ludwig's native Swabia, but the interior of the church derives from Roman sources, in particular the works of Carlo Fontana and his school, and the sculpture was commissioned from the most currently popular Roman artists.

Like Mafra the Royal Library, built between 1716 and 1728 and presented by João V to the University of Coimbra, was the result of collaboration between a team of international artists, but the result is a harmonious unity, clearly Portuguese in its total effect. It has been suggested that the design was made by Ludwig, but it has nothing in common with his work and is more likely to be by the local architect, Gaspar Ferreira, who was in charge of the building. The question is not of great importance, because the plan – a sequence of three rectangular rooms – is the least interesting feature of the library, which depends for its effect on its richly carved and gilded decoration. This is almost certainly by Claudio de Laprada, a French artist from Avignon, who had worked in Portugal since before 1700 and who probably designed the magnificent book-

408 *Opposite* Toledo, Cathedral, detail of the Transparente by Narciso Tomé, 1721

cases, painted black or red in alternate rooms and decorated with Chinoiserie scenes by the Tessinese artist Giorgio Domenico Duprà. The ceilings were decorated with illusionist frescoes by two Portuguese artists, Antonio Simões Ribeiro and Vicente Nunes.

The elements of which the decoration of the library is composed are extraordinarily disparate. The ceiling frescoes are Italian Baroque; the carved, gilt wood-work on the piers and round and over the full-length portrait of the king remind one of the interior of a North Portuguese church; but the pendentives which project from the soffits of the arches would not be out of place in an Elizabethan hall, and are certainly derived from Flemish engravings. The pilasters which support the galleries are in the *Régence* style, but the designer has made them taper to such an extent at the bottom that they hardly seem strong enough to carry the load which they have to bear.

In spite of the variety of components, the total effect of the library is one not only of gaiety but of unity. This is partly achieved by the careful control of the colour, which is dominated by the gold of the carving – broken with white, so that it does not seem heavy – which is carried on into the book-shelves and even into the gilt calf bindings of the books; warm colours are continued in the lacquer-red of the book-cases in the middle room, in the frescoed ceilings, and in the dull plum-colour of the marble floor – again broken with white; but unity is also imposed by the skilful control of the massing of the decoration, building up from the almost feminine delicacy of the book-shelves through the more massive decoration of the piers, to the climax in the portrait with its swinging drapery and canopy, topped by the trophy and the huge crowned coat-of-arms, which is repeated over the arches separating the three rooms which form the library.

In 1747, three years before his death, João V, perhaps because he had been frustrated in his plans to attract a major Italian architect to Portugal, tried another device and commissioned two of the most famous Roman architects of the day, Luigi Vanvitelli – later famous as the builder of Caserta – and Niccolò Salvi, the designer of the Trevi fountain, to produce for him a chapel which was to be entirely constructed in Rome and then dismantled, after being seen and blessed by the Pope, Benedict XIV, and shipped to Lisbon, where it was re-erected in the church of São Roco. As would be expected, the chapel is a pure example of Late Roman Baroque, literally transplanted to Lisbon, and exceptional only in the richness of materials, the inlay being in agate, onyx, and other semi-precious stones. It seems to have had no effect on the evolution of architecture in Portugal.

Apart from the great aquaduct built by João V between 1729 and 1748 to bring the Aguas Livres (Free Waters) to Lisbon, which, magnificent as it is, stands a little outside the history of Baroque architecture, the only other major royal building scheme of the reign, the palace at Queluz, was due not to the king but to his younger son, Dom Pedro. The palace was built in two campaigns. The main buildings were put up between 1747 and 1752 to the designs of the Portuguese architect Mateus Vicente de Oliveira (1706–86), who had worked with Ludwig at Mafra, but the garden front was extended in 1758 by two one-storey wings after the designs of the Frenchman Jean-Baptiste Robillon (d. 1782), who had been trained under the famous silversmith Thomas Germain.

For the general design of the garden façade, which consists of seven bays of two floors articulated by pilasters, with the middle

409 *Opposite* Oporto, exterior of the church of Santos Passos by André Ribeiro Soares, 1767–98

410 *Above* Guimarães, façade of the Lobo-Machado house

three bays covered by a straight pediment, Oliveira turned to an obvious French model, the Château of Marly, built as a country retreat for Louis XIV by J. H. Mansart, but he made a number of variations which changed the character of his design, in certain ways bringing it into line with later French taste, but also introducing elements which were entirely un-French. The façade at Marly was articulated with giant pilasters standing on high pedestals. Oliveira leaves out the pedestals and makes the pilasters spring from the ground – an arrangement justified by French precedent in Le Vau's Louvre designs – and he reduces the articulation to single pilasters at the corners and single pilasters supported by quarter-pilasters under the central pediment. In thus reducing the number of pilasters, Oliveira was following the taste of his French contemporaries in the designing of private *hôtels*, but he did not go as far as his Parisian colleagues who generally eliminated the Order altogether. In the shape of the windows, with their flattened

tops, he again followed French models, but in the hoods over them he broke away altogether from French taste and introduced curved pediments, which derive–at however many removes–from Borromini rather than from J.H. Mansart. Finally a local touch is given to the whole by the pink-washed walls of the palace itself and the blue and white ceramic pots which ornament the *parterre* in front of it.

The wings added in the second phase by Robillon follow French models, but with the addition of rather mean swags over the windows and heavy balustrades against the low roofs. The most remarkable feature of this added section is the ball-room, executed by Silvestre de Faria Lobo after the designs of the French decorator Antoine Collin. The design is somewhat conservative, for the walls are articulated with *Régence* pilas-

411 *Above* Queluz, garden façade of the Royal Palace by Mateus Vicente de Oliveira, 1747–52

412 *Opposite* Queluz, the ball-room by Silvestre de Faria Lobo after Antoine Collin, after 1758

ters, some of which end in herm-atlantes, and the central section of the ceiling, in the form of a cusped dome, goes back to the designs of Daniel Marot, but the decoration itself is in a fine and delicate Rococo style, which avoids the asymmetry and shell-forms characteristic of the 1730s and 1740s and seems to show an awareness of the tendency towards greater Classicism which marked French decoration of the 1750s.

The last chapter in the history of the Baroque in Portugal

centres mainly round the rebuilding of Lisbon after the earth-quake of 1755. This was made possible by the energy of the king's powerful minister, the Marques de Pombal, after whom the style of the period is called 'Pombaline'. The architect in charge of the replanning and rebuilding of the city was Eugênio dos Santos (1711–60), assisted by the Hungarian Carlos Mardel (active 1733–63). The lay-out of the city was planned round the Praça do Comércio, which occupied three sides of a rectangle facing the waterfront of the Ebro. In plan and in function as the business centre of the city it was like the Place de la Bourse facing the Garonne at Bordeaux, designed by Jacques V Gabriel some twenty years earlier, but the detail is Roman, not, however, based on Borromini but on the classicizing Roman architecture of the time as represented by Galilei, Fuga and Vanvitelli. The houses on the streets radiating from the square, however, have a functional simplicity not to be paralleled anywhere in Europe, a simplicity partly imposed by the ne-cessity of economy after the disaster of the earthquake.

At the same time many churches in Lisbon were recon-structed in a style which combines Borrominesque details in, for instance, the design of windows or pediments, with a severe use of the Orders and simplicity in the general planning or ele-vation, which reflects the Classical tendencies of the period.

In Oporto, which had been the centre of a lively Baroque style, the reaction towards Classicism happened earlier than in the South, partly through the influence of the powerful English colony which controlled the port-trade with England. An example of this influence is the fact that the hospital of São Antonio, begun in 1769, was designed by John Carr of York and is one of the largest and most impressive English Palladian buildings outside the British Isles. This neo-Palladian move-ment in the north, like the Italo-French Pombaline style in Lisbon, prepared the way for the full Neo-Classicism which dominated Portugal, as it did the rest of Europe, in the last years of the eighteenth century.

Brazil

The Portuguese carried European ideas with them to their colonies in all parts of the world, and in cities like Goa they erected buildings which show a charming mixture of local and European features, but it was only in Brazil that they created a real school of architectural design.[2]

The Portuguese discovered Brazil in 1500, but its potential-ities as a colony were not realized for more than a century. As a result there is no Manueline equivalent in Brazil to the Plater-esque churches of Mexico. Presumably the churches erected during this period were simple wooden structures, which have not survived. In the second half of the seventeenth century the severe style of church architecture which had prevailed in Portugal half a century earlier was introduced to such centres as São Salvador (Bahia), where the church of São Bento survives as an example of the style, most of the others having been either rebuilt or redecorated at a later date.

It was not till the discovery of gold in the province of Minas Gerais in 1693 that Brazil really began to prosper, but for nearly a century from that date Ouro Preto, the capital of the province, was one of the richest cities in the world, though much of its wealth spread to other parts of Brazil and to the mother country. This wealth was accompanied by an astonishing outburst of building activity, parallel to that of Mexico and Peru in the great days of the silver boom.

The relation of Brazilian to Portuguese architecture differs

413 Brazil, Bahia (São Salvador), detail of the nave of the church of São Francisco

from that of Mexico to Spain in several fundamental ways. Whereas in Mexico the Spaniards found a body of craftsmen trained in a great tradition of sculpture who could be employed on the building and decoration of their churches, the Indians of Brazil had hardly advanced beyond the Bronze Age and had no stone buildings or sculpture. The result was that artists– whether architects or sculptors–were completely dependent on the home country. Architects and sculptors came from Portugal to Brazil (in much greater numbers than from Spain to Mexico), and in many cases sculpture and architectural details, such as doors and windows, were carved in Portugal and shipped to Brazil as ballast, to be set up in the churches being built.

In plan Brazilian churches follow Portuguese models. Many are simple rectangles in form, and others have the elongated oval or octagon familiar in many churches in the north of the home country. Architects often used the twin-towered façade, but they introduced unusual variations on these models. In many cases the towers are round instead of square and, if they are square, they are sometimes canted at an angle of 45° to the plane of the façade itself, as at the Concecão de Praia at Bahia. In both cases the arrangement adds an effect of movement to the façade.

In the interiors gilding is used lavishly, usually over deeply cut wood carving or stucco moulding, as, for instance, at São Bento in Rio de Janeiro or São Francisco at Bahia. These interiors often include the gilded 'Romanesque' type of altar familiar in central Portuguese churches of the period. In more

413

remote districts the decoration, whether painted or carved, often has a certain rustic charm. As in Mexico, decorators had to rely on engravings for their models, and sometimes their choice was unexpected, as in the church of Nossa Senhora do Ó at Sabará, where the choir-stalls are painted with charming Chinoiserie scenes.

In the second half of the eighteenth century Brazil produced one architect-sculptor of real originality, Antonio Francisco Lisboa (1738–1814), called O Aleijadinho, 'the Cripple', because of a natural disability, the nature of which is still a matter of dispute.[3] He received some training as a sculptor from his father

and probably from a Portuguese die-engraver who worked for the royal mint at Rio, and – *pace* his admirers who speak of him as a great sculptor, even sculptor of genius – this training, coupled with a certain natural talent, would account for his achievement as a sculptor, of which the most remarkable manifestation is the series of life-size figures of prophets on the terrace in front of the church at Congoñas do Campo, vigorous, moving, but provincial.

On the other hand, his architecture – or to be more precise his architectural sculpture – is not only vigorous but highly sophisticated and seems to imply a personal knowledge of what had been produced in northern Portugal in the middle of the century. There is no evidence to show that Aleijadinho visited Portugal, but our knowledge of his career is fragmentary, and it

414 Brazil, São João del Rei, façade of the church of São Francisco by Aleijadinho

of the wall, and in the door of São Francisco at Ouro Preto this arrangement is carried over into the richly moulded architrave, thus creating a wave-movement of a kind which Meissonnier might have used in a two-dimensional engraving, but which few architects were bold enough to execute in three dimensions in stone. The movement in the architrave becomes even more complex across the top of the door. In elevation this has a form reminiscent of Manueline Gothic, but Aleijadinho gives it added richness by making it break forward and back half-way along the curve. The design culminates in an outburst of high-relief sculpture, rising over the door to the round window above, composed of wing-like forms, growing into shells, cut parchment, or skin – a device we have noticed in Spain – naturalistic flowers and ribbons, centring on a crown of thorns, above which rises a roundel containing a high-relief figure of the Virgin. All this is executed in the warm brown stone, streaked with greenish veins, locally called soapstone, which takes deeply cut carving even better than the granite of northern Portugal.

These doors of Aleijadinho represent a very high point in the development of Luso-Brazilian Baroque architecture, and their influence in Minas Gerais was enormous. Though none of his successors were his equals in inventive power, respectable works were still being produced in the style in the last decades of the eighteenth century, though the interior decoration of churches was gradually modified by the infusion of foreign elements, usually French. The church of the Rosario at Ouro Preto, is an unusual example of foreign influence because its façade is based on Fischer von Erlach's Kollegienkirche at Salzburg – a reminder of the fact that many of the religious orders responsible for the building of churches were international and not composed solely of members who were Portuguese by blood.

254

415 Brazil, São João del Rei, door of the church of the Carmo

is hard to believe that he could have acquired from drawings or descriptions the understanding of the Portuguese originals which his works seem to involve, and the possibility of a visit to the home country in his youth must be kept in mind.

Aleijadinho's most important buildings are to be found in Ouro Preto and the neighbouring town – also based on gold-mining – of São João del Rei, in each of which he built the Franciscan and Carmelite churches. Architecturally they conform to a normal Brazilian type, with twin-towered façades, sometimes with round towers, but their great novelty lies in their carved doors.

In their basic features these doors derive from the palaces of Braga and Guimarães, but Aleijadinho develops the style to a quite new imaginative level. In the Portuguese palaces the architraves surrounding the doors were kept fairly simple, though the pilasters flanking them were replaced by more complicated elements, canted and sometimes composed of scrolls. In Aleijadinho's doors the scrolls are broken in the middle by a kind of cusp projecting at right angles to the plane

Epilogue

About the middle of the eighteenth century a conscious return to the ideals of Classical antiquity in all European countries led to a revulsion against the Baroque and the Rococo. Architects were required once again to follow the precepts of Vitruvius, and Winckelmann and the group of enthusiasts round Cardinal Alessandro Albani proclaimed the supremacy of Greek art. The works unearthed at Herculaneum and Pompei gave a first impulse towards a return to Classicism but the 'discovery' of ancient Greek architecture – in Southern Italy and Sicily and then in Greece itself – gave substance to the claims of Winckelmann and led to an even more severely Classical doctrine.

In this scheme of things there was no place for the Baroque or the Rococo. The inventiveness of the former was condemned as license and the elegance of the latter as frivolity. Bernini and above all Borromini became monsters who had corrupted architecture, and even Michelangelo was condemned as the source of many errors. For more than a century and a half Baroque art received nothing but abuse from art historians. To the French it offended against the canons of le bon goût; to the Germans it was a licentious decadence from the art of the Renaissance; the Italians, who were inescapably surrounded by it, simply ignored it. English distaste for Baroque architecture sprang originally from a deeply ingrained belief that Palladio was the ideal architect, and English Palladians of the eighteenth century were among the most violent critics of Borromini and his contemporaries. Their Neo-Classical successors were almost equally vociferous, still on purely artistic grounds; but in the nineteenth century a new element appears in English criticism of the style, based on a Protestant suspicion of anything Roman Catholic: Baroque art was 'irreligious', 'profane', almost blasphemous, criticisms which can often be heard levelled at the style by English visitors to Rome or Naples today.

A new approach towards the Baroque first began to appear among German art historians of the 1880s. At first appreciation of the style was limited to specialists, but by the early years of the twentieth century interest spread more widely and in the years immediately after the First World War several general histories of the period were published in German. In addition detailed research began to be carried out on both Italian Baroque and that of Germany and Austria. The Italians slowly followed suit, though more with studies of individual artists or buildings than with general works. The French remained obdurately opposed to what they called – quite unreasonably – 'le style Jésuite'. It was, however, a French scholar, Emile Mâle, who is his L'Art Religieux après le Concile de Trente published in 1932, produced the first survey of the new iconography of the Baroque period.

England produced an isolated pioneer in the architect Martin Shaw Briggs whose book In the Heel of Italy, published in 1910, contains an enthusiastic account of the eighteenth-century architecture of Lecce. Later, in the 1920s, Osbert and Sacheverell Sitwell made the Baroque more widely known in a series of books which were as much concerned with the atmosphere of Southern Italy and Spain as with their architecture. In the years before and after the Second World War the study of the subject in English was greatly enriched by the arrival in England and the United States of German scholars such as Sir Nikolaus Pevsner and, above all, the late Rudolf Wittkower, whose books on the Baroque remain the most profound and satisfying treatments of the subject.

Now all German and American – and many British – universities have higher degree students preparing theses on the Baroque; guides conducting tours round Italy no longer pass hastily in front of Baroque churches with eyes averted; courses of lectures on the Baroque are given not only in university departments of art history but for adult education and other bodies with more general interests. Exhibitions of the previously despised Seicento and Settecento Italian paintings now draw large crowds, and coffee-table books on Baroque buildings are the stock-in-trade of Italian banks with capital to spare.

All these are the external manifestations of the fact that after its long period of neglect the Baroque is once more recognized as worthy to take its place beside the Gothic or Renaissance periods, as one of the great and creative periods of European art.

416 *Overleaf* Putto from the church of Neu-Birnau by Joseph Anton Feichtmayr

Notes and Bibliography

Introduction

1 The only general books on the Baroque in English are Norberg-Schulz's two volumes *Baroque Architecture* and *Late Baroque and Rococo Architecture* (New York, 1971). The best surveys of the period are the two admirably illustrated volumes of the *Propyläen Kunstgeschichte* (text in German): H. Hubala, *Die Kunst des 17ten Jahrhunderts*, and H. Keller, *Die Kunst des 18ten Jahrhunderts* (Berlin, 1970 and 1971). For a discussion of the meanings attached to the term Baroque see V.L. Tapié, *Baroque et Classicisme* (Paris, 1957) translated into English as *The Age of Grandeur. Baroque and Classicism in Europe* (London, 1960). For a general treatment of all the arts of the period see M. Kitson *The Age of Baroque* (London, 1966).

The history of Baroque architecture in individual countries is covered in many of the volumes of the Pelican History of Art mentioned in the sections below. Of these, R. Wittkower's *Art and Architecture in Italy 1600–1750* (Harmondsworth, 1973), now available in paperback, must be mentioned here since it contains brilliant analyses not only of Italian buildings but also of the basic problems of the Baroque as a whole.

For a good account of the Counter-Reformation and the Catholic Revival see the appropriate volume of the Cambridge Modern History.

2 For an analysis of the iconography of the painting of the Counter-Reformation and the seventeenth century, see E. Mâle, *L'Art religieux après le Concile de Trente* (Paris, 1932).

3 The relation of the Baroque to ancient architecture is discussed in A. Blunt's introduction to the section 'Baroque and Antiquity' in the *Acts of the Twentieth Congress of Art History* (New York, 1960; Princeton, 1963), III, pp 3ff., and his review of Margaret Lyttelton's very useful book, *Baroque Architecture in Classical Antiquity* (London, 1974), in the *Burlington Magazine* (CXVIII, 1976, pp 320ff.).

4 For a full discussion of the original application of the word *Baroque*, see O. Kurz, 'Barocco: Storia di una parola', *Lettere Italiane*, XII, 1960, pp 414ff., and 'Barocco: Storia di un Concetto', in *Barocco Europeo e Barocco Veneziano* (Florence, 1963), pp 15ff. For a summary of the later uses of the word as an art-historical term, see A. Blunt, *Some Uses and Misuses of the Terms Baroque and Rococo as applied to Architecture* (Oxford, 1973), pp 5ff.

5 Milizia was the author of lives of individual architects *(Le Vite dei più celebri Architetti d'ogni Tempo* (Rome, 1768), to which he added a general essay on the Neo-Classical view of architecture.

6 J. Burckhardt, *Die Kultur der Renaissance in Italien* (Stuttgart, 1860) and *Der Cicerone* (Basle, 1855). The theme of the Baroque is treated with greater sympathy in some of his later letters. Wilhelm Lübke, *Geschichte der Kunst* (translated by C. Cook, New York, 1879). Gurlitt, *Geschichte des Barockstils* (Stuttgart, 1887). H. Wölfflin, *Renaissance und Barock* (Munich, 1888); translation by Peter Murray (London, 1964), and *Kunstgeschichtliche Grundbegriffe* (Munich, 1915); translation by M.D. Hottinger under the title *The Principles of Art History* (London, 1932).

7 Max Dvořák's most important essay was translated as *El Greco and Mannerism* in the *Magazine of Art*, 1952. Walter Friedlaender, *Mannerism and Anti-Mannerism in Italian Painting* (translated from the German, New York, 1957). In 1921 W. Weisbach published *Der Barock als Kunst der Gegenreformation*, in which he identified the Baroque as reflecting the Counter-Reformation, but this view was challenged in a review by N. Pevsner who pointed out that late Mannerism was the art that really reflected the spirit of Trent and that the Baroque reflected the later stage of the Catholic Revival.

8 R. Hamann, *Geschichte der Kunst* (Berlin, 1933).

9 Eugenio d'Ors, *Teoria de los Estilos y espejo dela Arquitectura* (Madrid, n.d.).

10 The origin and early use of the term *Rococo* is discussed by Fiske Kimball in *The Creation of the Rococo* (Philadelphia, 1943, pp 3ff.). For a fuller discussion of the concept as a whole see J.P. Minguet, *L'Esthétique du Rococo* (Paris, 1966).

Part I Italy

Rome

1 The whole field of Italian Baroque is admirably covered in R. Wittkower, *Art and Architecture in Italy 1600–1750* (Pelican History of Art) referred to above, and many important individual themes are treated in his *Studies in Italian Baroque*, (London, 1975).

For plates of Roman Baroque buildings the most useful modern book is P. Portoghesi, *Roma Barocca* (American edition, Cambridge, Mass, 1970; the text however, is difficult in Italian and unintelligible in the American translation). Excellent photographs and reproductions of old engravings are to be found in

various volumes by Cesare d'Onofrio: *Le Fontane di Roma* (Rome, 1962), *Gli Obelischi di Roma* (Rome, 1967). The plates in G. Magni, *Il Barocco a Roma* (Turin, 1911) though old-fashioned as photographs are extremely useful.

Views, plans, and details of Roman Baroque buildings are also recorded in several volumes of engravings published in the late-seventeenth and early-eighteenth centures, of which the most important are the following: Falda, *Nuovo Teatro delle Fabriche di Roma* (Rome, 1665); P. Ferrerio, *Palazzi di Roma* (Rome, late-seventeenth century); and D. Rossi, *Studio d'Architettura Civile* (Roma, 1702–21). These are all available in modern facsimiles issued by the Gregg Press.

Much information can also be gleaned from the old guide books to Rome which are listed in L. Schudt, *Le Guide di Roma* (Vienna, 1940). Among the most useful of these early guides are two published since Schudt wrote, one by Fioravente Martinelli, a friend of Borromini, published by Cesare d'Onofrio under the title *Roma nel Seicento* (Florence, 1969), and the other, G.B. Mola's *Breve Racconto*, written in 1663, published in 1966 (ed. K. Noehles, Berlin). The most thorough guide is that of Titi which first appeared in 1674 and was repeatedly republished with additions. The last edition of 1763 was revised by Giovanni Gaetano Bottari under the title *Descrizione delle Pitture, Sculture, e Architettura esposte al pubblico in Roma*.

The most important early biographies of architects of the period are to be found in a series of works all entitled *Vite de Pittori, Scultori e Architetti* by G. Baglione (Roma, 1642), G.P. Bellori (Rome, 1672), G.B. Passeri (ed. J. Hess, Vienna, 1934), and L. Pascoli (Rome, 1730–36), and F. Baldinucci's *Notizie dei Professori del Disegno* (Florence, 1681–1728). The most important documents about Roman buildings of the period are to be found in O. Pollak, *Die Kunsttätigkeit unter Urban VIII* (Vienna, 1928); J.A.F. Orbaan, *Documenti sul Barocco in Roma* (Rome, 1920); V. Golzio, *Documenti Artistici sul Seicento nell'Archivio Chigi* (Rome, 1939).

2 The best account of the papacy of this period is to be found in Ludwig Pastor's monumental *History of the Popes* (English translation, London, 1952–58).

3 For the patronage of the period, see F. Haskell *Patrons and Painters* (London, 1963) which, though it deals mainly with painting, contains invaluable information about those who commissioned buildings.

Rome 1575–1625

4 For a general account of the architecture of this somewhat neglected period, see H. Hibbard *Carlo Maderno*, (London, 1971) which has a full bibliography. There are unfortunately no serious monographs on the other architects of this period. For plates of Vignola's work see J. Coolidge, W. Lotz *et al*, *La Vita e le Opere di Jacopo Barozzi da Vignola* (Vignola, 1974).

5 See Cesare d'Onofrio, *La Villa Aldobrandini a Frascati* (Rome, 1963).

6 For Maderno, see Hibbard, *op. cit.*

7 See Spagnesi, *Giovanni Antonio de Rossi* (Rome, 1964).

Bernini

8 For a general but comprehensive account of Bernini's life and works, see H. Hibbard, *Bernini* (Harmondsworth, 1965). For more detailed information, see M. Fagiolo dell'Arco, *Bernini* (Rome, 1967), and R. Wittkower, *Gian Lorenzo*

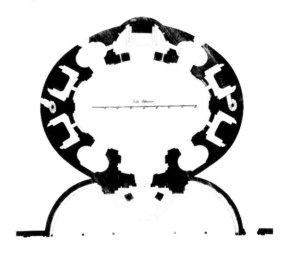

417 Rome, S. Andrea al Quirinale by Bernini, plan, 1658

Bernini (London, second edition, 1966) which, though it deals primarily with Bernini's sculpture, contains much valuable information about his architecture. For the drawings see H. Brauer and R. Wittkower, *Die Zeichnumgen des Gianlorenzo Bernini* (Berlin, 1931).

9 See I. Lavin, *Bernini and the Crossing of St Peter's* (New York 1968). Those who want further information can consult H. Thelen's very difficult *Die Entstehungsgeschichte der Hochaltar-Architektur von St Peter in Rom* (Berlin, 1967).

10 See Wittkower, 'A Counter-Project to Bernini's Piazza', *Studies in Italian Baroque* (London, 1975) p 61, and T.K. Kitao, *Circle and Oval in the Square of St Peter's* (New York, 1974).

11 See Franco Borsi, *La Chiesa di S. Andrea al Quirinale* (Rome, 1967).

12 See A. Braham and H. Hager, *The Drawings of Carlo Fontana at Windsor Castle* (London, 1978).

13 In the 'grand Marot', a volume of engravings published by Jean Marot, without a title.

Borromini

14 The monograph on Borromini (in German) by E. Hempel, *Francesco Borromini* (Vienna, 1924), remains the best treatment of the artist. P. Portoghesi's *Borromini* (Milan, 1967; English edition, London, 1968) has exciting, if often perversely taken, plates and the text is liable to the same criticisms as the author's *Roma Barocca*. A brief monograph by A. Blunt, with a full bibliography, is planned to be published by Alan Lane (London, 1979). For a documented survey of the events of Borromini's life see M. del Piazzo, *Ragguagli Borromini*, the catalogue of an exhibition held in the Archivio di Stato, Rome, 1968. Useful essays are to be found in the *Studi sul Borromini* (*Atti del Congresso Promosso dell'Accademia di San Luca*, Rome, 1967). For Borromini's drawings, see H. Thelen, *Francesco Borromini. Die Handzeichnungen* (Graz, 1967); so far only one volume, covering the early period (not including S. Carlo alle Quattro Fontane), has appeared.

15 The documents about the building of S. Carlino are published by Pollak (*op. cit.* I, pp 257ff.). For a detailed analysis of the formal and iconographical problems concerned see L. Steinberg, *S. Carlo alle Quattro Fontane* (Ph.D. Thesis, Garland, New York, 1977. Steinberg proved that the plans published

by Hempel as being for S. Carlino are for a different church and are probably by the architect's nephew, Bernardo.

16 See Borromini, *Opus architectonicum* (Rome, 1725) which has superb engravings and a long text written by Borromini and his friend Virgilio Spada.

17 For engravings see Borromini, *Opera* (Rome, 1720). The modern literature on S. Ivo is considerable. For the history of the building before Borromini was involved see Thelen, 'Der Palazzo della Sapienza', *Miscellanea Bibliothecae Hertzianae* (Vienna, 1961) p 285. For the iconography and symbolism see H. Ost, 'Borrominis Römische Universitätskirche', *Zeitschrift für Kunstgeschichte*, XXX, 1967, p 101, and P. de la Ruffinière du Prey, 'Salomonic Symbolism in Borromini's Church of S. Ivo della Sapienza', *ibid*, XXXL, 1968, p 215.

Pietro da Cortona

18 The most useful work on Cortona's architecture is K. Noehles, *La Chiesa dei SS. Luca e Martina* (Rome, 1970), which touches on many themes beyond the church which is the nominal subject of the book. Information about Cortona's career as a painter can be obtained from G. Briganti, *Pietro da Cortona* (Florence, 1962).

19 For S. Maria della Pace see the important article by H. Ost, 'Studien zu Pietro da Cortona's Umbau von S. Maria della Pace,' *Römisches Jahrbuch*, XIII, 1971, pp 231ff.

Rome   The last phase

20 See A. Pugliese and S. Rigano, *Martino Lunghi il Giovane, Architetto* (Rome, 1974).

21 See F. Fasolo, *L'Opere di Hieronimo e Carlo Rainaldi* (Rome, 1961).

22 The only work on del Grande is the article by O. Pollak, 'Antonio del Grande', *Kunstgeschichliches Jahrbuch der K.K. Zentral-Kommission*, III, 1909, p 135.

23 On illusionist frescoes see M.C. Gloton, *Trompe-l'oeil et Décor Plafonnant dans les Églises Romaines de l'Age Baroque* (Rome, 1965).

24 On Fontana, there exists a monograph by E. Coudenhove-Erthal (Vienna, 1930) which is now out of date but much valuable information about him is available in A. Braham and H. Hager, *The Drawings of Carlo Fontana at Windsor Castle* (London, 1978).

25 For the architecture of the early eighteenth century, the best plates, together with a fairly reliable summary of information, are to be found in Portoghesi's *Roma Barocca*.

26 For Fuga see G. Matthiae, *Ferdinando Fuga e la sua Opera Romana* (Rome, n.d.) and R. Pane, *Ferdinando Fuga* (Naples, 1954).

27 For the Fontana di Trevi, see d'Onofrio, *Le Fontane di Roma* (Rome).

28 See R. Wittkower, 'Piranesi as architect', *Studies in Italian Baroque* (London-New York, 1975, p 247) and J. Wilton-Ely, *The Mind and Art of Giovanni Battista Piranesi* (London, 1978).

418 *Below left* Naples, Palazzo Sanfelice, staircase by Ferdinando Sanfelice

419 *Below centre* Rome, Oratorio di S. Filippo Neri by Borromini, niche on façade

420 *Below right* Rome, Palazzo Barberini, door by Pietro da Cortona

Northern Italy

Piedmont

1 The most useful survey of the architecture of Turin and Piedmont is R. Pommer, *Eighteenth-Century Architecture in Piedmont* (New York-London, 1967), but much useful information is also to be obtained from the catalogue of the *Mostra del Barocco Piemontese* (Turin, 1963).

2 Guarini's *Architettura Civile* was published in Turin in 1737, and a critical edition with introduction and notes by N. Carbonieri appeared in 1968. The Acts of the Congress on Guarini, held in Turin in 1968, were published under the title, *Guarini e l'internazionalità del Barocco* (Turin, 1970). Good plates of Guarini's works are to be found in M. Passanti, *Nel Mondo Magico di Guarino Guarini* (Turin, 1967).

3 The most important passages are to be found in *Trattato I* chapter 3, observations 6 and 9, and *Trattato III,* chapter 13, observation 1.

4 A monograph on Juvarra by Henry Millon is in preparation. Meanwhile the most useful work on him is the catalogue of the *Mostra de Filippo Juvarra* (Messina, 1966).

5 The *Atti del Convegno internazionale dell'Accademia delle Scienze di Torino* (Turin, 1972) contain papers read at the Congress on all aspects of Vittone's architecture. Two very perceptive articles by R. Wittkower were reprinted in his *Studies in the Italian Baroque* (London, 1975).

Genoa, Lombardy and Emilia

6 There is no detailed treatment of Genoese Baroque architecture, but the subject is well covered in Wittkower's *Art and Architecture in Italy 1600–1750.* For good plates see O. Grosso, *Dimori Genovesi* (Milan, 1956), *Portali e Palazzi Genovesi* (Milan, n.d.) and A. Rossi, *L'Architettura Religiosa Barocca a Genova* (Genoa, 1959).

7 A complete and detailed record of Baroque architecture in the province of Lombardy is to be found in L. Grassi, *Province del Barocco e del Rococo, Lombardia* (Milan, 1966).

8 For a brilliant account of the various projects produced for the façade in the seventeenth and eighteenth centuries see R. Wittkower, *Gothic versus Classic* (New York, 1974).

9 A.M. Matteucci, *Carlo Francesco Dotti e l'Architettura Bolognese del Settecento* (Bologna, 1968).

10 For the architecture of the province of the Romagna, see A. Emiliani, *Architettura e Società del XVIII Secolo in Romagna* (Bologna, 1968). For the secular architecture of Bologna see G. Cuppini, *I Palazzi Senatorii a Bologna* (Bologna, 1974) and *Le Ville Bolognesi* (Bologna, 1967).

11 For the Bibiena family see A. H. Mayor, *The Bibiena Family* (New York, 1945).

Venice

12 The best account of Venetian architecture of the period is to be found in E. Bassi, *Architettura del Sei e Settecento a Venezia* (Naples, 1962).

13 For Longhena see the paper by R. Wittkower reprinted in *Studies in the Italian Baroque* (London, 1975).

The South

1 See however M. Mosco *Itinerario di Firenze Barocca* (Florence, 1974). Curiously enough the authoress does not mention the only major work of the Baroque in Florence, namely the rooms in the Palazzo Pitti decorated by Pietro da Cortona – perhaps because she considers Cortona a purely Roman artist.

2 A detailed account of the architecture of the period in Naples is given in A. Blunt, *Baroque and Rococo Architecture in Naples* (London, 1975).

3 For Fuga see R. Pane, *Ferdinando Fuga* (Naples, 1956). The fullest existing account of Vanvitelli's work is to be found in the volume of essays entitled *Luigi Vanvitelli,* edited by R. de Fusco, R. Pane and others (Naples, 1973). The Acts of the Congress on the architect, held in Naples in 1973, are due for imminent publication.

Sicily

4 For a brief account of Sicilian Baroque architecture, see A. Blunt, *Sicilian Baroque* (London, 1968). To the works listed in the bibliography should be added M. di Simone, *Ville Palermitane del XVII e XVIII Secolo* (Genoa, 1968).

5 For Serpotta, see G. Carandente, *Giacomo Serpotta* (Turin, 1967).

6 For the architecture of Catania see F. Fichera, *G. B. Vaccarini e l'Architettura del Settecento in Sicilia* (Rome, 1934).

Lecce and Apulia

7 A fairly full account of the architecture of Lecce and the Salento is given in M. Calvesi and M. Manieri-Elia, *Architettura Barocca a Lecce e in terra di Puglia* (Milan-Rome, 1971).

Part II   France

Louis XIII and Richelieu

1 For a general account of the architecture of the period see A. Blunt, *Art and Architecture in France 1500–1700,* (Pelican History of Art, Harmondsworth, 1970). For a more detailed treatment with full bibliogrpahy, see L. Hautecoeur, *Histoire de l'Architecture Classique en France,* II and III (Paris, 1948 and 1950). For Richelieu's patronage see L. Battifol, *Autour de Richelieu,* (Paris, 1937).

2 'Between good sense and good taste there is the difference of cause and effect.'

3 The literature on Sublet de Noyers and the Fréart brothers is very inadequate. The monograph by H. Chardon, *Les Frères Fréart* (Le Mans, 1867) contains much biographical material, and A. Fontaine's *Les Doctrines d'Art en France* (Paris, 1909) contains a summary of the views of the Classical party.

4 Sublet, for instance, wrote to Richelieu of 'le mérite et la fidélité' of Lemercier, recommending that he be paid more, on 28 January 1634 – well after Lemercier had entered the Cardinal's service, on the one hand, and, on the other, well before Sublet had officially assumed the functions of Surintendant des Bâtiments (L. Battifol, *Autour de Richelieu,* Paris, 1937, p 162).

5 Sauval in the seventeenth century, for instance, described Lemercier as 'prévoyant, judicieux, profond, solide, en un mot, le premier Architecte de notre siècle, et enfin s'il n'étoit pas le Vitruve de son temps, du moins en étoit-il le Palladio' *(Histoire et Recherches des Antiquités de la Ville de Paris,* I, p 330). To Blondel in the eighteenth century he was 'un grand maître' who had 'le mieux entendu le style convenable aux édifices sacrés', except for François Mansart who was superior in all fields, 'car on peut être un grand homme sans être un Mansart' *(Cours d'Architecture,* III, p 321).

6 A. Blunt, *Art and Architecture in France 1500–1700,* p 118.

7 That is to say the choice of an Order and the manner in which it is applied.

8 P. Moisy, *Les Églises des Jésuites de l'Ancienne Assistance de France* (Rome, 1958).

9 It is also worth noting that in a competition for the design of the transept façades for Sainte-Croix at Orléans in 1626 Lemercier had judged in favour of Martellange amongst entrants including Salomon de Brosse and Jean du Cerceau.

10 .... 'the only accomplished composition that he had seen in Paris'. P. Fréart de Chantelou, *Journal du voyage du Cavalier Bernin en France* (Paris, 1885), p 32 (13 June 1665).

11 Illustrated by Moisy *op. cit.* On the dispute over the façade of St Paul-St Louis see the same author's 'Martellange, Derand et le Conflit du Baroque' in *Bulletin Monumental,* CX, 1952, p 237.

12 *Op. cit.,* p 253 (19 October, 1665).

13 For Mansart, see A. Braham and P. Smith, *François Mansart* (London, 1973).

421 Paris, Sorbonne Chapel by Lemercier, façade

Mazarin and the minority of Louis XIV

14 For Mazarin as a patron see F. Haskell, *Patrons and Painters* (London, 1963), *Mazarin,* ed. by Mongrédien (Paris, 1959) and R. A. Weigert, 'Le Palais Mazarin, Architectes et Décorateurs', *Art de France,* II, 1962, p 147.

15 Illustrated by W. R. Crelly, *The Paintings of Simon Vouet* (New Haven and London, 1962) plates 117, 118.

16 *Ibid* plates 145–52.

17 V. L. Tapié, *The Age of Grandeur* (London, 1960, pp 88ff.).

18 Illustrated by W.R. Berger, *Antoine Le Pautre* (New York, 1969) plates 21–2.

19 There is no monograph on Le Vau, but much information about him can be gleaned from A. Laprade, *François d'Orbay* (Paris, 1960).

20 Discussed and illustrated by J. Montagu, 'The early ceiling paintings of Charles Le Brun', *Burlington Magazine,* CV, 1963, p 395.

Colbert and the maturity of Louis XIV

21 For Colbert see J. B. Colbert, *Lettres, Instructions et Mémoires,* ed. Clément (Paris, 1861–82).

22 'It was not that he particularly liked artists and men of letters; it was as a statesman that he protected them because he recognized that the Arts alone are capable of moulding and immortalizing great empires'. The writer was the Président Hénault.

23 The principal French and Italian projects for the completion of the Louvre are illustrated and discussed by L. Hautecoeur, *Le Louvre et les Tuileries sous Louis XIV* (Paris, 1923) and the same author's *Histoire du Louvre* (Paris, 1928). See also M. Whiteley and A. Braham, 'Louis le Vau's Projects for the Louvre and the Colonnade', *Gazette des Beaux-Arts,* II, 1964, pp 285, 347, where the problem of the authorship, touched on below, is discussed; this problem is further rehearsed by T. Sauval, 'Les Auteurs de la colonnade du Louvre' *Bulletin Monumental* CXXII, p 323.

24 Illustrated and discussed by A. Braham and P. Smith, *op. cit.,* chapter XV.

25 '. . . infuse the feelings of the people with respect and leave them with an impression of its strength'. J. B. Colbert, *Lettres, Instructions, et Mémoires,* ed. Clément (Paris, 1861–82, V, p 245).

26 '. . . But the Cavalier could not be persuaded to go along with it and wished only to follow his fantasy'. Chantelou, *op. cit.,* p 264.

27 Blondel condemned in particular: the impurity of the Order – a composite entablature above Corinthian capitals; the proportions – a balustrade too low for the entablature, windows too small for the diameter of the Order and a basement too low for the height of the Order; the expression and disposition of the Order – half columns, themselves deplorable, mixed with pilasters and unequally spaced, leaving, besides, large tracts of 'murs lisses qui se contredisent avec l'expression Corinthienne'; the arrangement of the openings – paired windows producing solids in the centre of intercolumniations and a transition from windows to arcades in the basement which, unannounced by a change of plane, inadequately emphasized the principal entrance; the division of the façade into a central *avant-corps* equal to half the length of the whole, and unrelated *arrière-corps* and side pavilions; and finally the sculpture – 'des figures gigantesques d'une composition triviale' ridiculously placed beside the main door, and the arms of the king sustained by no member of architecture but merely applied *hors d'oeuvre.*

28 '. . . of which one was adorned with an order of columns forming a peristyle or gallery above the first floor and the other was more simple and unified without an order of columns'. The register has been lost but extracts were published by Piganiol de la Force, *Description de Paris* 1742, II p 628ff.

29 C. Perrault, *Mémoires de ma Vie,* ed. P. Bonnefon (Paris, 1909). For a discussion of the evidence in support of the rival claims, see M. Whiteley and A. Braham, 'Louis Le Vau's projects for the Louvre and the Colonnade', *Gazette des Beaux-Arts,* II, 1964, pp 285, 347, where Le Vau is favoured, and a forthcoming article of my own supporting the Perrault case.

30 The dialogue is recorded in a document published by A. Laprade, *François d'Orbay, architecte de Louis XIV* (Paris, 1960 p 340).

31 Hitherto generally dated to 1664, the engravings of this project – by Olry Deloriandre – are reproduced by Laprade, *op. cit.* plates 2, 3 and Hautecoeur, *Le Louvre et les Tuileries sous Louis XIV,* plate 31.

32 The fact that Claude Perrault was nominated by Colbert to undertake the official translation of Vitruvius would seem to indicate that of all those involved in the design for the completion of the Louvre, he was the one likely to have been best qualified to provide the sort of academic corrections to the Roman High Baroque projects which formed the basis of the scheme actually adopted in 1667. The exact date of the Vitruvius commission is not known but it must have begun to occupy him at least as early as 1667 because the first plates connected with it were engraved in January 1668.

33 The works of Jules Hardouin Mansart are copiously illustrated by P. Bourget and G. Cattaui, *Jules Hardouin Mansart* (Paris, 1960). On Versailles

422 *Above left* Engraving of a triumphal arch designed by Le Brun for the entry of Louis XIV into Paris, 1661

423 *Above right* Paris, Saint Paul-Saint Louis, façade by Derand, 1629

see F. Kimball, 'The genesis of the Château-Neuf at Versailles, 1668–71', *Gazette des Beaux-Arts,* 1949, I, p 353; A Marie, *Naissance de Versailles* (Paris, 1960) and *Mansart à Versailles* (Paris, 1973).

The decline of Louis XIV, the Regency and Louis XV

34 The great contemporary records of the monumental projects of the period, especially beyond the French royal centres, include Boffrand's *Livre d'Architecture* (Paris, 1748) and Patte's *Monuments érigés en France à la gloire de Louis XV* (Paris, 1765). The principal projects are illustrated and discussed by Graf Kalnein in his section of W. Kalnein and M. Levey, *Art and Architecture of the Eighteenth century in France* (London, 1972) and P. du Colombier, *L'Architecture française en Allemagne au XVIII siècle* (Paris, 1956).

35 In particular in the important pioneering work of Fiske Kimball, *The Creation of the Rococo* (Philadelphia, 1943). For works of individual artists connected with the rise of the Rococo see R.A. Weigert, *Jean Bérain* (Paris, 1937); J. Mathey and C. Nordenfalk, 'Watteau and Oppenordt', *Burlington Magazine,* XCVII, 1955, p 132; N. Deshairs, *Nicolas et Dominique Pineau* (Paris, n.d.)

424 Vaux-le-Vicomte by Louis Le Vau, plan

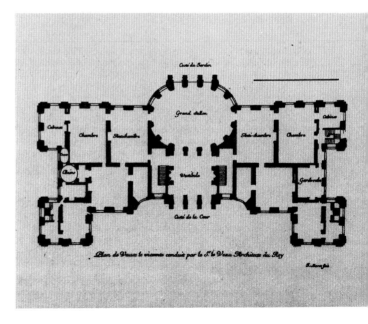

36 'There must be youthfulness in what is done' (quoted by Kimball, *op. cit.* p 58).

37 The engravings made for the *Livre d'Architecture*, post-date the actual work in this case by well over thirty years.

38 'Fountains, cascades, ruins, compositions of rocks and shells, architectural fantasies of bizarre effects, singular and picturesque in virtue of their piquant and extraordinary forms, of which one part rarely responds to another'. The principal engraved works of Meissonnier and his contemporaries are identified and discussed by Kimball, *op. cit.*

39 S. Eriksen, *Early Neo-Classicism in France* (London, 1974) reprints select passages from the writings of the principal critics including J.F. Blondel, the Abbé Le Blanc, C-N. Cochin and T-N. Loyer.

40 For Ange-Jacques Gabriel see E. de Fels, *Ange-Jacques Gabriel* (Paris, 1912) and my own monograph on the architect (London, 1978).

Part III Flanders, England and Holland

Flanders

1 The most useful general book on Flemish architecture in the seventeenth and eighteenth centuries is still J.H. Plantenga, *L'Architecture religieuse dans l'Ancien Duché du Brabant* (The Hague, 1926), which, in spite of its title, covers civil as well as ecclesiastical architecture.

For Rubens see A. Blunt, 'Rubens and architecture,' *Burlington Magazine*, CXIX, 1977, p 609.

England

1 For the historical background see, for instance, Maurice Ashley's *England in the Seventeenth Century* in the Pelican History of England (revised edition, Harmondsworth, 1975). General studies of the architecture of the period appear in J. Summerson, *Architecture in Britain 1530–1830* (Harmondsworth, 1953 and later editions) and M. Whinney and O. Millar, *English Art 1625–1714* (Oxford, 1957) while biographical details can be found in H.M. Colvin, *Biographical Dictionary of British Architects 1600–1840* (London, 1978). Baroque architecture in England is covered specifically, with many illustrations, in K. Downes, *English Baroque Architecture* (London, 1966).

2 See J. Summerson, 'The Classical Country House in Eighteenth-Century England', *Journal of the Royal Society of Arts*, CVII, July 1959.

3 For Gibbs, B. Little, *The Life and Work of James Gibbs* (London, 1955) should be supplemented by articles by S. Lang and J. Field in *Architectural Review*, CXVI, 1954, and CXXXI, 1962.

4 Campbell published three volumes, in 1715, 1717 and 1725. Reprint in one volume, New York, 1967.

5 Not published until the 5th edition of the *Characteristics* (London, 1732); Reprinted in B. Rand, ed, *Second Characters* (London, 1914).

6 For Jones's activity at court see now H.M. Colvin, ed, *History of the King's Works*, III (London, 1975); also J. Summerson, *Inigo Jones* (Harmondsworth, 1966).

7 See M. Whinney, 'John Webb's drawings for Whitehall Palace', *Walpole Society*, XXXI, 1946.

8 Jones's stage designs are extensively treated in S. Orgel and R. Strong, *Inigo Jones, the Theatre of the Stuart Court* (London, 1973).

9 Royal building of the period is fully and newly documented in H.M. Colvin, ed, *History of the King's Works*, V (London, 1976).

10 See K. Downes, 'Wren and Whitehall in 1664', *Burlington Magazine*, CXIII, 1971.

11 There are portraits at Audley End (Lely) and at Windsor Castle and his flamboyant signature appears in documents of the Royal Works. A monograph is hardly feasible on the basis of present evidence.

12 The Windsor interiors (except the staircases) are illustrated in J.B. Pyne, *Royal Residences* (London, 1819) and the exteriors are recorded in drawings by Paul Sandby (A.P. Oppé, *The Drawings of Paul and Thomas Sandby...at Windsor Castle*, London, 1947). See also Colvin (above, n. 9) and W.H. St J. Hope, *Windsor Castle* (London, 1913).

13 All modern studies of Wren depend on *Parentalia*, compiled by the architect's son and published by his grandson Stephen Wren (London, 1750; facsimile reprint 1965) and on the twenty volumes of the *Wren Society* (1923–43). See J. Summerson, *Wren* (London, 1953); E.F. Sekler, *Wren and his Place in European Architecture* (London, 1956); M. Whinney, *Wren* (London, 1971); K. Downes, *Christopher Wren* (Harmondsworth, 1971).

14 See J.A. Bennett, 'Christopher Wren: The Natural Causes of Beauty', *Architectural History*, XV, 1972.

15 For a history of the design and building, based on published sources, see J. Lang, *Rebuilding St Paul's* (London, 1956).

16 The designs are illustrated in *Wren Society*, VIII.

17 See F. Thompson, *A History of Chatsworth* (London, 1949); M. Whinney, 'William Talman' *Journal of the Warburg and Courtauld Institutes*, XVIII, 1955. Already in 1667 Sprat, the first historian of the Royal Society, had commented on the cultural importance of the country house in preference to city building in England. Some of the weekly illustrated articles on houses in *Country Life* have been collected and published in book form. H.A. Tipping and C. Hussey's volumes on *English Homes* (Period IV, London, 1920–28, Period V, London, 1921) remain invaluable for illustrations though their text has been largely superseded by the later series of *English Country Houses: Caroline* by O. Hill and J. Cornforth (London, 1966), *Baroque* by J. Lees-Milne (London, 1970) and *Early Georgian* by C. Hussey (London, 1955). For decorative adjuncts see E. Croft-Murray, *Decorative Painting in England* (London, 1962–70); G.W. Beard, *Georgian Craftsmen* (London, 1966) and the same writer's *Decorative Plasterwork in Great Britain* (London, 1975); C. Hussey, *English Gardens and Landscapes 1700–1750* (London, 1967).

18 See M. Whiffen, *Thomas Archer* (London, 1950, 2nd edition 1973).

19 On Bodt in England see articles by N. Pevsner and J. Harris, *Architectural Review*, CXXX, 1961.

20 See M.D. Ozinga, *Daniel Marot* (Amsterdam, 1938).

21 For Galilei in England in general see I. Toesca in *English Miscellany*, III (London, 1952). Galilei's initialled drawing for the Kimbolton portico is reproduced in J. Lees-Milne, *English Country Houses: Baroque* (London, 1970), p 106.

22 See T.P. Hudson, 'Moor Park, Leoni and Sir James Thornhill', *Burlington Magazine*, CXII, 1971.

23 See C.P. Curran, *Dublin Decorative Plasterwork of the Seventeenth and Eighteenth Centuries* (London, 1967).

24 K. Downes, *Hawksmoor* (London, 1959 and a new, shorter study, 1969).

25 L. Whistler, *The Imagination of Vanbrugh and his Fellow Artists* (London, 1954) should be used in conjunction with the Nonesuch edition of the architect's letters (London, 1928) and with K. Downes, *Vanbrugh* (London, 1977).

26 For Blenheim see also D. Green, *Blenheim Palace* (London, 1951).

27 See M. Girouard, *Robert Smythson and the Architecture of the Elizabethan Era* (London, 1966).

28 The first part of Leoni's translation appeared in 1716 with the imprint 1715. See R. Wittkower, *Palladio and English Palladianism* (London, 1974).

Holland

1 See J.H. Huizinga, *Dutch Civilization in the Seventeenth Century* (London, 1968). A summary history of architecture appears in J. Rosenberg, S. Slive and E.H. Ter Kuile, *Dutch Art and Architecture 1600–1800* (Harmondsworth, 1966).

2 K. Fremantle, *The Baroque Town Hall of Amsterdam* (Utrecht, 1959) deals with the context and meaning more than the history of the building. There is a factual monograph on van Campen in Dutch by P.T.A. Swillens (Assen, 1961).

3 See M.D. Ozinga, *De Protestantsche Kerkenbouw in Nederland* (Amsterdam, 1929).

4 See D.F. Slothouwer, *De Paleizen van Frederik Hendrik* (Leyden, 1945).

5 See M.D. Ozinga, *Daniel Marot* (Amsterdam, 1938).

Part IV Central and Eastern Europe

Introduction

1 Essential to any understanding of the Empire is a good historical atlas – preferably German, such as *Putzger* or *Westermanns*. No other book explains more succinctly the complexities of the Empire and sets the scene for the latter half of the seventeenth century better than C.V. Wedgwood, *The Thirty Years War* (revised paperback edition, London, 1964). The deficiency of books like W.H. Bruford, *Germany in the Eighteenth Century* (Cambridge, 1965) for the student of architecture is that, as the subtitle makes clear, they are more concerned with the background to the literature of the period – and hence biased towards the Protestant, urban North, the least fruitful ground for architecture. The judgements of travel-writers suffer from a similar bias, though the works of de Blainville, de Pollnitz, and Keyssler – all of which were translated into English in the eighteenth century – can still be warmly recommended. For a comprehensive survey of all the arts in this period, Eberhard Hempel, *Baroque Art and Architecture in Central Europe* (Pelican History of Art, Harmondsworth, 1965) is of course indispensable, as it is also for the minor, non-Baroque, or peripherally Baroque architects who could only have been covered here at the cost of the extreme fragmentation to which Hempel himself fell victim. Nicolas Powell, *From Baroque to Rococo* (London-New York, 1959) makes a vigorous attempt to reduce multiplicity to order in its

chapter divisions, but within these sometimes dwindles to an anthology; its chief strength lies in its consideration of the whole context in which architecture was produced. Essential both for the traveller and for quick reference are the regional guides published by Reclam and Dehio; the former are more selective, but also more verbose, the latter grittily factual, but not yet entirely republished in revised and expanded editions since the War. Most of the German *Länder* are in process of completing the inventories of all their monuments, begun at the end of the nineteenth century, and published under the title of *Die Kunstdenk-mäler (von Bayern, Württemberg,* etc.). The Austrian equivalents are the volumes of the *Österreichische Kunsttopographie,* whilst the Swiss are also publishing their *Kunstdenkmäler* canton by canton.

2 The Fascist Ministero degli Affari Esteri in Italy encouraged the publication of a series of books of variable depth under the general title *L'Opera del Genio Italiano all'Estero,* which at least gives an idea of the massive scale of Italian activity abroad. See especially: E. Morpurgo, *Gli Artisti in Austria* (1937 and 1962), F. Hermanin, *Gli Artisti in Germania* (1934 and 1943), and L.A. Maggiorotti, *Gli Architetti Militari* (1933 and 1935).

3 *Arte e Artisti dei Laghi Lombardi, II: Gli Stuccatori dal Barocco al Rococo,* ed. Edoardo Arslan (Como, 1964).

4 Wolfgang Braunfels, *Monasteries of Western Europe* (London, 1972, chapters 7, 9 and 10).

5 The fascinating speculative study of the iconology – the meaning as opposed to the content – of German church frescoes was inaugurated by an essay of Hugo Schnell's, and developed by Bernhard Rupprecht and Hermann Bauer, notably in the former's *Die bayerische Rokoko-Kirche* (Kallmünz, 1959), and the latter's *Der Himmel in Rokoko* (Regensburg, 1965).

6 An idea of the difficulties involved in trying to arrive at an *architectural*

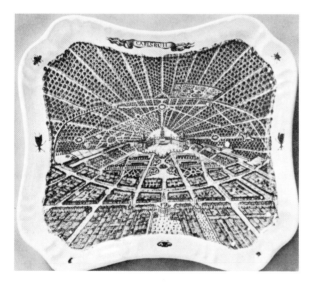

definition of Rococo can best be gained from Henry-Russell Hitchcock's essays in *Rococo Architecture in Southern Germany* and *German Rococo: The Zimmermann Brothers* (both London, 1968), whose *Leitmotiv* this is. Part of the difficulty arises from the fact that the canonical definition of Rococo derives from Fiske Kimball, *The Creation of the Rococo* (Philadelphia, 1943), which treats it purely as an internal development of French interior decoration, and has not been sufficiently understood in its isolation of the *'genre pittoresque'* as the essential Rococo in European terms. Hermann Bauer, *Rocaille* (Berlin, 1962) yields a subtle and penetrating analysis of the genesis and qualities of *rocaille*. A stimulating, if over-classified, study of Rococo as a style is that set out *sub voce* in the *Encyclopaedia of World Art*, XII (New York, 1966), written by Hans Sedlmayr and Hermann Bauer.

Austria

7 For this concept, see Hans Sedlmayr, *Die politische Bedeutung des deutschen Barock*, reprinted in his *Epochen und Werke*, II (Vienna and Munich, 1960).

8 Ernst Wangermann, *The Austrian Achievement: 1700–1800* (London, 1973), gives an illuminating and positive assessment of Austria in this century.

9 Alexander Hajdecki, 'Die Dynasten-Familien der italienischen Bau- und Maurermeister der Barocke in Wien', *Berichte und Mitteilungen des Alterthums-Verein zu Wien* (1906); Joseph Wastler, 'Die Verwelschung der Baumeisterzunft in Graz im XVIII Jahrhundert', *Mitteilungen der K.K. Central-Commission* (1893).

10 Reproduced in Victor Fleischer, *Fürst Karl Eusebius von Liechtenstein als Bauherr und Kunstsammler* (Vienna and Leipzig, 1910).

11 Hans Tietze, 'Domenico Martinelli und seine Tätigkeit für Österreich', *Jahrbuch des Kunsthistorischen Institutes, 1919* – but with dates corrected by Günther Passavant, *Studien über Domenico Egidio Rossi* (Carlsruhe, 1967, pp 109–23).

12 Hans Sedlmayr, *Johann Bernhard Fischer von Erlach* (Vienna and Munich, 1956) is massively authoritative, but is usefully condensed, together with fresh insights, by Hans Aurenhammer, *J. B. Fischer von Erlach* (London, 1973). Albert Ilg, *Die Fischer von Erlach* (Vienna, 1895) is a mine of information, not just upon the elder Fischer, but on the whole artistic situation in Vienna at this period.

13 Republished at Leipzig in 1725, and with an English translation by Thomas Lediard (London, 1730 and 1738).

14 For Fischer's and Hildebrandt's Salzburg employers, see Franz Martin, *Salzburgs Fürsten in der Barockzeit* (Salzburg, 1952).

15 The classic description of Viennese living-conditions at the beginning of the eighteenth century is that given by Lady Mary Wortley Montagu in her letter of 8/9/1716 to Lady Mar *(The Complete Letters,* ed. Robert Halsband, I, London, 1965). Very informative in a gossipy way about the life of the court and the nobility is the English translation of the appropriate volumes of E. Vehse's massive compilation *Geschichte der deutschen Höfe seit der Reformation – Memoirs of the Court and Aristocracy of Austria,* translated by F. Demmler (London, 1896).

16 Invaluable compilations of Viennese palaces and *Lusthäuser* were made at the time: those drawn by Fischer's son, Joseph Emanuel Fischer von Erlach, and engraved by J. A. Delsenbach, *Prospecte und Abrisse einige Gebäude von Wien* (progressively expanded editions 1713, 1715 and 1719); those included by Fischer himself in the last two books of his *Entwurff einer historischen Architektur* (1721); and Salomon Kleiner's four sets – the *Vera et accurata delineatio...* (1724 and 1725) and *Das vermehrte florirende Wien* (1733 and 1737).

17 The kind of architecture being built before the siege can be seen in the treatise by W. W. Prämer, edited by Hans Tietze in the *Jahrbuch der Kunsthistorischen Sammlungen des allerhöchsten Kaiserhauses* (1915).

18 A useful compilation, chiefly on the town palaces, is that by Bruno Grimschitz, *Wiener Barockpaläste* (Vienna, 1947), but the most thoroughgoing typological study is by Dagobert Frey, 'Johann Bernhard Fischer von Erlach: Eine Studie über seine Stellung in der Entwicklung der Wiener Palastfassade' *(Wiener) Jahrbuch für Kunstgeschichte* (1921/2).

19 See the (unillustrated) publication of Harald Keller's thesis, *Das Treppenhaus im deutschen Schloss- und Klosterbau des Barock* (Munich, 1935), which cries out for an illustrated translation, and F. Mielke, *Die Geschichte der deutschen Treppen* (Berlin, 1966).

425 Carlsruhe, from a decorated plate. Founded 1715 by Margrave Carl Wilhelm of Baden-Durlach

426 Vienna, Althan Palace, plan, by Fischer von Erlach, *c* .1693 (destroyed)

427 Bellotto, *View of Schlosshof*, built by Hildebrandt, 1729 (destroyed)

20 See Bruno Grimschitz, *Johann Lucas von Hildebrandt* (Vienna, 1959).

21 A vivid picture of Hildebrandt's role emerges from *Quellen zur Geschichte des Barocks in Franken unter dem Einfluss des Hauses Schönborn,* I, ed. H. Hantsch and A. Scherf (Augsburg, 1931) and II, ed. Max von Freeden (Augsburg, 1950–55).

22 See Hans and Gertrude Aurenhammer, *Das Belvedere in Wien* (Vienna and Munich, 1971), which also reproduces Salomon Kleiner's engravings of the interiors.

23 For ecclesiastical life and organization in Austria, see Anton Kerschbaumer, *Geschichte des Bistums St Pölten* (Vienna, 1875).

24 Hugo Hantsch, *Jakob Prandtauer: Der Klosterarchitekt des österreichischen Barock* (Vienna, 1926) and Rupert Feuchtmüller, *Jakob Prandtauer und sein Werk,* in a Melk exhibition catalogue, *Jacob Prandtauer und sein Kunstkreis* (1960).

25 I. F. Keiblinger, *Geschichte des Benediktiner-Stiftes Melk* (Vienna, 1851), pp 940–75. For the construction of the church, see F. Klauner, *Die Kirche von Stift Melk* (Vienna, 1946).

26 See Hans Reuther, 'Das Platzlgewölbe der Barockzeit', *Deutsche Kunst und Denkmalpflege* (1955).

27 Albin Czerny, *Kunst und Kunstgewerbe im Stifte St Florian* (Linz, 1886), for the documentary evidence; now usefully amplified and clarified, particularly over the staircase, by T. Korth, *Stift St Florian: die Entstehungsgeschichte der barocken Klosteranlage* (Nuremberg, 1975).

28 Emmerich Munggenast, *Joseph Munggenast, der Stiftsbaumeister* (Vienna, 1963).

29 Wolfgang Pauker, 'Die Kirche und das Kollegiatstift der ehemaligen regulierten Chorherren zu Dürnstein', *Jahrbuch des Stiftes Klosterneuburg* (1910); the problems newly discussed by Leonore Pühringer-Zwanowetz, 'Die Baugeschichte des Augustiner-Chorherrenstiftes Dürnstein', *Wiener Jahrbuch* (1963).

30 Wolfgang Pauker, 'Der Bildhauer und Ingenieur Matthias Steinl', *Jahrbuch des Stiftes Klosterneuburg* (1909); and L. Pühringer-Zwanowetz, *Matthias Steinl* (Vienna and Munich, 1966).

31 Bruno Grimschitz, *Johann Michael Prunner* (Vienna and Munich, 1960).

32 P. Arno Eilenstein, 'Abt Maxmilian Pagl von Lambach und sein Tagebuch', *Studien und Mitteilungen zur Geschichte des Benediktiner-Ordens* (1917–20); R. Guby, 'Die Dreifaltigkeitskapelle in Paura bei Lambach', *Jahrbuch des Kunsthistorischen Institutes (Wiener Jahrbuch,* 1919).

33 For this gargantuan project, see Wolfgang Pauker, *Donato Felice von Allio und seine Tätigkeit im Stifte Klosterneuburg* (Vienna, 1907), and for the clarification of the younger Fischer's share, T. Zacharias, *Joseph Emanuel Fischer von Erlach* (Vienna and Munich, 1960, pp 49–60).

34 Hans Reuther, *Des steirischen Baumeisters Joseph Huebers Weizbergkirche,* Erlangen thesis (published Hassfurt, 1947).

35 See Hans Tietze, 'Programme und Entwürfe zu den grossen österreichischen Barockfresken', *Jahrbuch der Kunsthistorischen Sammlungen des allerhöchsten Kaiserhauses* (1911 and 12). No student of Austrian or South German architecture can afford to pass over the wealth of research that went on in the 1950s into frescoes – their iconography, illusionism, and relation to the structure and decoration, notably: Hans Tintelnot, *Die barocke Freskomalerei in Deutschland* (Munich, 1951); Lucia Sigmeth, *Das Verhältnis von Malerei und Architektur,*

Bild und Rahmung in den Deckenfresken des österreichischen Barock (Vienna thesis, 1952); W. Mrazek, 'Ikonologie der barocken Deckenmalerei', *Sitzungsberichte der Österreichischen Akademie der Wissenschaften, phil.-hist. Klass* (1953); B. Rupprecht, *Die bayerische Rokokokirche* (Kallmünz, 1959).

Bavaria and Swabia

36 There have been no comprehensive surveys of Bavarian and Swabian church architecture since Max Hauttmann, *Geschichte der kirchlichen Baukunst in Bayern, Schwaben und Franken 1550–1780* (Munich, Berlin and Leipzig, 1921) and that included in Adolf Feulner, *Bayerisches Rokoko* (Munich, 1923), which, though inaccurate in places, are still both stimulating to read. Norbert Lieb, *Barockkirchen zwischen Donau und Alpen* (3rd, revised, edition, Munich, 1969) is a useful anthology of the main churches, with invaluable factual tables at the end. Henry-Russell Hitchcock, *Rococo Architecture in Southern Germany* (London, 1968) is a collection of chronological essays on individual architects of varying importance, that draws on all the available literature in German in the attempt to resolve the question of what Rococo architecture is; an unfortunate accident of publishing placed the crucial essay on the Zimmermann brothers between separate covers. John Bourke, *Baroque Churches of Central Europe* (2nd, revised, edition, 1962), though not intended as more than a select guide for travellers, contains a host of illuminating personal observations.

Essential reading for the religious background is Hugo Schnell, *Der baierische Barock* (Munich, 1936), which can be supplemented by L. Veit and L. Lenhart, *Kirche und Volksfrommigkeit im Zeitalter des Barock* (Freiburg, 1956). A sparkling attempt to relate plans to liturgy is made in Pierre Charpentrat, *Du Maître d'Ouvrage au Maître d' Oeuvre* (Paris, 1974).

In addition to the *Kunstdenkmäler* volumes inventarizing Bavaria, Swabia, the Upper Palatinate etc. (of which those for Upper Bavaria, having been the first, are unfortunately the least adequate), now being speeded up by the interim production of the *Kurzinventare,* this part of Germany in particular is supremely well covered by the *Kleine Kirchenführer* (with some *Grosse Kunstführer*) published by Schnell and Steiner, Munich. Now numbering over a thousand, these standardized little guides are written by expert authorities – clergy, archivists and art-historians – and are based on original research in the archives; one's gratitude to Dr Schnell for founding this series is immeasurable.

A comprehensive bibliography of Bavarian art has been edited by Hans Wichmann, *Bibliographie der Kunst in Bayern* (Wiesbaden, 1961–73).

37 The fundamental article on these is still Georg Hager, 'Die Bauthätigkeit und Kunstpflege im Kloster Wessobrunn', *Oberbayerisches Archiv* (1893/4).

38 See Wolfgang Braunfels, *op. cit.* (n. 4), and, for the economics of this, Matthäus Pest, *Die Finanzierung des süddeutschen Kirchen- und Klosterbaues in der Barockzeit* (Munich, 1937).

39 All but German studies tend to focus on the pilgrimage to Compostela, so see Georg Schreiber, *Wallfahrt und Volkstum* (Düsseldorf, 1934) and Rudolf Kriss, *Die Volkskunde der altbayerischen Gnadenstätten* (2nd edition, München-Pasing 1953/6).

40 For the Late-Gothic genesis of wall-pillar construction, see J. Büchner, *Die Spätgotische Wandpfeilerkirche Bayerns und Österreichs* (Nuremberg, 1964); the Baroque sequel set out by Gisela Deppen, *Die Wandpfeilerkirche des deutschen Barock* (Munich thesis, 1953), and Heinrich Hammer, 'Die St Jakobs-Pfarrkirche in Innsbruck und die süddeutschen Wandpfeilerkirche', *Zeitschrift des deutschen Vereins für Kunstwissenschaft* (1938).

41 Joseph Braun, *Die Kirchenbauten der deutschen Jesuiten,* suppl. vols to *Stimmen aus Maria-Laach* (1908/10).

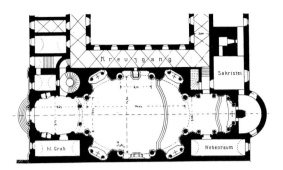

428 Weltenburg Abbey, by C. D. Asam, plan, 1716

42 For the Graubündeners, see A. M. Zendralli, *I Magistri Grigioni* (Poschiavo, 1958). For the Vorarlbergers, the superbly documented Norbert Lieb and Franz Dieth, *Die Vorarlberger Barockbaumeister* (2nd, revised and expanded, edition Munich and Zurich 1967) supplemented by the theoretical discussions in *Die Vorarlberger Barockbaumeister*, exhibition catalogue (Einsiedeln, Bregenz, 1973).

43 Wolfgang Hermann, 'Deutsche und österreichische Raumgestaltung im Barock', *Jahrbuch für Kunstwissenschaft* (1927).

44 Gebhard Spahr, *Die Basilika Weingarten* (Sigmaringen, 1974).

45 Richard Paulus, *Der Baumeister Henrico Zuccalli* (Strasburg, 1912); Karl-Ludwig Lippert, *Giovanni Antonio Viscardi* (Munich, 1969).

46 More useful than Erika Hanfstaengl, *Die Brüder Cosmas Damian und Egid Quirin Asam* (s.l., 1955), is the same author's earlier *Cosmas Damian Asam* (Munich, 1939); H-R. Hitchcock's essay on the brothers in his *Rococo Architecture in Southern Germany*, pp 19–88, is the most interesting in the book.

47 E. Guldan, *Die jochverschleifende Gewölbedekoration von Michelangelo bis Pozzo und in der bayrisch-österreichischen Sakralarchitectur* (Göttingen thesis, 1954), traces the origins of this.

48 The complicated issue of the kinds of perspective projection used in South German frescoes is handled by Hans Geiger, *Perspektivprobleme süddeutscher Deckenmalerei des Spätbarock* (Freiburg im Breisgau thesis, 1954).

49 The remarkable prevalence of this practice, which challenges any purely architectural treatment of Baroque and Rococo in the context of South German architecture, is exposed by Annemarie Thünker, *Die Barockisierung mittelalterlicher Kircheninnenräumen in Süddeutschland* (Munich thesis, 1945).

50 Here I am particularly indebted to the ideas thrown off by Pierre Charpentrat, *op. cit.* (n. 36).

51 See *Johannes von Nepomuk*, Exhibition catalogue (Münchener Stadtmuseum/Oberhausmuseum Passau/Österreichisches Museum für Angewandte Kunst in Wien, 1971).

52 See the exhaustive thesis by Christina Thon, *Johann Baptist Zimmermann als Stuckator* (Mainz, 1965), of which Dr Thon very kindly gave the writer a revised copy, now published as a well illustrated book (Munich, 1977).

53 Henry-Russell Hitchcock, *German Rococo: The Zimmermann Brothers* (London, 1968).

54 Ironically, though the architecture of the Asams, Dominikus Zimmermann, J. M. Fischer and Balthasar Neumann still await comprehensive scholarly monographs, H. J. Sauermost, *Der Allgäuer Barockbaumeister J. G. Fischer* (Augsburg, 1969) and K. H. Koepf, *Joseph Dossenberger* (Weissenhorn, 1973) have both recently been published.

55 See the essay on the Schmuzers in Hitchcock, *op. cit.* (n. 36) pp 127–50. His early stucco is handled in Karl Kosel, 'Die Stukkaturen der Schmuzergruppe 1695–1725', *Zeitschrift des historischen Vereins für Schwaben* (1969).

56 Since Hitchcock's essay on Thumb, *op. cit.* (n. 36) pp 151–74, H. M. Gubler, *Peter Thumb* (Sigmaringen, 1972) has appeared.

57 The most interesting works on special aspects of J. M. Fischer are: F. Hagen-Dempf, *Der Zentralbaugedanke bei J. M. Fischer* (Munich, 1954) and H. G. Franz, 'Johann Michael Fischer und die Baukunst des Barock in Böhmen', *Zeitschrift für Ostforschung* (1955). Hitchcock (*op. cit.*, n. 36) rather confusingly divides his discussion of Fischer between his essay on the architect himself and his essay on the Asams.

58 Several of the plans for Ottobeuren are published in Norbert Lieb, *op. cit.* (n. 36), figs 22–33, but for a full analysis the same author's *Ottobeuren und die Barockarchitektur Ostschwabens* (Augsburg and Memmingen 1933/4) should be consulted.

Bohemia and Franconia

59 There is no better depiction of the Schönborns as patrons than that evoked by their own vivid, macaronic letters, published as *Quellen zur Geschichte des Barocks in Franken unter dem Einfluss des Hauses Schönborn*, I, ed. H. Hantsch and A. Scherf (Augsburg, 1931), and II, ed. Max von Freeden (1950–55).

60 For those (including the present writer) who cannot read Czech, and who cannot obtain some of the key works produced under the German Occupation, the essential book on Bohemian architecture is H. G. Franz, *Bauten und Baumeister der Barockzeit in Böhmen* (Leipzig, 1962). The Dubček era produced a number of exhibitions and books on Bohemian Baroque, one of which was translated into English: Oldřich Blažíček, *Baroque Art in Bohemia* (London, 1968). See also *Barock in Böhmen*, ed. Karl Swoboda (Munich, 1964) with an essay on the architecture by Erich Bachmann; also Jaromir Neuman, *Das böhmische Barock* (Prague, 1970). Brian Knox, *The Architecture of Prague and Bohemia* (London, 1962) is a travellers' handbook with much useful information.

61 J. J. Morper, *Das Czerninpalais in Prag* (Prague, 1940) contains much valuable information, not just about the palace and its owner, but about the artistic life of Bohemia at the time.

62 See J. J. Morper, *Der Prager Architekt Jean Baptiste Mathey*, reprinted from the *Münchener Jahrbuch*, 1927.

63 The two fundamental works on the Dientzenhofer family are Hugo Schmerber, *Beiträge zur Geschichte der Dientzenhofer* (Prague, 1900), and Otto Weigmann, *Eine Bamberger Baumeisterfamilie um die Wende des 17. Jhs.* (Strassburg, 1902), though both were confused as to their numbers and exact relationships. Viktor Kotrba, 'Neue Beiträge zur Geschichte der Dientzenhofer', *Umění* (1973, pp 161–90), gives the latest state of research.

64 See Christian Norberg-Schulz, *Kilian Ignaz Dientzenhofer e il Barocco Boemo* (Rome, 1968).

65 See N. Pevsner, 'Bohemian Hawksmoor', *Architectural Review* (1957); H. G. Franz, 'Gothik und Barock im Werk des Johann Santini Aichel', *Wiener Jahrbuch für Kunstgeschichte* (1950); and Viktor Kotrba, 'Santini Aichl: seine Herkunft, sein Leben und Werk', *Umění* (1968, pp 563–66), resumé of preceding article in Czech, heralding forthcoming work.

66 Essential for an understanding of the vaults is Hans Reuther, 'Das Gewölbesystem der Benediktinerkirche Banz', *Das Münster* (1954, pp 358–66).

67 See Walter Boll, *Die Schönbornkapelle am Würzburger Dom* (Munich, 1925); a quite different account, crediting Hildebrandt with the chapel on the basis of an unsent letter in the Seinsheim archives, is given by Günther Passavant, 'Balthasar Neumann oder Johann Lucas von Hildebrandt: zum Problem der Kollektivplanung der Schönbornkapelle am Würzburger Dom'. in *Alte und Moderne Kunst* (1971, no. 115, pp 6–13).

68 Again a comprehensive monograph is wanting. Hitchcock's half-essay (*op. cit.*, n. 36, pp 208–23) only addresses itself to the somewhat metaphysical problem of whether Neumann was a Rococo architect, and ignores the lesson of Fritz Hirsch, *Das sogennante Skizzenbuch Balthasar Neumanns* (Heidelberg, 1912) that Neumann was not an ornamental draughtsman. Max von Freeden, *Balthasar Neumann: Leben und Werk* (2nd edition Munich and Berlin, 1963) gives an introduction to, and photographic survey of, all Neumann's work, with an invaluable table of dates. Hans Reuther, *Die Kirchenbauten Balthasar Neumanns* (Berlin, 1960) covers the churches, whilst his essay 'Balthasar Neumanns Gewölbebau', *Das Münster* (1953), pp 57–65 is essential to an understanding of his vaults.

69 See Richard Teufel, *Vierzehnheiligen* (Lichtenfels, 1957), though this is not entirely comprehensible without recourse to the original edition (s.d., circa 1936). Pierre Charpentrat, 'Politique et Dévotion. Réflexions sur une Eiglise de Pélegrinage Allemande du 18.e siècle', *L'Arte* 1969, overturns a number of *idées reçues* about Vierzehnheiligen in particular, and *Gesamtkunstwerke* in general, with great gusto.

70 Willy Fuchs, *Die Abteikirche zu Neresheim und die Kunst Balthasar Neumanns* (Stuttgart, 1914) gives the correspondence between Neumann and the abbot. Jörg Gamer, *Die Benediktinerabtei Neresheim*, in *Balthasar Neumann in Baden-Württemberg*, exhibition catalogue (Staatsgalerie Stuttgart, 1975), gives a lucid account of the stages of planning.

Palace architecture in the Empire

71 A. Fauchier-Magnan, *Les Petites Cours d'Allemagne au XVIIIe siècle* (Paris, 1947 and 1963), the first volume translated into English as *The Small German courts in the Eighteenth Century* (London, 1958), gives a wealth of amusing anecdotes about the petty German courts, with especial reference to Bayreuth, Ansbach, and Württemberg. The *Mémoires de la Margravine de Baireuth* (Paris edition, 1967) give an unforgettable account of the harshness of the Prussian court under Frederick William I and of her pinched existence in Bayreuth. The exhibition catalogue *Kurfürst Clemens August* (Brühl, 1961) gives a superb

picture of the several roles and extensive patronage of a truly resplendent prince (as did the summer exhibition devoted to Max Emanuel in Schleissheim in 1976).

There is no work that deals – the task is perhaps impossible – with the palace architecture of the Empire as a coherent whole. Hempel (*op. cit.*, n. 1) is indispensable for the lesser and the non-Baroque architects whom I have had to omit here. Karl Lohmeyer, *Die Baumeister des rheinisch-fränkischen Barocks*, reprints two articles in the *Wiener Jahrbuch* 1928/9 (Vienna/Augsburg, 1931) and does present a cohesive picture, copiously illustrated with plans, engravings, and drawings, of one of the most fertile regions for secular architecture, and one most rich in gentlemen-architects.

72 See the work by Lohmeyer cited in preceding note.

73 My drastic selectivity as to the architects and palaces treated in this chapter has chiefly been governed by the attempt to delineate the main lines of an indigenous Baroque palace architecture in the Empire, whose architects may, however, on occasion have been of foreign birth. Generally speaking, French, Dutch, and English influences acted in an anti-Baroque direction, and Italian influences in a Baroque direction, though there is generally an admixture of the two strains: it is rare to have as pure a Palladian building as von Knobelsdorff's Berlin Opera House (1741–3), or such unadulterated French influence as that prevailing in Cassel under the du Rys. I am particularly conscious of having shirked the problem of the hybrid architecture of Frederick the Great's Prussia, which the king himself urged in a steadily more Baroque direction, at a time when this was becoming outmoded. Also, despite the excuse contained in the title of the book by Pierre du Colombier, *L'Architecture Française en Allemagne au XVIIIe siècle* (Paris, 1956), and their deceptively Transitional/Louis Seize interiors, it is arguable that the masterpiece of Nicolas de Pigage – Schloss Benrath (1756–69) – and the two masterpieces of P.-L.-P. de la Guépière – Schloss Solitude (1763–7) and Schloss Monrepos (1764–7) – should have been treated. My excuse must be that they would have been plucked out of context on their own, and that the context is neither German nor Baroque.

74 Wholly new light has been shed upon the meaning of the – to our eyes – inessential suites of rooms in palaces by the seminal article of Hugh Murray Baillie, 'Etiquette and the Planning of the State Apartments in Baroque Palaces', *Archaeologia* (1967).

75 For this, see W. J. Hofmann, *Schloss Pommersfelden* (Nuremberg, 1968), esp. pp 39–60.

76 See Günther Passavant, *Studien über Domenico Egidio Rossi und seine baukünstlerische Tätigkeit innerhalb des süddeutschen und österreichischen Barock* (Carlsruhe, 1967).

77 See W. Fleischhauer, *Barock im Herzogtum Württemberg* (Stuttgart, 1958), pp 137–238.

78 H. Ladendorf, *Der Bildhauer und Baumeister Andreas Schlüter* (Berlin, 1935).

79 Jean-Louis Sponsel, *Der Zwinger, die Hoffeste und die Schlossbaupläne zu Dresden* (Dresden, 1924), which relates the architecture to the pageants, has never been superseded.

80 See Alfred Döring, *Mattäus Daniel Pöppelmann* (Dresden, 1930), now largely superseded by Hermann Heckmann, *Matthäus Daniel Pöppelmann* (Berlin and Munich, 1972).

81 See Eberhard Hempel, *Der Zwinger zu Dresden* (Berlin, 1961).

82 M. Hauttmann, *Der kurbayrische Hofbaumeister Josef Effner* (Strasbourg, 1913).

83 J. F. Oglevee, *Letters of the Archbishop Elector Joseph Clemens of Cologne to Robert de Cotte* (Bowling Green, 1956).

84 W. Kalnein, *Das kurfürstliche Schloss Clemensruhe in Poppelsdorf* (Düsseldorf, 1956).

85 See Hauttmann, *op. cit.* (note 82).

86 See W. Braunfels, *François Cuvilliés* (Würzburg, 1938), though the first half of this is an admirable study of the French revolution in interior planning. Friedrich Wolf, *François de Cuvilliés* (reprinted from *Oberbayerisches Archiv* 1967) contains some very erratic judgements.

87 E. Renard and F. Wolff Metternich, *Schloss Brühl* (Berlin, 1934) – one of the two model studies of German *Schlösser*, though now requiring to be supplemented by W. Hansmann, *Das Treppenhaus und das Grosse Neue Appartement des Brühler Schlosses* (Düsseldorf, 1972). A good short account in English is that by Marcus Binney in *Country Life*, Nov. 30th and Dec. 7th, 1972. To see Brühl in the overall context of Clemens August's patronage, consult *Kurfürst Clemens August* (exhibition catalogue, Brühl, 1961).

88 For an assessment of the positive aspects of Schlaun's intervention, see *Johann Conrad Schlaun* (exhibition catalogue, Münster, 1973), the essay by W. Hansmann pp 64–79.

89 For which, see W. Hansmann, *Schloss Falkenlust* (Cologne, 1973).

90 The extent of Cuvilliés' authorship of the ceiling designs in the Yellow

Apartment at Brühl is crucial to the question of his creative role in the design of the *Reiche Zimmer*. The matter is most judiciously handled by W. Hansmann, 'Die Stuckdecken des Gelben Appartements in Schloss Augustusburg zu Brühl', from Beiheft 16 of the *Beiträge zur rheinischen Kunstgeschichte und Dekmalpflege*, 1970.

91 See Christina Thon, *op. cit.* (n. 51).

92 K. Trautmann, *Die Reichen Zimmer der königlichen Residenz in München* (Munich, 1893), both for the archive-based text and Aufleger's photographs of the ceilings before their destruction.

93 K. Trautmann, *Die Amalienburg im königlichen Schlossgarten Nymphenburg* (Munich, 1894); Luisa Hager, *Nymphenburg, Schloss, Park und Burgen* (Munich, 1955 – summarized in the English translation of her official guide to the palace.

94 In addition to the literature cited in n. 67, see for Neumann's activity as a consultant on palace design *Balthasar Neumann in Baden-Württemberg* (exhibition catalogue, Staatsgalerie Stuttgart, 1975).

95 See not only W. J. Hofmann, *Schloss Pommersfelden* (Nuremberg, 1968), but also *Quellen*, I (cited in full, n. 59), *passim.*

96 For the full documentation, see Hans Rott, 'Quellen zur Kunstgeschichte des Schlosses und der bischöflichen Residenzstadt Bruchsal', *Zeitschrift für Geschichte der Architectur*, Beifeft 11, 1914; ably summarized and organized in O. B. Roegele, *Bruchsal wie es war* (Carlsruhe, 1975).

97 See Jörg Gamer, *Bruchsal*, in catalogue cit. (n. 94), pp 9–59.

98 For this there is the exemplary two-volume monograph by R. Sedlmaier and R. Pfister, *Die Fürstbischöfliche Residenz zu Würzburg* (Munich, 1923), though it unduly belittles Neumann's role and exalts Hildebrandt's. The *Quellen*, II (cited in full, n. 59) are a mine of information and entertainment.

99 Neumann wrote back regular letters reporting what he saw and learnt, published by Karl Lohmeyer, *Die Briefe Balthasar Neumanns von seiner Pariser Studienreise 1723* (Düsseldorf, 1911).

100 For which, see catalogue *cit.* (n. 94).

101 The authoritative account of this is now W. Hansmann, *Das Treppenhaus und das Grosse Neue Appartement des Brühler Schlosses* (Düsseldorf, 1972).

102 See *Johann Conrad Schlaun* (exhibition catalogue, Landesmuseum Münster, 1973).

103 See, not just for this episode, but for the whole subject of French architects in the Empire, Pierre du Colombier, *L'Architecture Française en Allemagne au XVIIIe siècle* (Paris, 1956).

Russia

104 The fullest account of Russian Baroque architecture available in English is in G. H. Hamilton, *Russian Art and Architecture* (Pelican History of Art, Harmondsworth, 1954).

105 I. Grabar's history of Russian art, originally written in Russian, has been published in an enlarged and revised German edition entitled *Geschichte der russischen Kunst* (Dresden, 1954). The Baroque is dealt with in volume five.

Part V The Iberian Peninsula and the New World

Spain and Spanish America

1 The literature on Spanish Baroque architecture is unsatisfactory. George Kubler gives a concise account in a volume of the Pelican History of Art, G. Kubler and M. Soria, *Art and Architecture in Spain and Portugal and their American Dominions* (Harmondsworth, 1959) His volume (in Spanish) in the *Ars Hispaniae*, *Arquitectura de los Siglos XVII y XVIII* (Madrid, 1957) is slightly more detailed and much more fully illustrated.

For a survey of the architecture of Granada, see A. Gallego y Tubin, *El Baroco Granadino* (Granada, 1956).

2 For this phase of Spanish architecture see R. Taylor, 'Francisco Hurtado and his School', *Art Bulletin*, XXXII, 1950, pp 25ff.

3 Kubler in the Pelican volume quoted above gives a fairly detailed account of the architecture of the Spanish Colonies in Central and South America. The subject is also dealt with in volume XXI of *Ars Hispaniae*, E. M. Dorta, *Arte en America y Filipinos* (Madrid, 1973).

Portugal and Brazil

1 For Portugal George Kubler's volume in the Pelican History of Art (see above under Spain) can be usefully supplemented by R. Smith, *The Art of Portugal, 1500–1800* (London, 1968).

2 For Brazil the most thorough treatment is to be found in R. Bazin, *L'Architecture religieuse baroque au Brésil* (Paris, 1956; in French).

3 For Aleijadinho, see R. Bazin, *Aleijadinho et la Sculpture baroque au Brésil* (Paris, 1963).

Glossary

Acanthus — A plant, native to the Mediterranean, the leaves of which are a favoured decorative feature in Classical architecture, e.g. in the Corinthian capital (see *Orders*).

Aedicule — From the Latin *aedicula*, a little temple or shrine; used to describe an architectural feature consisting of a pediment supported by two columns or pilasters, and enclosing a door, window or niche.

Ambulatory — An aisle continued round a central area (usually the choir of a church) to facilitate circulation.

Antependium — The front face or covering of an altar.

Apostle-light sconces — The ornamented candle-fixtures, usually twelve in number (and hence symbolic of the Twelve Apostles), habitually found as a feature of Central European Baroque churches.

Arch-band — An improvised translation of the German word *Gurtbogen*, meaning the arch-like element (which may be structural, or merely ornamental) dividing a *Tunnel-vault* (q.v.) into bays.

Architrave — See *Orders*.

Arrière-corps — The main part of a façade, which lies in a plane behind that of the projecting pavilions (see *Avant-corps*).

Ashlar — Smooth stone laid in squared, regular courses.

Astylar — Devoid of an *Order* (q.v.).

Atlas (plural Atlantes) — A colossal figure (named after the Titan who supported the world in Classical mythology), acting in place of a column to support an entablature, and often found flanking the portal of a palace.

Avant-corps — The pavilions which project in front of the façade of a building (cf. *Arrière-corps*).

Azulejo — Coloured tiles, used principally in Portugal for the decoration of walls in churches, houses and gardens.

Baldacchino (Baldachin) — Originally a canopy over a throne, but later used to describe the solid structure built over altars. The most famous baldacchino is that in St Peter's built by Bernini.

Barrel-vaulting — See *Tunnel-vaulting*.

Basilica — An aisled church of which the nave (generally lit by a *Clerestory* – q.v.) is higher than its aisles, in contrast to a *Hallenkirche*, in which the vaults of both spring from the same level.

Baumeister — A word, the significance of which varies from 'master-builder' to 'architect'.

Boiseries — Wooden panelling.

Bombé — A surface curved outwards.

Calotte — A semi-circular dome without drum or lantern.

Caul — One of the main stalks (from the Latin *caulis*) of a Corinthian capital (q.v. under *Orders*), out of which grow the lesser stalks, or *caulcoles* (Latin *cauliculus*) supporting the *Volutes* (q.v.).

Capital — See *Orders*.

Cartouche — An ornamental form, originally derived from heraldic shields shaped as if made from cut-out paper (It. *cartoccio*), frequently used as a framing or linking element in Baroque decoration.

Chamfer — The surface obtained by cutting off a square edge at an angle.

Chinoiserie — A form of decoration created by European artists in a very free imitation of Chinese motifs, derived from the Oriental porcelain brought to Europe in the seventeenth and eighteenth centuries.

Clerestory — The upper stage of a nave, lit by windows clear of the roofs of any aisles below.

Coffering — Decoration of a vault or dome with sunken panels, usually square.

Colossal order — See *Giant order*.

Comasques — Architects and craftsmen who came from the district round Lake Como.

Composite order — See *Orders*.

Console — A curved bracket, usually in the shape of an 'S', used to support architectural elements or busts.

Coretti — Small galleries like the boxes of a theatre, often inserted into the choir wall of Baroque churches.

Corinthian Order — See *Orders*.

Cornice — See *Orders*.

Corps-de-logis — One of the blocks of which a building is composed but often applied particularly to the main block of a house, as opposed to the flanking wings.

Cour d'honneur — The front court of a palace, where only distinguished guests might alight from their carriages.

Cove — The concave moulding between wall and ceiling.

Cross — The two forms of cross used by architects in the Baroque period were the *Greek Cross*, which had four equal arms, and the *Latin Cross* which had one arm much larger than the others. This arm corresponded to the nave of the church.

Cut-out, or cut-off dome — A dome, the top of which has been sliced off like an egg, allowing a view into a further dome or ceiling beyond.

Dentils — Small square blocks which occur in rows below the cornices of most of the Classical *Orders* (q.v.).

Diaperwork — A translation of the French *mosaïque*, meaning latticed patterning.

Diocletian window — See *Thermal window*.

Di sotto in sù — Literally '(seen) from below looking up', and applied to illusionist ceiling painting.

Doric Order — See *Orders*.

Enfilade — Disposition of the rooms in a house in a straight line, so that the doors form an unbroken vista.

Entablature — See *Orders*.

Estipite — A fantastically-shaped pilaster, used by Spanish architects of the early eighteenth century.

Exedra — A semi-circular recess.

Festsaal — The largest room in a *Schloss* (q.v.) or abbey, used for ceremonial occasions.

Frieze — See *Orders*.

Gartensaal — See *Sala terrena*.

Gesamtkunstwerk — A term originally employed by Wagner to describe the aspiration of opera to embrace all the arts, and subsequently, sculpture, painting, and decoration within a building (literally: 'total work of art').

Giant order or Colossal order — A Classical *Order* (q.v.) extending through two or more storeys.

Gigantomachia — Battle of giants.

Gnadenaltar — The altar upon which a miraculous image is placed.

Greek Cross — See *Cross*.

Grotesques — A fanciful type of decoration consisting of arabesques mixed with figures which often merge into vegetable forms. They derive their names from the fact that they were first discovered, at the time of the Renaissance, in the half-buried ruins of Roman palaces, which were referred to as grottos.

Gurtbogen — *Arch-band* (q.v.).

Guttae — Small trianglar features which originally appeared under the triglyph of a Doric frieze, but in the Baroque period were often used as decorative features in their own right.

Herm — A figure with a pillar or pilaster in place of its lower parts. An angel-herm has wings growing from its back; a seraph-herm uses its wings to cover its body.

Hipped roof — A roof of which the two sides rise at the same angle to the horizontal.

Hofbaumeister — Court architect.

Hôtel — French for 'town-house'. Eighteenth-century usage tended to make a distinction between *hôtels*, which belonged to the aristocracy, and *maisons*, which were owned by the *bourgeoisie*.

Imperial staircase — A form of staircase of a single flight dividing into two at right angles, to right and to left, each of which then doubles back to become parallel to the first flight.

Impost — Flat lintel over a door or flat entablature over a row of columns or piers.

Ionic Order — See *Orders*.

Jagdschloss — Hunting-lodge.

Jalousie — An open-work grille covering a gallery in a church, or a box in a theatre.

Kaisersaal — The *Festsaal* (q.v.) of a direct feudatory of the emperor, designed in theory (and, when need arose, in practice) for the reception of the latter, and expressing this right in its decoration.

Latin Cross	See *Cross*.
Lunette	A semi-circular surface, or opening, above a cornice. Sometimes misapplied to the penetration of this into a *Tunnel-vault* (q.v.), called in German *Stichkappe* (q.v.).
Lusthaus (Lustgebaüde)	A pavilion built in the park of a royal or princely palace, or a villa set in its own grounds, designed for spending the day in. The German equivalent of a *Maison de plaisance* (q.v.).
Maison à l'italienne	In French eighteenth-century usage, a single-storey villa.
Maison de plaisance	A country or suburban retreat (a 'villa' in the old sense).
Mansard roof	A roof of which the slope is broken into two sections, the lower steeper than the upper.
Mascaron	A frontally-viewed face (usually exotic in character) used as a decorative motif.
Mensa	The table of an altar.
Metope	See *Orders* (Doric).
Oculus	A round window.
Oeil-de-Boeuf	A round or oval window.

Orders

	A Entablature	1	Guttae
	B Column	2	Metope
	C Cornice	3	Triglyph
	D Frieze	4	Abacus
	E Architrave	5	Echinus
	F Capital	6	Volute
	G Shaft	7	Fluting
	H Base	8	Dentils
	I Plinth	9	Fascia

Piers	usually (in English) the first (in American the second) floor, except in Naples, where it is usually one or even two storeys higher.
	A load-bearing mass upon which the downward thrust of a dome or vault is concentrated.
Pietre dure	Semi-precious stones used for the decoration of furniture.
Pilaster-strip	A narrow vertical band, like the shaft of a pilaster, but without base or capital.
Plinth	Properly, the lowest part of a pedestal, but used to describe any form of defined base.
Polier	See *Palier*.
Quadratura	An architectural composition painted illusionistically in perspective on the walls or ceiling of a palace or church.
Quadri riportati	Pictures on panels or canvas let into a vault, or frescoes painted as if so let in.
Quatrefoil	An ornamental shape divided into four petal-like parts.
Quoins	The dressed stone wall at the corner of a building, usually in the form of alternately long and short stones.
Ramping arches	Arches which are made asymmetrical to follow the ramp of a staircase.
Régence	The kind of ornament invented by Jean Bérain, Daniel Marot and Claude Audran in the early years of the eighteenth century, characterised by the use of *Diaper-work* and *Ribbonwork* (q.q.v.).
Reichsfreiheit	Lit. 'Empire's freedom': i.e. owing allegiance to no one but the emperor.
Reichsstift	A religious foundation owing direct allegiance to the

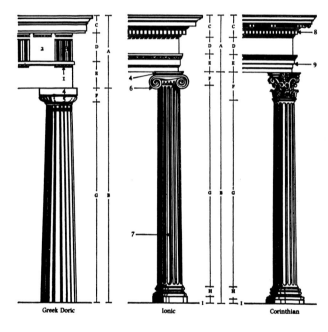

Greek Doric   Ionic   Corinthian

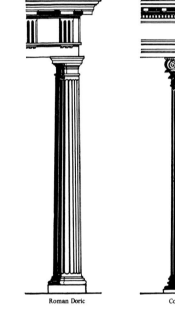

Tuscan   Roman Doric   Composite

Ordonnance	A term used by French writers on architecture in the seventeenth and eighteenth centuries, to cover the choice of an *Order* (q.v.) appropriate to a building, and the way in which it is applied.
Palier (or Polier)	Site manager, builder's foreman, or architect's deputy – a necessary stage on the way to becoming a *Baumeister* (q.v.) in the guild system.
Pediment	A triangular or curved covering, recalling a gable end, used to crown a door or window, or a block or central feature of a building.
Pendentives	A spherical triangle of masonry; one of the two ways (cf. also *Squinch*–q.v.) of effecting the transition between a cubical structure and a dome.
Penetration	See *Stichkappe*.
Pfuscher	A 'scab', or non-guild craftsman not entitled to work independently on his own account.
Piano nobile	The floor containing the principal rooms of a palace,

	emperor.
Retable	The rear superstructure of an altar.
Revet	To clad with some (usually precious) material.
Ribbonwork	A kind of ornament found in the early eighteenth century, the chief constituent of which is ribbon-like staves.
Ricetto	Literally, a shelter, but used to describe the ante-room, including a staircase, which Michaelangelo built to join the Laurentian Library in Florence to the cloister below.
Rocaille (Rockwork)	Amorphous, rock-like, ornamental material, originally used in grottoes, and on fountains, and hence suggestive of water and mutability, which, together with shells, became the point of departure for Rococo ornament.
Rotunda	A circular structure.
Rustication	The use of masonry deliberately left with a rough surface, though coursed, to suggest the primaeval rock out of which a building is shaped and over which it is raised.
Sail vault	A vault shaped like a billowing sail, formed like a *Saucer*

dome (q.v.) cut into by the arches linking the four piers or columns sustaining it.

Salomonic columns	Spiral columns based upon those preserved in St Peter's which were traditionally believed to come from Solomon's Temple.
Sala terrena (Gartensaal)	A ground-floor room giving direct access to the garden, often decorated naturalistically or like a grotto, to suggest its function as a mediator between the built and the natural.
Salle des gardes	The first and largest room of an *apartement*, in which the bodyguard attended, and which was used as a general dining-hall.
Saloon nave	A translation of the German *Saalkirche*, denoting a church without aisles.
Saucer dome	A domical vault of less than semi-circular section.
Scagliola	A composition based on powdered marble used to make imitation marble columns or inlaid patterns.
Schloss (plural Schlösser)	An untranslatable term, equivalent to the French *château*, which may denote anything between the country-house of a private individual and the castle or palace of a prince.
Serliana or Serlian Arch	A round-headed arch flanked by two narrow bays covered by flat imposts. It was first used in Rome in the early sixteenth century (Bramante inserted one in the Sala Regia of the Vatican), but it was popularized by Serlio in his treatise. It was much used by Palladio and is often called the 'Palladian arch', or, in England, a 'Venetian window'.
Severy	A section of a vault.
Socle	A base or pedestal.
Spandrel	The area between the shoulder of one arch and the next underneath the *Entablature* (see *Orders*).
Squinch	An arch constructed across the corner of a square space to make the transition to a dome on a circular plan; the alternative to a *Pendentive* (q.v.).
Stereotomy	The art and science of pre-cutting stones to fit in their allocated place, especially in an arch or vault, where the geometry of their planes is particularly complex.
Stichkappe	The German word for the intrusion into a tunnel vault caused by an arch rising above the level at which the vault springs. The least inadequate English equivalent is 'penetration'.
Strap-work	A form of stucco decoration, invented by the artists of the school of Fontainebleau, particularly Rosso, in the 1530s, which simulated strips of leather or parchment cut into elaborate patterns.
String-course	A light moulding running horizontally across the surface of a building.
Stucco-lustro	Composition mixed and polished to simulate marble.
Surintendant du Bâtiments	The minister in charge of royal buildings and other artistic activities in France.
Tabernacle	The receptacle for the reserved Host, which, it has been decreed since shortly after the Council of Trent, should be placed upon the altar.
Three-dimensional ribs	A rib which arches not merely upwards, but also outwards, thus twisting in its course.
Tester	The sounding-board above a pulpit.
Theatra sacra	The liturgical dramas enacted in the Catholic Church, especially during Passion week, in temporary sets erected around the high altar, or the altar of the Sacrament.
Thermal window (Diocletian window)	A semi-circular window created in a *Lunette* (q.v.), divided into three by two sturdy mullions. It derives its name from the fact that it occurs in the *thermae* (hot chambers) of the Baths of Diocletian in Rome.
Trabeation	A flat lintel placed across the top of two columns or piers.
Trefoil	An ornamental shape divided into three petal-like parts.
Triconch	A church ending in three apsidally-ended arms at right-angles to one another.
Tunnel-vaulting	Continuous vaulting shaped like a (usually semi-circular) tunnel, also called *Barrel-vaulting*.
Triglyph	See *Orders* (Doric).
Tuscan Order	See *Orders*.
Tympanum	The area between the lintel of a door or window and the arch above it.
Utraquist	A heretical group connected with the Hussites, who

demanded Communion for the laity in both species, bread and wine.

Velarium	An awning hung over a court-yard, or, in ancient Rome, over a theatre or amphitheatre.
Villa suburbana	A country retreat on a comparatively intimate scale, built just beyond the confines of a city.
Volute	A spiral scroll, as on an Ionic capital (see *Orders*) but often curling in different directions at either end, and used as a linking ornament.
Voussoir	The wedge-shaped stones which form an arch.
Wall-pillar Church	An aisleless, tunnel-vaulted church with internal buttresses connected by small transverse tunnel-vaults springing at the same level as the main vault.
Welsch	Literally 'foreign' but applied in the German Empire especially to the Italians, and hence to the immigrant architects and craftsmen who established themselves in South Germany and Austria in the decades after the Thirty Years War.
Zopfstil	The German name for a form of decoration inspired by the French *goût grec* or Louis Seize style, so-called from the German word *Zopf* used to describe the queues in which men's hair was worn in the period.

429 Mexico, Ocotlan, façade of the church

List of plates

Acknowledgements

The editor, the authors and the publishers would like to thank all those individuals and organizations who have helped to provide the photographs reproduced in this volume. In particular, Wim Swaan was afforded great courtesy and assistance during his journeys to photograph all the buildings he visited and to all those who gave permission for him to photograph interiors he would like to accord his special thanks. There were a great many buildings that he was, for a variety of reasons, unable to visit and those who provided additional copyright photographs are acknowledged below, with thanks for permission to reproduce. A major source of such photographs was the Courtauld Institute of Art, London, and a special debt of gratitude is due to them. Christopher Newall kindly photographed a great many of the documents reproduced. Photographs of works in museums or private collections are usually acknowledged in the captions.

Alinari, Florence: 19, 26, 34, 42, 65, 69, 90; Courtauld Institute of Art, London: 23, 24, 60, 64, 72, 78 (Mrs Wiggin), 88 (Georgina Masson), 95, 97–99, 105, 113 and 114 (Tim Benton), 116–119 (Tim Benton), 120–22, 123 (Tim Benton), 124 (Canon Brookes), 128 (A. F. Blunt), 129 (Tim Benton), 132 (Kersting), 141, 144 (P. Smith), 145, 151, 152, 160 and 161, 164, 172 (A. F. Blunt), 183 (T. Friedman), 189, 199, 234, 235 (Kersting), 276 (T. Friedman), 282 (Wickham), 283 (C. N. P. Powell), 286, 290, 292 and 293, 299, 301, 309, 310 (Marburg), 313, 315, 316, 320, 322, 346, 350, 357 and 358, 375 (Marburg), 382 and 383 (Alan Braham), 384, 401 (Robert Kraus), 403 (A. F. Blunt), 404, 414, 417–20, 421 (James Austin), 423 (Colin Tubbs), 424, 427, 428; Gabinetto Fotografico Nazionale, Rome: 67; Edwin Smith: 74; Paolo Portoghesi, Rome: 93 and 94; Trustees of the British Museum, London: 100; Reproduced by gracious permission of Her Majesty the Queen: 104; Fondazione Giorgio Cini, Venice, 111; O. Böhm, Venice: 112; Foto Rigamonti, Rome: 151; Eric de Maré: 158, 175, 178 (the last two reproduced by kind permission of Penguin Books Ltd); Bibliothèque Nationale, Paris: 170; The Louvre, Paris: 171; Giraudon, Paris: 191; National Trust, Waddesdon Manor: 196; Rubenshuis, Antwerp: 202; Musées des Beaux Arts, Brussels: 203; Albertina, Vienna: 205; Kerry Downes: 208, 211 and 212, 217, 219, 221 and 222, 226, 228 and 229, 231; Bank of England: 213; Department of the Environment: 218; Alexander Paul, Prague: 262, 323, 325, 327–44; Bildarchiv Foto Marburg: 311, 324; Alex Starkey: 354, 372, 373, 380; Kunsthistoriches Museum, Vienna: 424. The illustration reproduced on page 341 under the heading *Orders* is reprinted by permission of Penguin Books Ltd.

Index